HEBREW GOTHIC

JEWISH LITERATURE AND CULTURE

Alvin H. Rosenfeld, *Editor*

HEBREW GOTHIC

History and the Poetics of Persecution

Karen Grumberg

INDIANA UNIVERSITY PRESS

This book is a publication of

Indiana University Press
Office of Scholarly Publishing
Herman B Wells Library 350
1320 East 10th Street
Bloomington, Indiana 47405 USA

iupress.indiana.edu

© 2019 by Karen Grumberg

All rights reserved
No part of this book may be reproduced or utilized in any form or by any means, electronic or mechanical, including photocopying and recording, or by any information storage and retrieval system, without permission in writing from the publisher. The paper used in this publication meets the minimum requirements of the American National Standard for Information Sciences—Permanence of Paper for Printed Library Materials, ANSI Z39.48-1992.

Manufactured in the United States of America

Cataloging information is available from the Library of Congress.

ISBN 978-0-253-04225-5 (cloth)
ISBN 978-0-253-04226-2 (paperback)
ISBN 978-0-253-04229-3 (ebook)

1 2 3 4 5   23 22 21 20 19

*For Astrid Leah, Daniel Per,
and Øystein*

CONTENTS

Acknowledgments   ix

Note on Translation and Transliteration   xi

Introduction: Gothic Matters   1

Part 1   A Spectralized Past   35

   1   Always Already Gothic: S. Y. Agnon's European Tales of Terror   37

   2   Maternal Macabre: Feminine Subjectivity at the Edge of the Shtetl in Dvora Baron and Ya'akov Shteinberg   74

   3   After the Nightmare of the Holocaust: Gothic Temporalities in Leah Goldberg and Edgar Allan Poe   113

Part 2   Haunted Nation   145

   4   Dark Jerusalem: Amos Oz's Anxious Literary Cartography between 1948 and 1967   147

   5   Historiographic Perversions: Echoes of *Otranto* in A. B. Yehoshua's *Mr. Mani*   187

   6   A Séance for the Self: Memory, Nonmemory, and the Reorientation of History in Almog Behar and Toni Morrison   223

Coda: "Here Are Our Monsters": Hebrew Horror
from the Political to Pop 260

Bibliography 277

Index 297

ACKNOWLEDGMENTS

For the better part of a decade, various interlocutors have reacted to the ideas in this study with enthusiasm and encouragement. This book would not have come into being without their open-mindedness, collegiality, and generosity of spirit. I am especially grateful to Adriana X. Jacobs, whose perceptive comments were instrumental as I wrote and revised the manuscript. I feel exceedingly fortunate to have had such an engaged reader. Blake Atwood, Maya Barzilai, Sidra DeKoven Ezrahi, Sheila Jelen, Neta Stahl, and Ilana Szobel read and commented on the manuscript or on drafts of particular chapters. Their insights and suggestions were invaluable in clarifying and refining my ideas. At various junctures, I have benefited from the comments of other colleagues, including Marc Caplan, Rebecca Hopkins, Lital Levy, Jerome Singerman, and Melissa Weininger. As I navigated the terrain of gothic studies, Carol Margaret Davison, Catherine Spooner, and Sara Wasson, all of whose work leaves its imprint throughout this study, extended a warm welcome.

Many others have responded to my work with curiosity and interest, recommending texts, questioning points, and expressing support. I am indebted to those who provided feedback on my work in progress at annual meetings of the American Comparative Literature Association, the Association for Jewish Studies, the Modern Language Association, the National Association for Professors of Hebrew, and the International Gothic Association, as well as at symposia and colloquia, including "All That Gothic" at the University of Łódź, Poland; the Gruss Colloquium at the Katz Center for Advanced Judaic Studies at the University of Pennsylvania on "Jews Beyond Reason"; and "Gothic Trespass: Borders, Bodies, Texts" at the University of Texas at Austin.

I wish to thank my friends and colleagues in the Department of Middle Eastern Studies and the Program in Comparative Literature at UT, who have helped nurture an intellectually stimulating and supportive environment. I reserve deep gratitude for UT's remarkable Hebrew and Judaica librarian, Uri Kolodney, for whom no text is too rare, too geographically distant, or too difficult to locate. His instinct, skills, and perseverance have unearthed gems. Special thanks to my dear friends Na'ama Pat-El and Esther Raizen, who, over the years, have offered their wisdom, steadfast support, and patient guidance through various grammatical and historical nuances of the Hebrew language. I am grateful to Leonor Diaz, whose perspicacity and warmth put everything into proper perspective. My students, both graduates and undergraduates, have allowed me to indulge my love of the gothic and provided a forum for discussing the ideas informing this book. I owe much to my editors at Indiana University Press, Dee Mortensen and Paige Rasmussen, for seeing this project through to its completion with astuteness and integrity.

This book could not have been completed without the support of several fellowships, including the American Association of University Women Postdoctoral Research Fellowship, which allowed for a leave in the early stages of research; a Humanities Research Award from UT's College of Liberal Arts, which offered three years of support; and a College Research Fellowship from UT's College of Liberal Arts, which provided leave in the final stages of writing.

Finally, the personal reverberations effected by the labyrinthine process of writing a book deserve special acknowledgment. My parents, Simi and Alex, and my parents-in-law, Grethe and Hans Gunnar, have accompanied this project with love and encouragement over the years. My husband, Øystein, has shared all the moments of exhilaration and frustration that have attended my research. He is a true partner in life, as he has proved in part by his willingness to spend many an evening by my side watching *Penny Dreadful*. Our children, Astrid Leah and Daniel Per, were born and have grown alongside this book. They are my wondrous progeny; they make everything possible.

* * *

An earlier version of chapter 3 was originally published as "Gothic Temporalities and Insecure Sanctuaries in Lea Goldberg's 'The Lady of the Castle' and Edgar Allan Poe's 'Masque of the Red Death,'" in *Comparative Literature* 68, no. 4: 408–26. Copyright 2016, University of Oregon. All rights reserved. Republished by permission of the copyright holder and the present publisher, Duke University Press (www.dukepress.edu).

NOTE ON TRANSLATION AND TRANSLITERATION

IN TRANSLITERATING HEBREW TERMS IN THIS BOOK, I follow the recommendations of the Library of Congress Romanization Table for Hebrew, with minor modifications to enhance readability. I retain diacritic marks only in the *ḥet* and dispense with the final *he* (*he sofit*) in most cases, with a few specific exceptions (such as in *agunah* and *Haskalah*) to accord with publication conventions. For proper names, I defer to the preferred or conventional English spelling, designating *ḥet* only to provide clarification regarding texts that have not been translated to English. For example, referring to Ḥana in Ya'akov Shteinberg's story, which has not been translated, I retain the subscript dot beneath the *H* to distinguish between *ḥet* and *he*, while in other references to the name Hana, I dispense with the dot. Throughout, I cite English translations when available but modify when necessary; these modifications are noted and refer to the Hebrew original. In these cases, and for texts that have not been translated to English, the translations from Hebrew are mine.

HEBREW GOTHIC

INTRODUCTION
Gothic Matters

How does fiction factor into our understanding of the past? Literature might challenge long-held assumptions of historical truth, offering other stories to displace or complement them; or it might, more radically, expose historical narrative as itself constructed. To varying degrees, literature can contaminate the "purity" of history. Alon Hilu's Hebrew novel *Aḥuzat Dajani* (*The House of Rajani*, 2008) opens with a preface that claims its historical basis: "This book is based on the letters and personal diaries of Ḥayim Margaliyot-Kalvarisky (agronomist, member of the First Aliya, 1868–1947), kept in the Central Zionist Archive in Jerusalem." The author explains that he has chosen to retain the language of these documents, "the authentic Hebrew of the late nineteenth century," and to translate and publish alongside them the Arabic journal entries of Salaḥ Dajani, a Palestinian Arab.[1] Kalvarisky is an actual historical figure; the preface heightens the sense of historical veracity through the use of explanatory footnotes, absent from the novel itself. Subsequent Hebrew printings of the novel as well as its English translation, published in 2010, end with an author's note clarifying that *"The House of Rajani* is absolutely a work of fiction and is not based on any so-called 'diaries.' *The House of Rajani* is in no way or form a historical document. It is a work of fiction."[2] The overwrought and repetitive author's note and the replacement of the historical surnames with fictional ones were consequences of a scandal and legal row that ensued upon the novel's publication. Kalvarisky's family accused Hilu of tarnishing their forebear's reputation, while critics from the right and left found fault with his representation of the history of the Zionist narrative.[3]

The tension between history and fiction that has come to define the novel calls to mind a novel published 250 years earlier, Horace Walpole's *The Castle of Otranto*, considered the first gothic novel. Published in 1764 under the pseudonym William Marshal, *Otranto* opens with a preface claiming the historical authenticity of the text, supposedly discovered "in the library of an ancient catholic family in the north of England" and translated by Marshal from "the purest Italian."[4] Walpole revealed himself as the author and the work as fiction in the preface to the second edition in 1765, only after the purportedly historical document had been favorably received. This conceit of "the discovered manuscript" has, over time, become one of the favored conventions of the gothic mode. It is a formal manifestation of one of the foremost preoccupations of the gothic: the tension between counterfeit and authenticity, artifice and truth, fictions and histories.

Hilu's novel expresses this preoccupation not only in the liberties it takes with history but also more generally in the author's intentional participation in and emulation of the gothic tradition. When he was asked, in a 2010 interview, to name the "best books on Israel and Palestine in art," he listed a novel by the revered Hebrew Nobel laureate S. Y. Agnon, two historical accounts of the Israel-Palestine conflict, and Ann Radcliffe's *The Mysteries of Udolpho* (1794), a mainstay of British gothic literature. When asked to explain what Radcliffe's novel has to do with Israel and Palestine, he recalled facing similar skepticism from his editor when he approached him with the idea of writing a gothic novel set in Palestine: "But it's always sunny there!" Despite its climate, though, "Palestine can be gothic," he explains, because of traces of "old empires" dating back several millennia. The gothicism of *Dajani* is deliberate and strategic: "I decided I wanted my book to be gothic, which meant it would involve supernatural events, ghosts, murder in the night—all the motifs of gothic novels." He cites *Hamlet* (also admired by Walpole) and *Udolpho* as important influences: "If you Google gothic you can find the name Ann Radcliffe and this is one of her most famous books. So I summarized it and made a list of the gothic motifs I would like to include in my book, like events taking place at night and a raven."[5]

This facile presentation of the gothic notwithstanding, Hilu clearly is aware that there is something behind this catalogue of aesthetic conventions. He invokes them in the service of *Dajani*'s position as "part of a new trend in Israel to be critical of the way we tell our history," which he associates with the Israeli New Historians. But this so-called trend is not new. The revisionist historians Hilu cites and with whom he explicitly aligns himself had been at work for nearly three decades when *Dajani* was published, and even if they were a minority, authors such as S. Yizhar had been critically engaging with the official Israeli narrative since the birth of the state. Nor is Hilu by any means the first Hebrew author to turn to the gothic to express these historical and historiographic modifications. To the contrary, though up to now unacknowledged, the gothic has played a role in the development of modern Hebrew literature at least since the fin de siècle, not as a curiosity on the sidelines of the Hebrew literary landscape but as a constitutive force.

Why the gothic? What does this mode—notoriously difficult to define adequately, seemingly incompatible with the aesthetic and the setting of Israel/Palestine, and frequently dismissed as a popular and even vulgar mode—contribute to Hebrew literature? Particularly given the antisemitism lurking in British gothic literature, why would Jewish authors of Hebrew turn to the gothic? *Hebrew Gothic* responds to these questions by locating the gothic within modern Hebrew literary discourses engaged with history, historiography, and collective identities and putting these works in conversation with key British and American gothic texts and theoretical paradigms. Hebrew authors' appeal to the gothic mode, I argue, shapes the literary engagement with the Jewish past. As such, the gothic helps authors revise the dynamics of powerlessness and victimization associated with the Jewish conception of history, central in contemporary Israeli cultural and political rhetoric. In their appropriation and revision of particular gothic themes and devices, the Hebrew works included in this study, which span from the early twentieth century to the early twenty-first, offer unconventional approaches to power and powerlessness, vulnerability and violence. As this study shows, the Hebrew adaptation of the gothic adds a new dimension to the mode writ large. The very devices that inscribed the Jew as the cursed wanderer who threatened the moral and social order in European gothic literature were taken up by Jewish authors of Hebrew to subvert such paradigms. Significantly, as the object of the gothic became its author and its agent, he or she did not necessarily reassign villainy to the non-Jewish other but rather used the gothic to critically examine the collective Jewish self.

The gothic is widely regarded as having been inaugurated by the publication of Walpole's *Otranto*. Its popularity gave rise to other texts that, like *Otranto*, used imagery and devices that have become the conventions of the gothic: ghosts, vampires, and vulnerable heroines occupy foreboding castles and navigate subterranean labyrinths, eliciting the reader's suspense and terror. Primarily between the 1760s and the 1820s, Walpole, Radcliffe, Matthew Lewis, and others associated with "first wave Gothics" produced gothic works that shocked the English public with their violence, excess, transgressions, and explained or unexplained supernatural events—but, as numerous studies have shown, their narratives are never detached from the social and political milieu in which they were produced.[6] The gothic not only provided a paradigm through which to express the violence and fear in Britain; it also made an important contribution to a discourse, just beginning to take shape, on national identity, by producing an apparatus of monstrosity to account for alterity within and beyond the borders of Protestant England.[7] American gothic, too, contends with the shadows and specters of those eradicated and suppressed from the national sensibility that they threatened.[8] As we shall see, certain gothic elements have been instrumental in the Zionist imagination. This book's primary concern is with the fundamental tasks performed by the gothic in these works: the reconceptualization of the past and the development of new, alternative historiographies. These tasks, in turn, encompass the gothic engagement with and against the national endeavor, a phenomenon that informs my analysis particularly in the second half of this study.

The Hebrew plays, stories, and novels analyzed in *Hebrew Gothic* revise gothic literary conventions to reinterpret elements of the Jewish past and their place in the present. More specifically, their authors summon the gothic for several reasons: to engage with a particular historical event that continues to haunt the Jewish Israeli sensibility, such as the Holocaust or the wars of 1948 and 1967; to modify a historiographic practice, such as the conceptualization of the Eastern European Jewish past or the revisionist Israeli histories that emerged in the 1980s; or to confront historiographic injustice, as in the erasure of the Arab Jewish past in Zionist Israel. My main point of entry to the gothic in Hebrew literature, then, is history, broadly defined to include representations of a hostile but seductive past, the reconfiguration of temporality and the mechanics of time, and fragile narratives of family and nation. The literary expression of this confrontation with history is shaped through a poetics of persecution, which itself is based on adaptations of specific gothic conventions. Inscribing the ongoing revision of the categories of victim and oppressor and exposing them as historically unstable and ambivalent, this poetics forces us to reevaluate assumptions about political power and powerlessness in the past and the present. The implicit or overt violence exhumed by the formal, thematic, and aesthetic appropriation of the gothic, as well as the shifting dynamics of victim and persecutor it engenders, are at the heart of my investigation.

The "Para-site" of History

As a field, gothic studies spans a broad spectrum, temporally and geographically as well as in terms of its critical and theoretical focal points.

Centered in the United Kingdom, it is supported by a robust scholarly society, the International Gothic Association (founded in 1991), and a biannual academic journal, *Gothic Studies* (first published in 1999). Centers of gothic studies and related graduate degree programs can be found throughout the United Kingdom. Since the 1990s, which saw an efflorescence in research of the gothic, the field has nourished its own expanding boundaries and is well established in the Anglophone world, including Scotland, Ireland, Australia, Canada, and New Zealand. Though in the American academy the gothic tends to be subsumed under other literary categories, individual American scholars have contributed prolifically to gothic studies.[9]

This global network helps renew, invigorate, and sustain the field's multilingual, transnational, and interdisciplinary nature. Studies of gothic from the perspective of feminism, postcolonial studies, queer studies, new historicism, and cultural studies have built on a broad body of scholarship on British and American gothic literature from the eighteenth and nineteenth centuries, demonstrating the mode's elasticity and wide applicability beyond its original context.[10] Scholars specializing in literature produced from Canada to the Caribbean to Japan have drawn on the gothic as a framework to articulate new modes of thinking. More recently, "globalgothic" has emerged as the identification of gothic themes and devices with global trends in market capitalism and technology.[11] The turn of the millennium saw a global proliferation of literature and film that contribute to the ever-evolving phenomenon known as contemporary gothic, which indicates the malleability of the historical and territorial features that made earlier gothic texts gothic. This elasticity is a primary attribute of contemporary gothic as well as its eighteenth- and nineteenth-century precursors. Broadly speaking, the gothic, like its subjects, is defined partly by the constant flux of its own generic, geographic, temporal, and linguistic boundaries, a necessary trait for its continued adaptation beyond its original time and place.

This adaptability, however, is the same feature that makes the gothic so difficult to pin down. Despite certain tendencies and conventions associated with gothic fiction, one would be hard-pressed to settle on a definition of the gothic. Even the designation of its basic category—is it a genre, a mode, an aesthetic?—is contested. The first task at hand, then, is to explain what I mean by *gothic*. Clearly, the gothic is more than the sum of its familiar conventions: the presence of a ghost does not, in itself, make a text gothic, and gothic texts do not all contain ghosts. The broad issue at stake in gothic texts is the contamination, disruption, or transgression of established social, cultural, and national boundaries. Unsettling notions of national identity and of historical narrative, the gothic reveals the fear and anxiety at the heart of these seemingly fixed entities and forces a reassessment of the present and future. Not all texts that deal with the past or its unstable narratives, however, are gothic. Unlike other narrative modes or approaches that engage with these themes, the gothic produces a particular atmosphere and mood that prioritize the terror they evoke, creating a dynamic of victimization that feeds this terror. Gothic conventions and devices matter because they literalize the horrific nature of the past. In other words, it is not only *what* gothic texts do but also *how* they do it that makes them gothic.

In gothic subject and form alike, one of the mode's chief characteristics is readily evident: its signification of instability. As David Punter puts it, the gothic encompasses an "*awareness* of mutability, an understanding of the ways in which history itself, and certainly narratives of history, are not stable."[12] Instead of stability, there is "only distortion—slips of the tongue, tricks of the eye, which ensure that what we see is always haunted by something else, by that which has not quite been seen, in history or in text."[13] The gothic itself is subject to the same mutability of what it represents, with its repertoire of lost, misread, miscommunicated, or misunderstood texts, indicating "the attempt to validate that which cannot be validated, the self-sufficiency, the autonomy of a textuality that is always ruined beyond repair."[14] The instability of the gothic is a function of narrative, both at the level of the text itself and in a broader historical sense: a dominant story gives way to those that have been stifled, clamoring to be told. As such, diverse cultural, historic, and geographic contextualizations of the gothic have led to its interpretation, in Carol Margaret Davison's words, as "the site of a multiplicity of discourses whose authors do not share a single coherent world-view."[15] Simply put, suggests Punter, in "dealing with terror, Gothic deals with the unadmitted," a preoccupation that makes gothic "a mode—perhaps *the* mode—of unofficial history."[16] British imperialism and American slavery, for example, sustained glossy narratives of cultural and economic success at horrific cost to those whose stories were unacknowledged. The threatened exposure of these histories, long buried, provokes the dread associated with the gothic. Besides functioning as a repository of suppressed historical narratives, the gothic, asserts Markman Ellis, "is itself a theory of history: a mode for the apprehension and consumption of history."[17] Through dark, irrational, and excessive plots, it "offers a critique of the Enlightenment construction of history as a linear account."[18]

Building on this foundation, much gothic criticism has come to identify its engagement with history as one of its most consequential features. Born of fissures in the facade of social or political stability, the gothic provides an idiom for the literary articulation of and response to these moments of rupture and a distinct aesthetic expression for the historiographic revisions they invite. As such, as we have already seen, history itself often becomes a subject of or in gothic texts. The relationship of the gothic to history is threefold. It is evident in the gothic's representation and thematization of the past; in its theorization of history, time, and historiography; and in the specific historical circumstances of its own production, which are often subject to the same occlusion they thematize. I locate the gothic in Hebrew literary texts at this intersection of history as the subject of gothic fiction and gothic fiction as a history in and of itself. For the Hebrew authors in this study—S. Y. Agnon, Dvora Baron, Ya'akov Shteinberg, Leah Goldberg, A. B. Yehoshua, Amos Oz, and Almog Behar—cultural anxieties regarding the development of Hebrew culture inform a reflection on the role and representation of the past.

Though both contemporary gothic fiction and its "classic" textual predecessors can seem removed from the "real world" of politics, history, and social issues, they both work to challenge not reality itself but the well-lit, seemingly stable and coherent narratives that lay a claim on the "real." Conceptualizing the gothic as a "para-site," in Punter's words, can help us envision the relation between gothic fiction and the narratives from which it so decisively departs: the gothic "*perversion* of other forms . . . serves to demonstrate precisely the inescapability of the perverse in the very ground of being."[19] As a "para-site," the gothic is not only compatible with but also necessary for the functioning of the real world: "The parasite supports the host as much as vice versa, as the pragmatic daylight world survives only in its infolding of the spectral world of desire."[20] The terror of the gothic is in its confrontation with darkness, not as a fantastic force with no bearing on our lives but as a force that is constitutive of our world. Urging nothing less than the reevaluation of reality itself, the gothic, observes Punter, "demands that we reject the narrative of cultural cleansing and engage instead with a textual and psychic *chiaroscuro* where plain sight is continually menaced by flickerings from other worlds."[21] The sanitized present gives way to a past of inconvenient truths, moldering secrets, and buried transgressions.

The confrontation staged by the gothic between the past and the present to disinter obscured narratives of family and nation has created the perception that the gothic is, at heart, a subversive form. This is often the case, as many studies on postcolonial, postnational, or queer gothic can attest. Yet the motives behind such exhumations and their consequences vary from text to text. As Sara Wasson reminds us, "eighteenth-century Gothic regularly tames subversion into an enlightenment narrative, ending by reasserting conventional family structures and the power of modernity to vanquish the ghosts of the past."[22] In other words, the gothic can be claimed by no single political or ideological project but can be appropriated to serve either conservative or progressive ends. The authors in this study demonstrate this pliability of the gothic. Though they are all subject to a degree of ambivalence regarding their personal subjectivity or their national identity, urged by different motivations and circumstances to engage with the past, they all call on the gothic to do so. Some use it to express anxiety at the dissipation of "an enlightenment narrative," while others expose the violence of this narrative's suppression of others.

The authors and texts included in this study are intended to reflect the pervasiveness of the mode in Hebrew literature and its adaptability to a wide spectrum of ideological concerns. I do not propose that these authors be designated "gothic," but, more modestly, that their adaptation of gothic elements be acknowledged as a significant feature of their literary repertoire and of the Hebrew literary landscape. I have chosen to include these authors, a sampling of those who call on gothic aesthetics and thematic preoccupations in Hebrew, for several reasons. Though they are not all canonical authors, they have all left an indelible mark on Hebrew literature, and thus their use of gothic cannot be dismissed as irrelevant, coincidental, or anomalous to the concerns of Hebrew culture more broadly. The texts at hand span a good part of the twentieth century and into the twenty-first, with the earliest story, by Agnon, published in 1916 (but probably composed in prior versions as early as 1906 or 1907), and the latest, by Almog Behar, published in 2005. They all engage, in some way, with the past and its representation: the first half of the study focuses on the use of the gothic to grapple with the European Jewish past, while the second half is concerned with Israeli history.

This study does not aspire to an exhaustive survey or complete history of Hebrew gothic literature with a distinct starting point, a particular instigating event, or a unified and homogeneous ideological purpose.[23] Nor is it primarily interested in making a claim of direct influence. Though, being educated and well read, the authors in this study almost certainly read European gothic texts in their English or German originals or in Hebrew translation, I have not tried to unearth such encounters. I do not contend that A. B. Yehoshua read *The Castle of Otranto* and decided to emulate it (though Hilu does engage in this prototypically gothic process of imitation and fakery). Rather, I analyze a number of case studies to ask, What does the gothic *activate* in these Hebrew authors' visions and revisions of the past? *Hebrew Gothic* confronts this and other questions I have posed to investigate how Hebrew literature's gothic expressions of and about history are effected by an ambivalent poetics of persecution. As such, the gothic helps Hebrew authors respond to and represent formative moments of historical rupture. Contrary to the perception of it as external to the concerns of Hebrew writing, a misconception I will address in the individual chapters, the gothic has—since the revival of modern Hebrew literature—been intimately intertwined with it. Exposing this intimacy and questioning the boundaries separating the Jewish from the non-Jewish is one of the main aims of this book.

At the outset, I want to emphasize that certain demonic or supernatural figures that are associated primarily with the Jewish and, particularly, the Yiddish folk tradition, such as the dybbuk and the golem, are not included in this study. Their fantastic nature suggests an affinity to the gothic mode that is unsurprising, given the European setting that nurtured them for centuries.[24] What interests me in this study, however, is the way Hebrew authors engage with figures, themes, and imagery supposedly *outside* the Jewish repertoire, exposing the artifice of perceived divisions between the Jewish and the non-Jewish.[25] The gothic in the Hebrew works I examine is in dialogue with the themes borne of Christian European gothic—a literary tradition associated with reactionary politics and antisemitism as much as with subversive ideologies. Moreover, this study focuses on Hebrew, a language whose narrative of resurrection can itself be conceptualized in gothic terms. The authors who chose to write in Hebrew in the early decades of the century were Europeans who had to renounce Europe's culture and languages in allegiance to the Zionist project. Hebrew, as such, encompasses both an acknowledgment of the diasporic Jewish powerlessness that instigated Zionism and a resolve to attain political power through nationalism and the resurrection of a "dead" tongue.[26]

Theorizing Hebrew Gothic:
The "Spectral Turn" and Affect Theory

Having summoned the image of Hebrew's resurrection, I want to turn for a moment to the contemporary era to address two theoretical orientations that inform this study. The first is the far-reaching and influential cultural theory phenomenon known as the "spectral turn." The spectral turn refers to growing scholarly interest, since the 1990s, in interdisciplinary engagements with ghosts and haunting. Its defining concept, spectrality, posits the haunting ghost as a "conceptual metaphor" primarily (but not solely) concerned with "elucidating issues of memory and history."[27] Jacques Derrida's *Specters of Marx* (1993), though by no means the first work to invoke the ghost as a metaphor, is considered to have sparked the spectral turn in cultural criticism. In this text, Derrida revises ontology to arrive at the concept of "hauntology," which acknowledges the prominence of haunting in being itself: "It is necessary to introduce haunting into the very construction of a concept. Of every concept, beginning with the concepts of being and time."[28] Taking aim at what he sees as Marx's impulse to exorcise necessary ghosts in the name of revolution, Derrida promotes a universalizing conceptualization of haunting in the name of ethics and justice vis-à-vis the other, urging an acceptance of and cohabitation with specters. Critics of this broad notion of spectrality have argued for a more historically specific understanding of ghosts and haunting.[29] These two modes of interpretation—general and broadly ontological, on the one hand, or historically determined by specific events and experiences, on the other—continue to inform spectrality.

The question of whether we ought to consider the metaphor of the ghost to be general or specific is accompanied by another: that of the specter's purpose. Tracing two models of ghostly interaction, Colin Davis characterizes Derrida's paradigm as one in which we speak with specters not so that they will divulge their secrets but rather to "open us up to the experience of secrecy as such" and thus "ensure respect for otherness."[30] By contrast, Davis notes, the psychoanalysts Nicolas Abraham and Maria Torok, who wrote about haunting in the context of transgenerational trauma, argue that the ghost's return neither clarifies mysteries nor restores justice. For them, "the phantom is a liar; its effects are designed to mislead the haunted subject" and safeguard its own secret.[31] Psychoanalysis is necessary to air the secret and exorcize the ghost, a goal at odds with Derrida's famous exhortation "to learn to live *with* ghosts."[32]

What is the relationship of spectrality to the gothic? The spectral turn coincided with what María del Pilar Blanco and Esther Peeren, among others, characterize as "a surge in gothic scholarship" since the 1990s; the ghost has become a key "generic marker" in gothic studies. Yet as they point out, the ghost appears in other literary modes, such as magical realism; it predates the eighteenth-century heyday of British gothic literature; and it is just one of the fear-inducing conventions of the gothic. As such, they insist that "by no means all ghosts are Gothic and that each haunting should be read on its own terms."[33] Just as the gothic cannot contain the ghost, so can spectrality not encompass the gothic. Decrying the "spectralization of the Gothic," Roger Luckhurst critiques spectrality as an overdetermined cultural concept, wielded by critics to legitimize broad generalizations.[34] "No concept, no self-identity, no text, no writing that is not haunted," he laments.[35] The application of Derrida's universalist hauntology in gothic literary criticism has led, argues Luckhurst, to a "meta-Gothic discourse" that is not adequately attentive to the specific historical and political contexts of gothic texts.[36] The gothic and spectrality, then, "are far from equivalents—while they do frequently impinge on each other, each also has its own (after) life to live," as Pilar Blanco and Peeren assert.[37]

In this study, spectrality provides a conceptual framework that allows me to situate my inquiry within a broader, transnational interest in ghosts and haunting. Several concepts that have emerged to dominate the discourse of haunting in literary criticism are relevant to this study: the idea of "spectralized modernity" and the haunted city;[38] the ghost's disruption of historical narrative and chronology and its exposure of alternative narratives; the specter's spectatorship and invisibility; its relation to repressed secrets; and the notion of ghostly inheritance. The literary gothic, while also concerned with these matters, expands the scope of inquiry while remaining attentive to its particularities. Allowing for an engagement with specific histories and their narratives, constellations of political and social circumstances, and textual encounters with other gothic figures, themes, and experiences beyond spectrality, the gothic designates the tenor of these texts. Haunting is one among many modes of confronting the past.

The second theoretical orientation that warrants discussion is affect theory. Though only one chapter (chap. 2) engages with affect theory in a sustained manner, considerations of affect inform my analyses throughout this study and are critical to the gothic more broadly. Affect theory, like spectrality, is identified with its own moment in cultural theory, the "affective turn" of the mid-1990s. As Melissa Gregg and Gregory J. Seigworth have pointed out, though, no single theory of affect exists—nor should it. Rather, they suggest striving to maintain the multiplicity that informs our understanding of this concept: "theories as diverse and singularly delineated as their own highly particular encounters with bodies, affects, worlds."[39] Defining affect entails navigating and disentangling a web of interrelated concepts, including emotion and feeling. While acknowledging that these concepts are closely related, numerous theorists have identified distinctions among them, pointing to differences in their formation, expression, and consequences (or lack thereof). Brian Massumi's elucidation of affect is among the most influential: "*L'affect* (Spinoza's *affectus*) is an ability to affect and be affected. It is a prepersonal intensity corresponding to the passage from one experiential state of the body to another and implying an augmentation or diminution in that body's capacity to act."[40] A bodily inscribed intensity, an experiential state, a potentially political positionality—though it is not difficult to see how the boundaries separating emotions, feelings, and affects might blur, Massumi's emphasis on the body's engagement with and expression of experience, and the complementary notion that these processes can catalyze or limit action, are central to affect theory.[41]

One might expect, given gothic literature's obsession with intense experience, that the gothic would offer fertile ground for the exploration of affect. Gothic studies, however, is curiously devoid of sustained critical considerations of affect, save for a few exceptions. Pointing to the gothic as "primarily structured so as to elicit particular responses in the reader," George E. Haggerty has identified gothic affect as central to, and even interchangeable with, gothic form. This affective structure is what allows the gothic to achieve its notoriously wide "range of interpretive possibility"—the "mutability" that Punter identifies.[42] Jerrold E. Hogle has identified gothic affect as "primordial fear made 'sublime' by safe fictional distancings from the ultimate threat of death." Hogle argues that the real is always enfolded within the exaggeration, hyperbole, and excess of the gothic, thus producing its affect, "its pulling us back to safety as much as it draws us towards the fear it keeps arousing."[43] Xavier Aldana Reyes, lamenting that "the purpose of the gothic—to scare, disturb, or disgust—has often been neglected," calls for a more thorough critical investigation of affect in gothic studies, one that prioritizes the gothic's concern with "readerly effect and immersion."[44] Bruno Lessard has written about "affect-value," the commodification of gothic affect in film.[45]

These studies all consider the affective consequences of the reader's or viewer's encounter with the gothic text. One of the ways the gothic works to frighten and distress its readers, though, is by depicting extremely affected characters: gothic victims are subjected to situations that elicit almost unbearably intense psychological, emotional, and physiological responses. With this in mind, my own considerations of affect, most prominent in chapter 2, shift the focus to the affective dynamics of the characters rather than of the readers. The two approaches, however, are inextricable: implicit in an investigation of character is the notion that the character's affect bears consequences for the reader who encounters him or her. Divergent subjects notwithstanding, Hogle's multilayered conceptualization of gothic affect—a manifestation of the tense coexistence of the real and the fake, proximity and distance, present and past—percolates this study.

Gothic in Hebrew Translation: A Brief Nonhistory

The Hebrew authors who call on the gothic do not do so in a vacuum. Those who immigrated to Palestine from Europe were, without exception, well read in European literature and had certainly encountered European gothic texts in their original language. In fact, this was the only way to access most of these texts, since scarcely any were translated to Hebrew until the 1980s. The Hebrew translation enterprise that thrived in Europe and Palestine in the early decades of the twentieth century was positioned as an arbiter of literary greatness; deciding which books to translate to Hebrew was a strategic act, calculated to enhance Hebrew literary culture and, finally, to legitimize the Zionist aspiration to be "a nation among the nations."[46] Clearly, the translation of melodramatic tales of the supernatural did not accord with these goals. Walpole's *Otranto* was not available in translation until 2014, but even more canonical gothic works, known beyond their affiliation with the gothic and widely considered "great books," were left out of Hebrew translation until late in the twentieth century. The first Hebrew translation of Mary Shelley's *Frankenstein* was published in 1983; Bram Stoker's *Dracula* was published a year later. Although German authors with gothic proclivities, such as Goethe and E. T. A. Hoffmann, were widely admired as great romantic authors, the dearth of translations of classic English-language gothic works to Hebrew demonstrates the low status of these works in the eyes of the Hebrew literary establishment.

There is one notable exception. In Warsaw, a small Hebrew edition of stories by Edgar Allan Poe was published in 1921 as part of the Biblioteka universalit (Universal Library) series of Lapid Press.[47] Readers of Hebrew could, as early as 1914, read Poe in Hebrew. That year, Ze'ev Jabotinsky (1880–1940), the polyglot right-wing ideologue best known as the founder of Revisionist Zionism, published the first Hebrew translation of Poe's poems "The Raven" and "Annabel Lee." His translations were reprinted throughout the twentieth century, ensuring that generations of Hebrew readers would recognize Poe's haunting refrain, "nevermore," rendered in Jabotinsky's iconic line: "אל עד-אין-דור" (*al ad-ein-dor*).[48] Jabotinsky himself counted "The Raven" as his most beloved work "of the world's poetical treasury."[49] The introduction to the 1964 bilingual edition of the translations was written by the Hebrew and Yiddish poet Uri Zvi Greenberg (1896–1981), a key figure in Revisionist Zionism and its right-wing politics. Strikingly, Greenberg casts Jabotinsky himself as a gothic figure whose Hebrew is possessed by and possesses Poe's poems:

> Had Edgar Allan Poe known Hebrew such as that in the translations by my dear sir, Poe would have bared his soul in just such Hebrew—and not in English—when he wrote "The Raven" and "Annabel Lee." . . . And since . . . Poe did not know such Hebrew but English, he was fortunate that the visionary spirit of the raven's nightly terror and the lovelorn pain for Annabel Lee flowed in the blood of the Hebrew wolf (זאב, *ze'ev*), who sat and wrote both of the poems *instead* of Poe—and on Poe's behalf—in superior Hebrew (עברית נעלה). A resonant Hebrew poetry that is among the most beautiful foreign poetry— with Hebrew tools.[50]

For Greenberg, the spirit of Poe's poetry inhabits Jabotinsky, who, in turn, uses Hebrew to possess the poems. Exemplifying the tenet that the translation of great works would enhance the Hebrew literary canon, Poe's works are "among the most beautiful foreign poetry" at the same time that they are Jabotinsky's original Hebrew creations, written "instead of Poe—and on Poe's behalf." Remarkably, "The Raven" has undergone more than a dozen different translations to Hebrew since Jabotinsky's, and new translations of his stories continue to appear well into the new millennium. Poe's popularity in Hebrew has not waned. Hillel Halkin remarks that "Jabotinsky's 'Annabel Lee,' like his Hebrew version of Poe's 'The Raven,' remains a highwater mark of Hebrew translation to this day."[51] Adam Rovner concurs, noting that even "today his translation of Poe's gothic verse is considered a masterpiece."[52] The prominent place that Poe has inhabited in the Hebrew literary consciousness for over a hundred years, however, is anomalous, unmatched by any other gothic author.[53] Until the late twentieth century, Hebrew readers and authors could access gothic literature only in its original language.

Nationalisms and the Undead: The Jew as Gothic Object

While direct literary influence may well play a role in Hebrew texts that employ the gothic, I am less interested in tracing self-conscious adaptations such as Hilu's. Rather, I want to indicate the extent to which gothic imagery and themes that informed the popular sensibility of Christian Europe were relevant to Jewish authors, who would later adapt and revise them to their own ends. The deployment of these widespread and persistent gothic images to construct a monstrous Jew against which Christian Europe would define itself suggests that the gothic is always already linked, in a fundamental way, to the Jew.

What is critical to this study is the consequence of this figuration: the experience of the Jew in Europe is necessarily shaped by the popular understanding of Jews in gothic terms. This conceptualization was adopted later by Jews, as well, in the articulation of their own national aspirations. Initially, this took the form of uncritical appropriation, whereby European Jews subscribed wholesale to existing Christian European notions identifying Jews with these gothic figures. Later Hebrew adaptations would divorce such images of their antisemitic provenance and claim them on their own terms, revising them to suit the needs of Hebrew national culture. These mutually informing points of convergence between the Jewish and the gothic, then, suggest that the experience of Jews in Europe is inextricable from the European perception of Jews as gothic figures. As such, these figures and their central role in defining and challenging national identities, both in the Christian European context and in the Jewish Zionist context, point to a fertile cultural precedent for the use of gothic in Hebrew literature. To give a sense of the influence they exerted in their respective cultural milieus, I want to outline several figures positioned at the juncture between Jewishness and the gothic. These figures demonstrate the centrality of the gothically figured Jew in the literary articulation of a rhetoric of national belonging and alterity. In this context, this section briefly addresses the vampire and the Wandering Jew, while the next section considers a third figure, *ha-met ha-ḥai*, or the "living dead" (המת החי).

For centuries, Christian Europe nurtured the stereotype of the Jew as a vampire, a creature simultaneously defiling and drinking the pure blood of his host nation.[54] This figure found a permanent place in the popular imagination with the publication of Bram Stoker's *Dracula* in 1897 and the myriad literary and cinematic adaptations that it continues to inspire, some of which, like F. W. Murnau's *Nosferatu* (1922), amplify the antisemitic inclination of the novel. The notion of the Jew-as-vampire, however, predates *Dracula*, as is no more strikingly evident than in the persistent blood libel narratives in which the Middle Ages are steeped. Even before the rise of European nationalisms in the nineteenth century, the vampiric nature of the Jew—imagined both as a literal impulse to consume blood and as an economic metaphor signifying greed and usury—designated his radical alterity vis-à-vis Christian Europe. The most far-reaching and grotesque consequence of imagining the Jew as a vampire was the adaptation of this stereotype as a centerpiece of the propaganda efforts of the Third Reich.[55]

A century and a half before the Holocaust, however, British gothic literature was mobilizing another archetype as a counterpoint to British nationhood: the Wandering Jew, a figure intimately related to and sometimes conflated with the vampire. The legend, which can be traced to antisemitic Christian treatises in the thirteenth century, tells of a Jew condemned to eternal wandering for his refusal to allow Jesus to rest on the Via Dolorosa.[56] Though the Wandering Jew is a stock character in gothic novels such as Matthew Lewis's *The Monk* (1795) and Charles Maturin's *Melmoth the Wanderer* (1820), his depiction in gothic literature strips him of his ethnic and historical specificity. At the same time, it relies on specifically antisemitic stereotypes, calling on him to signify what Michael Ragussis describes as "a homelessness that is almost metaphysical, a weariness and alienation that is fantastic as opposed to real."[57] As a figure seemingly resistant to the vicissitudes of time and history, argues Davison, the Wandering Jew was seen as a threat to an already fragile sense of progress, "a compelling agent of the uncanny upon whom are projected ambivalent feelings about modernity and the modernization process."[58] The "Jewish Question" in Europe is thus inextricably linked to the European preoccupation with "the undying and uncanny Wandering Jew spectre who haunts European nations."[59] To illustrate this connection, Davison opens her study with a quotation from the famous German essay by the Russian Zionist Leo Pinsker, "Auto-emancipation" (1882). "Auto-emancipation" vividly articulates the Christian fear of the uncanny spectral Jew. Though not literary, this foundational text of national Jewish culture adapts the images promulgated in gothic literature and shows how easily they could be invoked as a shared cultural currency in disparate national contexts.[60]

How do the gothic dynamics of this relationship shift when considered from the perspective of the feared and despised Jews with whom Pinsker identified and whom his essay addressed, rather than from the viewpoint of those Christian Europeans they supposedly threatened? Pinsker, a physician and outspoken public figure, anonymously published "Auto-emancipation" in the midst of violent pogroms in Russia in the early 1880s.[61] Through its gothic portrait of the relations between Jews and Christians in Europe, it argues that national sovereignty offers the only tenable solution for European Jewry. As an essay proposing a Jewish solution to the Jewish Question, it draws on gothic imagery not to denounce it but to affirm it and motivate the Jews to action. The story undergirding the nationalist call to action emerges, in Pinsker's essay, as a gothic story, the Jews as gothic figures.

Pinsker refers to the image of the Jews that had taken hold of the Christian European imagination sometimes as a reanimated corpse, "the uncanny form of one of the dead walking among the living," and others as a collective "wandering Jew."[62] These related images and the fears they evoke engender what he diagnoses as "Judeophobia" and indicate the need for the Jews to embrace nationalism. In other words, though he pathologizes antisemitism as "a form of demonopathy," he does not dispute the imagery that informs it.[63] The Jews, for Pinsker, *are* "a ghostlike apparition," a "dead and yet living nation." Their loss of national independence led to "a decay which is not compatible with existence as a whole vital organism," a liminal state of national living death.[64] Faced with this specter, Europe understandably developed its "fear of ghosts . . . the mother of Judeophobia."[65] Exorcism, not denial, will deprive Judeophobia of its subject. Furthermore, it is the Jews themselves who are responsible for this exorcism. Arguing that "the misfortunes of the Jews are due, above all, to their lack of desire for national independence," Pinsker insists that nationalism offers the only viable path for Jews to overcome this spectral condition as well as the demonic antisemitism it provokes.[66] Only when Jews stop wandering can they come back to life, and only as a living nation can they escape, finally, Europe's fear of ghosts.

Ghosts, vampires, and eternal wanderers are figures eminently suited to the representation of otherness. Pinsker, writing to an audience of "others," draws from this gothic lexicon to call for the realization of Jewish national aspirations. What is compelling is not necessarily that Zionists accepted ideas informing antisemitism, but that they adopted the language and aesthetic of these ideas to promote their own national ideology. "We, too, must not sit a moment longer with folded hands," cautions Pinsker. "[We] must not admit that we are doomed to play on in the future the hopeless role of the 'Wandering Jew.'"[67] Yet Pinsker's appropriation of gothic rhetoric belies far more than unquestioning acceptance of a rigid non-Jewish/Jewish dyad neatly paralleling related binaries such as home/exile and self/other. European Jewry is neither the only ghost he identifies nor the only wanderer. In his account, the Jews are both haunter and haunted, as antisemitism itself is identified as a spectral force: "Thus have Judaism and Anti-Semitism passed for centuries through history as inseparable companions. Like the Jewish people, the real wandering Jew, Anti-Semitism, too, seems as if it would never die."[68] As Pinsker reimagines Judeophobia itself as the eternal Wandering Jew, so does Davison articulate antisemitism as "a disturbing revenant that has been variously repressed and expressed throughout history," identifying it, in the British context, as "the real vampire that has birthed demons by projecting its macabre tendencies onto the Jew."[69] The specters of Europe and the vampires imagined to drink and defile its blood are mediated by the figure of the Wandering Jew, who, in British gothic literature, incorporates elements of both. Whether interpreted as the victim of a Christian European pathology or as the embodiment of this pathology, whether invoked as a bogeyman threatening European identity or as a rallying cry for Jewish nationalism, the Wandering Jew has been central in the conceptualization of national selves.

Ha-met ha-ḥai: Hebrew and Gothic

As the primary representatives of national Hebrew culture, authors and poets, too, turned to gothic imagery to imagine the Jewish nation as rising from the dead, reborn from the living death of diasporic Jewish existence and, in later decades, from the ashes of the Holocaust. Though in this study I have chosen to focus almost exclusively on prose, which historically has been the primary medium of gothic literature, Hebrew poetry was instrumental in forging and popularizing a lexicon of enduring images to articulate the national endeavor. Well established in nationalistic poetry from the early twentieth century, the image of the nation and its people extricating themselves from the tomb of the diaspora invokes death to affirm rebirth, the grave to affirm the cradle. Uri Zvi Greenberg, for example, the Hebrew and Yiddish poet, essayist, journalist, and leading figure of Revisionist Zionism, produced Hebrew poetry that was at times unrelentingly macabre in its portrayal of diasporic existence through graphic images of death, decay, and blood.[70]

The most salient and sustained example of gothic imagery in the service of Jewish nationalism is the figure, central in works by the modernist poet, essayist, and translator Nathan Alterman (1910–70), of ha-met ha-ḥai, or the "living dead," the third character positioned at the juncture of the gothic and the Jewish. Like Greenberg, Alterman was an intensely political poet and a critical force of Hebrew modernism. Ha-met ha-ḥai, a romantic figure crossing the boundary between life and death, has spurred diverse interpretations over the decades. In Alterman's earlier poems, such as those collected in *Kokhavim baḥuts* (Stars outside, 1938), it was associated primarily with love and personal loss. Later works by Alterman and other poets saw the figure mobilized to political ends such as secular martyrdom and nationalist self-sacrifice, whether to support or to subvert these ideals. The ubiquity of the living dead in Hebrew poetry from the 1930s on shows that gothic elements were shaping Hebrew literary culture long before Hilu googled Ann Radcliffe.

As a key figure in Alterman's oeuvre, ha-met ha-ḥai has elicited a wide range of critical interpretations, from the perspectives of symbolism, decadence, Romanticism, the medieval ballad, and, of course, modernism.[71] The figure is primarily understood in the context of the poet's response to contemporary events, including the rise of fascism in Europe and the war of 1948. As Hanan Hever has noted, the status of ha-met ha-ḥai as a national symbol rooted in an urgent contemporary political reality suggests that the figure's return from death amounts to "a spiritual, collective-national life and not a physical, individual one."[72] Other critics are more concerned with the personal dimension of ha-met ha-ḥai, interpreting the figure through Alterman's internal confrontation with his own experiences as the culmination of his love poems.[73] Focusing on the poetic provenance of ha-met ha-ḥai, these critics use it to position Alterman within a broader literary tradition.

In one such article about *Simḥat aniyim* (*The Joy of the Poor*, 1941), a long poem about a dead husband who returns from the grave and observes his living wife and daughter, Dan Miron proposes the gothic as a forceful influence. In this poem, which Miron considers comparable to works by Nathaniel Hawthorne or Edgar Allan Poe, Alterman "consciously and intentionally exploits the atmosphere of the gothic tale."[74] Indeed, insists Miron, "the use of macabre gothic effects is absolutely legitimate within the fairytale frame of *Simḥat aniyim*, and in truth, is characteristic of a significant portion of Alterman's poetry as a whole."[75] Ha-met ha-ḥai is the exemplar of these effects. Other gothic motifs and characteristics complement this figure, as Miron shows, including Alterman's use of candles and gas lamps, the demonic gaiety of his settings, and the marked mobility of ha-met ha-ḥai himself, who sometimes crosses the line from life to living death while walking, a macabre take on the picaro, himself a species of wanderer.[76]

The interpretation, in 1961, of Alterman's *Simḥat aniyim* as participating in a well-established gothic tradition provoked a hostile response from a founding father of modern Hebrew literary criticism, Baruch Kurzweil. Kurzweil argued that, though an affinity between macabre European and American literature and Alterman "admittedly exists," the poetry of Alterman demands not such an external comparative reading but rather one that attends to the internal, immanent rules governing Alterman's poetry specifically and modern Hebrew poetry more broadly.[77] Ha-met ha-ḥai in Alterman "is more than a fashionable game with a macabre subject," Kurzweil asserts, adding that "we do not require the external aid of the motif of the macabre" to understand Alterman's poetry.[78] Seen as merely the subject of a "fashionable game," the gothic, for Kurzweil, lacks the solemnity required for the interpretation of Alterman's poetry in its political and historical contexts.

Yet as is evident from gothic criticism published in recent decades, the gothic, however alien or fantastic, never strays far from the concerns of its time. Furthermore, Kurzweil's dismissal of the mode accords precisely with the critical reception of British gothic literature, which, from the eighteenth century to the twentieth, tended to dismiss gothic works as lacking literary value, except for a handful of authors and texts. Most critically, Kurzweil's heated rejection of Miron's reading suggests that turning to the gothic to explain key Hebrew literary images and motifs, such as ha-met ha-ḥai, denies Hebrew its aesthetic and thematic autonomy. This autonomy can be understood in direct relation to the autoemancipation Pinsker urged. If Hebrew readers must turn to the gothic to interpret Hebrew literature, then that literature still relies on Europe, like the vampire who parasitically consumes the blood of others to survive, or the spectral nation-not-nation that haunts the territory of others for lack of its own land. For Kurzweil, reading Alterman through the gothic signals a failed cultural emancipation and casts the poet himself as a vampire.

To the Victim Go the Spoils

Perhaps the most gothic attribute of ha-met ha-ḥai is its signification of transgression, ambiguity, and the tense cohabitation of unlikely forces and states of being. The trespass between life and death as an act amenable to both personal and political interpretation exposes the artifice of the boundary between them. Ha-met ha-ḥai, understood thus, is an individual and also a collective, a lover and also a soldier, a human and also a symbol, living and also dead, hero and also victim. In many of these poems, dead men continue to speak from beyond the grave, whence they reaffirm the moral purpose of their death in the context of the national endeavor. The "theme of the victim," as Ortsion Bartana calls it, that informs this paradoxical figure offers a particularly productive approach to the gothic in Hebrew literature.[79] Read as the national symbol of the Zionist idealization of self-sacrifice, ha-met ha-ḥai "assumes his full national identity" upon making the choice that transforms him, simultaneously, into a hero and a victim, proposes Bartana.[80]

Yet the victim position itself is rife with ambiguity and ambivalence. Published during the Holocaust, Alterman's historic poetic cycle "*Shirey makot Mitsrayim*" ("Poems of the Plagues of Egypt," 1944), which invokes ha-met ha-ḥai in the setting of the biblical exodus, offers an unexpected extranational perspective on the history of the Jews' persecution. In it, Alterman reconceptualizes the historical narrative to emphasize the personal rather than the collective aspect of violence and victimhood.[81] The twilight existence shaped by a heroic invitation of one's own death or by the renegotiated ethics of powerlessness sets the stage for other manifestations of victimization and responses to persecution in the Jewish context, vis-à-vis the vulnerability of life in the diaspora, the gendered powerlessness of traditional domestic life, strength in the wake of debilitating loss, and damaged or unwritten histories. Whether read as a melancholy lover or a hegemonic national symbol, ha-met ha-ḥai indicates a forceful affinity among victimization, power, and the culture of death that would help shape the twentieth-century Hebrew imagination.

A preoccupation with victims, villains, and persecution is evident in all the major gothic literary works. In Walpole's *Castle of Otranto*, a horrified Isabella flees from her lecherous father-in-law; in Lewis's *The Monk*, Ambrosio sells his soul to the devil upon ravishing and murdering the innocent Antonia; in Radcliffe's *Mysteries of Udolpho*, the brigand Montoni imprisons the blameless Emily St. Aubert in an isolated castle. Several traits typify such characters in gothic novels: the hyperbolic malevolence of the gothic villain, the naivete and goodness of the gothic victim, and the sensational twists and turns of a fast-paced but long-winded plot that either restores the victim to safety and punishes or banishes the villain, or sees the demise of the victim at the villain's hand. These conventions suggest a clear-cut binary dynamic governing victims and villains. Indeed, many gothic villains are marked as "other" by their names, such as, for example, Radcliffe's Italian villains, Montoni, Schedoni, and Mazzini, or Bram Stoker's Count Dracula. Their status as foreign heightens the sense of essential difference between the victim and the villain and makes the victim/oppressor construct eminently applicable to the delineation of a distinct national identity *against* another. As psychoanalytic theory shows, the persecutory anxieties brought on by the threat of victimization and the dissolution of the self are a prerequisite to the formation or maintenance of a coherent sense of self.[82] Some critics have astutely argued that the ostensibly rigid binary structure of victim/oppressor is often subverted in gothic texts, offering compelling new readings of apparently straightforward plots.[83] Whether read at face value or as a performance of a more subversive effort, the victim/oppressor construct and the plot it structures are defining conventions of the gothic mode.

Since notions of victimization and suffering have dictated critical debates on Jewish historiography throughout the twentieth century, an analysis of the gothic expression of the Jewish past in Hebrew literature must contend with what Adi Ophir calls the "identity of the victims."[84] While Hannah Arendt argued that "Jews have always been objects and not active forces in their own history," the historian Salo Wittmayer Baron spent much of his career refuting this view of the Jews as passive victims of history.[85] More broadly, he opposed the conceptualization of Jewish history as one of endless suffering and antisemitic persecution, a stance that he saw other historians promoting to the detriment of more positive forces and developments in Jewish history through the ages. "The lachrymose conception of Jewish history" that Baron famously rejected underpinned a force motivating political Zionism: the renunciation of the identity of the victim, which came to be seen as the purview of life in the diaspora. As Pinsker asserts in "Auto-emancipation," political powerlessness, the consequence of statelessness, made Jews vulnerable; a state would make them strong. Though early Zionists considered Jews to be the historic victims of antisemitism, however, "they did not assume the victim position" themselves, as Adi Ophir points out.[86] Established in 1948, in the wake of the Holocaust, the State of Israel defined itself in accordance with Zionist ideology, which repudiated the perceived powerlessness of the diaspora. It called, instead, for the formation of a New Jew who would defy this weakness by being an active agent of his own history rather than the passive object of others' actions. Though Zionists sought to renounce victimhood, victimhood came to be seen as a necessary condition for the practical realization of the Zionist dream.

Until the Eichmann trial, the topic of the Holocaust was almost taboo in the Israeli public realm, partly because of the perception that Jews should have somehow acted against their persecution.[87] The trial was a turning point because it invited the Nazis' victims to tell their stories publicly, and it encouraged Israeli Jews to identify with their victimization in the interest of fostering a sense of collectivity, giving rise to what Martin S. Jaffee has called a "victim-community." Publicly telling the story of the victim consolidates the victim-community through memorialization, solidarity, and identification, "bringing into its history the power of its myth and mapping onto its own political and social reality the mythic plot through which it comes to self-understanding as a community of suffering."[88] The Jewish Israeli collective's self-perception as a "community of suffering," as Idith Zertal has shown, constitutes an "essential stage in the formation and shaping of a national community," based on the shared and unifying memory and narration of "catastrophes, suffering, and victimization."[89] Thus, Zertal argues, the victim-community maintains itself by resisting the past's finality, compelling its ghosts to haunt in perpetuity: "The dead do not belong solely to the past; they are a vital and active part of the present."[90] In Israel, she notes, both Holocaust victims and the historical event itself "were brought to life again and again" in the context of present-day political and military deliberations and dilemmas. Auschwitz, "as the embodiment of the total, ultimate evil," is conceptualized as "not a past event but a threatening present and a constant option."[91] To ensure that the Holocaust never return, then, Israeli Jews preserve its spectral presence. The Eichmann trial provided a major public forum for the consolidation of the Israeli victim-community.[92]

The dynamics of victimization shifted once more after the Six-Day War of 1967, when Israel, now an occupying power, came to be seen as an aggressor and the Palestinians as its hapless victim. Since at least the sixties, the Holocaust has provided a vocabulary of victimization for both sides: Israelis have mobilized it to justify their actions, accusing the Arab nations of desiring, like the Nazis, to obliterate the Jews, while the Palestinians have harnessed it to indict Israel and its prolonged occupation. The Intifadas, settlement building, failed peace talks, and terror attacks that have defined Israeli-Palestinian relations for decades have engendered a sophisticated media apparatus through which both the Israelis and the Palestinians vie, before the world, for the position of the victim. This cynical competition has created a sense of what might be called "victim fatigue." When examples of historic persecution such as the Holocaust are invoked so often, so predictably, and in justification of such a wide range of actions, even this horrific event loses its force.[93] Furthermore, such competitions accomplish little more than the disparagement and even the denial of the suffering experienced by the other, a defiant performance of antiempathy that has permeated rhetoric and praxis on both sides. Ironically, to legitimize its military strength and power over the Palestinians, Israel finds itself continuing to cultivate the very victim position it yearned to escape.

The prominent role of victimization in questions of Jewish and Israeli historiographic practice might help explain the attraction of the gothic mode to Hebrew authors whose writing complicates "the lachrymose conception" of the Jewish past. Drawing from the gothic to revise or reconceptualize the past, these authors subscribe to a different poetics of victimization, one that looks beyond the standard paradigm that pits victim against oppressor, suffering against blame, and Jew against non-Jew. As such, they create unexpected new modes for the confrontation with and representation of history. The appropriation of the gothic to this end is innovative in the context of Hebrew literature as well as in gothic studies, where even subversions of the victim position seem only to reinforce the binary that structures it.[94] The Hebrew gothic revision of the victim position, though manifested differently in different texts, is concerned less with redrawing and reversing dividing lines and more with dismantling these divisions altogether, creating the conditions for a critique of the collective Jewish self.

* * *

Though my approach varies from text to text, I employ a comparative methodology that combines critical theory, much of it in conversation with the field of gothic studies, and close readings of literary texts. Each chapter of this book focuses on a different episode or era in the Jewish or Israeli past and its historically conditioned power relations, diversely expressed and exemplified by one or two fictional texts that draw on gothic conventions and devices. The chapters are organized around theoretical paradigms that stress salient dimensions of the literary texts' gothicism. In several chapters, I turn to American or British gothic narratives to help excavate certain points and to highlight proximity or disjunctures vis-à-vis the Hebrew texts. Reading these Hebrew texts side by side with their English-language counterparts is imperative for their conceptualization as part of a broader discourse about the gothic thematization of history. It invites us to consider Hebrew literature globally *beyond* the conventional cultural or historical contexts that tend to define comparative studies of Hebrew. Though such studies have yielded important critical work on Hebrew's engagement with Yiddish, German, Arabic, and Russian literatures, we stand to gain much by broadening the comparative scope to include points of contact with other traditions, ones that may not have a "biographical" or "genealogical" claim on Hebrew literary culture.

The first chapter focuses on two macabre short stories by the most prominent and influential author of modern Hebrew, S. Y. Agnon: "Meḥolat ha-mavet" ("The Dance of Death," 1916) and "Ha-adonit ve-ha-rokhel" ("The Lady and the Peddler," 1943). The gothic in these stories is readily apparent in their supernatural figures and violent plots. In one, a famished vampire dies when her bloodlust is thwarted; in the other, a bridegroom murdered on his wedding day rises nightly from his grave to dance with his bride, who dies a melancholy death after being kidnapped by his murderer. Reading closely the stories' invocation of blood and wandering, themselves prevalent gothic themes, I point to the stories' depiction of violent episodes in an Eastern European past that cannot be confined to its grave. This restless past invades the present to suggest that turbulent contemporary events, namely the two world wars and the Holocaust, are another manifestation of the cyclical temporality defining Jewish history. Thus gothicized, the European Jewish past is intimately entangled with the present that would leave it behind. The Jewish experience is always already gothic, and history is never past.

The second chapter considers early twentieth-century representations of Eastern European Jewish motherhood and femininity in two stories: "Shifra" (1927) by Dvora Baron, one of the first women authors of modern Hebrew, and "Ha-iveret" (The blind woman, 1923), by Ya'akov Shteinberg, a Hebrew and Yiddish poet. In both stories, a young woman is forced to leave her mother's home to conform to the social norms of her time and place. Both heroines find themselves in profoundly unwelcoming and even sinister spaces that indicate a critique of the social norms that consigned the women there. Centered on a tension between visibility and seeing, the gothic paradigm of a "domestic carceral" structures these women's experiences at the margins of their Eastern European communities.[95] Their affective reactions to this tension and its spatial circumstances unveil an alternative feminine narrative of the place of women in the Eastern European Jewish past. Though these stories' expressions of space and subjectivity in some ways accord with the tenets of "gothic feminism," in others they depart from it decisively, reflecting the authors' complex relations with the places of their past.

Chapter 3 exposes the relation between gothic temporality, characterized by spatiotemporal disjunctures, and the impossibility of a safe haven. Contextualizing these concerns within the period immediately following the Holocaust, this chapter underlines Jewish ambivalence regarding Europe as well as regarding the national homeland established as its only viable alternative. How can we long for a beautiful European past, if its beauty depends on a deadly stasis seemingly divorced from reality? How can we inhabit a present deformed by ideologies stripped of all aesthetic sensibility, no matter how dynamic and inclusive? Bringing together "Ba'alat ha-armon" ("The Lady of the Castle," 1954), a play by Leah Goldberg, one of the foremost Hebrew poets, and Edgar Allan Poe's story "The Masque of the Red Death" (1842), I consider the relation between art, as the representative of a beautiful, static temporality, and the safe haven, which works to preserve this stasis or eradicate it, but does both at a steep cost. Read thus, the anxious post-Holocaust present gives rise to a provocative revision of victimization and a critique of the accomplishments of nationalism.

After reading texts that engage primarily with the Jewish past in Europe, I turn to those that grapple with the historical reverberations of 1948 and the establishment of the State of Israel. Chapter 4 considers Jerusalem, a blood-soaked city perpetually situated at the crosshairs of history and on the verge of religious and political violence. Its geography, its ethnic and religious heterogeneity, its historically steeped sensibility, and even its architecture and design create the ideal conditions for a gothic cityscape characterized by claustrophobia and paranoia. Amos Oz's 1967 novel *Mikhael sheli* (*My Michael*) portrays a partitioned Jerusalem whose dark, tense atmosphere sets the stage for his heroine's paranoia and whose images and symbols of the past threaten the fragile stability of the present. Time, the agent of the uncanny in Jerusalem, activates anxiety on a personal level as well as on broader historical levels. On the eve of 1967, Oz brings to the fore Jerusalem's inherent gothicism to contend with the war of 1948, an event formative in his own experience and in Zionist history, which would return in triumph and ambivalence in Israeli culture and historiographic discourse.

Chapter 5 approaches the question of origins more broadly. Stepping outside the contested geographic terrain of Israel/Palestine and into a splintered cartographic and historical perspective, it examines the multilayered, pseudohistorical genealogical narrative of A. B. Yehoshua's novel *Mar Mani* (*Mr. Mani*, 1989). Comparing *Mr. Mani* to the first gothic novel, Walpole's *The Castle of Otranto*, I demonstrate how Yehoshua's novel, written just as the "New Historians" were calling for a new conceptualization of Israeli history and specifically of the war of 1948, calls on the gothic in the service of its own revisionism. Both works illuminate threats to national identity through the corruption of filial bloodlines through incest and other transgressions identified with the gothic. Both, too, raise questions relevant beyond the immediate historical circumstances of their writing, indicating the gothic elements of their plots as highly consequential in the production of historiography itself. The chapter seeks not only to consider the process by which stories are told and become fixed as "history" but also to address the ways historical narrative is manipulated, erased, propagated, and perceived.

The final chapter picks up where chapter 5 leaves off, considering how official histories underpin power structures rooted in past injustice. Ghosts unsettle and disrupt these power structures, but the trajectory of haunting can challenge our expectations. Rather than representatives of the forgotten come to force their way into the forgetful consciousness of the hegemon, specters may haunt versions of themselves, those who *ought* to have remembered. They might focus their attention less on the perpetrators of historiographic injustice and more on those who have, through cultivated forgetting, enabled it, though they themselves have been its victims. In this light, this chapter compares the return of repressed histories in Almog Behar's story "Ana min al-Yahoud" (2005) and Toni Morrison's novel *Beloved* (1987). Both texts depict transgenerational hauntings that amount to a haunting of the self, attentive to the nuanced struggle within the self over and above that between the victim and the perpetrator. The gothic revenants who literalize both texts' preoccupation with memory and forgetting also work to reappropriate language. Haunting, therefore, not only activates the characters' reclamation of their own occluded narratives but also allows them to tell their stories on their own terms.

The study's coda arrives at the contemporary popular moment. I close by considering how the ethical and ideological implications of negotiating the Jewish past through the gothic relate to the emergence of popular contemporary gothic works in Israel today, such as Gal Amir's Galilean gothic novel *Laila adom* (Red night, 2003), Vered Tochterman's vampire erotica *Dam kahol* (Blue blood, 2011), and a veritable onslaught of "Hebrew Horror" films and television series. The undeniable surge in popular gothic suggests that in Israel's charged contemporary political climate, the questions and anxieties that motivated the authors in this study are still relevant and increasingly urgent. At a time when the official gatekeepers of Israeli identity show no signs of relinquishing their claims of victimization, the ambivalent poetics of persecution exposed in *Hebrew Gothic* suggests a far more nuanced notion of Hebrew national culture.

Notes

1. Hilu, *Ahuzat Dajani*, 13.
2. Hilu, *The House of Rajani*, author's note (n.p.).
3. For more on the responses to Hilu's novel, see Eshel, *Futurity*, 155–60.
4. Walpole, *Castle of Otranto*, 3.
5. Hilu, "Alon Hilu Recommends."
6. The term "first wave Gothics" is Ridenhour's. See *In Darkest London*, 1.
7. Numerous studies examine the role of the gothic in the formation of British identity, including Wein, *British Identities*; Schmitt, *Alien Nation*; Edwards, "British Gothic Nationhood"; and Miles, "Abjection, Nationalism, and the Gothic."

8. For more on the gothic in the formation of an American national identity, see Goddu, *Gothic America*; on gothic in a Canadian national context, see Edwards, *Gothic Canada*.

9. Teresa A. Goddu published her landmark study *Gothic America* in 1997, with the goal of "resurrecting the gothic as a critical term in American literary studies" and contributing to "the destabilization of traditional readings of the American literary canon" (8). Goddu identifies the gothic in an array of American texts typically classified as romantic and even realist, arguing for the acknowledgment of the gothic as a pervasive force in American literature writ large.

10. Some examples are Rudd, *Postcolonial Gothic Fictions*; Hughes and Smith, *Queering the Gothic*; Sugars and Turcotte, *Unsettled Remains*; Khair, *Gothic, Postcolonialism and Otherness*; Haggerty, *Queer Gothic*; Hoeveler, *Gothic Feminism*; Wolstenholme, *Gothic (Re)Visions*; and K. Ellis, *Contested Castle*.

11. See Byron, *Globalgothic*.

12. Punter, *New Companion to the Gothic*, 3.

13. Ibid.

14. Ibid.

15. Davison, *Gothic Literature 1764–1824*, 10.

16. Punter, *Literature of Terror*, 1:18, 2:187.

17. M. Ellis, *History of Gothic Fiction*, 11.

18. Ibid., 14.

19. Punter, "Introduction: Of Apparitions," 3.

20. Ibid.

21. Ibid.

22. Wasson, *Urban Gothic*, 23.

23. Despite the absence of a distinct historical starting point or clearly delineated trajectory of the use of gothic in Hebrew literature, it is worth noting Kalman Schulman's wildly popular Hebrew translation of Eugène Sue's melodramatic serialized French novel *Les mystères de Paris* [*The Mysteries of Paris*, 1842–43], one of the first European literary works to be translated to Hebrew. Published in four installments from 1857 to 1860, the Hebrew translation's popularity, rivaled in Hebrew at the time only by Avraham Mapu's *Ahavat Tsiyon* [*Love of Zion*, 1853], sparked a heated debate about the adaptation of Hebrew to the novel form. Though more of an urban thriller or a crime novel than gothic, its melodramatic tone, its unsavory events and characters, and its wide accessibility and popularity evoked in some critics a skepticism or anxiety that presaged that of later readers toward the prospect of Hebrew gothic.

For more on how translations of *Les mystères* to Hebrew, Yiddish, Judeo-Arabic, and Ladino helped create "a transnational network of Jewish literary culture," see Levy and Schachter, "Jewish Literature/World Literature" (99).

24. The scholarship on these figures, particularly on the golem, is abundant. Recent studies include Barzilai, *Golem: Modern Wars*; Baer, *Golem Redux*; Gelbin, *Golem Returns*; and Dauber, *Demon's Bedroom*.

25. This artifice is borne out not only by Hebrew authors' deployment of the gothic, supposedly incompatible with their experience, but also by the fact that figures such as the golem, as Barzilai points out in her study, regularly appeared in narratives produced by non-Jews: "The modern golem narrative has been adapted and readapted, written and rewritten by Jews and non-Jews alike" (Barzilai, *Golem: Modern Wars*, 8).

26. Though not regularly spoken among Jews since the late biblical period, the Hebrew language never died. Throughout the Middle Ages, it was used as the language of Jewish liturgy, of rabbinic literature, of correspondence, of record keeping, and of philosophy, and as the lingua franca connecting Jews from disparate geographical locales. For more than three hundred years, starting in the tenth century, authors on the Iberian peninsula produced secular poetry and even prose in Hebrew, a tradition that continued in Italy well into the modern period. The secular Hebrew culture that emerged in the context of the Haskalah, the Jewish Enlightenment, in eighteenth-century Prussia, produced self-consciously ideological literature. With the onset of political Zionism in the 1880s, the transformation of Hebrew from a lively, if still awkward, secular literary language to a spoken national language became a central preoccupation. The rhetoric of Hebrew as "dead," however, was invoked to emphasize the accomplishments of Zionism, which catalyzed its revival as a spoken language.

27. Pilar Blanco and Peeren, "Introduction: Conceptualizing Spectralities," 15.

28. Derrida, *Specters of Marx*, 202.

29. For a critique from the perspective of trauma studies, for example, see Pilar Blanco and Peeren, "Introduction: Conceptualizing Spectralities," 11–15. For a broader critique of the spectral turn as expounding a "very generalized economy of haunting," see Luckhurst, "Contemporary London Gothic," 534.

30. C. Davis, "État présent," 56; Pilar Blanco and Peeren, "Spectral Turn/Introduction," 34.

31. C. Davis, "État présent," 54.

32. Derrida, *Specters of Marx*, xviii.

33. Pilar Blanco and Peeren, "Introduction," *Popular Ghosts*, xvi.

34. Luckhurst, "Contemporary London Gothic," 536.

35. Ibid., 535.

36. Ibid., 536.

37. Pilar Blanco and Peeren, "Introduction," *Popular Ghosts*, xvi.

38. Luckhurst, "Contemporary London Gothic," 528.

39. Gregg and Seigworth, "Inventory of Shimmers," 4.

40. Massumi, "Pleasures of Philosophy," xvi.

41. For some, this interpretation of affect creates a problematic dichotomy that separates cognition and intention, body and mind. In her thoughtful critique of some of the key currents of affect theory, Ruth Leys writes that its central thinkers in the humanities and social sciences, including Massumi and Eric Shouse, "suggest that the affects must be viewed as independent of, and in an important sense prior to, ideology." As a result, "action and behavior are held to be determined by affective dispositions that are independent of consciousness and the mind's control" ("Turn to Affect," 437, 443). Leys challenges this notion through an examination of affect theory's engagement with neuroscience, accusing the affect theorists she examines of operating according to a "false opposition between the mind and the body" (ibid., 458).

42. Haggerty, *Gothic Fiction/Gothic Form*, 8, 10.

43. Hogle, "Hyper-reality," 166, 169.

44. Aldana Reyes, "Gothic Affect," 12.

45. Lessard, "Gothic Affect."

46. In the period of the Yishuv (the pre-state Jewish settlement in Palestine), as Zohar Shavit has shown, works deemed worthy of translation to Hebrew and publication fell into two categories: either they qualified as "great books" or "classics" of world literature, or they promoted "educational values" ("Status of Translated Literature," 47). She identifies two trends in translation policy in the Yishuv. The first, promoted by the labor parties, "empha-

sized the need to publish books of perceived ideological value. Both original and translated literature was required to suit the needs of the Hebrew laborer" (48). The second, expounded by Ze'ev Jabotinsky, stressed the need for a wider variety of translated texts. Jabotinsky advocated for "a comprehensive project of translation and original writing" to bolster national culture: "since there could be no national culture without literature, . . . any void would be filled by foreign literature" (48–49). In other words, though Jabotinsky did not consider explicit ideological themes to be the primary determinant of whether texts should be translated to Hebrew, ultimately, he, too, understood the act of translation as an ideological one central to the development of a national Hebrew culture.

47. The collection, entitled simply *Sipurim* [Stories], includes Hebrew translations of Poe's "The Black Cat," "The Masque of the Red Death," and "Silence." Only the initials of the translator are supplied, *yod alef*; this likely refers to Yisrael Eliyahu Handelzats (1879–1942), a Hebrew teacher and translator in Poland, who also translated Poe's "The Pit and the Pendulum" to Hebrew in 1920.

48. For an account of "Poe's literary afterlife" in Hebrew poetry and translation, see Dykman, "Poe's Poetry in Israel (and Russia)" (33).

49. Jabotinsky, *Story of My Life*, 44.

50. Greenberg, "Ze'ev Jabotinsky," 13 (emphasis in original).

51. H. Halkin, *Jabotinsky: A Life*, 121.

52. Rovner, *Shadow of Zion*, 132.

53. In the Hebrew literary milieu, Poe was known primarily as a progenitor of symbolism and decadence and associated with the French poets Charles Baudelaire (1821–67), Paul Verlaine (1844–96), and Arthur Rimbaud (1854–91). While this association likely bestowed on Poe a measure of literary status that eluded other gothic authors in Hebrew eyes, it does not diminish the gothicism of his works nor explain why they have continued to attract the attention of Hebrew readers and translators throughout the twentieth century. In 2016, the prominent academic publishing house Resling published an essay by a highly regarded contemporary translator of Poe, Oded Wolkstein, titled "Ani omer lakhem she-ani met!" [I'm telling you I'm dead!]. The essay's primary concern is not translation but the struggle between the author and the interpreting reader. Of note in the context of this study is Wolkstein's focus on Poe as, first and foremost, a gothic author.

54. Numerous studies have examined the Jew-vampire association in Europe. Brenda Gardenour traces it to medieval discourses of law. She asserts that "the vampire Jew reflects a long history of anti-Judaism in European culture that began in the late-twelfth and early-thirteenth centuries with the systematic application of Aristotelian natural philosophy to issues of theology," resulting in the creation of the "pure" body of the Christian male and the corrupt, feminized, and bloodthirsty body of the Jewish other ("Biology of Blood-Lust," 51–52). Marie Mulvey-Roberts observes that one "of the most damaging conflations of monstrosity and race has been that of vampire and Jew," a link that "goes back to the Middle Ages and has been perpetuated through folklore, literature, and cinema" (*Dangerous Bodies*, 129). Other studies examining the correlation between Jews and vampires in European culture include, for example, Davison, *Anti-Semitism*; Halberstam, "Technologies of Monstrosity"; Gelder, *Reading the Vampire*; and Robinson, *Blood Will Tell*.

55. On the continuity between the anti-Jewish blood myths of the Middle Ages and Nazi antisemitism, see Biale, "Power in the Blood: The Medieval and the Modern in Nazi Antisemitism," in *Blood and Belief*, 123–61. See also Davison, "Afterword: Pathological Projection and the Nazi Nightmare," in *Anti-Semitism*, 158–65.

56. For more on the legend of the Wandering Jew, see Hasan-Rokem and Dundes, *Wandering Jew*.

57. Ragussis, *Figures of Conversion*, 136.

58. Davison, *Anti-Semitism*, 22.

59. Ibid., 1. Davison's important study *Anti-Semitism and British Gothic Literature* makes a substantive contribution to the efforts to recuperate the ethnic and historical specificity of the Wandering Jew, and to indicate his central role in the development of a British national identity. Pointing to a shift in the basis of antisemitism from religion to race in the eighteenth century and to the related specters of Jewish difference and assimilation, she argues that the "Wandering Jew in British Gothic fiction functions . . . to both strengthen and unsettle an idealized vision of Englishness" (ibid., 8). Gothic fiction invoked this figure not, like medieval uses of the tale, to justify or promulgate acts of persecution and violence against Jews, but rather to raise "the question of the nature and parameters of European national identity" (ibid., 2). For more on British national identity and the "Jewish Question," see Ragussis, *Figures of Conversion*; and Shapiro, *Shakespeare and the Jews*.

60. Davison, *Anti-Semitism*.

61. The broader historical trajectory that led many Jewish intellectuals to Zionism can be traced to the Enlightenment. The Enlightenment's rejection of superstitions associated with the Middle Ages sparked hope among Europe's Jews and gave rise to a Jewish counterpart, the Haskalah. One of the central tenets espoused by the proponents of the Haskalah, the *maskilim*, was that assimilation would lead to the acceptance of the Jews as equals in Europe. Yet despite the Enlightenment rhetoric that suggested a tolerant, rational Europe, and despite the best efforts of the maskilim, who learned German and French, intermarried, and abandoned Orthodox Judaism, antisemitism never disappeared. The outbreak of anti-Jewish violence in Eastern Europe in the 1880s proved a tipping point for the maskilim, who sought alternatives to assimilation in the Socialist Bund or in political Zionism. Among those who cast their lot with the latter was Leo Pinsker. His "Auto-emancipation" is recognized as a key Zionist text.

62. L. Pinsker, "Auto-emancipation," 7, 9.

63. Ibid., 8.

64. Ibid., 7.

65. Ibid., 8.

66. Ibid., 6–7.

67. Ibid., 18.

68. Ibid., 9.

69. Davison, *Anti-Semitism*, 14.

70. For more on Greenberg's aestheticization of violence, see Hever, *Moledet ha-mavet yafa*.

71. See, for example, Bartana, "Image of the 'Living-Dead'"; Z. Shamir, "Ha-met ha-ḥai"; Oppenheimer, "Gilgulav shel degem ha-met ha-ḥai"; Miron, "Ha-met ve-ha-re'aya"; Shaham, "Bein mithizatsya le-demithizatsya"; Hever, "Ḥai ha-ḥai"; Arpali, "Ha-met ve-ha-re'aya."

72. Hever, *Sight of War*, 42.

73. For example, see Miron, "Ha-met ve-ha-re'aya."

74. Ibid., 92.

75. Ibid., 94.

76. Numerous critics have pointed to the link between ha-met ha-ḥai and the biblical figure of Cain, doomed to wander in perpetuity after he murdered his brother Abel. The

figure of Cain was also associated with Ahasureus, cursed to become the eternal Wandering Jew because he refused to grant Jesus a resting place on the Via Dolorosa. See, for example, Z. Shamir, "Ha-met ha-ḥai." On the Jewish literary adaptation of the picaresque as a function of "minor" or marginal modernism that both aligned with and diverged from European literary traditions, see Udel, *Never Better!*

77. Kurzweil, "Mahuta shel simḥat aniyim," 127.
78. Ibid., 129.
79. Bartana, "Image of the 'Living-Dead,'" 193.
80. Ibid.
81. For more on the subversive nature of Alterman's representation of violence and his revision of victimization in *Makot Mitsrayim*, see Hever, *Sight of War*, 123–33.
82. Paranoia is a good example. On the role of paranoia in the formation of a unified self, see M. Klein, *Psycho-analysis of Children*; Kristeva, *Melanie Klein*; and Lacan, *Psychoses*.
83. See, for example, Hoeveler, *Gothic Feminism*. Hoeveler defines "gothic feminism" as a precursor to the contemporary antifeminist notion of "victim feminism," defined as "an ideology of female power through pretended and staged weakness" (*Gothic Feminism*, 7). Provocatively, she argues that women authors of gothic "have not simply been the passive victims of male-created constructions but rather have constructed themselves as victims in their own literature" (ibid., 4). Colluding in the performance of their vulnerability and powerlessness becomes the ironic and subtle basis for a questionable female empowerment.
84. For more on the victim identity in the Israeli sensibility, see Ophir, "Identity of the Victims."
85. Liberles, *Salo Wittmayer Baron*, 11.
86. Ophir, "Identity of the Victims," 192.
87. Anita Shapira argues that, though the Holocaust was always present in the public consciousness as an abstract historical event, private memory was repressed both by the victims themselves and by Israeli society, producing the widely accepted perception of Israeli silence regarding the Holocaust in the first decade of statehood. Shapira, "Holocaust." For more on the Israeli relationship to the Holocaust and to Holocaust survivors, see Segev, *Seventh Million*.
88. Jaffee, "Victim Community," 231.
89. Zertal, *Israel's Holocaust*, 2.
90. Ibid., 3.
91. Ibid., 4.
92. Commenting on the Israeli consolidation of national unity based on an identification with Holocaust victims, Ella Shohat focuses on Mizraḥim, Jews of Arab descent who, though not subject to the same violence as their European coreligionists, were nevertheless encouraged to identify with Israel's "master narrative of universal Jewish victimization" (Shohat, "Invention of the Mizrahim," 6).
93. Zertal elaborates on Israel's "devaluation of the meaning and enormity of the Holocaust" in her Introduction (*Israel's Holocaust*, 4).
94. See n. 83 on Hoeveler's notion of "gothic feminism." These ideas, and Hoeveler's concept of "professional femininity," are discussed in further detail in chap. 2 of this study.
95. The phrase "domestic carceral," which designates domestic "feminine" spaces as sites of gothic horror, is Paul Morrison's ("Enclosed in Openness"). Chap. 2 of this study elaborates on this notion.

PART 1
A SPECTRALIZED PAST

1

ALWAYS ALREADY GOTHIC

S. Y. Agnon's European Tales of Terror

IN 1916, A GERMAN LITERARY ANTHOLOGY ENTITLED *TREUE* (Fidelity) was published and presented as a Passover gift to Jewish soldiers serving on the German front during World War I. The anthology included works by the foremost Hebrew and Yiddish authors of the day, but it is perhaps best remembered today for cementing the importance of the renowned Hebrew author S. Y. Agnon (1888–1970) in the discerning German Jewish intellectual milieu.[1] Printed as a preface to Agnon's contributions to the volume and, more broadly, as an introduction of Agnon to a German audience was an admiring letter from Martin Buber to the editor, Leo Herrmann. In his letter, Buber prophetically asserts that Agnon's "vocation is to be the poet and chronicler of Jewish life; of that life which is dying and changing today, but also of the other life, still unknown, that is growing."[2] Buber's enthusiastic public endorsement of Agnon helped establish his reputation as a leading Hebrew literary figure whose writing mediates not only between Europe and Palestine but also between fiction and history. *Treue* included German translations of two stories by Agnon: "Aliyat neshama" (Ascent of the soul), about an untimely death brought about by Hassidic fervor for the coming of the Messiah; and "Meḥolat ha-mavet" ("The Dance of Death"), a gothic story involving the kidnapping of an innocent maiden and ghosts rising from their graves for a midnight dance.[3]

Almost three decades later, another wartime literary anthology, this time in Hebrew, hosted fiction by Agnon. Titled *Ba-sa'ar* (In the storm) and described as a literary response to the horrific news from Europe, it was published in 1943 by the Union of Hebrew Authors (Agudat ha-sofrim ha-ivriyim) and included contributions from the most highly regarded authors and poets of the time, such as Leah Goldberg. Whereas *Treue* was distributed to Jewish soldiers on the German front in 1916, *Ba-sa'ar* was produced for the Hebrew Brigade, Jewish soldiers from the Yishuv who volunteered to fight with the British Army during World War II, and was small enough "to fit into their kit bags."[4] The story that Agnon chose to submit to the collection, "Ha-adonit ve-ha-rokhel" ("The Lady and the Peddler"), was not an obvious candidate for the explicitly political endeavor, rooted in contemporary events, undertaken by the Union of Hebrew Authors in *Ba-sa'ar*. Like "The Dance of Death," it is a gothic story, complete with a foreboding forest, a bloody dagger, and a murderous vampire.

Agnon's contribution to *Ba-sa'ar* departs from the others, and more generally from literature produced, translated, and consumed in the Yishuv during the war.[5] As Sidra DeKoven Ezrahi notes, Hebrew authors at that time subscribed to a "mandate to reenter history as acting [subjects]" through "revisionist symbols that invert the archetypes of martyrdom."[6] She points to the poetry in *Ba-sa'ar* as exemplifying the call for "heroic acts of revenge."[7] Agnon diverges from these poetic tendencies, offering no semblance of valor in "The Lady and the Peddler." If heroism, revenge, and defiance were seen by his contemporaries as paving the way to reenter history and assert a Jewish presence in the here and now, then Agnon's characters challenge the binary logic undergirding heroism and cowardice and offer a different historical orientation in the face of violence and war—one that is not linear but cyclical, not liberated from the past but perpetually revisited by it. This engagement with history is the first indication of a shared sensibility with gothic fiction, in which, as Catherine Spooner puts it, the "past chokes the present, prevents progress and the march towards personal or social enlightenment."[8]

Furthermore, Agnon's choice to respond to contemporary violence through narratives set in the distant and unspecified past complements his consistent borrowing from the themes and imagery of European gothic. Deeming the gothic a literary mode devoid of literary prestige, many readers of Agnon have tended to disparage its role in his oeuvre. For Agnon as for its most enduring eighteenth- and nineteenth-century practitioners, however, the gothic not only provides an alluring aesthetic but also allows for serious social and historical commentaries. This point is lost if we dismiss the pervasive, persistent, deep-seated gothic sensibility in his fiction as the awkward birth pangs of an author destined for greatness. Agnon without the gothic would not be Agnon.

In this chapter, I argue that taking Agnon's gothicism seriously sheds new light on his engagement with the Jewish past, which has been conceptualized primarily in terms of loss and memorial. Agnon's unconventional figuration of key themes at the intersection of Jewishness and the gothic, blood and wandering, in "The Dance of Death" and "The Lady and the Peddler" suggests a disconcertingly active past that invades and affects the Jewish present. The gothic evocation of fear, anxiety, and persecution structures these stories' vision of a restless past and links it to an uneasy present. Even as the past shapes the present, the stories themselves shape the past, as evidenced by Agnon's appropriation of familiar antisemitic tropes. By exposing the affinity of the gothic to the Jewish experience, Agnon recalibrates the dynamics between Christian and Jew, fiction and history, and, in particular, the past and the present. Though in the popular Hebrew imagination his fiction is associated, sometimes nostalgically and sometimes ironically, with an irrevocably lost Eastern European Jewish world, Agnon's gothic stories bring us face-to-face with a violent history that refuses to retire into the grave.

What does Agnon gain by summoning these ghosts of history, both literal and metaphorical? What does he disrupt by delineating Jewish history as gothic? One of the most productive critical approaches to the gothic situates it vis-à-vis national narratives and their need to maintain coherence through exclusion. As Teresa A. Goddu notes, the gothic's restoration of repressed narratives "disrupts the dream world of national myth with the nightmares of history." At the same time as it discloses a haunting past as the source of the instability of national self-representation, she points out, it paradoxically "can also work to coalesce those narratives."[9] Agnon's gothic, however, is not positioned politically; it addresses the past of the Jewish people rather than that of the Jewish (or Polish) state. Furthermore, the violence his stories expose is not intended to restore a marginalized or suppressed narrative. It is accessible not to the descendants of its perpetrators but to those of its victims: readers of Hebrew, who, in the first half of the twentieth century, were grappling with a relentlessly increasing barrage of anti-Jewish violence that would culminate in the most incomprehensible event in Jewish history. Agnon's gothic, then, invites his Jewish readers to confront the violent past to better understand their brutal present—indeed, the gothic in Agnon unsettles the very boundary between the past and the present.

I begin with a discussion of Agnon's gothic oeuvre and of the discomfort his gothicism has engendered among some critics. I then consider his historic vision, first in terms of his fiction's relation to specific historical eras or events such as the Holocaust, and then through broader conceptualizations of the past. Moving to the two stories at hand, I examine their multiple modes of temporality and historicity as evidence of a restless past that intrudes on the present. The final two sections of this chapter closely read the motifs of wandering and blood in the stories to show how the gothic complements the Judaic and activates Agnon's history not only temporally but also thematically and aesthetically.

In "The Dance of Death" and "The Lady and the Peddler," the gothic shapes Agnon's vision of Jewish history on several levels: in the emphasis on fear and anxiety as defining features of the Jewish presence in Europe; in the depiction of time as cyclical and the past as perpetually returning to and rupturing the present; in the thematization of these phenomena through supernatural figures; and, finally, in the portrayal of historic Jewish experiences in terms of certain key motifs that mediate between the gothic and the Judaic. The persistent gothic image of the past that accompanies Agnon's modernism points to anxieties of the present and parallels similarly jarring encounters in gothic literature, in which, as Fred Botting notes, "gothic figures have continued to shadow the progress of modernity with counter-narratives displaying the underside of enlightenment and humanist values."[10] As the dreams of Zionism came ever closer to realization while blood flowed in the fields of Agnon's lost world, the lines collapsed between the gothic and the modern, the past and the present, the dead and the living, creating fertile ground for these stories.

Agnon's Jewish Gothic: Critical Repressions

Though doomed love, death, and violence are prominent themes in Agnon's oeuvre, they are not the ones with which he is primarily correlated. As the inimitable master of the Hebrew language in all its forms, a practitioner of a densely nuanced and allusive poetics, and the gatekeeper of the Eastern European Jewish past, Agnon is imbued with a gravitas that precludes the thrills and chills associated with the gothic. As such, Miriam Roshwald's denial of Agnon's gothicism, though perhaps more explicit than most, is typical. "Agnon could have been compared with the nineteenth-century Gothic writers in England, notorious for their flair for mystery and terror set among medieval castles, ruins, and cemeteries," she observes. "But the similarity is totally misleading. Ruins and cemeteries in Agnon's writings are not settings for theatrical effects, but form an integral part of the scheme of the Jewish shtetl. Even though occasionally Agnon indulges his gnomish imagination in a 'Gothic' prank, ultimately it leads to a serious ... purpose and not to a cathartic thrill."[11] This evaluation is based on a misrepresentation of the gothic, which, as a vast body of criticism attests, amounts to more than the "theatrical effects" and "cathartic thrills" with which it is often disparagingly associated.

Numerous critics have acknowledged Agnon's proclivity for the macabre and the supernatural, but most consider it a characteristic of the great author's unrefined first steps. Gershon Shaked, for example, observes that "the sentimental foundation dominated" in Agnon's early works.[12] These features, he argues, provided the counterpoint to the ironic distance that Agnon was developing and for which he would become famous; as the author matured, the poetics of "emotional excess," associated with the "nonrealistic" (בלתי-ריאליסטי or לא-ריאליסטי) mode of some of his stories, diminished.[13] Some critics invoke the term *gothic* to signal the triviality of characteristics associated predominantly with Agnon's early style, while others eschew this term altogether in favor of the more serious *romantic*, a related term more acceptable for an author of Agnon's stature.[14] Shaked attributes the author's "sentimental topics," preoccupation with death, and "melodramatic style" primarily to the German and Scandinavian romantic traditions and to neoromanticism, read as antithetical to Judaic motifs.[15] That Romanticism offers a more palatable framework for Agnon's gothic writing is evident even in Arnold Band's monograph on Agnon's work, *Nostalgia and Nightmare*, one of the only studies to have recognized and meaningfully engaged with Agnon's gothicism as an integral component of his poetics.[16]

The critical literature on Agnon attributes his gothic propensities, however they are designated, to two influences that were formative in Agnon's education and background: European, especially German, secular literature by authors such as E. T. A. Hoffmann, and the Jewish mystical tradition. Though both these influences undoubtedly played a role in the development of Agnon's gothic poetics, I am interested more in the tendencies with which they are associated in Agnon's writing than in identifying their source. Moreover, this approach not only fails to differentiate between the gothic and Romanticism, resulting in the occlusion of significant forces in Agnon's stories, but it also, as we see in Roshwald's statement and in studies by Shaked and others, presumes an inherent antithesis between the concerns of secular European literature and those of a world governed by Jewish tradition.

The latter point speaks to one of the most popular critical orientations toward Agnon and his work: the author's duality. This duality takes several frequently cited forms: Agnon's works encompass both the realistic and the nonrealistic; they both conceal and reveal; they can be characterized as both nightmare and nostalgia; they are both "revolutionary and traditionalist"; and, most significantly for my analysis, they subscribe to incompatible themes espoused by European Romanticism and Jewish tradition.[17] Yet certain expressions of Judaic faith, such as Jewish mysticism and Hassidism, are readily associated with a spiritual fervor similar to that of Romanticism. The intense emotions brought on by the romantic encounter with nature and the sublime find expression in the extreme emotional and psychological states depicted by gothic literature.

Positioning the gothic as a counterforce to Agnon's Judaism, then, charts a rigid literary cartography of mutually exclusive poetics and praxis, despite the constant trespass evidenced by Agnon's texts. Further, it discounts key characteristics of these texts' representation of the past. Whereas romantic authors and poets idealized the past—particularly the medieval era—imagining it in terms of a "lost paradise," authors of gothic texts look to the distant past with fascination tinged with dread.[18] The past in the gothic threatens rather than comforts because it is not fully consigned to the past: it repeatedly breaches its own bounds and disrupts the present, exposing its dark underpinnings. Band titled his study *Nostalgia and Nightmare* to express what he saw as the two "antithetical but complementary" focal points of Agnon's "sentiment," the romantic and the modern, because they offer different modes of engagement with the past.[19] Nostalgia is aligned with the lost traditional Jewish world, while nightmare expresses its violent destruction. If, in addition to the *attitude* Agnon's stories convey regarding the historical past, we also consider the *structure* of history as it emerges in his fiction, then we can understand how the "nightmare" of Band's title encompasses not only the modern but also the gothic.

Already evident in his earliest stories, written at the turn of the century, Agnon's gothic inclinations intensify in the two decades or so after his return to Palestine from Berlin, from the 1920s to the 1940s. Though his "neoromantic" stories are identified primarily with his period in Jaffa and considered representative of youthful literary experimentation, his post-Weimar years spawned some of the most gothic stories in his oeuvre, including "Yatom ve-almana" (An orphan and a widow, 1931); "Ha-yalda ha-meta" (The dead girl, 1932, 1935); "Kol ha-em" ("The Mother's Voice," 1941); "Ha-lev ve-ha-einayim" ("Heart and Eyes," 1943); and "The Lady and the Peddler"; as well as revisions of earlier stories, such as "The Dance of Death" and "Ḥupat dodim" (The bridal canopy, 1931), originally published in 1913 as "Ha-ḥupa ha-sheḥora" (The black bridal canopy).[20]

In these stories and others, the gothic sensibility prevails not as a counterforce to the Jewish world of the past but as an integral component of it: a gaunt orphan's corpse prays with other departed souls in the great synagogue; a Polish king's Jewish wife wanders restlessly after death; a girl rises from the grave after being buried prematurely in an effort to comply with halacha. Here, then, the opposition between the gothic and the Judaic collapses. Far from posing a challenge to the "portrayal of a traditional Jewish milieu," the gothic mode in these stories intensifies their Jewish mores, offering concrete manifestations of otherwise abstract Judaic notions such as *ha-olam ha-ba* (the world to come), *tohara* (purity), and *galut* (exile). Clearly, the young Czaczkes who conceived of "Ha-panas" (The lantern) in Buczacz and revised it for publication during World War I was not so far removed from the revered S. Y. Agnon who, almost four decades later, would use the same gothic motifs to comment on contemporary Jewish crises. Like the vision of history his gothic tales espouse, Agnon returns again and again in his career to the terror, fear, and anxiety that characterize both the gothic and the modern confrontation with the present.

Agnon's Historiography

Though the preoccupation with the past is one of the characteristic features of gothic literature, the gothic has little interest in historical veracity, revealing more about the present's anxieties than about the past as it was. The gothic past is the site of paradox, housing the finest and most virtuous sentiments as well as the most barbaric and violent ones. Gothic authors strove to evoke the distant past not only by setting their narratives in medieval times but also, occasionally, by fabricating their historicity, through devices such as the discovered manuscript. Such devices operated both outside and inside these texts, ascribing to them a sense of historical authenticity and contributing to the aura of mystery suffusing their plots.[21]

Perhaps the most forceful feature of gothic historicity has to do with the supernatural figures that populate this fiction, calculated to terrify readers because of their ability to cross back over the boundary between life and death. Reanimated representatives of the past, they threaten the present with long-forgotten curses, buried secrets, and unfinished business. Explained or unexplained supernatural figures and events distort temporal progression and contribute to the subjective affective experience of reading gothic texts. Invasive, disruptive, and violent, the past in gothic fiction surfaces in a present trying desperately to maintain an illusion of wholeness and peace, exposing the chaos that reigns.

This gothic vision of the past helps shape "The Dance of Death" and "The Lady and the Peddler." Agnon's pronounced historicity is often conceptualized as a window into the lost world of Galician and Polish Jewry, affording a gaze that is nostalgic and wistful at the same time that it is critical and ironic.[22] In these gothic stories, Agnon structures the past poetically: not as a rupture of linear progress—since history for him is not linear, even when it involves redemption—but as a repeated series of ruptures. The cyclical temporality that operates in many of his stories gestures to the modern and its redemptive possibilities. At the same time, it adorns the experience of modernity with the inescapable shadows of a dark and violent past—a specific historical event or a more general pattern—destined to repeat itself. Agnon also invites the past's returns by evoking multiple temporalities through his distinctively historicized Hebrew and through allusion and intertextuality. In these stories, those temporal and historical frameworks are complemented by elements more readily associated with gothic literature: supernatural beings, a macabre atmosphere, and the central gothic motifs of blood and the Wandering Jew.

The gothic, which works to resist both historical forgetting and romantic idealizing of the past, is certainly not the only force that shapes European Jewish history in Agnon's fiction. Still, even texts that are not predominantly gothic articulate key historical tensions by drawing from gothic conventions. The morbid essay "Ir ha-metim" (City of the dead, 1907), about Agnon's hometown, Buczacz, and its inhabitants' "fondness for death," signals one of Agnon's earliest forays into this mode and coincides with the publication of "Ha-panas" and "Toitentans." The fact that it is nonfiction makes Agnon's invocation of gothic imagery noteworthy, suggesting that his aesthetic repertoire developed in tandem with his preoccupation with history. The collection *Sipurey Polin* (*Stories of Poland*), whose tales engage with Jewish settlement in Poland, demonstrates the primacy of the Jewish past and of historiography in Agnon's mind.[23] The gothic framework of many of these historicized depictions enables the mediation between the Jewish and the non-Jewish elements of this history and exposes their interdependence. Straddling the line between legend and history, the stories in *Sipurey Polin* are set in an "Agnonian time and space," in Boris Kotlerman's phrase, distinct from concrete events and historical conventions.[24] Beyond *Sipurey Polin*, several stories about ravaged Jewish communities probe questions of historical memory and forgetting by drawing on gothic imagery and atmosphere. These include "Bein ha-bayit la-ḥatser" (Between the house and the fence), later titled "Im knisat ha-yom" ("At the Outset of the Day," 1943); "Ba-derekh" ("On the Road," 1944); and "Ha-siman" ("The Sign," 1943). "On the Road" evokes medieval elements in its depiction of this destruction, telling of a narrator who finds himself in the midst of a small remnant of a massacred medieval German Jewish community. The medieval revisits the present, framing the contemporary events that are themselves seldom articulated explicitly.

Agnon was not alone in evoking the medieval past to comment on (or avoid) the violent events of the present. In his preface to a 1945 collection of Hebrew narrative and liturgical poems written in response to contemporary antisemitism in Germany and France, Abraham Meir Haberman asserts, "These days it is incumbent upon us to read again these ancient texts. We have not expected that the Middle Ages would come back to haunt us.... The Middle Ages are back with us, on a greater scale, and with even greater ferocity."[25] Explicitly linking the barbaric historical past with the violence of the present, Haberman calls on Jewish readers of Hebrew to return to their ancient texts to help exorcise the specter of the Middle Ages. Zalman Schneour's 1913 poem "Yemei ha-beinayim mitkarvim" ("The Middle Ages Draw Near"), written in the aftermath of the Beilis blood libel, makes dramatic use of gothic imagery such as the raven to personify this historical era as an embodiment of antisemitic violence risen again in the present. Shaul Tchernihovsky's ballad "Shney ha-kvarim" (The two graves, 1942) forges a connection between the persecution of the Jews during the Crusades and the growing awareness of the scope of the Holocaust. As in Agnon's stories, these texts' disconcerting depictions of the barbaric past threatening the present exemplify one of the gothic's paradigmatic features.

Agnon's historical sensibility, as expressed in his fiction, changed over the course of his life. Gershom Scholem notes that after World War II, Agnon shifts from a poetic historicity to a more "ethnographic" one charged with the task of memorialization and preservation.[26] The seeming absence from

Agnon's works of the Holocaust, the greatest catastrophe in modern Jewish history, has attracted critical attention. Sidra DeKoven Ezrahi charts the shifts in Agnon's understanding of the role of the Jewish author who represents catastrophe "from chronicler to threnodist," from an author "who had set out to write of the internal collapse of European Jewish civilization" to one "who finds himself bereft of his subject."[27] Identifying cyclical phases in his fiction moving from irony to elegy and, finally, despair, she points to his use of diverse historical-literary approaches to these events, including straightforward ethnographic preservation, piyyut or lamentation, and restoration. Dan Laor argues that the Holocaust reverberates in a sizeable portion of Agnon's oeuvre, but he points to Agnon's "spiritual and esthetic predicament in addressing it" as evidenced through "unfinished stories, ideological contradictions, even return to traditional literary genres."[28] He observes Gershom Scholem's disappointment regarding what he considered to be increasingly ethnographic tendencies in Agnon's writing, and ultimately asserts that "the artistic enterprise of Agnon after the Holocaust [is] commemorating the Holocaust."[29] Alan Mintz, too, interprets Agnon's literary confrontation with the Holocaust as "an alternative to forms of memorialization that brought destruction and loss to the forefront," an authorial choice "to recreate in words what is lost."[30] Hillel Weiss, addressing those works that deal indirectly with the Holocaust, identifies Agnon's employment of "unique disguises to escape into the German past in its encounter with the Jewish past."[31] They all concur that the historical dimension of Agnon's fiction, despite its lack of explicit engagement with the events of the Holocaust itself, is profoundly affected by it.

Beyond specific historic frameworks such as that of the Holocaust, Michal Arbel interprets Agnon's "constant engagement with the past" as producing writing that is "a gravestone" for what has been and no longer exists.[32] Identifying a mystical, redemptive "historiosophy" at odds with and critical of the present-centered Zionist notion of redemption, she contrasts the cyclical temporality of certain Agnon stories with the "realistic" linear history associated with nationalism. The act of writing, defined by this tension, is linked to the memory of loss and catastrophe but ultimately consigns the past to its grave. Yet how is it then possible to reconcile the circular temporality she rightly identifies with the stasis and finality of the grave? By contrast to Arbel, I interpret this temporality as evidence that the past *cannot* be buried. Rather, it constantly and energetically impinges on the present. This is clear in both the explicit thematization of revenants in Agnon's plots and the stories' more subtle metatextual investigations of the past's role in the present. In other words, if we consider Agnon's stories as a gravestone, we must acknowledge that the grave it marks will, inevitably, open.

As Agnon's use of the Hebrew language makes clear, his writing not only memorializes but also actively intervenes in history, inviting the past into the present. Gershom Scholem, the philosopher and historian recognized as the foremost modern scholar of Jewish mysticism, met Agnon in Germany, maintained a lifelong friendship with him in Israel, and translated his work into German. In his essay "Reflections on S. Y. Agnon," he discusses the Hebrew language as inherently weighted with history.[33] Whereas authors after Agnon are liberated from this heavy burden, Agnon and his contemporaries, writing at a critical moment for the transition of Hebrew into a spoken national language, had to shoulder it.[34] Jewish history resides in the Hebrew language itself, which was subject to modernization through literature at the same time as it had to contend with the perpetual revisitations of its own past. Agnon, Scholem points out, with his mastery of midrashic and biblical Hebrew and his prolific reading of secular Western literature, was well positioned to delve into various historical forms of the Hebrew language while shaping its most modern contours.

Commenting on Scholem's essay, Kenneth Hart Green argues that Agnon's idiosyncratic, self-consciously historicized Hebrew expresses Scholem's nonrational Jewish historiography.[35] Agnon's language operates via "a conscious memory of the past as marching (even if unseen) alongside the present and the future."[36] In the historic transition of Hebrew from a literary to a spoken language in the late nineteenth and early twentieth century, Agnon maintains Hebrew's past within his development of the language in a contemporary cultural milieu. Hebrew "is not only the product of history, but it is also the shaper of history," and no author has been better equipped to carry out this process than Agnon, whose Hebrew uncovered for Scholem "poetic truths about history."[37] As such, Agnon plays a central role in the development of Scholem's historiography. "If Scholem 'invented' a historical unfolding of medieval Jewish mysticism for the benefit of modern Jews," argues Green, "he did so with the aid of Agnon, who showed in his unique Hebrew literary style how it is possible to historically express, preserve, and advance (rather than betray) an ancient wisdom by letting it speak in a modern 'dialectical' idiom."[38] This interpretation presents Agnon's language as epitomizing a vision of history that brings the past into inevitable, dynamic interaction with the present. Though one may argue that modern Hebrew, rooted in biblical Hebrew and necessarily dependent on classical texts for its development, by definition (not only in Agnon) brings its own history into the present, Agnon's self-conscious use of the language's myriad historical manifestations points to a highly considered historiographic strategy residing in his poetic language.

Agnon's mastery of Hebrew means that his evocation of diverse points in its history through a tactical use of language is fully accessible to a handful of erudite readers. But the gothic, too, hosts the coexistence of the past and the present, offering an expression of the dynamic presence of history that is immediately evident. Indeed, the resurrection of spoken Hebrew is itself a gothic story.[39] Just as the gothic affords the ability to sustain the dead in the world of the living, so does it create the conditions for the past's sustenance in the present. In Agnon's narratives, the gothic vision of history invites and accommodates the intrusions of the violent past in an uneasy present.

Temporality and Historicity in "The Dance of Death" and "The Lady and the Peddler"

It is clear why a story like "The Dance of Death," which Agnon wrote before bursting into the Hebrew literary scene in Palestine, was later included among the folkloristic-historical tales of *Sipurey Polin*. It offers a poetic ethnography chronicling certain customs of Polish Jewry at the same time that it narrates a melodramatic tragedy culled from the annals of Polish Jewish folk history. "The Lady and the Peddler" looks to the timeless past of the folktale to subvert contemporary antisemitic propaganda.[40] Both stories structure history through a gothic temporality characterized by the compulsive returns of a barbarous, threatening past. The ideal vehicle for the expression of the fear and anxiety provoked by antisemitic violence in Europe, this temporality also articulates the dynamism of the Jewish past— the way it revisits, affects, and clings to the no less frightening present.

"The Dance of Death" is perhaps the most quintessentially gothic tale in Agnon's oeuvre. Set in a Polish town in an unspecified past, it depicts a wealthy father of a beloved only daughter on the eve of her wedding. The father is denied a request to allow his daughter to wear silk on her wedding day, and though he accepts the ruling, he remains uneasy and preoccupied with it. As the couple stands beneath the wedding canopy surrounded by guests, the arrival of a feudal lord or count (פריץ) on horseback evokes a fearful tremor from the celebrants, who meekly invite him to join the wedding party. Struck by the bride's beauty, though, he unsheathes his sword, slits the throat of the groom, and kidnaps the young woman. The guests can only watch this horrific scene unfold, and the bride's cries for help are for naught. In her kidnapper's castle, the bride spends her days gazing from the window in the direction of her town, eventually dying of grief. After death, she rises from her grave every midnight for a danse macabre with the specter of her murdered groom.

The danse macabre motif illuminates the affinity between the Christian European sensibility and the Judaic.[41] The term *meḥolat ha-mavet*, which ostensibly refers to the spectral dance of the tragic couple, is a Hebrew rendering of the French *danse macabre*.[42] One of the most popular nineteenth-century motifs in European arts and literature, the danse macabre can be traced back to performances in Christian weddings in the fourteenth century and in Jewish weddings by the seventeenth century, a reminder, in the midst of the most joyous occasion, of the universality and inevitability of death.[43] In Agnon's hands, the danse macabre motif brings together death and power not to demonstrate that the finality of death equalizes the powerful and the powerless but that it actually makes possible the transgression of the boundary dividing them.

The groom's kittel, a key image in the story, offers a direct parallel to the danse macabre: the kittel, a simple white linen robe worn by Ashkenazi Jews in weddings and on certain holidays, is also used as a burial shroud for men.[44] Emblematic of purity and simplicity, the pocketless kittel disallows the deceased to bring his earthly possessions to his grave, signifying the equality of all in death—precisely the motivation of the danse macabre. In the story, however, burying the groom in his bloodstained kittel will not only equalize power relations but will also compensate for his powerlessness in life by fueling his vengeful resurrection: folk belief transforms the kittel into a vehicle of revenge. Yet the groom declines this opportunity, instead using his supernatural ability to return from death to consummate his interrupted love.

The full title of the story, "The Dance of Death, or the Beloved and the Pleasant," links the European danse macabre to the citation in the story's epigraph from *Kinat David*, King David's lamentation for Shaul and Yonathan after their death in battle with the Philistines: "Beloved and pleasant in their life, in death they were not parted." Agnon's reference to

Kinat David alters the purpose of the danse macabre: whereas the dance of death reminded its medieval audience that death spares no one, from the poorest beggar to the most powerful pope, the epigraph suggests that love can transcend death, allowing the persecuted to overcome their earthly oppressors—whether Philistine warriors, Central European crusaders, or Polish aristocrats. In its juxtaposition with the epigraph, the danse macabre motif not only harks to the generally gothic theme of the intertwining of love and death but also alludes to various flash points in Jewish history: biblical, medieval, and post-Enlightenment.

The story's subtly multifaceted historicity complements its narrative temporality. "The Dance of Death" is a frame story. Its opening paragraph creates suspense and temporal displacement between the narrative frame, in which the narrator announces his intent to tell the story, and the story he will tell, which is embedded within it.[45] The first sentence of the embedded narrative offers its only temporal marker: "בימים מקדם" (long ago), suggesting an ahistorical, folkloric notion of time. The frame device, however, suggests that the narrator and the reader occupy a shared present, another of the story's multiple historical moments. Supplementing the distinctive historiography that Scholem identified in Agnon's Hebrew, the title, the epigraph, and the various intertextual allusions to both ancient and modern enemies of Israel, from the biblical battles against the Edomites to the pogroms of Eastern Europe, confirm this temporality.[46] The story is structured on the basis of both folkloric time and historical time, as Kotlerman has argued for the *Polin* collection as a whole. This is further complicated by an ambiguous narrative temporality: the narrator does not reveal how much time passes in any of the main sections of the story—before, during, and after the wedding. Though some readers have assumed that the bride spends months or even years with the count after she is kidnapped, the story provides no definitive evidence for such interpretations, resisting attempts to pin down its temporality.

These multiple temporalities and historical moments contribute to the story's different historiographic modes. Its attentive chronicling of Polish Jewish customs—related to weddings, burials, and legal decrees—point to a documentarian impulse that positions the text as recording or memorializing a community that no longer exists. The frame narrative, however, suggests a different engagement with history, situating the narrator in the reader's present and pointing to the cyclicity of the dramatic plot. Before the melancholy bride dies, she dons her wedding dress, the object of so much tension earlier in the story, revisiting her moment of historical rupture. She dies wearing her dress and is buried not according to Judaic custom in a Jewish cemetery but in a non-Jewish grave, "קבר בקברות אל נכר"[47]—literally denoting "a grave among the graves of a foreign god," the phrase emphasizes the bride's estrangement from Judaic practice and identity.

However, though the bride's exile as a Jew in Eastern Europe reaches a tragic apex in her foreign burial, it is this improper burial that loosens the nail from her coffin, so to speak: this foreign grave will not be her final resting place. Her nightly reappearance as a ghost provides a consistent respite from the grave. The same is true for the groom. Buried on the spot where he was murdered in front of the old synagogue to allow him to avenge himself, he, too, is denied a proper grave. Instead of taking revenge on his murderer, though, he returns after death to dance with his spectral bride. Their regular nocturnal visitations, rather than a singular return of revenge, point to the same cyclical temporality that compels the bride to wear her wedding dress on the day she dies. Whether interpreted as triumphantly redemptive or tragically doomed, the spectral dance evokes an infinite loop. The two conceptions of history that emerge from the narrative structure are evident also in the plot: linear, documentary, and objective, on the one hand; and cyclical, fantastic, and subjective, on the other. As a chronicle, the story is situated in the lost past documented by the narrator at a later time. As a myth, it operates not in the historical past but in a timeless, recurrent past, illustrated by the repeated dance of death.

Like "The Dance of Death," "The Lady and the Peddler" is set in an unspecified past. It opens with a Jewish peddler wandering the Eastern European countryside with his wares on his back. He arrives at the isolated home of a crude woman who threatens him but eventually buys a hunting knife. When a storm approaches, he wanders around the forest and loses his way, returning to the woman and asking for shelter; she allows him to sleep in the barn. As the rain continues, he begins doing odd jobs for the "lady," who eventually invites him into the house and finally into her bed. As their relationship develops, it becomes clear to the reader that the woman is dangerous. Indeed, she makes little effort to conceal her intention of drinking the blood of the peddler, who is so naive that he cannot recognize the danger. She prepares food for him, yet she never eats; when he asks about the whereabouts of her previous husbands, she gestures at her belly. When he probes further, she warns him explicitly about her intentions: "'I drink men's blood and I eat human flesh.' As she spoke she embraced him with all her might and placed her lips against his and sucked. 'I never imagined,' she said to him, 'that a Jew's flesh would be so sweet. Kiss me, my raven. . . . O my own sweet corpse!'"⁴⁸ Ignorant in love, he tries to quiet his nagging sense that something is not quite right: "This is the kind of poetic language that noblewomen must use when they address their husbands with affection."⁴⁹ Indeed, his fundamental misunderstanding of romantic love reveals a comic strain in the otherwise grim story. What does a Jewish peddler know about romantic love? Here Agnon acknowledges explicitly the kind of disjuncture that readers might expect between a practicing Jew and bourgeois romantic love, which parallels the assumed incompatibility between the Judaic and the romantic.

Whether he is truly in love with the lady or just victim to a perception of love that has invaded even the highly proscribed personal world of pious Jews, however, is irrelevant, because he does, in fact, become involved in a love affair with the lady. He finally senses danger—"even the bed made up for him shrieked, 'Pick up your feet and run!'"—and decides he must leave, but can only bring himself to move to the storeroom after having two ominous dreams.⁵⁰ One night, he suddenly feels compelled to recite the Shema, going outside to pray because of the crucifix on the wall. When he returns, he finds the lady on the floor of his room, bleeding from wounds she sustained while violently attempting to murder him in the darkness of the room. As he tries to revive her, she bites him, but she finds his Jewish blood intolerable and dies after a few days. The icy ground is too hard for burial, so he places her coffin on the roof, where birds devour her corpse.

Unchanged by the violent episode with the lady, the peddler continues to wander with his wares on his back, the archetypal Wandering Jew—without the characteristics that frightened British readers of nineteenth-century gothic. He is not threatening but pathetic, not cunning but naive, not evil but kind. Much as the circular temporality and perpetual returns of "The Dance of Death" are ambivalent, lending themselves to several contradictory interpretations ranging from triumph to futility, the same characteristic in "The Lady and the Peddler" courts ambiguity. The depiction of the peddler as hopelessly naive suggests a critique of his unreflective reentry into the circular temporality of wandering. At the same time, though, the story as a whole impugns the European stereotype of the Wandering Jew.

As in the earlier story, this one delineates a narrative temporality that mirrors the recurrence of violence in European Jewish history. The story begins with a folkloristic ahistoricity, offering specificity in neither time nor place: "One day," recounts the omniscient narrator, the peddler "found himself in a wooded region far from any settlement."[51] It ends on the same note: "And that peddler took up his pack and traveled on from place to place, traveling and crying out his wares."[52] The story's final sentence might easily serve as its own first sentence, a narrative mirroring of the peddler's ceaseless meandering.

The story thematizes repetition in other ways. The peddler sells the lady the knife and then gets lost in the darkening forest, only to arrive at the lady's house once more. The lady herself has sated her bloodlust by murdering several previous husbands and intends to reenact the ritual on the peddler. In this story, unlike in "The Dance of Death," the timelessness suggested by the peddler's meanderings and by the fairy tale conventions to which Agnon seems to adhere in tone and diction are continually disrupted by markers of temporal specificity that provide a clear sense of time's passing: a sunset, the end of the rainy season, several months passing, five days later, and so on. Even these seeming disruptions, however, contribute to the story's cyclic temporality, as their main purpose is to indicate the perpetual stasis of the peddler regardless of time's passing. "I have to get out of here," thinks the peddler when he finally begins to comprehend that he is in danger. "If not now, then tomorrow morning. . . . When day broke, he would be on his way."[53] Yet he stays: "A day passed, a week passed, and he did not leave her house."[54] It is difficult to imagine that Agnon, in Palestine following reports of the atrocities blackening Europe a decade after Hitler's rise to power, could write such lines without awareness of their applicability to the events at hand.

The repetitions of both plots gesture at the returns of the stories themselves on the timeline of Jewish history, all the way to the contemporary events that contextualize their publication. The performance of this temporality is made possible by the most explicitly gothic elements of both stories: the ghosts in "The Dance of Death," who are able to traverse the boundary between death and life and return from the grave; the peddler in the "The Lady and the Peddler," whose resumed wandering restores the Jew to his gothic place and time, even as it reassigns his bloodlust to the Christian lady; and the vampiric lady herself, whose intolerance of Jewish blood confirms the Jew's inherent difference and ultimately makes possible the peddler's return to wandering and to his Jewishness. Agnon revisits these gothic devices to undermine and revise common antisemitic stereotypes while maintaining the notion of Jewish difference. In these two stories, two themes, in particular, host these subversions and mediate between the gothic and the Jewish: wandering and blood. These themes trace a direct route from medieval folk beliefs to their consolidation in popular European gothic literature in the century and a half before World War I, and finally to their terrible apex in the anti-Jewish ideology of the Third Reich.

Perambulatory Narratives: The Wandering Jew

The legend of the Wandering Jew, a prominent figure in the gothic imagination, can be traced to the 1602 publication of a pamphlet in Germany by a student of Martin Luther's, at the height of Luther's antisemitic activity. The pamphlet builds on earlier versions of the story, in which the figure, not specified as Jewish, is punished with eternal life after he refuses to let Jesus rest on the Via Crucis; it replaces his eternal life with eternal wandering and his unspecified identity with a concrete Jewish identity.[55] Folklorists agree that the legend of the Wandering Jew took shape after the publication of the 1602 pamphlet and the subsequent rapid spread of the legend throughout Europe, as part of the Christological worldview. As R. Edelmann puts it, it was "a cunningly camouflaged statement of the new theology about its attitude towards the Jew and his position in the world, an attitude which in itself was not new but had only to be restated."[56] Jesus condemned the Jew to eternal wandering, and the figure, which became associated with Cain, emerged in British gothic literature as an archetype. Seldom the main character, he haunts the pages of gothic novels, entering, departing, and reappearing in the narrative. Having accumulated a wealth of knowledge over the centuries of his wandering, this supernatural, immortal being is highly intelligent and usually portrayed as either evil or miserable, desperate to do the one thing his immortality does not allow him: to die. The spatiality of the Wandering Jew complements the temporality of the Eternal Jew: he lacks a place and suffers from an overabundance of time.

The archetypal Wandering Jew reflects the antisemitism of British gothic literature since its inception, as Carol Margaret Davison argues in her important study. In the pages of gothic fiction, she shows, "wherever he appears... the question of the nature and parameters of European national identity, as constituted by various commercial, religious, and social practices and values, is raised."[57] The Wandering Jew came to represent the antithesis of the various European national identities that were coming into being. Stateless, unbound to temporal and physical laws, desiring death yet unable to attain it—the Wandering Jew compelled European readers because he embodied difference. His representation in gothic fiction provided a useful contrast against which to define British national identity and helped crystallize this contrast in the popular imagination.

The Wandering Jew signifies twin specters haunting gothic literature, as Davison points out: Jewish assimilation and Jewish difference.[58] Jewish difference threatened the stability of European national identities from the outside, while the prospect of assimilation threatened to corrode it, unsuspected, from within. In Germany by the early nineteenth century and in England by the late eighteenth century, the medieval legend of the Wandering Jew began to be associated with the "Jewish Question" that emerged in the wake of debates about Jewish assimilation, transforming the Jew from a religious to a secular, political, racialized figure and rendering his representation increasingly sinister.[59] The legend itself is markedly ambivalent, regarding the Wandering Jew by turns with sympathy, admiration, and scorn, and depicting him as intelligent, handsome, or tragic.[60] His post-Enlightenment literary manifestations in both the German *Schauerroman* (terror novel) and British gothic literature, however, focused increasingly on the threat he posed. In Germany, France, and Britain, the birth pangs of national identity in the nineteenth century were accompanied by and defined against the development of the Wandering Jew from a religious outcast to a demonic vampire.[61] It is not difficult to identify parallels between these anxieties, articulated in the context of newly defined national identities, and those that would culminate in National Socialist ideology in the fourth decade of the twentieth century. The Nazi regime notoriously exploited antisemitic stereotypes, foremost among them that of the Eternal Jew, "*Die Ewige Jude*," in its propaganda materials. Though invoked in the service of genocide, the grotesque figure the Nazis reproduced on posters, newspapers, and films disseminated throughout the Third Reich was a direct descendent of the Wandering Jew who appeared in gothic literature as a counterpoint to rooted nativeness.[62]

The Wandering Jew as the figure haunting the margins of gothic literature and threatening national stability is maintained in "The Lady and the Peddler": he still haunts the margins, and he is still different. But Agnon appropriates his position and embraces the Jew's difference as a way of proclaiming his ever unassimilated national-cultural sensibility as distinctly Jewish. Maintaining the equation of Jewishness and difference, the story outlines the dangers of assimilation not to the rooted European Christian but to the wandering European Jew himself. Furthermore, Agnon's story undermines the binary logic of home and exile, rootedness and wandering: rejecting assimilation as the means to rootedness, the story also challenges the stereotyped perception of wandering as profoundly derogatory.

Introduced as the familiar Wandering Jew, Agnon's peddler has an outward appearance that projects the despised Christian stereotype as it had developed by the nineteenth century: he carries a heavy pack on his back, wears distinctively Jewish clothes, and is obsequious in his interaction with the lady. That the narrator does not reveal the names of the two main characters, Joseph and Helen, until well into the story confirms the reader's understanding of them as archetypes.[63] However, despite the seeming concord between Agnon's peddler, most at home in wandering, and his predecessor in gothic literature, it becomes clear fairly quickly that neither he nor the lady conforms to associated stereotypes. As the story progresses, the peddler is revealed to be naive, vulnerable, kind, and rather stupid, a far cry from the worldly, cunning, sometimes tragic figure encompassed by the gothic paradigm of the Wandering Jew in novels such as Matthew Lewis's *The Monk* (1795) and Charles Maturin's *Melmoth the Wanderer* (1820). Similarly, the so-called lady is crass, violent, and threatening—anything but noble. Beginning with its title, the story invites readers to rely on existing archetypes even as it almost immediately works to dismantle them.

Agnon's peddler gradually penetrates the most intimate recesses of the lady's home, but he does so by her own invitation and at his own peril. His increasing sense of security and comfort in the lady's house is inversely proportional to his observation of the *halachic mitzvoth*, the commandments of Jewish law, which proscribe every act. He stops eating kosher food, exchanges his peddler's clothes for "the garments of aristocracy," and falls in "with the people of the place until he [is] like one of them."[64] As the narrator asserts explicitly, "he had forgotten that she was a lady and he a Jew."[65] The lady, however, does not forget, referring to him as a Jew: "I never imagined . . . that a Jew's flesh would be so sweet," she exclaims while kissing him aggressively.[66] After their relationship deteriorates, he persistently questions her about her murdered husbands, and she asks: "You're a Jew, aren't you? . . . Well, the Jews don't believe in God, for if they believed in Him, they wouldn't have murdered Him. But if you do believe in God, pray to Him that you won't end up the way they did."[67] Though he sheds outward trappings of his Jewishness as he becomes more intimate with the lady, they both remain alert to their differing cultural sensibilities. It is this awareness that allows him to explain away the most egregious signals she sends of her intention to devour him. Despite the comedic effect of this endeavor, the humor is laced with anxiety, not least on the part of the presumably distraught reader. How can the peddler not recognize the danger that openly announces itself? Does he believe that she accepts him as one of hers because he eats her food and dresses like a forest dweller? These questions would have surely resonated profoundly with Jewish readers in the 1940s.

It is worth noting that the sinister hospitality experienced by the peddler recalls a key motif in perhaps the most famous vampire narrative, Bram Stoker's 1897 novel *Dracula*. Hospitality in *Dracula* is a grotesque business, whether in the experience of the hapless Jonathan Harker, who finds himself a prisoner in Dracula's castle, or in the broader implications of Count Dracula's attempt to inhabit England, adulterating it with Transylvanian soil and with his own contaminating presence.

Though Agnon's unassuming and guileless peddler attributes his confusion regarding the lady's behavior to his being a (formerly) pious Jew, the narrator suggests that it is the peddler's naivete that prevents him from recognizing the lady's dark but readily apparent intentions. After the lady smiles ominously at him, the narrator observes that her smile is subject to interpretation: the "peddler, who was a naïve man, interpreted the laughter of that woman in his own favor and for his own benefit."[68] Though a practicing Jew like the peddler, the narrator is knowledgeable about romantic love. Drawing on biblical narrative to illustrate his knowledge, he delegitimizes the supposed incompatibility between romantic love and Judaic practice: "Anyone who has to do with women knows that a love that depends upon the physical bond alone will come to an end before long. And even if a man loves a woman as Samson loved Delilah, in the end she will mock him, in the end she will oppress him, until he wishes he were dead."[69] Nevertheless, the peddler's assumption that his ignorance of romantic love prevents his recognition of the many hints and even explicit assertions of the lady's murderous intent reveals the chasm between Jews and the hegemonic cultural sensibility that they have resisted and within which they have maintained this difference.

The story associates the act of wandering with Jewishness itself: the pause in the peddler's wandering not only results in his abandonment of Judaic practice and observance but also nearly costs him his life. He can resume his wandering and reclaim his Jewishness only after his sudden urge to recite the Shema saves his life by taking him outside just when the lady enters the room to murder him. The lady's rejection of his blood at the end of the story, even as she hovers at the threshold of death, indicates that beneath his clothing, he is still a Jew. She cannot tolerate the taste of his "icy" Jewish blood, spits it out, and dies. At the same time as this scene corroborates Christian European fears that the assimilated Jew will always be different, it also demonstrates that it is precisely this difference that ultimately saves the Jew from the lady's fangs.

Agnon's rendition of the Wandering Jew explicitly restores *Jewishness* to a key gothic figure, one who was "a Christian invention" from its origins and subject to a "problematic de-historicization" in British gothic literature, to cite Edelmann and Davison, respectively.[70] The key transformation of the basis of the antisemitism undergirding representations of the Wandering Jew, from religious principles to secular, racialized notions, occurred in Germany in the mid-nineteenth century and in Britain by the fin de siècle.[71] This shift finds expression in Charlotte Dacre's *Zofloya, or the Moor: A Romance of the Fifteenth Century* (1806), ostensibly about a black-skinned Moor, but which arguably deflects its Jewish author's internalization of contemporary British antisemitism onto a racial Other depicted as the Wandering Jew.[72] It is not by chance that the gothic emphasis of the Jew's ethnic difference over his religious difference coincided with the development of race-based nationalism in Europe.

By depicting the centrality of the Judaic in this gothic archetype, Agnon resists the Christian European attempt to appropriate Jewishness for its own purposes, reclaims religious practice and identity as central to the Jew, and reintroduces the European Jew into history, even as he critiques the repeated returns of this history in the continued wanderings of the peddler, who, as Band observes, is "probably no wiser for the nightmarish experience."[73] In the context of World War II, the Holocaust, and the looming establishment of the Jewish state, Agnon appropriates the Wandering Jew from what had become his dehistoricized antisemitic provenance, reinscribing his Judaism as a practice, as a confirmation and affirmation of his difference, and as the primary basis of his identity.

At the same time, in Agnon's vision, the Jew's return to history is not a return to *linear* history. By invoking multiple narratives and historicities in the story, he positions the peddler's cyclical movements as geographic as well as, and perhaps primarily, temporal. Agnon's Joseph wanders not only in the Eastern European forest where the story is set but also, via allusion, through biblical Egypt and Hellenistic Greece, and via the legend of the Wandering Jew through eighteenth- and nineteenth-century Britain and Germany—themselves literary conduits into chronotopes as varied as Inquisition-era Spain and nineteenth-century Transylvania. As such, he evokes a multilayered historicity of recurrent returns that invites this figure, again, to haunt 1940s Europe.

Circulatory Stories: Blood

One of the distinctive traits of the European gothic representation of the Wandering Jew is his vampiric impulse: he must drink blood to sustain his immortality. The gothic representation of vampires coalesced various "discourses of blood," in David Biale's phrase, that predated it in centuries of European folk tradition.[74] The popularity of gothic literature ensured that these symbols and associations would be firmly entrenched in European minds by the fin de siècle. Besides its role as an elixir of supernatural power and immortality, blood in the gothic context carries multiple related significations. A currency of life and death, it courses through gothic fiction, signifying violence, transgression, corrupt genealogies, power, and vulnerability. From Joseph Sheridan Le Fanu's *Carmilla* (1872), which briefly portrays a Wandering Jew who is also a vampire, to Stoker's *Dracula*, British literature by the early nineteenth century increasingly identified the vampire with the Wandering Jew.[75] Indeed, as Davison asserts, Stoker's infamous Count "represents the apogee in the development of the vampiric Wandering Jew in British gothic literature."[76] The vampire's mobility, indicated by his transnational inclinations, generates as much anxiety as his thirst for blood.[77] In the stories at hand, the significance of blood is evident not only in the convergence of the Wandering Jew and the vampire but also in the intersection of other blood idioms: its role in Judaic practice and law, its folk interpretations, and its signification of violence. In Agnon's appropriation of the "blood language" of the gothic, blood emerges as the very ink of the Jewish experience in Europe.[78]

In the Judaic context, the Torah states unequivocally "הדם, הוא הנפש" (the blood is life), a point that becomes the ironic motto of Count Dracula himself (Deuteronomy 12:23). The prohibition of the consumption of blood forms the basis for the Judaic dietary injunction to drain meat of its blood (Leviticus 7:26–27, 17:10–14). The rigorous rabbinic interpretation of this law, which instructs Jews to salt, broil, and boil meat until no drop of blood remains, tinges with irony the tragedy of the centuries-long persecution of Jews on the basis of their supposed bloodlust. Indeed, it is impossible to reflect on the Jewish experience in Europe without considering the blood libel, the accusation, which persisted in Europe for centuries, that Jews kidnapped Christian children to use their pure blood in religious rituals such as the preparation of Passover matzah.[79] There is evidence linking the blood libel to the crucifixion of Christ, an event marked in Christian practice at around the same time that Passover is observed by Jews. This link takes us back to the Wandering Jew, whose interaction with Christ dooms him to eternal life—a punishment sustained, in gothic literature, by the consumption of blood. Further, the Jew's bloodlust was figured as a literalized manifestation of his parasitic nature, expressed through his involvement in commerce and usury as well as through his menacing sexuality, which threatened the social and moral fabric of the societies he penetrated.

Manifestations of the demonic Jew, Davison has shown, emerge in several gothic works explicitly in the context of posing a threat to British women, expressing "what was clearly regarded by many at the fin-de-siècle as the extremely unsettling idea of the physical union of male Jew and female non-Jew."[80] The blood spilled by the lady when she tries to kill the peddler points to Agnon's dismantling of such gender dynamics in the relations between Christians and Jews. To the antisemitic mind, the Jewish man was effeminate and lacking virility, a consequence of his circumcision, which has historically been confused with castration; at the same time, he was lascivious and lustful, and his eagerness to violate and corrupt pure Christian womanhood was a metaphor for his corrosive desire to take over the world.[81] Agnon's depiction of a lady as a bloodthirsty vampire threatening a foolish but kind peddler not only disrupts the Christian-versus-Jew dynamic of violence and power but also upends the notions of femininity and masculinity that so often inform this dynamic, from gothic tales of helpless heroines imprisoned and dominated by evil men to Nazi images of hook-nosed men leering at Aryan milkmaids. As Biale has shown in the context of National Socialist ideology, the "main corporeal anxiety was sexual. . . . Because this kind of pollution required injection of the pure essence of blood, the obvious vector was a Jewish man assaulting an Aryan woman. While the blood libel was less gender-specific, *Rassenschande* had a rigid gender code."[82] It is blood that activates the heart of these gendered anxieties. The Nazis' racial utopia depended on, first and foremost, the protection of the purity of German blood. "If the blood libel reflects fear of the *extraction* of Christian blood for Jewish rituals," Biale points out, "'race pollution' involves the *injection* of alien blood into the bloodstream of the Aryan nation."[83]

The blood libel, which promoted the depiction of the Jew as a parasite or a vampire sucking the lifeblood of his host society, is one of several "discourses of blood" that expressed different historical dimensions of antisemitism, from the medieval to the modern. While the blood libel spoke to a medieval Christian suspicion of an isolated, alien community, the fear of Jewish blood pollution reflected modern secular apprehensions about assimilation and integration, which belied an essential, radical difference that threatened the hegemony of European culture and biology.[84] The characterization of "Nazi anti-Semitism as *both* medieval and modern" is based on the Nazi mobilization of various "blood languages" rooted in diverse historical stereotypes that converged in the gothic representation of vampires.[85] Observing that "vampire stories and the blood accusation against Jews have a family resemblance, if not more," Biale connects "the same kind of anxieties over race, nationalism, and sexuality that pervade modern vampire stories" to the blood libel: "It may well be a coincidence that Bram Stoker's *Dracula* (1897) was published just as the modern ritual-murder accusation was reaching its crescendo, but both traffic in the same idea that those who threaten the stability of the nation do so by sucking its blood."[86] As numerous studies have shown, it was no coincidence. Gothic fiction in Europe buttressed an energetic public interest in vampires, explicitly linked to antisemitism and to fears related to modernization, that persisted into World War I.[87] Agnon's revisions of these "blood languages" respond to the multilayered historicity of antisemitic blood discourse and imagery in kind.

Several studies have noted explicit allusions to the blood libel in Agnon's writing, reading it as one component of his literary-historical project.[88] Though the two stories at hand do not engage directly with historical instances of the blood libel, they represent blood in ways that subvert the stereotype associating Jews with bloodlust, reassigning this bloodlust to Christians. Band addresses this phenomenon specifically in the context of the blood libel allusion in "The Lady and the Peddler," pointing to the story's "paradigmatic projection of Christianity's guilt and desires, its imaginary construction of those they dominate."[89] Agnon thus not only disrupts the Christian worldview and the Jew's assigned place within it but also holds up a dark mirror to European antisemitism. The thematization of the blood libel in the figure of the vampire writes the violent history of European Jews in the literary language of those eighteenth- and nineteenth-century European texts that continued to propagate, popularize, and legitimize this violence.

In Agnon's story, the lady's dependence on human blood for sustenance establishes a fundamental difference between her and the peddler by dehumanizing her. Even before the peddler finally understands the fate that is about to befall him, he is puzzled and disturbed by her refusal to join him at meals and questions her abstention from food on several occasions. Unable to participate in the social act of taking meals together with her companion, the lady is beholden to a perversion of Jewish dietary laws—the same dietary laws that the peddler has abandoned. The complex, highly proscribed laws of kashruth not only made social relations between Christians and pious Jews nearly impossible in Europe, but they were also the basis for some of the worst misconceptions about Judaic practice writ large, feeding extant suspicions about Judaism. Though the narrator informs us that Joseph himself had taken upon himself the customs of food and dress of "people of that place," the truth is that the lady herself, his hostess and the house's owner, does not share these customs, having abandoned human habits long ago. In fact, despite Joseph's ministrations, she finally dies five days after wounding herself because "whatever food she tried to eat she would throw up, for she had already forgotten the science of eating ordinary human food, as it was her practice to eat the flesh of her husbands whom she slaughtered and to drink their blood."[90]

The gulf of difference between the lady and the peddler exists, just as the antisemitic worldview insists; but its contours are dictated first and foremost by the nefarious needs of the lady and not by the naive foolishness of the peddler. She thus takes on the role of caricatured Jew in the story, not only owing to her bloodlust but also in her extreme perversion of Jewish difference, which takes her beyond the realm of the human. For his part, the peddler's abandonment of Jewish dietary laws implies that he has transgressed and consumed blood literally by eating nonkosher meat, suggesting that it is assimilation into a Christian milieu that can transform the Jew into the monstrous stereotype promulgated by non-Jews.

As the lady brings to life an inverted version of the antisemitic stereotype of the bloodsucking Jew, the peddler takes on the characteristics of the gothic victim. On the night the lady will attempt to murder him, he is compelled to go outside: "That night was a winter night. The earth was covered with snow and the sky was congealed and turbid. He looked up to the sky and saw no spark of light; he looked to the ground and he could not make out his own feet. Suddenly he saw himself as though imprisoned in a forest in the midst of the snow around him that was being covered over by new snow. And he himself was also being covered over. He uprooted his feet and began to run."[91] Evoking imprisonment in the form of one of the most terrifying conventions in the gothic arsenal, live burial, Agnon's portrait of the peddler suggests that he is the victim not only of the vampire-lady but also of her milieu. Live burial, a phenomenon that famously preoccupied Edgar Allan Poe in life, is depicted as a central horror in many of his stories, including "Berenice" (1835), "The Fall of the House of Usher" (1839), "The Premature Burial" (1844), "The Cask of Amontillado" (1846), and others. Agnon himself was no stranger to the concept. As Dov Sadan has shown, his stories indirectly express the opposition by the maskilim (proponents of the Haskalah, or Jewish Enlightenment) to the Judaic custom of interment soon after death, an act that risked premature burial.[92] In "Ha-yalda ha-meta" (The dead girl, 1932), Agnon depicts premature burial literally; in "The Lady and the Peddler," the burial is less literal but nevertheless material and real. The foreboding forest, the suffocating snow, the dark night—all conspire against the Jew, delaying his departure, imprisoning him, swallowing him alive. He is saved only when he finally "uproots" himself (עקר את רגליו) and returns to wandering. The return to wandering, however, is clearly not accompanied by increased wisdom. The inversion of the gothic victim and perpetrator results in a Jew who is a victim of his own naivete as much as of the vampire who would consume him.

"The Lady and the Peddler" maintains the Jew's difference. At the same time, it subverts the antisemitic image of the vampiric Jew by assigning bloodlust to the Christian hostess, illustrating the idea that antisemitism, in Davison's words, "has been the real vampire that has birthed demons by projecting its macabre tendencies onto the Jew."[93] Following Adorno and Horkheimer, Davison discusses Nazism in the context of the dark mirror that antisemitic rhetoric holds up to those who propagate it: "Ironically, in its organization and belief system, Nazism resembles Judaism as it had been demonically portrayed in the European world-view: it was a conspiratorial, millenarian, kabbalistically grounded secret society whose leader regarded himself as the new German messiah."[94] Agnon's story confronts the insidious, centuries-old stereotypes of Jewish bloodlust and the Wandering Jew to rewrite European history, undermining the stereotypes that dictated the terms of Jewish-Christian relations as cemented in the popular European imagination by gothic literature, and adapting their symbols to confront the demons that threatened Jewish particularity.

In "The Dance of Death," too, "blood languages" circulate between the Jewish and the anti-Jewish, locking these two worldviews in their own macabre dance. The frame narrative of "The Dance of Death" opens and closes at the scene of the crime, the square before the great synagogue. Already in the second sentence, blood emerges as a central symbol. Foreshadowing the tragedy of the embedded narrative, the narrator describes the red weeds sprouting from the site of the groom's murder, a spot where weddings are not performed and where Kohanim, priests, do not tread. We learn later that the groom has been interred in the spot of his murder to facilitate vengeance. His corpse contaminates the earth and bars the proximity of priests. The spilled blood, "the soul of the flesh" in Jewish tradition, becomes a metonymy of the groom's murder.[95]

Despite the arid, measured symmetry of the narrator's words, the melodramatic moment of the groom's death is repetitive and excruciatingly concrete:

> The groom fell to the earth and a sad laugh hovered on his lips. He silently spread his arms to dance with the bride. In his throat was an oily, sweet moistness. The skin of his neck contracted and his lifeblood flowed from his neck. A hint of laughter played on his lips, his tongue between his lips. He silently lifted his eyes before the face of his bride, and his bride he did not see. His blood flowed in his eyes, and in his blood he wallowed. The groom died. Before the great synagogue he lay dead. From his neck flowed his blood on the whiteness of his clothes and on his wedding attire.[96]

The vivid depiction of the groom's blood—seeping into the earth in the square in front of the great synagogue, staining his white wedding attire, hemorrhaging from his slit throat—is uncharacteristic for a story whose characters are enigmatic and whose plot hints at cryptic undercurrents. A decidedly physical depiction, it contrasts with the spectral form the groom will take at the end of the story.

Blood in this scene is a material substance, as concrete as the silk gown on which the narrator elaborates in the first half of the story. Whereas the narrator's disproportionate focus on the matter of the silk clothes links them to power and money, suggesting a symbolic relation to the blood that will be spilled at the wedding, the materiality of the blood in the moments following the murder reveals its substance. The celebrants-turned-mourners, though utterly impotent themselves, believe that burying the groom in his bloodstained clothing and shoes will avenge his murder. As a physical element and not only a symbol, blood is power. As such, this story, too, appropriates the antisemitic vocabulary utilized by gothic literature to express fear of corrupting external elements. In Agnon's adaptation, however, the power offered by blood goes unclaimed. With its potential to disrupt the victim/oppressor dichotomy that structures many European gothic narratives, the burial of the groom in his bloody kittel only demonstrates his dissociation from such earthly concerns. While he does rise from his grave, he does so not to exact vengeance but to reunite with his bride.[97]

Where the Jewish groom is ultimately spirit, the Polish count is entirely physical. His blood, the story suggests, primarily functions as the source of his violent lust: on seeing the bride at her wedding, his "blood vessels became confused."[98] His physical and political power belies a profound moral weakness, signified by his confused blood, and satiated only through the *spilling* of blood. In the story's penultimate scene, he returns from the hunt to find his Jewish bride, clad in her wedding gown, dead. His hunting clothes, "soiled with blood," mirror the bloodstained kittel of the unfortunate groom, paralleling the transgression of murder with the distinctly un-Jewish pastime of hunting animals for sport.[99] Both acts revise the lust for sex and for blood ascribed in the antisemitic imagination to Jews, exposing how these traits actually correspond to the nature and practice of the murderous Pole. Besides enhancing the macabre atmosphere of the story, the juxtaposition of the bloody garments—the count's hunting attire and the groom's pure white kittel—forcefully announces their difference and coalesces the tension between power and powerlessness even as it laces both with ambivalence. If the Torah instructs us that "the blood is the life," the gothic tradition suggests that it is also very much *the death*, an idea that was always already enfolded in the rabbinic understanding of blood. Blood goes both ways: it sustains, purifies, and empowers, but it can also defile, corrupt, and weaken. Acknowledging this tense duality in the figures of the groom and the count, Agnon's story accentuates the gothic tenor in the experience of Eastern European Jews.

The story clearly invokes the gothic economy in which blood is the foremost currency, first through the preoccupation with material wealth, conveyed through the father's dissatisfaction with the matter of the silk clothing, which may have precipitated the tragedy. It also calls on this gothic economy through the white kittel, whose bloodstains imbue the groom with the ability to avenge himself after death, and through the Polish count's nonchalant and unimpeded spilling of blood, a habit that indicates his political power. At the same time, the story inscribes the count's power as a moral failing and indicates that the groom is not the sort of man whose blood vessels would become confused. Renouncing the opportunity offered by his spilled blood to overturn in death the power relations that sealed his fate in life, the groom chooses instead to dance with his spectral beloved. In this story, as in the later one, the treatment of blood helps dismantle antisemitic stereotypes and reflect them back at their inventors.[100] The language of blood circulates from the medieval anti-Jewish lexicon to the nineteenth century and into the 1930s, appropriated by Agnon to express the history of persecution of Eastern European Jews. Even as these stories disown and reassign the most insidious and persistent antisemitic tropes, they look back to the images and devices of the gothic to do so.

Back to the Present

"The Dance of Death" and "The Lady and the Peddler," as noted early in this chapter, were written in the context of key moments in twentieth-century history. Though neither story comments directly on the turbulent historical events that accompanied its writing and publication, both were first published in an explicitly political contemporary context. For an author like Agnon, who generally refrained from involvement in political activities, this is unusual.[101] *Treue* and *Ha-sa'ar* bookend the two world wars, defining events of the twentieth century, and both collections were specifically intended to be read by Jewish soldiers fighting in those wars. Agnon's choice to contribute these stories on two of the few occasions he agreed to participate in such projects suggests that the gothic offered a way of responding to the events at hand without actually engaging with them.

It is possible that Agnon intended these stories, with their supernatural figures and historical displacement, to provide escapism to the soldiers who would read them in the trenches, tents, or battlefields of war. On the other hand, though, it is difficult to imagine a Jewish soldier who would read these gruesome stories about Jewish life in Europe without linking their events to those unfolding there in the second and fourth decades of the twentieth century. In other words, just as Agnon addressed the historical trauma of the Holocaust indirectly in much of his later work, so does he represent the implications of volatile contemporary events implicitly. Though the gothic deflects realism through its devices, style, and historical setting, it is also, by definition, amenable to a multivalent temporality, refracting historical reality through its shadowy lens. It thus allows Agnon to connect contemporary events to key moments in the Jewish past, producing a historiography that encompasses and links diverse historical moments.

Agnon's gothicism is evident in the macabre atmosphere and supernatural devices of many of his stories as well as in the fear and anxiety emanating from his depictions of the relations between Christians and Jews. Hosting a literary repository of antisemitic imagery and discourse, the gothic provides an idiom for Agnon to subvert and appropriate anti-Jewish stereotype from within, while maintaining the notion of Jewish difference. Revising antisemitic iconography, his stories mirror and recalibrate the dynamics of victims and oppressors associated with Jews and Christians in the European past, a textual vindication of past misrepresentations.

At the same time, though, these devices leave the past restless. Wanderers return to their travels; ghosts emerge from their graves; narrators end their tales midcycle. This cyclical temporality operates together with the multiple historical layers informing these stories—through language, allusion, and, critically, the revision of antisemitic images and themes integral to the gothic—to activate a vision of the Jewish past that is itself gothic, perpetually returning to inform and disrupt the present. Actively intervening in the past, Agnon's stories both recall and revise multiple layers of Jewish history, not as eulogies to a finalized past but as disturbing mirrors of history's continued violations of the vulnerable present. The result is a gothic historiography at odds with the kind of static "ethnographic impulse" Scholem identified in Agnon's post-Holocaust fiction. In his ironic exposure and appropriation of the gothic forces always underlying Jewish histories, Agnon disrupts the boundary between the past and the present, an act that can be understood as one of the defining characteristics of his distinctive brand of modernism. The next chapter considers how such gothic disruptions are deployed in distinctly feminine narratives of the traditional Eastern European Jewish world.

Notes

1. Other notable contributors included Zalman Schneour, David Frischman, and Shalom Aleichem. For more on the role of *Treue* in Agnon's reception among German Jews, see Laor, "Agnon and Buber." See also Barzilai, "Agnon's German Consecration."

2. Laor, "Agnon and Buber," 54.

3. "The Dance of Death," the seeds of which appear as early as 1906 in the Hebrew story "Ha-panas" [The lantern, 1906–7] and the Yiddish "Toitentans" [Dance of death, 1908], was written during a period of multiple transitions in Agnon's life: from Buczacz to Jaffa, from writing in both Yiddish and Hebrew to writing solely in Hebrew, from the position of a promising writer to that of an acclaimed one. Likely one of the last stories he conceptualized before leaving Buczacz in 1907, its publication coincided with that of his macabre composition on the city, "Ir ha-metim" [City of the dead]. The story underwent further revision during Agnon's period in Germany and was published in the *Polin* cycles of 1919 and 1925 together with "Bimtsulot" ["In the Depths," 1917], another markedly gothic story.

4. Roskies and Diamant, *Holocaust Literature*, 39.

5. Translation of world literature to Hebrew thrived in Europe and Palestine in the early twentieth century because of the widely held conviction that it was integral to the formation of a Jewish national culture. The major works of gothic literature, however, except stories and poems by Edgar Allan Poe, remained untranslated until late in the twentieth century. Until then, Hebrew readers could access gothic works only in their original language. On the dearth of Hebrew translations of gothic literature in the twentieth century, see the introduction to this study, specifically the section entitled "Gothic in Hebrew Translation: A Brief Nonhistory."

6. DeKoven Ezrahi, "Revisioning the Past," 251.

7. Ibid.

8. Spooner, *Contemporary Gothic*, 18–19.

9. Goddu, *Gothic America*, 10.

10. Botting, *Gothic*, 1.

11. Roshwald, *Ghetto, Shtetl, or Polis*, 63. Roshwald later discusses the "macabre touches of death, shrouds, spectres, and grotesque desecration" in Agnon's *Sefer ha-ma'asim* [The book of deeds] as kabbalistic (ibid., 147). There is no doubt that, as numerous studies on folk elements in Agnon's fiction suggest, Judaic folk as well as mystical traditions provide Agnon with an array of specifically Jewish demons and monsters. See, for example, Shenhar, "Motivim amamiyim." Other critics, however, regard similar devices of a non-Jewish European provenance as superficial, insignificant, and irrelevant to the Judaic.

12. G. Shaked, *Omanut ha-sipur*, 33.

13. Ibid., 41, 89. Shaked argues that even in the early gothic story "Be'era shel Miryam" [Miriam's well], which was lamented by his contemporaries as overly sentimental, Agnon was already attempting to moderate emotion both thematically and stylistically, and to establish ironic self-awareness as the dominant mode of his poetics.

14. The slippage in the critical literature between the terms *gothic* and *romantic* warrants brief clarification. Most scholars agree that the historical boundaries of British gothic writing predate Romanticism, beginning in 1764 and winding down by 1820. Despite their aesthetic and poetic overlap, the gothic and romantic fulfilled two different needs in the literary economy of their time and place. Romantic authors in early nineteenth-century England saw themselves as participants in high culture, whose literary productions were far removed from the vulgar popular fiction of the "German School." Even as they themselves borrowed from the "lowbrow" poetics of the gothic, they were often its most vociferous detractors. While some contemporary critics argue that gothic and romantic are essentially one and the same, or that the gothic is a darker subset of Romanticism, others insist on fundamental differences in their confrontation with moral ambiguity, fear, and transgression; still others contrast the romantic embrace of nature as leading to "emotional certainty" with the gothic rejection of

the very notion of transcendence. See Gamer, *Romanticism and the Gothic*; Williams, *Art of Darkness*; and Hume, "Gothic versus Romantic."

15. G. Shaked, *Omanut ha-sipur*, 33, 36–37.
16. Band, *Nostalgia and Nightmare*, 91.
17. For example, citing "the fascination with the macabre" in Agnon's *Ve-haya he-akov le-mishor* [*And the Crooked Shall Be Made Straight*], Band writes: "We are here confronted with the same romantic ethos that militates against the portrayal of a traditional Jewish milieu governed by divine providence and halakha" (*Nostalgia and Nightmare*, 91). See also G. Shaked, *Omanut ha-sipur*, especially "Galui ve-samui ba-sipur," 89–132. An exception is Shenhar. Though she describes Agnon's fiction as indicating his "dualistic world-view" and the broader dialectic that governs his fiction (gothic, romantic, and "international," on one hand, and Jewish, on the other), she is more inclined to see these forces as mutually reinforcing than opposed (Shenhar, "Motivim amamiyim," 61). In an altogether different approach to Agnon's duality, Weiss proposes a "dual generic reading" that melds gothic and magical realism (V. Weiss, "Generic Hybridity," 69). *Shmuel Yosef Agnon: A Revolutionary Traditionalist* is the title of a monograph by Gershon Shaked.
18. For more on the romantic view of the past, see Löwy and Sayre, *Romanticism*.
19. Band, *Nostalgia and Nightmare*, 449.
20. This list includes the most explicitly gothic of Agnon's stories in this period, but it is not exhaustive; it excludes several stories that are not as a whole gothic but that make use of certain gothic devices or conventions (such as ghosts or other figures who return from the dead)—for example, "Ha-mikhtav" ["The Letter," 1940] and "Le-veit aba" ["To Father's House, 1941"].
21. For more on the gothic's relationship to history and on related conventions such as the discovered manuscript, see the introduction and chap. 5 of this study. See also Dent, "Contested Pasts."
22. Other notions of Agnon's historicity consider his historiographic tendencies in relation to particular works. Roman Katsman, for example, argues that *Ir u-melo'a* [*A City in Its Fullness*] showcases Agnon as a writer of alternative history; see Katsman, *Literature, History, Choice*. Several recent studies focus on Agnon's relationship to Buczacz specifically. See, for example, DeKoven Ezrahi, "Shtetl and Its Afterlife"; and Mintz, "Building a City." For a comprehensive study of Buczacz, see Bartov, *Your Brother's Blood*.
23. For more on *Sipurey Polin*, see DeKoven Ezrahi, "Shtetl and Its Afterlife," especially 134–39; Ben-Dov, "Poland as 'Promised Land'"; and Boris Kotlerman, "Historical Time and Space."
24. Boris Kotlerman, "Historical Time and Space," 361, 372.
25. Quoted in Laor, "About the Holocaust," 41.
26. Scholem, "Reflections on Agnon."
27. DeKoven Ezrahi, "Agnon Before and After," 85, 86.
28. Laor, "About the Holocaust," 63.
29. Ibid., 55–57.
30. Mintz, *Translating Israel*, 109.
31. H. Weiss, "Presence of the Holocaust," 432.
32. Arbel, "Ha-ktiva ke-matseva."
33. Scholem, "Reflections on Agnon," 59.
34. See Alter, *Invention of Hebrew Prose*.
35. For more on Scholem's notion of history, see Biale, *Gershom Scholem*.

36. Green, "What Agnon Taught Scholem," 163.
37. Ibid., 163, 175.
38. Ibid., 175.
39. Gershom Scholem, in his famous 1926 letter to Franz Rosenzweig, writes of the resurrection of Hebrew in a modern secular context that represses its religious force as necessitating a "demonic courage." The consequence of this undertaking, a "ghostly" Hebrew, poses a threat to Zionism that is "more uncanny than the Arab nation, . . . one that of necessity the Zionist undertaking has summoned up." Scholem, "A Confession," in Cutter, "Ghostly Hebrew, Ghastly Speech," 431.
40. For more on time and history in the folktale, see Nicolaisen, "Past as Place."
41. Malka Shaked reads the motif as a Christian-European one distinct from and inherently at odds with the Judaic, evidence of the influence of German literature on Agnon. She does not point to specific German literary examples but rather states that "the German Gothic world . . . includes the tragic intensity of the *danse macabre*" ("What Dances," 162). Asserting the danse macabre as an indicator of the "German Gothic" that influenced Agnon, she suggests that its juxtaposition with the Judaic in the story reflects "the two cultural sources of the story" (ibid.). DeKoven Ezrahi writes against the broad critical tendency to read Christians against Jews in Agnon, offering a different interpretation of his story "Ma'agelei tsedek" ["Paths of Righteousness"]. See DeKoven Ezrahi, "S. Y. Agnon's Jerusalem," 146–48.
42. For a discussion of possible literary influences related to the danse macabre in the story "Toitentans," see Ber Kotlerman, "His Heart."
43. On the dance of death motif, see Goodwin, *Kitsch and Culture*. For more on the dance of death in the Jewish context, see Elstein and Lipsker, "Homogeneous Series."
44. Agnon would most likely have been familiar with Goethe's 1815 ballad "Der Totentanz," which blends humor and tragedy in its adaptation of the famous motif. Notably, the ballad's tension hinges on the lost shroud of one of the skeletal dancers, recalling the centrality of clothing (both the groom's kittel and the bride's wedding dress) in Agnon's story.
45. Agnon, "Meḥolat ha-mavet," 290. All citations from this story are my own translation.
46. For more on the story's intertextual allusions, see Ben-Dov, "Biblical Allusion." See also M. Shaked, "What Dances."
47. Agnon, "Meḥolat ha-mavet," 292.
48. Agnon, "Lady and Peddler," 203. All citations from this story are from this translation unless otherwise noted.
49. Ibid.
50. Ibid., 206.
51. Ibid., 198.
52. Ibid., 210.
53. Ibid., 206.
54. Ibid., 208.
55. Edelmann, "Ahasuerus, the Wandering Jew," 8.
56. Ibid., 9.
57. Davison, *Anti-Semitism*, 2.
58. Ibid., 7. Davison expands on this notion in the context of *Dracula*, which "taps two joint fears at the fin de siècle—the alien 'invasion' and domination of Britain by Eastern European Jews from without, and the threat of Anglo-Jewish takeover from within" (*Anti-Semitism*, 125).

59. Ibid., 7.
60. Anderson, "Popular Survivals."
61. Davison, *Anti-Semitism*, 5.
62. Davison identifies "a reciprocal German-English dialogue at the end of the eighteenth century when the German Terror-novel, or Schauerroman, was popular in Britain, and British gothic literature was garnering great attention in Germany" (*Anti-Semitism*, 160). Picking up the German thread of her investigation by way of Nazi propaganda cinema, she observes that, while the vampiric Wandering Jew "was central to the consolidation of national identity in both countries, his religious affiliation remained unidentified in Stoker's gothic *fantasy* in stark contrast to his more *realistic* treatment in Germany," and identifies the medium of cinema as more amenable to this treatment (ibid.).
63. The names themselves invoke the Judaic past through the allusion to the story of Joseph and Potiphar; see Kurzweil, "Lady and the Peddler." The names also allude to the clash between Hellenic and Hebraic civilizations. Davison discusses Matthew Arnold's conceptualization of Hellenism and Hebraism in *Culture and Anarchy* (1869), arguing that his lamentation of the Hebraism that dominated British society belies "the racial ideology underpinning his ethnically inflected terminology" (*Anti-Semitism*, 12).
64. Agnon, "Lady and Peddler," 202.
65. Ibid., 203.
66. Ibid.
67. Ibid., 205.
68. Ibid., 201.
69. Ibid., 204.
70. Edelmann, "Ahasuerus, the Wandering Jew," 3; Davison, *Anti-Semitism*, 4.
71. Davison, *Anti-Semitism*, 129.
72. See Hoeveler, "Charlotte Dacre's Zofloya."
73. Band, *Nostalgia and Nightmare*, 402.
74. Biale discusses "discourses of blood," such as Jewish ritual murder, specifically in the context of Nazi propaganda, but stresses that they were rooted in medieval folk beliefs. See Biale, *Blood and Belief*, 125.
75. Davison, *Anti-Semitism*, 114. Davison locates the origin of this vampiric Wandering Jew in Schiller's incomplete novel *The Ghost Seer*, though its wanderer is Armenian and not specified as Jewish (*Anti-Semitism*, 90–92). She writes that in "their supernatural abilities to recognize and expose real and figurative vampires, Apollonius and Schiller's Wandering Armenian influence the Wandering Jew's earliest incarnation in British gothic literature" (ibid., 95). From the German genesis of the Wandering Jew, Davison charts his "progressive 'fall' from supernatural vampire-detector to figurative vampire and, finally, to actual vampire in the pages of British gothic literature" (ibid.).
76. Davison, *Anti-Semitism*, 120.
77. Goddu links the vampire's mobility to that of the gothic as a literary mode: "traveling vampires remind us of the gothic's mobility" and signify "the genre's movement across diverse geographical spaces" (Goddu, "Vampire Gothic," 126–27).
78. Blood is central in less paradigmatically gothic stories in Agnon's oeuvre, as well—for example, "Kisuy ha-dam" [Covering the blood, published posthumously in 1975] and "Agadat ha-sofer" ["Tale of the Scribe," 1919]. In the former, the use of blood is particularly compelling for its role in relating different periods in Jewish history and its implications about the Jews' role in the Holocaust.

79. For a wide-ranging survey on the blood libel, see Dundes, *Blood Libel Legend*. For a detailed history, see O'Brien, *Pinnacle of Hatred*. For an analysis of historiographic approaches to the blood libel, see Johnson, *Blood Libel*.

80. Davison, *Anti-Semitism*, 133–34.

81. For more on the role of circumcision in the othering of the Jew, see Gilman, *Jew's Body*.

82. Biale, *Blood and Belief*, 139

83. Ibid., 138.

84. Ibid., 139.

85. Ibid., 125.

86. Ibid., 172.

87. For a comprehensive study, see Robinson, *Blood Will Tell*; and Robinson, "Novel Anti-Semitisms." For more on *Dracula* as representing Jews via "reverse colonization," see Arata, "Occidental Tourist." For a consideration of *Dracula* as a critique of contemporary race discourse, see Ewence, "Blurring the Boundaries."

88. Band discusses "The Lady and the Peddler" specifically as alluding to the blood libel through the evocation of the Eucharist. See Band, "Refractions of Blood Libel." See especially 128–30. See also Werses, "Bein metsiyut historit le-te'ur sipuri."

89. Band, "Refractions of Blood Libel," 130.

90. Agnon, "Lady and Peddler," 210.

91. Ibid., 208.

92. For more on Agnon's stories in relation to the maskilic protest of this custom, see Sadan, *Al Shai Agnon*, 94–97.

93. Davison, *Anti-Semitism*, 14.

94. Ibid., 165.

95. A related idea, which builds on the notion of the blood as the "soul of the flesh" (Leviticus 17:11) is *kisuy ha-dam*, the covering of the blood, the injunction that ritual slaughterers must cover the blood they spill when slaughtering a wild animal (Leviticus 17:13: "And he shall pour out its blood, and cover it with earth"). "Kisuy ha-dam" is also the title of a late Agnon story, published posthumously.

96. Agnon, "Meḥolat ha-mavet," 291–92.

97. The groom's rejection of revenge situates this story at odds with the sentiment behind the myth of the golem, associated, in its best-known Prague tradition, with violent vengeance on behalf of blood-libeled Jews. Literature attesting to the association between the golem and the blood libel abounds. For some examples, see Biale, *Blood and Belief*; and Sherwin, *Golem Legend*.

98. Agnon, "Meḥolat ha-mavet," 291.

99. Ibid., 292.

100. See Biale, *Blood and Belief*, chap. 5, especially 172–75, where he discusses late nineteenth- and early twentieth-century Jewish defenses against the blood libel and other blood-related antisemitic accusations. Agnon's treatment is not so nationalist, and it is fraught with the ambivalence of a man torn between the indictment of Christian Europe for what it has done to its Jews and his critique of the Jews for what they do to themselves. This assessment aligns with DeKoven Ezrahi's contention that the "intractability" of the story "Kisuy ha-dam" "may be in the inherent tension between the conflicting mandates to mourn and to judge the victims" ("Agnon Before and After," 92).

101. Laor, who has argued that Agnon's oeuvre actually engages with the Holocaust despite very few explicit references to it, also wryly comments that his contribution to *Ha-sa'ar* was anomalous. The rest of his publications, "including those that were published after November 1942—were completely independent of the political situation." As World War II raged, Agnon "did not change the way of his writing and continued to write tales of bygone days or of the Land of Israel" (Laor, *Ḥayey Agnon*, 349, 350). In a similar vein, DeKoven Ezrahi remarks that, in general, "political upheavals in the modern era do not determine Agnon's fictional timeline, and even the Holocaust and the birth of the State of Israel are inscribed less as events than as continuous with processes already in place" ("Shtetl and Its Afterlife," 147–48).

2

MATERNAL MACABRE

Feminine Subjectivity at the Edge of the Shtetl in Dvora Baron and Ya'akov Shteinberg

At around the same time that Agnon published his morbid story "The Dance of Death" in *Treue*, two other authors, also recently arrived in Palestine from Eastern Europe, were revising and rewriting their own dark tales. Dvora Baron (1887–1956) and Ya'akov Shteinberg (1887–1947), like Agnon, were anomalous in their ongoing literary preoccupation with the Eastern European Jewish milieu even after their immigration to Palestine. Baron, the first woman author to be included in the canon of the modern Hebrew renaissance, and Shteinberg, a Yiddish and Hebrew poet, essayist, and author, emigrated in 1910 and 1914, respectively. I bring them together in this chapter for several reasons: they both chose to emigrate though neither was an outspoken nationalist, they both contributed prolifically to the cultural milieu of the Yishuv, and they both wrote in Hebrew. Though she wrote her earliest stories in Yiddish, Baron eventually became known as one of the most important authors of modern Hebrew. Shteinberg relinquished Yiddish in Palestine. Both, though, continued to write about traditional Eastern European society. Most of the Hebrew authors in the Yishuv, by contrast, preferred to leave the Eastern European past behind and turn their literary attention to the historic settlement enterprise in which they were participating. Furthermore, both Baron and Shteinberg are known for their empathetic representations of marginalized characters, such as women, the disabled, and the poor. Their focus on such figures immediately deflates any notion of sentimentality or idealization in their depictions of traditional Jewish society, though it also does not preclude the possibility of happiness in that milieu. In their stories, neither Shteinberg nor Baron disowns the shtetl or the social system that sustains it.[1] The authors' refusal to reify the shtetl, its inhabitants, and their relationships contributes to a complex portrayal of a space that, by the third decade of the twentieth century, was on the verge of extinction. From their vantage point in a Jewish state-in-the-making, both authors looked back to the place they had left behind as a chronotope, to use Mikhail Bakhtin's term, a phenomenon defined by its geographical location in Eastern Europe as well as its association with the Jewish past.[2] Though their continued attention to this chronotope is considered a digression from the here and now of the Yishuv, their writing on social justice constitutes an important contribution to the creation of the new Jewish society they had joined.

Born in Uzda, a shtetl near Minsk, Baron was raised in a rabbinic home; her father, a rabbi, allowed her a religious education usually reserved exclusively for boys. This education, and her experience observing the collective and procedural application of halacha, or Jewish law, in her community, would mark her writing and her social sensibilities. Having published numerous stories as a young woman, most in Hebrew but some in Yiddish, she was already established as a promising author of Hebrew upon her immigration to Palestine in 1910. Soon after her arrival, she married Yosef Aharonowitz, a founder of the socialist Zionist group Ha-po'el ha-tsa'ir (the Young Worker) and the editor of its weekly newspaper by the same name, where Baron worked as the literary editor. Like other cultural and intellectual figures in Jewish Palestine, Baron and her family were exiled to Alexandria by the Ottoman government during World War I. They returned to Palestine in 1919, settling in Tel Aviv and continuing to participate in the literary life of the Yishuv. Baron's public activities came to an end in 1922, when she withdrew to her apartment for the rest of her life. Many of the stories she continued to write reflect her enduring interest in social environments like the one she had left behind in the Lithuanian shtetl, particularly in the lives of girls and women in that context.

Like Baron, Shteinberg began publishing at a young age after leaving his Ukrainian home for greener literary pastures in Odessa and, later, Warsaw. His poetry and stories in Hebrew and Yiddish attracted the attention of no less a figure than the celebrated Hebrew poet Ḥayim Naḥman Bialik, who heralded him as a rising star of Hebrew verse.[3] Until his emigration to Palestine in 1914, Shteinberg published some of his most important and best-known Yiddish stories. In Palestine, he married the sister of the prominent Zionist political leader Ḥayim Arlozorov and began writing exclusively in Hebrew and translating his own Yiddish stories to Hebrew. Besides a two-year hiatus from 1922 to 1924 in Berlin alongside Bialik, he spent the rest of his life in Palestine. Like Baron, he was involved with the weekly *Ha-po'el ha-tsa'ir*, as an essayist, in addition to producing poetry and prose in a distinctive Hebrew that seemed resistant to the shifts occurring in the local Palestinian poetic milieu. Perhaps the most concrete evidence of this resistance is his continued use of Ashkenazi Hebrew, a linguistic form that, though used in poetry by Bialik, was abandoned by other Hebrew poets in Palestine. Like Baron, Shteinberg maintained a separation in much of his writing from his immediate surroundings, in terms of his poetics as well as the themes and atmosphere of his writing.

The two stories I examine in this chapter, Shteinberg's "Ha-iveret" ("The Blind Woman"; 1923 in Hebrew) and Dvora Baron's "Shifra" (1927), expose another link between Baron and Shteinberg, one that is particularly germane to this study: their occasional turn to the gothic to express the dark side of Jewish Eastern Europe, particularly its marginalized figures.[4] The Eastern European Jewish world is a repository of dybbuks, golems, goblins, and other supernatural beings sprung from Yiddish folk culture. From S. Ansky to I. L. Peretz to I. B. Singer, the shtetl, a key setting in Yiddish literature, has hosted haunting and possession. Though in form these demons and goblins may resemble the supernatural beings that populate gothic literature, they emerge from a different tradition and to different ends than those in the gothic. Further, as noted in the introduction to this study, the gothic comprises more than the conventions with which it is identified: a work need not contain ghosts to be gothic, and the presence of a ghost does not, in itself, render a work gothic. In stories by Baron and Shteinberg, the gothic accords with Sarah Wasson's characterization of the mode: it produces an "intense affect [that] accompanies a particular experience of spatiality."[5]

Conceptualizing gothic thus brings to mind the stories of Edgar Allan Poe, who, as we saw in the introduction to this study, was the only gothic author widely available in Hebrew translation when Baron and Shteinberg were in Palestine; Poe's spatial anxieties and their relation to his characters' profound affective reactions are hallmarks of his writing. In Baron's early stories, affect is particularly pronounced in plots that emphasize confinement and claustrophobia or menacing, bleak settings.[6] The narrator of the story "Kaddish" (1908 in Hebrew, 1910 in Yiddish), for example, describes her grandfather's house thus: "Inside the house, mute, terror-black shadows would wrap my grandfather in dark shrouds. . . . Outside—a disheveled, lumbering sky over the congealed, dead earth. It's quiet and dismal. Every now and then a flock of black crows flies by, hurls a few curses into the air, and then disappears, and again it's quiet."⁷ Evoking a similar mood of quiet dread in the familiar spaces of family and community, many of Shteinberg's works, such as "Mot ha-zkena" (The death of the old woman, 1917), are preoccupied with death and dying; some, such as "Bat ha-rav" (The rabbi's daughter, 1914 in Hebrew, 1912 in Yiddish), narrate subtly erotic encounters that culminate in tragedy.

Several readers have acknowledged the gothic atmosphere of fiction by both authors. For example, Aharon Komem identifies Shteinberg's tendency to portray "experiences on the borderline between reality and nightmare" as a basic feature of his writing.⁸ Shteinberg's biographer, Yisrael Cohen, writes that his stories "are anchored in a Jewish experience that bleeds (שותתת דם)."⁹ Explicitly calling "Ha-iveret" "a gothic horror story," Ziva Shamir relates specific motifs and figures such as ravens and dogs to "gothic horror literature," specifically the fiction of Poe.¹⁰

Baron, too, has been ascribed gothic influences, particularly evident in her early stories.¹¹ Her fiction evokes "the unrest of a ghost being called back from the dead," in Sheila Jelen's words, thus aiding the revival not only of the Hebrew language but of an "entire culture."¹² Comparing the Hebrew and Yiddish versions of several of Baron's gothic early stories published between 1908 and 1910, including "Kaddish," "Bubbe Henya," and "Aḥot" ("Sister"), Naomi Seidman makes a compelling case for an explicit gothicism in the Yiddish versions' ambivalence and their suggestion of incest and infanticide. She links the Hebrew stories "to the realist literature of social protest" and the Yiddish "to expressionism, or, more specifically, to the gothic family tale."¹³ The intensified gothicism of the Yiddish derives from the association of the macabre and the supernatural with Yiddish folk culture, posits Seidman, "although they find their place in Hebrew as well." Further, as the feminine counterpart to the "masculine sphere of Hebrew," Yiddish was better equipped to express the gothic dramas of Jewish women's lives.¹⁴ As we shall see, though, Hebrew, too, hosts the gothic to this end. In Hebrew works by both Shteinberg and Baron, gothic devices function, as in nineteenth-century gothic works, not separately from but in tandem with the social and ideological critiques that have been identified in their writing.

The matter of language, however, does warrant consideration. Though both the stories I discuss are written in Hebrew, Shteinberg wrote the first version of "Ha-iveret" in Yiddish and later translated it to Hebrew; both stories' sparse Hebrew dialogue is understood to represent Yiddish.[15] Yiddish literature, like gothic literature, has been historically associated with women readers and with popular literary sensibilities. Yet the Yiddish language is absent from the pages of these two stories, haunting both and gesturing toward the ideological convictions that were at least partly responsible for bringing their authors to Palestine. In the context of these stories' alternative feminine narratives, the turn to a Hebrew expression of the gothic is especially compelling.

In this chapter, I propose that the invocation of the gothic in Shteinberg's "Ha-iveret" and Baron's "Shifra" produces a metaphor of *staying*, an alternative to the key "departure metaphor" that Dan Miron identifies in literature set in the shtetl. The emphasis on staying in these women-centered narratives calls attention to the dark undercurrents of Eastern European Jewish social norms in the late nineteenth and early twentieth centuries. Even those women who leave their homes, as we shall see, do so only to maintain the social and domestic order. They find themselves not journeying to the metropolis or emigrating to another country, like the men, but relegated to the social and geographic margins of their own communities. In fact, the women in these stories bypass altogether the binaries established as the basis of social relations in Eastern European Jewish society on the eve of modernization: home and exile, "nonimmigration" and departure, the "women left behind" and "the men who have traveled on."[16]

Though my focus is on gender, social class plays an important role as well. Radcliffean "female gothic" fiction depicted noble or formerly privileged heroines subjected to a threatened or destabilized social order that would ultimately be restored. Charles Dickens's works, on the other hand, are widely recognized for their depiction of social stratification. The perceived dissonance between the gothic and social commentary is likely one reason that Dickens's works, though indisputably gothic in many respects, are seldom categorized as such. Both Shteinberg and Baron recast the privileged social orientation associated with the gothic, representing characters who suffer as much for their socioeconomic powerlessness as for their gender. With this in mind, I interpret these women's experience of motherhood through the stories' gothic expressions of space, subjectivity, and visibility.

I begin with an examination of the homes portrayed in the stories as carceral domestic spaces that evoke an uncanny, multigenerational feminine genealogy of *aginut*, of staying (chained). I then show that the mothers' presence in these spaces, which upends the convention of absence in portrayals of the gothic mother, is expressed through tropes of affect and visibility. These paradigms establish these women's embodied subjectivity as a precarious position, but one that locates them within a distinctively feminine history. In their gothic spatiotemporality and their unresolved negotiations of maternal identity between society and individual feminine subjectivity, both stories provide historical insight but resist interpretation as mere ethnography, suggesting a critique of the Jewish social milieu that is both politically and poetically charged. As such, reading these heroines and their spaces through the gothic leads to a more complex interpretation of their victimization: They react to their plight not by helplessly lamenting it, nor by radically rejecting it, nor by strategically manipulating it. Rather, they try—impossibly—to negotiate the fine line between social norms and expectations and their own invisibility. The gothic sensibility suffusing these stories, then, unveils an alternative feminine narrative of ambivalence regarding the place of women in the Eastern European Jewish past. Positioned within the Jewish collective but at its margins, this narrative neither disowns the Eastern European Jewish social order nor wholeheartedly affirms it—neither indicts traditional society nor excuses its flaws.

The Shtetl Chronotope and History

In his authoritative study of the shtetl in literature, Miron argues for a "metaphorical" reading of the shtetl and a disengagement from the conventional discursive and metonymic interpretations that approach shtetl stories as "sociohistorical documents."[17] The fact that the shtetl, as a distinctive space, disappeared almost completely by the 1930s intensified readers' hopes and expectations that such works would function as historical documents primarily for the purpose of preservation. Without denying these stories' "complex and sometimes ambivalent sociohistorical commentary," Miron argues that literary representations of the shtetl were pointedly *not* historical in this way, and he calls for an attention to poetics generally and to metaphor specifically.[18] He rejects not the idea that the shtetl occupies a central place in the Jewish past, but rather the unproblematized acceptance of artistic representations of this past as "authentic" and "true" depictions of the shtetl. Even more emphatic than Miron regarding the dissociation of shtetl representations from history, Arnold Band argues that, "even when treated by historians," the shtetl is a "synthetic" construct that references a particular period of the past at least as much as a specific geography: "As such, the 'shtetl' is less a specific place than a shorthand way of referring to the life of Jews in Eastern Europe in the late-nineteenth and early twentieth centuries."[19] The shtetl is both a place—a distinctive Jewish topos, with its own legal and political structures—and a time—the past. The interdependence of time and space in the representation of the shtetl, as well as its recognizable spatiotemporal contours, make it an ideal chronotope despite its "synthetic" representation in literature: a shtetl can no more convincingly be represented outside Eastern Europe than it can be situated after the 1930s.

The motifs and metaphors that Miron identifies as recurring in literature of the shtetl, such as the great fire, the departure, and the arrival of a mysterious stranger, all designate a mythical connection to the biblical past, "referents to the largest patterns of Jewish history and . . . intertextual links to the classical Jewish sources," in Seidman's words.[20] Thus, multiple temporalities overlap in the image of the shtetl: it is the site of the intersection of the biblical past, the European Jewish present, and the uncertain future. Likewise, diverse spatial paradigms collide: the non-Jewish space out of which Jews carve their polity, the distinctly Jewish spaces that comprise it, and the mythical space of Jerusalem. The shtetl represented in fiction is a complex amalgam of time and space, as Miron observes; he goes on to argue that Baron's fiction offers little by way of contribution to this historical complexity.[21] Baron and Shteinberg, however, produced narratives that not only engage with the paradigm Miron outlines but also illuminate other aspects of the spatiotemporal experiences of Eastern European Jews. The multidimensionality of the Eastern European Jewish space as it is represented in these stories by Baron and Shteinberg suggests that other temporal narratives play a role in this complex chronotope—narratives beyond the religious-mythical or national-collective. Though neither story actually takes place in a shtetl, both are shaped by its social dynamics. Addressing their gothic poetics adds another facet to our understanding of these alternative stories of time and space, recalibrating our engagement with the Jewish past.

Departure and Staying, *Tlishut* and *Aginut*

It is in this light that I would like to examine more closely the metaphor of departure that Miron identifies as central in shtetl literature. "The chief function" of the shtetl in the writings of S. Y. Abramovitsh, he asserts, is that it is "a place to be left."[22] Two distinctive types of departure from the shtetl, exile and exodus, evoke the departure from Jerusalem and from Egypt, respectively. The common thread in these departures is their conveyance of "messages of *galut*, alienation, uprootedness."[23] The figure primarily associated with departure is the luftmensch, but his description as rootless and disconnected from place also brings to mind another figure of cultural transition who would come to play a central role in the literature of the Hebrew Renaissance: that of התלוש (the *talush*, the uprooted).[24] "Distinguished by an inability to return to the traditional Jewish world he left behind and to fit into the secular European world he seeks to break into," observes Jelen, "the *talush* is literally uprooted from any collective identification."[25] The experience of the talush emphasizes the alienation resulting from cultural and geographic transition.

The formulation of the shtetl as "a place to be left" necessarily invites a corollary: the shtetl is a place to be left *by men*. Lamenting the critical tendency to read Baron's stories as autobiographical, Jelen notes that her stories were generally viewed "not as the expression of a generation undergoing modernization, migration, and cultural transition. Rather, they were seen as the isolated autobiographical expression of a woman."[26] She reflects on whether there could be a female counterpart to the talush, a *tlusha*. It is a question worth asking. Conceptualizing a tlusha, however, suggests an interpretation of women's narratives according to the same cultural indexes that shaped the talush. Most women, as Jelen points out, experienced disillusionment with tradition differently than men because of their differing social roles: "The *talush* had to be male because he was seen as the collective expression of a generation of *yeshiva* students struggling to become modern. Women, barred from the *yeshiva* world, could not share the biography of the *talush*. Most important, the *talush* had to be male because all the ideologies that formed him ... were all male types."[27] It is clear that Miron's predominantly masculine departures from the shtetls tell just part of the story.

To help excavate other parts, I propose linking the chains of the agunah (עגונה) to the shackles of the gothic heroine. Literally "an anchored woman," *agunah* is translated to English as "forsaken wife," its meaning in the halacha, Judaic law. *Agunah* is a legal designation for a woman whose husband has disappeared and may be dead. Without witnesses to attest to his death, his wife cannot obtain a writ of divorce and is left chained to him legally, unable to remarry or to make financial claims that her marriage contract stipulates in case of death or divorce. Neither of the stories I examine here depicts an agunah in the technical, halachic sense. But both texts portray a sinister, distinctly gendered enchainment that is the basis for my reading of these heroines in terms of what I call the gothic agunah, a concept meant not to designate a discrete type of agunah but rather to call attention to the shared features and intersecting concerns of the gothic heroine and the agunah.

The liminal situation of the agunah—neither married nor divorced, her husband neither clearly dead nor certainly alive—opens diverse avenues of representation and interpretation. Seidman notes that Miron, in his discussion of the departure motif in classic shtetl literature, sees the figures of the widow and the agunah "not so much as unfortunate individuals in a broadly mimetic canvas of social upheaval as richly symbolic emblems of national lamentation and bereavement."[28] Seidman observes that while the agunah symbolizes national destruction in both the literature of the shtetl and *aggadic* literature, the fiction connects her symbolic role to a mimetic one: "she functions *both* as a metonym for nineteenth-century social upheaval *and* as a metaphor in a national-religious epic."[29] Miron foregrounds the latter aspect in the context of the shtetl's disintegration, as Seidman notes.

Miron similarly prioritizes the symbolic function in his interpretation of the shtetl in Baron's fiction, which he characterizes as a "generalized social arrangement that transcends the specifics of time and place." Baron, he writes, "transforms units of personal, social, and national experience into a zone of fictional, independent, symbolic existence, which become a metaphor for human life as a whole."[30] Several critics have reacted against this universalist reading as one that resists the distinctly gendered perspective of Baron's fiction. Jelen and Pinsker take Miron to task for his insistence that "Baron's world is mythological and ahistorical" and that "fundamentally, [Baron] negates historical time."[31] Rather than represent or reject the ubiquitous nationalist male narrative, they assert, Baron's fiction worked "to create an alternative subject."[32] Orly Lubin more vehemently denounces Miron's interpretation and those who subscribe to it: "These critics' copious attempts to resolve the 'problem' of writing about details and individuals are thus based on identifying the universal aspect of her work, which they use to recruit [Baron] into the camp of national writing."[33] Her reading of Baron's *Ha-golim* (The exiles) is informed by this insistence that "gender cannot be expunged in favor of universalism."[34]

I concur: though we might recognize a cyclical, nature-based temporality operating in some of Baron's stories, this does not preclude their energetic engagement with specific histories and social questions—which, in turn, does not lessen their aesthetic, artistic impact. The social questions that concern Baron, such as those regarding marginalized Jewish women, occasionally find forceful expression through the gothic. Far from diluting or obscuring the reality she details, the gothic only intensifies it, allowing for a balance between a collective feminine narrative and one specific to the European Jewish world. The gothic exposes connections between these women and others inhabiting similarly confining domestic spaces (in works by Charlotte Smith, Jane Austen, the Brontës, and others) while also highlighting these Jewish women's specific social and historical circumstances. The social upheaval referenced by the agunah, as Seidman asserts, is "the historical situation of women and marriage in the disintegration of the shtetl. Her presence is shorthand for the differential effects for men and women of the processes of modernization, immigration, and urbanization."[35] Her symbolic, national-religious function in aggadic literature can obscure the specificity of this contemporary sociohistorical situation as well as the distinctly feminine gendering of the figure, in her reference to a predominantly male collective. "By contrast," writes Seidman, "in the mobilization of the *agunah* in modern Jewish literature, the femininity of her plight continues to register."[36] I would add that the mythical function of the agunah not only neuters her femininity but also, in transforming her into a symbol of "the ultimate Jewish exile," alters the mechanics of the metaphor itself. Whereas the root of the word *agunah*, ע-ג-ן, denotes an anchor and indicates an emphasis on enchainment, the mythical representation of the agunah underscores separation.[37]

Unlike the talush, as Seidman observes, the agunah is "enchained by and to the past that has rejected her," a symbol of "an alienated entanglement, or an entangled estrangement," exemplified by Agnon's famous story "Agunot."[38] Thus, the agunah as a metaphor can signify not only the exile of Israel but also the Jew's continued enchainment to the spectral past. Thinking metaphorically about the agunah while reappropriating her femininity from its universalist Agnonian application invites new possibilities of conceptualizing the experience of Eastern European Jewish women in terms not of rootlessness but of chains, not of absence and departure but of continued, excessive, haunted presence. These divergent experiences accord with Kate Ferguson Ellis's interpretation of the gendered relations between characters and home in gothic narratives, resulting in the archetypes of "male exile" or wanderer and "female prisoner" in the home or the castle.[39] Shackled to her absent husband, the agunah is amenable to the archetypal gothic motif of the imprisoned woman. Rather than seeking a *tlusha*, then, we might reflect on the potential of the agunah to express poetically the gothic experience of some Eastern European Jewish women.

The Present Mother

By now the concepts of a "female gothic" and of "gothic feminism" are well established, and it is taken for granted that, as Sue Zlosnik points out, the fear central to the gothic "manifests itself in the specifically female terrors experienced by women in patriarchal society."[40] Directing its critique at "public institutions that have been erected to displace, contain, or commodify women," Diane Long Hoeveler asserts, the female gothic novel represents women as victims not only of "gender politics" but also of the social, economic, political, and religious constructs that limit or exclude them.[41] Gothic heroines' strategy of resistance to this victimization is described by Hoeveler as "professional femininity," defined as "a cultivated pose, a masquerade of docility, passivity, wise passiveness, and tightly controlled emotions."[42] This textual strategy, she argues, was inversely proportional to the authorial impulses that spurred them on: "Gothic feminist authors are angry while their heroines are pointedly controlled and strategically not angry. These heroines are characterized, unlike their creators, by repression and silence, acceptance or at least the pose of complaisancy."[43] Gothic heroines collude in their own oppression to resist their victimization by the patriarchy. Restraining their emotions in a pretense of docility is a feminist strategy, but it ultimately maintains the structures of oppression. Other interpretations, such as that by Ellis, identify a similar paradox shaping gothic femininity. Though she diverges from Hoeveler by reading gothic femininity as subversive, she, too, emphasizes the gothic novel's paradoxical "resistance to an ideology that imprisons [women] even as it posits a sphere of safety for them."[44]

Given the significance of the domestic realm and of family narratives in gothic literature, the centrality of the figure of the mother in the theorization of gothic femininity is not surprising. One compelling feminist paradigm, delineated by Ruth Bienstock Anolik, emphasizes "the absent wife and the missing mother in the Gothic text."[45] The gothicism of the mother and wife is related not to an internal "other," as is the case with so many other modes of gothic subjectivity (for example, the doppelgänger), but rather to external social and political factors. In the English context Anolik analyzes, the gothic depictions of marriage and motherhood express two legal principles that governed women's lives until the middle of the nineteenth century: coverture (whereby "the woman's legal identity was 'covered' by that of her husband") and primogeniture (which "effectively erased the female presence from the line of property transmission").[46] Gothic narratives render wives and mothers invisible, through death or absence, to literalize these legal principles that amount to "a metaphoric civil death."[47] The gothic's literalization of these legal and economic structures thereby exposes "the horror implicit in seemingly mundane systems of oppression." Some gothic texts forego this passive act of literalization, depicting instead an active presence in the form of women's successful negotiations with and within the oppressive structures. Anolik, discussing this textual strategy in Anne Brontë's *The Tenant of Wildfell Hall* (1848), deems it a "political fantasy" for its denial of "social and legal realities of its time."[48] Regardless of the way different authors of gothic texts contend with the oppression of mothers, a shared perception of the mother's institutional and social erasure motivates these authors to address "dangers that have become invisible through daily practices and that become visible only when literalized in the Gothic text."[49] The tension between absence and presence, literalization and abstraction, and visibility and invisibility undergirds this theorization of the mother in the gothic.

These factors all come into play in the maternal attributes of the agunah, who, like the gothic wife and mother, is subject to a legal status imposed on her by patriarchal institutions.[50] In marked contrast to the gothic mother as theorized by Anolik, however, the gothic agunah is not absent but excessively present, unlike the fathers and husbands who, in these narratives, are all but nonexistent. Her presence is expressed not just in the central position of the woman in the home and in the narrative, but also in her defiant affect, which, as opposed to the repressed emotions of canonical gothic heroines, suggests an explicit resistance to the patriarchal powers that regulate women's behavior. These women subscribe, to a point, to social structures and expectations that push them into unhappy domestic situations, but their affect defies this compliance. The gothic agunah does not enable her own victimization because she cries out against it, literally. Though they do not effect change or allow her to "unshackle" herself in a productive way, her outbursts establish her presence and an embodied subjectivity, providing a counterparadigm to the metaphor of departure and to the spiritual division of the man who left.

Further, in these stories, the woman's presence is figured not as a "staying behind" to passively lament her lonely state in the shtetl, nor as "nonimmigration" that contrasts with men's departures, nor as a reinscription of exile as home, nor as a fantastic negotiation with an oppressive system. Rather, these women experience their own, distinctly feminine trajectories that unsettle neatly bifurcated notions of place as home or not home, of leaving or staying, of power and powerlessness. Just as she revises the conventions of the legal or mythopoetic agunah, this figure also rewrites the gothic heroine, known more for her repression than for her resistance. While the gothic heroine performs in the very dramas that stage her oppression, stifling her desire to upend the status quo, the gothic agunah disrupts her own performance by unapologetically expressing her emotions. Physical, nonverbal expressions of affects such as intense sadness and anger in "Ha-iveret" and "Shifra" signify neither the passivity and helplessness associated with the tearful agunah left behind in the shtetl, nor the carefully repressed emotions of the gothic heroine. Rather, they indicate her only possible means of breaking her chains—even if the attempt is ultimately futile.

Before looking more closely at the stories at hand, I want to point out that traditional Jewish societies in Eastern Europe participated in very different institutionalized paradigms of gender than their non-Jewish counterparts. Since these societies valorized Torah study above all else as the single greatest aspiration for men, women were expected not only to fulfill the functions that the West has long associated with them—such as childrearing and caring for the domestic realm—but also to participate actively in the public sphere to ensure the economic stability of the household. While this paradigm of Jewish femininity is radically different from those of non-Jewish English women in the eighteenth and nineteenth centuries, these women, too, were conceptualized as fulfilling the practical needs of the household, as opposed to the intellectual and spiritual riches for which the ideal man would be responsible; moreover, the domestic realm in both societies is the exclusive purview of women.[51]

I begin my analysis of the stories with a brief summary. In Shteinberg's "Ha-iveret," Hana's mother, desperate to marry her off, realizes that her daughter's blindness makes her a less desirable bride. She lies to persuade Hana to agree to marry a man whose trade, age, and social status have relegated him to the lowest rungs of society. The wedding itself is a non-event in the narrative, which skips over it to the first night after the nuptials. From this point, the story takes on the tone and devices of a suspenseful thriller. Ḥana feels her mysterious husband's beard while he sleeps, slithers across the floor to investigate his boots, listens to his gait as he walks—all to pick up subtle clues about who he really is and what he really does. "So who is this, her husband, and what is his profession?" wonders the ever-suspicious blind woman.[52] Shortly after she gives birth to a baby girl, her husband comes home from town one day and, indifferent to and oblivious of her fear, tells her that children are dying from a diphtheria epidemic in town. Panicked, she neglects her household chores to sit and watch over her baby, who eventually falls ill and dies. After a night of despair, Ḥana awaits the gravedigger and, reaching to touch her baby one last time, finds the crib empty. In the final lines of the story, she has, for the first time since her marriage, broken away from her home to find her husband outside, only to run into one large stone after another. She finally realizes that her husband is the gravedigger and their home is adjacent to the cemetery.

Baron's story "Shifra" begins with a young widow living with her mother and two small children in squalor. The mother's hopes that her neighbor will marry her newly widowed daughter are dashed in the first pages of the story, and she decides to send Shifra to be a wet nurse to a wealthy family. The lady of the house comes to Shifra's mother's home to negotiate the terms of Shifra's contract, which stipulate that she must leave her own infant behind. Soon, Shifra finds herself in a carriage on the way to the estate. She is well received at the large manor house and is given a bath, fresh clothes, and a mug of hot chocolate. The situation deteriorates very quickly, however; she manages to nurse the lady's baby only once before breaking out in uncontrollable sobs, raising the ire of the mother, who angrily releases her from her position. Another wet nurse arrives to replace Shifra, and Shifra is left to find her own way home. She begins walking and stops to rest by a bridge, where she falls asleep, hallucinating the spectral image of her beloved, deceased husband. She is found frozen, the brilliance her blue eyes had lost in life now restored in death.

Men are almost entirely absent from both stories. In "Ha-iveret," Ḥana's mother plays an important role, particularly in the beginning of the story, while no mention is made of her father. Her husband is mysteriously away from home most of the time, and when he is present he hardly speaks, communicating instead with grunts and growls that suggest his distance from human social relations. "Shifra" similarly depicts present women and absent men. Shifra's mother's concerns govern the first part of the story, and other women populate the narrative: Shifra herself, the agent who comes to arrange for her work, the wealthy woman who hires her, the servant who warns her to restrain her emotions, and the wet nurse who replaces her at the end of the story. Shifra's father, like Ḥana's in "Ha-iveret," is never mentioned. Shifra's husband is dead; the men of the manor house are present only in the background of the women's drama. In both stories, the men's absence is secondary to the presence of the women and their narratives. The reader does not know where Ḥana's and Shifra's fathers are or even whether they are alive or dead, and it does not matter. The initially unexplained absences of Ḥana's husband at odd and irregular times and intervals *are* relevant to the story, insofar as they stoke Ḥana's extant suspicions.

Ultimately, both Ḥana and Shifra, like their mothers, navigate a bleak social landscape on their own. The grown daughters inhabit their mothers' homes: Ḥana stays with her mother until she is ready to give birth, and Shifra returns to her mother's house after her husband's death. Both stories outline the maternal dynamic as the primary one in the life of the woman, the one that shapes the woman's sensibilities and the day-to-day aspects of her life. To this end, both stories represent multiple mothers. The mothers of Ḥana and Shifra are responsible for painful decisions that shape their grown daughters' futures, while Ḥana and Shifra themselves are both mothers to infants who depend on them for survival.

In both stories, it is the mother who determines the fate of her daughter. "Ha-iveret" opens with an unspecified third-person plural pronoun, a "they" discussing the widower whom Ḥana is to marry. The narrative soon melds this collective perspective with that of the mother, who extolls Ḥana's future husband in vain. It is clear, the narrator observes, that Ḥana "did not believe her mother's talk; and the old woman did not keep talking, . . . and her pursed lips whispered something—the blocked secret of a miserable mother."[53] Though the narrator reveals from the beginning that Ḥana's mother lies to her, and that it is most likely not the first occasion on which she has done so, the reader also understands that the mother herself suffers from her role in her daughter's entrapment. The man Ḥana's mother convinces her to marry is older than she reveals. His livelihood is not in tobacco, as she insists, but in death. He is not childless, as she first claims, but has two speech-impaired children from his previous marriage. Though her mother deems these deceptions necessary, securing Ḥana's future brings misery to both mother and daughter.[54]

Baron's narrator begins the story by relating the tragedy of Shifra's husband Pinchas's brief illness and tragic death, his grave destined to be covered by the first snow of the season. The winter grows harsher, and with it the poverty of Shifra's mother's household. The mother's only hope is that her neighbor's uncle, a wealthy shoemaker who had desired Shifra years before, would marry her; but when she understands that he means to marry another, she makes a choice she has resisted: "The old woman bitterly made up her mind, and when the agent's wife appeared again with her idea of sending Shifra off to the estate as a wet nurse she put her off no longer; she only tried to argue that the two-month-old baby be allowed to accompany her."[55] Like Ḥana's mother in "Ha-iveret," Shifra's mother makes a choice about her daughter's future, one that is in the daughter's best interest socially and economically but that underscores her lack of subjectivity and her dependence on others for social worth and even for basic survival. Both daughters are undesirable matches: Ḥana because she is blind, Shifra because she is a poor widow. In both stories, the mother understands all too well the difficulties that her choice will bring upon her daughter. In both, she makes the choice because she has no other. The mothers' difficult choice indicates that the mothers, too, are victims of the social paradigm that necessitates the daughters' departures from the maternal home. It is not only the young women who can be conceptualized as anchored through transactions conducted on their behalf—Ḥana, deceived into marrying a cruel gravedigger, and Shifra, a widow who must abandon her infant to care for another—but also their mothers, chained to social expectations that pressure them to expel their daughters from their homes and uphold gendered conventions.

The most critical paradigm of aginut emerges from these stories in the excessive maternal presence of Ḥana and Shifra. This presence finds negative expression as enchainment in these women's bondage to social norms and their carceral, transactional relation to their new home. It is subversively reappropriated as visibility through the women's expression of anger. Ultimately, this tense matrix of space and visibility, affect and subjectivity, is the basis for an alternative shtetl chronotope that exposes women as part of a tragic multigenerational genealogy that precedes them and that will survive them.

"Seeing Suffering": The Domestic Carceral, Surveillance, and Visibility

The synagogue and the bathhouse, two of the three social institutions that Miron identifies as the most significant in literary representations of the shtetl (the third is the cemetery), are both conceptualized as predominantly masculine spaces.[56] Though women might be present on the other side of the partition, or *meḥitsa*, the synagogue as a "replica of the Temple" required a quorum of ten men for prayer. Likewise, its political function as "a kind of parliament" necessitated, in the words of Abramovitsh, "a special committee of honorable and venerable Jews who [sat] there all the livelong day—abandoning wives and children and devoting themselves to all of these matters."[57] The bathhouse, similarly, was ostensibly a space for both sexes, but it, too, promoted the primacy of men in collective Jewish life. Women used it for ritual cleansing without which "they could not be sexually accessible to their husbands" for the fulfillment of the commandment to be fruitful and multiply.[58] The bathhouse also signified "shtetl intimacy": "Here every shtetl man knew from early childhood the entire male population of his hometown in total nakedness."[59] There is little doubt that these spaces encompassed alternative feminine collective experiences, hidden from the eye of the men who dominated them; but in the "classic" collective Jewish cultural imagination that Miron examines, these experiences are unacknowledged.

In representing places that emerge as formative in the experience of their heroines, Shteinberg's and Baron's stories do not endeavor to offer an idealized "feminized" version of these social spaces (though in other stories, Baron, especially, is attuned to the drama on the women's side of the meḥitsa or in the rabbinic court). This spatial trinity plays no role in these stories.[60] The stories subvert another of the conventions of the spatiality of shtetl stories by acknowledging the Christian dimension of their environment. From the beginning of "Ha-iveret," Ḥana suspects her husband of living among ערלים, non-Jews, or even of being one himself, citing her intimate knowledge of the difference between the design of Jewish and non-Jewish homes, the sound of Jewish and non-Jewish footsteps, and more. In "Shifra," the peal of church bells marks time alongside the falling snow and the darkness, accompanying Shifra to and from the grand estate. These stories forego the sites of collective Jewish spatiality to focus on their heroines' divergent experience of space, whether through the exposure of heretofore seldom acknowledged spatial elements or through a focus on the domestic. Even as the emphasis on the home accords with broad literary conventions associating women with domestic space, these narratives' revisions of gothic spatial tropes suggest a more sophisticated critique that foregrounds the dark dimension of the domestic. Namely, they evoke a version of what Paul Morrison calls "the domestic carceral," spaces defined not only by imprisonment but also by their porousness and vulnerability.[61]

"Horror," writes Morrison, "begins at home."[62] Arguing for "the synonymy or continuity between the practices of the gothic and the domestic," he theorizes a "domestic carceral" spatiality as the basis of a broader reading of women's domestic life as gothic.[63] Ellis, in her influential study *The Contested Castle*, also addresses the domestic setting in gothic literature. Demonstrating that the gendered separation of spheres in eighteenth-century England was intended partly to maintain women's idealized femininity, she argues that gothic novels offered subversive representations of the confinement of women in domestic spaces. Her focus is on the castle, a classic gothic site. Morrison expands the range of gothic spatiality. The gothic resides not only in the shadowy castles, dark woods, and winding labyrinths of classic gothic texts like Ann Radcliffe's *The Romance of the Forest* (1791) and *Mysteries of Udolpho* (1794); it also inhabits the supposedly antigothic, well-lit domestic space, which "reinscribes gothic incarceration in and as a generalized economy of surveillance."[64] Following Foucault's discussion of the panopticon, Morrison reminds us that surveillance is aided not by the darkness and concealment of the dungeon—a conventionally gothic space—but rather by circumstances that expose and render their subjects highly visible. This sort of space is easy to overlook because of its banality: "far from being opposed to the dungeon as darkness is to light, the parlor reinscribes gothic claustration in the mode of light or visibility, all the more effectively for eschewing the obvious mechanisms and paraphernalia of gothic enclosure."[65] These Hebrew stories diverge from the effects of gendered gothic claustration by appropriating visibility from the oppressive purpose of surveillance to the defiant assertion of subjectivity.

For Ḥana and Shifra, motherhood as a function of social value is, in a fundamental sense, transactional. In this light, it is unsurprising that the homes that host their experience of motherhood accord more with the cold economics dictating their function and less with the warm hearth of idealized domesticity. Both stories portray the home as a carceral space of aginut: it limits the movements and autonomy of the women within, and it subjects them to discipline and surveillance. The home incarcerates them thus not only for being women but also for being poor, unlike the middle- or upper-class heroines of so many gothic narratives. In both stories, the heroines find themselves on a transitional carriage ride from the known territory of the mother's house to the alien space intended to incorporate the heroine back into the social life of the Jewish collective by offering her a domestic purpose and economic security. In these disconcertingly similar scenes, both women sit silently in a carriage and wonder about the whereabouts of their destination, underscoring that neither has been an active party in the arrangement that takes her to a new home. Ḥana tries to guess her surroundings, while Shifra entertains visions of her mother, her baby, and her deceased husband.

Both stories bring their heroines to secluded homes at the outskirts of town. Yet this geographic remove hardly renders them unseen. To the contrary, their marginalization subjects them to a particularly mundane mode of surveillance: their commodification as the voiceless objects of an economic negotiation invites the evaluative gaze of those who would acquire them. Ḥana's husband in "Ha-iveret" confirms this transactional state as a precursor to literal confinement. When she periodically hears the sound of a crowd and, "longing for human voices," asks her husband what it might be, he angrily chastises her: "You don't need to know. Sit at home—that's enough!"[66] Ḥana's new home offers social salvation to a woman considered an undesirable *shiddukh*, but it also imprisons her. Noting that it "becomes a prison almost in the literal sense," Hana Naveh cites the cold winter and Ḥana's pregnancy as her husband's allies in the "conspiracy of silence" that keeps her confined and maintains her oppression.[67] This carceral quality also finds expression in the house's proximity to death, both geographically, in its abuttal of the cemetery, and figuratively, in its vulnerability to deleterious external forces, expressed here as the diphtheria that eventually takes the life of her baby. When the disease penetrates the boundaries of the house, Ḥana is transformed into an archetypal nurse-mother and the home itself into a hospital, a "temple of death," in Foucault's words, the site of her hopeless ministering to her ill-fated baby.[68] As the blind woman cares for the baby she knows will soon die, she begs her husband to "see" the baby's condition for her, to survey the baby's state, but he refuses. It is left to Ḥana, the blind woman, to examine her daughter. Though she has taken on the role Foucault attributes to the doctor, who relies on his "loquacious gaze" to diagnose patients, her blindness renders her gaze silent.[69]

In "Shifra," too, the house stages a transactional domesticity fundamental to its evocation of sickness, suffering, and death. The heroine must endure first the negotiations between the agent, the lady of the estate, and her own mother regarding the fate of her milk and her baby. At the estate, she submits to the disciplinary gaze of the nurse, doctor, and lady, a gaze that further commodifies and possesses her maternal body. In contrast to her mother's cramped, squalid house, the manor home is bright, airy, and secure, smelling of "abundance" and faultlessly clean. But in Baron's hand, this cleanliness takes on ominous undertones. The bath, the robe, the physical examination, "the watchful eye of the doctor," the many mirrors, even the mug of hot chocolate—her various preparations to receive the hungry infant remind her uncannily of her stay in a hospital many years before, when she was a little girl fallen ill.[70] A nurse hands Shifra a shift to wear and takes her to a room for a medical examination, "and the feeling she had in the hospital never left her after that."[71]

When the narrator describes Shifra's encounter with the baby in the manor house explicitly in terms of a vampire feeding on his victim, the uncanny makes way for the morbid: "A tiny creature was brought to her chest, who fell upon her with a drooling mouth, a strange heat, and a new thirst she had never experienced—the thirst of a bloodsucking leech."[72] Shifra's milk, Shifra's body, her time, her closeness, now belong to *him*. This vampire baby's ravenousness echoes Shifra's baby's hunger, destined now to increase in inverse proportion to the sating of the doppelgänger's milk lust. His pouncing on Shifra's breast links her milk to her lifeblood and confirms the transactional nature of her presence at the estate.[73] The ritualized preparations for their initial encounter concretize Shifra's contractual obligation to submit her body to the clinical gaze. Finally, the repeated mention of the mug of hot chocolate brings to the fore that this mechanized ritual has been performed countless times in this house. Like Ḥana, Shifra finds herself in a domestic carceral space that subjects her to evaluative gazes and reminds us that her condition is a function not only of gender but also of class.

In these two stories, however, processes of seeing and blindness, visibility and invisibility are not limited to the panoptic paradigm of surveillance. Both stories are preoccupied with the interplay of seeing and visibility beyond this model, and with how these concepts relate to questions of social justice. Both Shteinberg and Baron make visible their heroines' suffering by depicting their eyes and their vision or blindness as vehicles for the pain, anger, and frustration they cannot restrain. In both stories, vision and visibility relate to external, institutional power and powerlessness, as well as to a subversive—if ultimately unsuccessful—assertion of feminine subjectivity from within.[74] The domestic carceral space, in these stories, encompasses both the institutionalized power relations that lead to the women's aginut and the personal struggles they instigate within these women, as they are left trying to maintain a coherent sense of self. Before examining the relations between vision, surveillance, affect, and subjectivity more closely, though, I want to consider the way the literary representation of seeing and blindness has been theorized.

Poets since antiquity have established the "blind bard" as an archetype, positioning the one who cannot see as the one who has special access to knowledge and truth, even a representative of the gods themselves. This figure represents a view that is diametrically opposed to the popular association of blindness with ignorance. Contemporary critical theory, particularly in the context of postcolonialism and feminism, has rallied around analyses that expose a direct connection between vision and power.[75] Foucault's exposition on Jeremy Bentham's panopticon has led to a host of astute variations on the theme of vision in the context of surveillance, while psychoanalytic theory following Jacques Lacan has shed light on the power of the gaze and the uneven dynamics between subject and object, the gazer and the gazed. The historian Martin Jay has written extensively about the transformation of the status of vision in the western intellectual tradition. Historically conceptualized as the basis of knowledge about the world, vision in the twentieth century has been devalued and denigrated, occasioning a broader "crisis of ocularcentrism."[76]

More recently, Donna Haraway has theorized vision and visibility as processes of "embodied subjectivity." Acknowledging the "premium on establishing the capacity to see from the peripheries and the depths," she warns against romanticizing "the vision of the less powerful while claiming to see from their positions.... Vision is *always* a question of the power to see—and perhaps of the violence implicit in our visualizing practices."[77] She calls for partial—rather than totalizing—perspectives: "An optics is a politics of positioning."[78] As such, the model she proposes for reading vision and visibility is one that considers the way we relate to, perceive, and try to take on the vision of subjugated others. It is a paradigm of partiality and plurality of visions and perspectives, sometimes conflicting and contradictory, based on the local, specific, physically grounded nature of bodily experience. Relating science to "the cacophonous visions and visionary voices that characterize the knowledges of the subjugated," she argues for "knowledges . . . ruled by partial sight and limited voice. . . . The only way to find a larger vision is to be somewhere in particular."[79] While other theoretical paradigms point to the relation between vision, visibility, and power in various ways, Haraway is not content to leave undisturbed the notion that an all-seeing eye translates to boundless power, but revises this model to empower the partial, the relational, and the limited, in the highly localized physical context of the individual body.

Several studies have considered the significance of seeing, visibility, and blindness in specific cultural and ideological contexts. Asserting that "the structure of looking has gendered consequences," Rebecca Stern argues that the gothic upends the binaries associated with light and darkness whereby light is "good" and darkness is "bad."[80] In accordance with Morrison's ideas about the domestic carceral, she proposes that, in gothic texts, light "is instrumental in *creating* fear by making visible the threats that hover in a novel's darkened passages" or by threatening "to expose a hiding heroine."[81] While total darkness can be threatening in these narratives, illumination does not extinguish this threat but only exacerbates it. Twilight, shadow, and "flickering," modes of partial illumination, on the other hand, empower or aid gothic heroines.[82] This privileging of partial illumination echoes Haraway's privileging of "partial perspective" in the analysis of female subjectivity. In addition to the role of illumination and perspective in the dynamics of vision and subjugation, we can consider the connection between vision and subjectivity. According to Elizabeth Dolan, two cultural preoccupations in the late eighteenth century—"the materiality of vision and pressing social justice issues—created new modes of 'seeing' (and thus of expressing and alleviating) suffering in the Romantic era."[83] Aligning with Haraway's notion of "the embodied nature of all vision," this romantic interest in a physiological, "embodied vision" reframed women's cultural invisibility as a matter of perception and perspective rather than as absolute.[84]

Haraway's "joining of partial views" speaks directly to the question of perspective so critical to the recognition of independent subjectivity.[85] It points to what is at stake in the critical debate on Baron's designation as "universal" or "particular." The emphasis in both these narratives of feminine subjugation on eyes and blindness, seen in this light, is not coincidental. Ḥana's blindness in "Ha-iveret" is her primary characteristic, the one that instigates the plot and dictates its development. Her mother's decision to marry her to an undesirable man is a consequence of her blindness and its designation of Ḥana herself as limited and therefore undesirable. Ḥana's continued effort to uncover the truth about her husband is shaped by her inability to see, prompting her to hypothesize desperately and creatively regarding her surroundings and her circumstances on the basis of nonvisual clues. With her arrival in the unfamiliar territory of her new home, she loses her bearings, and the clues she thinks lead her to an acquaintance with her new place actually mislead and confuse her. When she hears the driver knocking on a distant window, she thinks the window sounds small, like those belonging to non-Jews. When she enters the house for the first time, the wide hallway and the sudden heat seem to suggest an organization of the home that is distinctly not Jewish. In a marked reversal of the trope of the blind bard, who "sees" the truth despite his blindness, Ḥana's keen attunement to her auditory and tactile surroundings does not reveal the truth about her husband and his home. Her blindness renders her vulnerable to the very thing she detests: deceit. From the first lines of the story, the narrator relates, through the lying mother, that Ḥana cannot abide lies, but as someone who cannot see, she is all too easy to lie to.

Her maternal identity, however, is so strong as to enable her to overcome the grim circumstances of her life, and even, the story suggests, to overcome the physical limitations of her blindness itself. When the midwife removes the newborn infant from Ḥana's bed for fear that Ḥana would accidentally suffocate her while sleeping, Ḥana chuckles to herself: "Does she not know everything that needs to be done around the house, even if her eyes do not see?"[86] Three days after the birth, when the midwife hands Ḥana a bowl of soup, Ḥana instinctively lifts the baby and lays her far from her and the soup, "and then the old woman, who had watched the blind woman and her movements, mused that the new mother was not totally blind and that her eyes see something of the light of day."[87] It is the strength of her identity as a mother, however, and not the physical strength of her eyes, that renders her keenly attuned to the dangers that threaten her daughter. This maternal instinct is allowed her despite the physical limitations that dictate her social marginalization and lead to her grim fate. Indeed, her maternal role almost saves her, offering an outlet for her isolation and loneliness, granting her the ability to "see," distracting her from her unbridled anger at her husband, at her mother, and at the abusive world. When that identity collapses upon her infant's death, she not only is left childless but also discovers that her home itself has been a lie—and it is one that she cannot escape.

The preoccupation with vision in "Shifra" is evident from the story's first line, which refers to Shifra's "light eyes" and soon establishes them as the canvas on which her life's events are inscribed: "Later, after Pinchas died, . . . the azure of her eyes also dimmed and grew murky from her tears."[88] Those "same tears that first saddened and then dimmed their blueness" are echoed in her infant's blue eyes, which, on her carriage ride to the estate, "looked at her as if through a fog, miles away."[89] After her outburst at the manor house, as she sets out, she encounters the kind shepherd who shows her to the exit, and his kindness calls to mind her infant through the shared blue of their eyes: "At the sight of his blue eyes under his sheepskin hat, . . . she felt as if a sob were about to burst from her throat."[90] The baby's eyes appear again when she falls asleep on a bridge blanketed by snow: "From within the web of dreams that caressed her, the azure eyes of the two-month-old baby gazed at her again, as they had during the carriage ride."[91] Finally, when she is found frozen to death at nightfall, the "blue that glistened between her eyelids was as bright as if it had never in her life been touched by a tear," having reverted in death to the tranquility of a life without suffering.[92]

In her feminist reading of "Ha-iveret," Naveh notes that Ḥana's blindness "is a fundamental, literal confirmation of culturally sanctioned symbolic concepts. . . . The woman, the blind Ḥana in this case, is presented as a pure object for the totalizing gaze of the man and she does not have the ability to gaze at him."[93] The vulnerability that is a consequence of Ḥana's blindness in "Ha-iveret" is immediately evident to the reader, since the narrator reveals her mother's conscious decision not to lie to Ḥana, "who tends to become angry at every lie she is told."[94] In stressing Ḥana's anger, Shteinberg's delicately rendered portrait of her ill-treatment, a direct consequence of her blindness, does not translate her vulnerability into the repressed, affectively paralyzed victimization we might associate with gothic heroines. Most critically for the theorization of Ḥana's blindness as a function of "seeing suffering" is the fact that, as others have noted, the narrative enacts Ḥana's blindness upon the reader. Shteinberg's use of suspense and his delay of revealing the narrative "truth" to the reader until Ḥana herself has discovered it work to blind the reader, and thus to force upon him or her an empathetic perspective of Ḥana's suffering. Ḥana's blindness provides her with only a partial picture of her circumstances—a partiality she recognizes and that she tries to redress—and the reader shares this partial picture. While this situation may not bode well for Ḥana, whose suspicions are confirmed finally, though not as she expected, on the narrative plane it operates precisely to make this invisible woman visible in the eyes of her Hebrew readers. Privy to her partial perspective, the reader is able to see her suffering clearly.

It is critical to recognize that, for Shteinberg, Ḥana's suffering is as much a consequence of being a woman as it is of being blind. As Naveh argues, Ḥana's blindness is intended to expand our understanding of the suffering of women: "The lack of images, the lack of knowledge, the lack of freedom of movement, the nonstop silence—all these were ascribed [by most critics] to the heroine's blindness and were reasoned using mimetic justifications linked to the facts of the world of a blind person."[95] Yet all these lacks also more broadly represent the experience of women in patriarchal societies.

In Baron's story, it is precisely when Shifra closes her eyes, first on the carriage ride to the estate and then again when she stops to rest on a ramshackle bridge after her departure, that her vision expands beyond the limited scope of the real, inviting the abandoned infant and the deceased husband into her line of sight. Shifra's eyes signal the emotional trajectory of her life; her inner vision grants her access to those from whom she has been separated.

Another manifestation of the visual in the story explicitly reveals the dynamics of power implicit in these processes: Shifra's position as the object of the scrutiny of her employer. Upon her arrival at the estate, she is lifted down from the carriage and rushed into the dark house, where "she found herself suddenly face to face with her own reflection in a mirror."[96] Seeing herself in the mirror disconcertingly forces her to confront her lamentable circumstances and distorts her already fragile sense of self. As the new wet nurse, she is subjected to a series of medical examinations and procedures of hygiene. Like the nurse in a hospital she remembers from long ago, the maid at the estate "had stripped her naked in broad daylight," scrutinizing her and advising her to gain weight.[97] The pointed reference to the illumination that leaves her bereft of all modesty and enhances her sense of vulnerability recalls Stern's claim that gothic heroines are exposed and compromised by light. The narrator relates that Shifra "was brought to the next room for a medical examination," where she is dressed in a mirrored room and given hot cocoa.[98] Only "after the new mother had looked her over for herself, under the watchful eye of the doctor," do they finally bring the hungry baby to Shifra.[99] The proliferating eyes in this scene—the nurse's, the mother's, the doctor's—conspire with the mirrors that emphasize her body's objectification to disempower Shifra. With unimpeded visual access to her body, they scrutinize her, assess her, evaluate her, reducing her to pure physicality, a milking body, robbed of subjectivity and even of objectivity and constructed in terms of abjection, of the milk that crosses the border of her body.

The screens, mirrors, and many doors of the house, which conceal, distort, and blur Shifra's view, can be understood as architectural manifestations of her "partial perspective" vis-à-vis the disciplinary procedure of the household. Though Shifra's eyes remind her of her own humanity by inviting the gaze of her far-off husband and infant, they are restored to their former glory only when death relieves her of her suffering. The visual, for Shifra, brings pain: her eyes are constant reminders of her suffering, and others' sight operates only to amplify her social invisibility.

Embodied Subjectivities: Affect and the Eye

Feminist theorists have written about the role of affect both in expressing the injustice women have historically faced and in the development and articulation of feminist thought as an intellectual or activist response to such injustice.[100] As Ann Cvetkovich notes, feminists responded to "the sense that an absence of outlets for the expression of rage and sadness not only prevented political action but constituted a form of oppression."[101] The scholarship on gothic affect is surprisingly sparse, given the centrality of affect in the structure of gothic literature both in its evocation of the reader's terror and in its depiction of intense emotion.[102] Since gothic works "are primarily structured so as to elicit particular responses in the reader," George E. Haggerty points out, "gothic form" is, by definition, affective.[103] Indeed, he insists, without acknowledging "the extent of their affective rationale," our understanding of gothic works is inadequate.[104] Continuing to probe "how the gothic works on its readers/viewers," Xavier Aldana Reyes's more recent investigation proposes an affective critical approach that might help identify narrative strategies calculated to elicit particular reactions.[105]

In the Hebrew stories at hand, as in the nineteenth-century sensation novels Cvetkovich examines (such as Mary Elizabeth Braddon's *Lady Audley's Secret* [1862] and George Eliot's *Daniel Deronda* [1876]), it is neither the presence of the anger within these women nor the evocation of physical affect in the reader that commands our attention so much as the characters' *expression* of their anger.[106] The manifestation of anger, its emergence from the private recesses of the self to the external, discernable, embodied manifestation of it—this is the "affective rationale" that thematizes the subtle but potent political statement of these stories.[107] The expression of anger disrupts the dynamics of ocular power, making these heroines visible, establishing their presence, and calling attention to them as subjects. Finally, it is a forceful if futile rejection of the repressed emotions integral to the "professional femininity" Hoeveler identifies in gothic fiction.

Throughout Baron's story, Shifra remains silent in the face of the increasing tension between the presence of her body and its insignificance, her corporeal being and her social not-being. After the mistress of the house pulls Shifra off the couch where she had collapsed, Shifra falls "the way an old, worn dress finally drops, without making a sound as she fell."[108] On the carriage ride to the estate, "Shifra hunched over and shut her eyes, and with the swaying of the carriage and the pinpricks of cold, her own body seemed to her insubstantial and lost, a lonely bird by the roadside."[109] Later, when the robust new wet nurse arrives, the sensation recurs: "In the face of this substantial villager . . . Shifra felt insignificant, and she seemed to herself frail and terribly short."[110] As her body seems to weaken, recede, and finally disappear in the face of her difficult circumstances, Shifra loses the only commodity she has to offer.

The insignificance Shifra ascribes to her embodied self in contrast to that of the sturdy peasant girl is confirmed by her employer's perception of her as *only* a body. Unseen as she stands exposed before her new mistress, the maid, and the doctor, she also remains silent, in stark contrast to the "loquacious gazes" devouring her. Before long, though, her body begins to speak. Dusk has fallen, and true to the sensibility of the "flickering" partial illumination that replaces the "broad daylight" of her humiliating medical examination, Shifra's silence cracks under the weight of her subjectivity asserting itself: "She was passing through one of the darkened parlors with a glowing stove in it when she heard from afar, from the direction of town, the tolling of the evening bells, and that was when the moan rose in her throat, and since she could no longer find the door because tears were blinding her eyes, she sank right down onto a sofa."[111] The maid, though apparently unsurprised, warns her to stop or risk upsetting their employers, who "like good spirits in a wet nurse": "'You get up, take a walk outside, cheer yourself up or something. Main thing is—hold back, hold it back.' But Shifra could no longer restrain herself by any effort of will."[112] Shifra's display of grief is defiantly embodied, resisting the maid's exhortations to repress her emotions ("התאפקי, התאפקי").[113] Her affective assertions, as conveyed through her tears, her unsuppressed anger and disillusionment, her inability to "hold back"—*these* render her finally visible. Despite the maid's exhortations that Shifra erase herself by banishing her tears and even going outside, Shifra's lack of control over her emotions makes her presence at the estate impossible to ignore and transforms her milk—her body's currency—into סם-מות, "deadly poison."[114]

Shifra's outburst instigates that of another mother: the "heavy old lady, who was forbidden any excitement by the doctor's orders."[115] When they encounter Shira prostrate and weeping on the sofa, the lady drags and drops her to the floor: "'No, no, no, no,' [Shifra] shrieked with a terrible hoarseness, drenched in tears, stubborn and ungrateful from her head to her toes."[116] The dramatic release of her pent-up emotions evokes no empathy from the lady, who "ran shouting at the top of her lungs to the furthest parlor, despite her doctor's warnings and the midwife's pleas to have mercy on herself and refrain from getting angry, since her health was at stake."[117] The lady, like Shifra, is subject to the disciplining gaze of the doctor. Like Shifra, she has been ordered to restrain herself, to avoid excitement, to stifle anger. Far from providing a shared feminine perspective, however, this experience has the opposite effect, prompting the lady to inscribe *herself* as the victim, having been subjected to "the torments of the negotiations in the shtetl, in that suffocating little house, over the children's wails and the shrieking of the goat."[118] Shifra's suffering is invisible to the wealthy woman, though both of them have had to submit to a pathologizing gaze upon their maternal bodies. Rather than recognize this shared experience as the basis for empathy or even the most minimal identification, the wealthy woman turns a blind eye to it. Shifra's only resistance to this insistent blindness is the expression of her anger.

In "Ha-iveret," the narrator establishes Ḥana's pronounced affect from the beginning, when her mother remembers that Ḥana is angered by lies. As Shifra sits and says "not a word" during the negotiations over her baby's access to her breast milk, so, too, does Ḥana "listen in silence to her mother's many words," as the old woman sings the praises of her intended match: "Her eyes were open and her lashes didn't tremble, even though the heart of the blind woman stormed within her. And after her silence the blind woman felt with her hand along the table once and again and asked in repressed anger (מתוך רוגז עצור): how old is he? . . . It was clear that the blind woman's heart stormed within her and that she didn't believe what her mother said."[119] In a departure from the conventions associated with victim-heroines, Hana, a truth seeker in a world of liars, is no gullible girl but a wise woman attuned to the subtlest truths. After the wedding, when Hana has a chance to feel her sleeping husband's beard and realizes that she has, indeed, been deceived about his age, "her heart raged within her with wrath. . . . She tossed and turned in anger."[120] Initially according with the behavior of repressed gothic heroines by containing her agitation, Hana is angry and bewildered more than she is frightened. She sits in silence, "only her large eyes wide open and her face expressing astonishment," as the mystery of her husband's occupation deepens; "this is the emotion that fills her heart so frequently."[121] On one of the rare occasions when she has a conversation with her taciturn husband, who prefers growling to words, he dismisses her questions: "Hana lowers her eyebrows, as she always does when she is angry."[122] Her affect, though repressed for the time being, is discernable, despite her own inability to see.

Her anger gives way to curiosity and finally to fear only after her baby's birth, when her husband announces indifferently that a diphtheria epidemic is killing babies every day: "The slice of bread stuck in her throat and a great amazement came over her face: why does he say these things and awaken fear and panic in her heart?"[123] Every day, she inquires about the disease, and her husband responds impatiently and cruelly that infants are dying "like flies."[124] Finally, "the things that were concealed in her heart for several days burst forth from Hana," and she asks him to look at the girl, whose breathing seems heavy.[125] When he refrains from responding and goes about his business, Hana is struck by fear not only because of the sudden certainty that her daughter is sick and destined to die but also because she realizes that her husband is unperturbed by this prospect. As the child's illness worsens, the husband remains indifferent both to her and to his wife, who is "immersed in sorrow" and neglects all her domestic chores: "From day to day her heart accrued more hatred toward her husband. . . . And once it happened that the blind woman couldn't contain her anger and pounced on her husband with cries and wails: 'Murderer, you have eyes, tell me what's happening to the girl?'"[126] Apathetic, he extricates himself and leaves the house.

Hana, certain of the infant's impending death, sits by the crib all night, too tired to cry. After falling asleep at the baby's side, she awakens with a start to the absence of her breathing and jumps up with a great cry: "The blind woman passes the whole night moaning, but she sits by the crib by herself, because her husband enters and exits in turns.... With the light of day, the blind woman ceases crying because she has become exhausted,... her hair disheveled, her head moving constantly, and her lips moving and whispering again and again: 'the gravedigger will come.'"[127] The phrase becomes a macabre refrain: "יבוא נא הקברן."[128] When she lays her hand on the crib to feel her infant once more, she finds it empty: "A horrible wail bursts from the blind woman's throat," and she cries out to her absent husband, making her way outside for the first time.[129] She runs into one large stone after another, until she realizes that she is standing in a cemetery: "a terrible wail bursts from the blind woman's throat."[130]

The twin discoveries she makes in these final lines of the story—of the disappearance of her dead infant's body, and of the true occupation of her husband—evoke the same affect, an expression of grief that caps a lifetime of anger. As Naveh argues, Shteinberg's empathy for Ḥana is evident throughout the story and serves "to sound the woman's silenced voice."[131] It is not only her newfound willingness to speak that breaks the silence but also the affective expression of her anguish, the bursting forth of her frustration and agony. Though her husband refuses to see both his daughter and his wife, Ḥana resists this erasure. The blind woman's ability to express her wrath and her suffering rescues her from invisibility. Like Shifra, the visibility that Ḥana achieves through the expression of her anger does not resolve her pain or the injustice she suffers. The affect that makes visibility possible, though, helps establish each of these women "as a feeling subject," to adapt Cvetkovich's term, and thereby acknowledge their alternative narratives.[132]

An Uncanny Feminine Historiography "From Time Immemorial" and "For the Rest of Her Days"

Forged through the transactional aginut of the domestic carceral space, maternal subjectivity in these stories is predicated on paradigms of seeing and visibility, blindness and invisibility. Having considered the relation of these ocular processes to individual maternal subjectivity, I conclude by examining the way both stories relate the inhospitable domestic space not only to the forceful presence and individual subjectivity of their main characters but also to a collective, perpetually replicated maternal archetype, shaped by suffering and proximity to death. Acknowledging the stories' broader social orientation invites us to recalibrate the figure of the gothic agunah collectively and over time. Not only are these particular mothers figured in terms of presence rather than absence, but the distinctive temporality of their presence also indicates a broader, historical, collective presence.

Exposing a repetitive rhythm in the collective feminine experience of these spaces, both these stories harness the uncanny to cast the mothers as archetypes in a forlorn feminine genealogy. In "Ha-iveret," Ḥana spends her days in the house, where she marks time according to her perception of the seasons: the rain and howling wind announce autumn; falling snow signals winter; dripping icicles herald spring. Time is concretized for Ḥana by the weather, which constitutes one of the only tangible markers of the world outside the home. The temporal cyclicity represented by the story's attentive recording of the weather is linked to a repetition of women's suffering. The night her baby dies, while Ḥana sits "with her head down and her lips moving—it seemed to her that many years have already passed with her beside the girl's cradle and that until the end of her days she would sit like that in this place."[133] Tending to her sick child in the vulnerable home, she becomes an archetypal mother, destined to repeat her maternal suffering "until the end of her days."

In "Shifra," the mug, "the one that had been set aside in this house from time immemorial for wet nurses," signifies the long line of women who preceded Shifra and the women who would follow her in this sad charge.[134] Like her, they are driven to it out of loss. Indeed, her replacement at the estate, a sturdy peasant girl, had lost her own infant merely days before arriving at the manor house. She, too, must "undergo the entire series of preparations again: a bath, a medical examination, a complete change of clothing, and finally, the hot cocoa, as well."[135] The manor house, like a hospital, is large and well stocked. The women employed there are surveyed and assessed, admonished to gain weight, and given chocolate to drink. The professional, antiseptic exterior, however, barely covers the suffering just beneath the surface, the ghosts of the women and their lost husbands, infants, selves. It is no coincidence that Shifra is called to her death by a vision of her deceased husband. The lady of the house, herself under medical observation, is given a tranquilizer by the doctor.[136] Though unacknowledged by the lady herself, the link between her experience of the maternal and Shifra's is exposed and filtered through the challenges of maternity, be they physical or psychological. Baron's critique is first and foremost social, and it is shaped by the recognition that gender dictates the social paradigm.

Like the ice and snow that silently accumulate in both these stories, destined to melt and reappear, the suffering of these women is not limited to their discrete narratives. Rather, it signifies a maternal temporality dictated by a transgenerational feminine presence in the domestic space to which they are bound.

The home stages the repetition of women's domestic incarceration and reinscribes temporality as also cyclical, in accordance with the weather that marks time in both stories. This cyclicity, associated with monumental or eternal time, structures the paradigm of "women's time" that Julia Kristeva defines in contrast to linear, historical masculine temporality. Pinsker identifies this feminine temporality in Baron's rereading and reinterpretation of Judaic texts to produce a "women's narrative."[137] The stories at hand, though, create a feminine space-time by integrating these two contrasting temporal models: the cyclical, multigenerational historic paradigm is interwoven into the linear history, exposing the way domestic spaces write the history of women as a carceral gothic history. Ultimately, their domestic incarceration is instigated primarily not by a "male gaze" but by the gaze of their mothers—who, themselves confined to seeing the world through eyes shaped by institutionalized male privilege, send their daughters away with a heavy heart. Thus, the mothers themselves rehearse the excessive presence of the mother and the multigenerational drama of maternal carceration.

The genealogy expands beyond the particular feminine stories the narratives tell, extending back to a past at which they only hint. In "Ha-iveret," the gravedigger's first wife, the one with whom he had two children, is never mentioned, but in its portrayal of the beastly husband, the story leaves little doubt that that Ḥana's predecessor, like Ḥana, suffered. In "Shifra," the heroine participates in an endless cycle of women struck by their own maternal tragedies—whether the prior or subsequent wet nurses, forced by poverty or loss to take on the position, or the mothers who were unable to feed their own infants. As women denied a place in "History," Ḥana and Shifra indicate tragic maternal archetypes, which, though oppressive, help articulate alternative feminine narratives. The domestic carceral finds expression through these women's individual experiences of motherhood as well as in a broader, historical structure of anguish.

This is not to suggest that women in traditional Eastern European Jewish milieus all suffered. Rather, it calls attention to one way that twentieth-century authors articulated alternative feminine versions of this chronotope. Their reappropriations of shtetl time-place through these macabre maternal narratives issue a scathing critique, creating the possibilities for these invisible women to assert their subjectivities and thus positioning them within an all but unseen feminine history. It is a history that not only adheres to the conventions of linear temporality but also melds it with a historicity delineated by "time immemorial" (מאז) and "to the end of her days" (עד קץ ימיה), stretching into the past only to reach the inevitable future.[138]

At the same time, moments of beauty and quiet contentedness break through these bleak stories to complicate their critiques. Ḥana remembers the tranquility of her mother's home during the Sabbath and experiences moments of maternal bliss at her daughter's side. Shifra knew great happiness before her husband's untimely death, and she remembers him with longing and sorrow. Clearly, these stories aim not to subvert, disown, or discredit the social machinery of traditional Jewish society. Rather, they call attention to its shortcomings, making visible those women who are otherwise relegated to invisibility. The "mixed feelings" these women experience regarding their society thwart attempts to designate the heroines as *only* defiant or victimized. This characteristic, together with specific narrative features the stories elicit and revise—the morbid sensibility, the oppressive carceral domestic, the preoccupation with death, a particular "affective rationale" that exhibits previously repressed anger—shapes the gothic sensibility undergirding these alternative feminine histories. The next chapter invites us to confront another layer of complexity and ambivalence in the gothic Jewish engagement with the European past, this time from the mid-century, post-Holocaust perspective of a conflicted Zionism.

Notes

1. *Shtetl*, literally "town" in Yiddish, refers to small, pre–World War II Central or Eastern European towns with a large Jewish population.

2. Bakhtin posits the "chronotope" as a cohesion of particular paradigms of temporality, spatiality, and narrative, characteristic of the specific historical circumstances in which they are rooted. See Bakhtin, *Speech Genres*.

3. In his famous 1907 essay "Shiratenu ha-tse'ira" [Our young poetry], Bialik lyrically expounds on the newly emergent generation of Hebrew writers and praises the originality and great promise of Shteinberg's Hebrew poetry.

4. "Ha-iveret" was first published in Yiddish as "Di Blinde" in *Der Fraind* in 1912. Shteinberg's own Hebrew translation was published eleven years later in the first volume of *Sipurim* [Stories]. "Shifra" appeared in two prior versions. The first, "Hitparets . . ." ["Erupt . . ."], was

published in Vilna in the Hebrew newspaper *Ha-zman* in 1907. The second, titled "Atsbanut" [Nervousness], was published five years later, after her 1910 emigration to Palestine, in *Ha-zman*. The final version, "Shifra," published in 1927, underwent substantive changes.

5. Wasson, *Urban Gothic*, 2.

6. Baron's biography itself, which includes over three decades of self-imposed isolation in her Tel Aviv apartment, is reminiscent of the well-known gothic convention of the confined woman. Jelen cites the classic study by Sandra Gilbert and Susan Gubar, *The Madwoman in the Attic: The Woman Writer and the Nineteenth-Century Literary Imagination*, to contextualize Baron's withdrawal from the world. Like Baron, "many women writers of the eighteenth and nineteenth centuries developed a rhetoric of 'confinement' and enclosure in their literary works" (*Intimations of Difference*, 134).

7. Baron, *First Day*, 156.

8. Komem, "Use of Setting," 179.

9. Cohen, *Ya'akov Shtainberg*, 433.

10. Z. Shamir, "Isha Ivriya," 76n33.

11. See Kronfeld and Seidman, introduction to *The First Day*, xxii.

12. Jelen, *Intimations of Difference*, 43.

13. Seidman, *Marriage Made in Heaven*, 96. For more on the comparison of gothic elements in the Hebrew and Yiddish versions of Baron's early stories, see especially pp. 95–100. For detailed publication information of these stories, see Govrin, *Ha-maḥatsit ha-rishona*, 313–25.

14. Seidman, *Marriage Made in Heaven*, 100.

15. Baron and Shteinberg were far from anomalous for writing in both Hebrew and Yiddish. In her study *Lingering Bilingualism*, Naomi Brenner examines the ongoing contact between Hebrew and Yiddish in the twentieth century, and argues that this bilingualism enriched both literatures.

16. Thanks to recent scholarship on Baron, such binaries have been reoriented through a feminist lens to reveal an alternative perspective of these forces in Jewish life. Wendy Zierler points to Baron's "persistent focus on female nonimmigration and her preference of exile rather than homecoming as the site of her woman-centered fiction" (Zierler, "In What World," 129). Seidman cites Baron's focus "on the women left behind" rather than "the men who have traveled on" (Seidman, "Gender and the Disintegration of the Shtetl," 207). The same essay appears also in Jelen and Pinsker, *Hebrew, Gender, and Modernity*, 173–87.

17. Miron, *Image of the Shtetl*, 13, 11.

18. Ibid., 12.

19. Band, "Agnon's Synthetic Shtetl," 234.

20. Seidman, "Gender and the Disintegration of the Shtetl," 194.

21. Miron, "Endless Cycle," 18. In Baron's work, Miron writes, "*shtetls* do not play any role except for the obvious one of providing a necessary reality in which poetry seeks the existential principles that lie beyond the descriptive sequence of historical, geographical, and ethnographic reality." In other words, according to Miron, the shtetl as represented by Baron is dictated by biographical coincidence, a concrete setting marginal to her fiction's universal concerns, whereas for S. Y. Abramovitsh and other canonical shtetl authors, who "seek out what is unique or different about the Jewish *shtetl* life," it is central (ibid.). For critiques of this interpretation, see the section "Departure and Staying, *Tlishut* and *Aginut*" in this chapter.

22. Miron, *Image of the Shtetl*, 21.

23. Ibid., 23.

24. For more on the talush, see S. Halkin, *Mavo le-sifrut Ivrit*; and Govrin, *Telishut ve-hitḥadshut*.

25. Jelen, "All Writers Are Jews," 189. See also Jelen, "Strange Sympathy: The Talush Imperative," in *Intimations of Difference*, 25–50.

26. Jelen, "All Writers Are Jews," 197. Jelen and several other scholars have, over the last two decades, persuasively argued for gender as a fundamental interpretive framework for Baron's fiction. Among these studies, see Jelen, *Intimations of Difference*; Seidman, *Marriage Made in Heaven*; and Zierler, *Rachel Stole the Idols*.

27. Jelen, "All Writers Are Jews," 197.

28. Seidman, "Gender and the Disintegration of the Shtetl," 194.

29. Ibid., 195. *Aggadah* (lore) or *aggadic literature* refers to nonlegalistic rabbinic exegetical texts that transmit rabbinic traditions to readers through practical and moral advice, historical anecdote, and folklore.

30. Miron, "Endless Cycle," 18, 20.

31. Ibid., 21, 23.

32. Jelen and Pinsker, *Hebrew, Gender, and Modernity*, 7.

33. Lubin, "Tidbits from Nehama's Kitchen," 91.

34. Ibid., 92.

35. Seidman, "Gender and the Disintegration of the Shtetl," 195. Seidman draws a distinction between the literary figure of the agunah and her real-life counterpart. She argues that the almost total absence of abandoned children in literary depictions of aginut helps reify it into a decidedly gendered "struggle between mythical opposites": though historically both women and children were abandoned, "in the *literature* that describes the departure from the shtetl, what is left behind is gendered as feminine and emblematized by the figure of a woman" (ibid., 199).

36. Ibid., 196.

37. Ibid., 202.

38. Ibid., 203. This interpretation of the agunah is in keeping with her ambiguous historical resonance. Seidman points out that in the cultural milieu of the Haskalah, women were understood sometimes as the force of tradition burdening men on the path to modernization, and sometimes as the victims of this very tradition: "victim and victimizer both, the *agunah* indeed embodies the past in its nagging demands and impossible claims" (ibid., 198). Seidman reads the agunah in Baron's fiction as divergent from those in men's shtetl narratives, part of a broader reconceptualization of exile and modernity.

39. K. Ellis, *Contested Castle*, xv.

40. Zlosnik, "Gothic," 147. Ellen Moers first used the term *female gothic* in her 1978 study *Literary Women*. The concept has since seen substantive revision. For more on female gothic and gothic feminism, see Becker, *Gothic Forms*; Hoeveler, *Gothic Feminism*; Moers, "Female Gothic"; and Kahane, "Gothic Mirrors." See also Smith and Wallace, "The Female Gothic" (a special issue of *Gothic Studies*).

41. Hoeveler, *Gothic Feminism*, xiii.

42. Ibid., xv.

43. Ibid., 15.

44. K. Ellis, *Contested Castle*, x.

45. Anolik, "Absent Mother," 96.

46. Ibid., 97, 103.
47. Ibid., 97.
48. Ibid., 106.
49. Ibid., 113.
50. Both Seidman and Shamir discuss Y. L. Gordon's "Kotso shel ha-yod" [The point of the *yod*] in the context of reformist Haskalah fiction and gender. Seidman brings the poem into conversation with Dvora Baron's "Agunah" and Shamir with Shteinberg's "Ha-iveret," which Shamir argues engages in a sustained dialogue with the poem (Seidman, "Gender and the Disintegration of the Shtetl"; Z. Shamir, "Isha Ivriya").
51. For an illuminating analysis of gender roles in traditional European Jewish society, see Boyarin, *Unheroic Conduct*.
52. Shteinberg, "Ha-iveret," 13. All citations from Shteinberg's story are my own translation.
53. Ibid., 12.
54. Hana Naveh accuses Ḥana's mother of leading the patriarchal "conspiracy" against her daughter: by deceiving her daughter, the mother "collaborates with the establishment, which wants to perpetuate the woman's childlikeness and her dependence." Along with other women as well as children in the story, she participates in a broader "conspiracy of silence" that serves "the needs of the male establishment" (Naveh, "Politika shel hashtaka," 153–54).
55. Baron, "Shifra," 102. All citations from "Shifra" are from this translation unless otherwise noted.
56. Miron, *Image of the Shtetl*, 36.
57. Ibid., 36–37.
58. Ibid., 37.
59. Ibid.
60. The cemetery is the obvious exception, as it appears in Shteinberg's story. Its function there, however, differs substantively from the function of the cemetery that Miron delineates in his typology. Whereas in "classic" literature of the shtetl the cemetery might signify the Judaization of the non-Jewish territory, the moribund state of the shtetl, or, by contrast, the shtetl's vivacity, in Shteinberg's story it indicates the metaphorical burial of the marginalized blind heroine and her proximity—symbolic and literal—to death.
61. P. Morrison, "Enclosed in Openness."
62. Ibid., 21.
63. Ibid., 11–12.
64. Ibid., 11.
65. Ibid.
66. Shteinberg, "Ha-iveret," 20.
67. Naveh, "Politika shel hashtaka," 155–56.
68. Foucault, *History of Madness*, 415.
69. Foucault, *Birth of the Clinic*, xii.
70. Baron, "Shifra," 105.
71. Ibid., 104.
72. Ibid., 105.
73. Joan Copjec argues that the political advocacy of breastfeeding that emerged in eighteenth-century England "is the precise equivalent of vampire fiction." In psychoanalytic terms, both can be understood as "a cry for the object-cause of desire" (Copjec, "Vampires," 26, 42).

74. Naveh elaborates on the failure of most of the critical responses to "Ha-iveret" to address the gender-specific dynamics of the story, and on their interpretation of the heroine's blindness in universalist terms: "The criticism poses no questions on the matter of the difference between the blindness of a man and that of a woman, or questions regarding the reason that Shteinberg chose a blind heroine and not a blind hero." She argues that "Shteinberg had a special intuition in regards to the world of women, and that a character that was not a woman could not have played Ḥana's role" ("Politika shel hashtaka," 148, 149). This claim is especially compelling if we consider that Shteinberg calls on the female gothic at a time when prevailing notions of Jewish masculinity, influenced by Zionism and the West more broadly, associated femininity with the diaspora.

75. For example, see Mohanty, "Under Western Eyes."

76. For more on ocularcentrism, see the following studies by Jay: *Downcast Eyes*; "Disenchantment of the Eye"; and "Rise of Hermeneutics."

77. Haraway, "Persistence of Vision," 679–80.

78. Ibid., 681.

79. Ibid., 684.

80. Stern, "Gothic Light," 28.

81. Ibid., 27.

82. Ibid., 28.

83. Dolan, *Seeing Suffering*, 1.

84. Ibid.

85. Haraway, "Persistence of Vision," 684.

86. Shteinberg, "Ha-iveret," 21.

87. Ibid., 22.

88. Baron, "Shifra," 99.

89. Ibid., 100, 104.

90. Ibid., 107.

91. Ibid., 108.

92. Ibid.

93. Naveh, "Politika shel hashtaka," 150.

94. Shteinberg, "Ha-iveret," 11.

95. Naveh, "Politika shel hashtaka," 166.

96. Baron, "Shifra," 104.

97. Ibid.

98. Ibid.

99. Ibid., 105.

100. For a succinct review of the theoretical literature on feminist theory and affect, see Gorton, "Theorizing Emotion and Affect."

101. Cvetkovich, *Mixed Feelings*, 1.

102. For a study on the gothic's development of "an emotional and imaginative vocabulary," see Howells, *Love, Mystery and Misery*, 2. For more on affect theory in the context of the gothic, see the introduction to this study.

103. Haggerty, *Gothic Fiction/Gothic Form*, 8.

104. Ibid., 13.

105. Aldana Reyes, "Gothic Affect," 15, 16.

106. The idea that the expression of anger is a primary force of social change has been a mainstay in feminist thought since it was famously expressed by Audre Lord, the African

American author and civil rights activist, in her scathing keynote address at the National Women's Studies Association conference in 1981, "The Uses of Anger: Women Responding to Racism." Following Lord, Sara Ahmed argues that pain evokes a "call to action" that demands anger: "an interpretation that this pain is wrong, that it is an outrage, and that something must be done about it" (Ahmed, *Cultural Politics of Emotion*, 174). Thus feminism "moves from anger into an interpretation of that which one is against, whereby associations or connections are made between the object of anger and broader patterns or structures" (ibid., 176).

107. The distinction between the privately experienced emotion of anger and its public expression is critical. Cvetkovich cautions against the tendency to sweep anger and other emotions into the private, pathologizing realm of therapy instead of using it as an instigator for social change, the only means of actually overturning oppressive structures that drive women to repress their feelings: "Rather than leading to social change, the expression of feeling can become an end in itself or an individualist solution to systemic problems. . . . Often therapy becomes a substitute for political action, a privatized and personalized solution to problems that are ultimately social and collective" (*Mixed Feelings*, 1–2).

108. Baron, "Shifra," 106.
109. Ibid., 103.
110. Ibid., 107.
111. Ibid., 105.
112. Ibid.
113. Baron, "Shifra" [in Hebrew], 184.
114. Ibid., 185; "Shifra," 106.
115. Ibid.
116. Ibid.
117. Ibid.
118. Ibid. For an analysis of a similar phenomenon in "Ha-iveret," see Naveh, "Politika shel hashtaka": "One of the typical coping mechanisms of a socio-cultural minority is the adoption and internalization of the values of the majority culture. This internalization includes a silent agreement with the values of the majority culture, and the hope that adopting them will yield gains and achievements" (152).
119. Baron, "Shifra," 103; Shteinberg, "Ha-iveret," 11–12.
120. Shteinberg, "Ha-iveret," 12–13.
121. Ibid., 17.
122. Ibid., 20.
123. Ibid., 23.
124. Ibid., 24.
125. Ibid.
126. Ibid., 25.
127. Ibid., 26–27.
128. Ibid.
129. Ibid., 27.
130. Ibid.
131. Naveh, "Politika shel hashtaka," 159.
132. Cvetkovich, *Mixed Feelings*, 7. It is worth noting that neither story challenges the narrative of domestic joy in and of itself, but rather portrays women whose individual circumstances position it beyond their reach.

133. Shteinberg, "Ha-iveret," 26.
134. Baron, "Shifra," 107.
135. Ibid.
136. Ibid., 106–7.
137. S. Pinsker, "Unraveling the Yarn," 160.
138. Baron, "Shifra" [in Hebrew], 185; Shteinberg, "He-iveret," 26.

3

AFTER THE NIGHTMARE OF THE HOLOCAUST

Gothic Temporalities in Leah Goldberg and Edgar Allan Poe

IN A TELLING DIARY ENTRY DATED JULY 22, 1952, the Hebrew poet Leah Goldberg (1911–70) relates a conversation typical of the ones intellectuals were having in the 1950s about the future of Israeli culture. At a meeting of the Supreme Council for Culture, a fellow poet, Avraham Kariv, had derided Goldberg for her prolific translation of foreign literature, accusing her of contributing to "a translated nation" rather than to the creation of a purely Hebrew culture. In his view, Goldberg represents those who "have no need for 'roots' in Israel, who know what the *goyim* did to us, and bow down before the goy. Why do we need all these Balzacs and Stendhals! We have no need for any Balzacs, they're only good for degenerate conversation (שיחה מנוונת) in cafes. All this European culture is worthless, and L. G. and her journal that has memorial days (*yahrtzeiten*) for some goy 50 weeks of the year."[1]

His sentiments, which troubled Goldberg deeply but were not exceptional at that time, reflected a profound anxiety regarding the development of a national culture: it should be rooted in its time and place, expressing the concerns and values of contemporary readers of Hebrew rather than the bourgeois, moribund European cultural sensibility they rejected as irrelevant. Like one of its most famous literary protagonists, this new culture would "come from the sea," divorced from its multispatial histories.[2] Kariv's emphasis on the utility of art introduces the idea that art must be political, engaged, practical, and productive—not merely beautiful.

Moreover, his characterization of Hebrew translations of European literature as *yahrtzeiten* establishes the latter as a manifestation of death and the past and positions Hebrew writing as living, dynamic, and present. Though the centrality of Europe in the development of modern Hebrew culture—through translation, literary influence, and the biographical circumstances of Hebrew authors—is undisputed, its acknowledgment, for Kariv, amounts to a perpetual state of mourning a dusty past, a threat to Hebrew culture. This conviction echoes earlier debates in the Yishuv about whether translated literature might cannibalize original Hebrew literary culture, with an added stress on the contrast between Hebrew's lively vigor and Europe's sarcophagal rot.[3]

Reflecting on Kariv's outburst, Goldberg becomes distressed: "What a terrible development! On the one hand socialist realism, the Stalinist line in literature, on the other the 'Blubo' (*Blod und Boden*), of the type of things I heard in Germany in 1933, the 'roots,' and the hatred for all that is good and beautiful in the world. Where else can we escape this despair?"[4] Seeking to disown the Europe that engendered the Holocaust amounted, in Goldberg's eyes, to another expression of fascism. Beauty for its own sake becomes anathema in the practical worldview of 1950s Zionism precisely because it offers an illusory escape from the tribulations of the real. It was a view that had already taken shape decades before. In a 1935 review of Goldberg's volume of poetry *Taba'ot ashan* (Smoke rings), the critic Y. Sa'aroni, writing as Y. Sin, accused Goldberg of vacillating, in her poems, between her room and the museum: "Paintings, statues, and books might rouse her imagination. . . . But life itself says almost nothing to her. . . . The poetess is outside time and place."[5] There could be no greater failure for a Hebrew poet in Palestine. Failing to represent the truth or to reveal the real, art is distracting at best and deceptive or even destructive at worst. In this context, the definitions of art and reality are both at stake. Should art reflect reality or shape it? Should art and reality be considered distinct entities, or are they intertwined and interdependent?

In her remarkable neogothic play "Ba'alat ha-armon" ("The Lady of the Castle"), published in 1956 and first performed in 1959 at the Cameri Theater, Goldberg attends to these questions and related ideological issues that preoccupied Israeli Jews in the 1950s and 1960s. The play reflects on the past's relation to the present and the future, on the role of Europe in the collective Jewish Israeli memory, and on what Israeli culture stands to gain or lose from its incorporation of its European past or, conversely, from its divestment from this past.⁶ An important question the play raises concerns art itself: In the wake of the destruction of war, the horror of the Holocaust, and the Zionist endeavor to disown the past and enact a collective national Jewish rebirth, what value does art have, particularly given its association with the European past? It was a question that left a mark throughout Goldberg's literary production as well as on her academic work.⁷

"The Lady of the Castle" was produced during a critical historical moment just a few years after the end of the war and the declaration of Israel's statehood. Israeli Jews in the young state renounced Europe not only because of the Holocaust but also in the name of a defiantly presentist Zionist ideology, which encouraged a broad, willful detachment from diasporic Jewish history, associated with weakness.⁸ For Goldberg, this was an impossible and undesirable endeavor. Though she refused to set foot in Germany, her birthplace, after the war, her academic and literary production is steeped in Europe. Her poetry, nonfiction essays, and translations of European literature from seven different languages—including works by Tolstoy, Shakespeare, Chekhov, Rilke, Mann, and others—were no less than prolific, and they attest to the forceful presence of the European past in her sensibility.

Goldberg also published short stories, a few plays, and longer prose works, among them an autobiographical novel. Her poetry is characterized, in Robert Alter's words, by its "subtle sense of beauty in small words and small things," by its attention to the minor details of landscape, to the quiet wonder of nature, and to unrequited love.⁹ One of her best-known essays, "Ha-omets le-ḥulin" (The courage for the mundane, 1938), points to the significance of these individual experiences but positions them as part of what Anat Weisman describes as "a painful oscillation, a stubborn dialogue between alternating interpretations of the world . . . , between the exalted and the mundane."¹⁰ This defining tension of Goldberg's poetics demonstrates the uneasy interdependence of art and reality. Her era, seething with war, revolution, displacement, and upheaval, could not possibly allow Goldberg to deny or resist the power exerted by ideology over the experience of quotidian reality, or to disregard the question of the ethical responsibility of art. Though art can reveal or represent truth, it can also be mobilized to guard against an overwhelming reality. In subscribing to both these possibilities, Goldberg illuminates a complexity that both creates and is born of art itself.

Written and performed less than a decade after Theodor Adorno penned his famous dictum that "to write poetry after Auschwitz is barbaric,"

"The Lady of the Castle" foregrounds the preoccupation with the relation between reality and art as an ethical one.[11] For Adorno, this constitutes the final stage of the "dialectic of culture and barbarism," instigating the loss of cultural particularity to totality and singularity.[12] Goldberg's play configures this tension vis-à-vis temporality. The absolutism of ideology is positioned against the beauty of art: the former represents the tyranny of present time, while the latter signals the past as an illusory and futile resistance to this barbaric present. Evoking concerns regarding the relationship between art and reality that were taken up as far back as Plato in his *Republic* and in the twentieth century by figures such as Adorno, Erich Auerbach, and Walter Benjamin, the play addresses questions relevant beyond specific Jewish, Hebrew, and Israeli contexts.

The gothic mode employed by "The Lady of the Castle" allows it to enter a global discourse on art and reality despite its historical specificity because the gothic itself, with its reliance on the mystery and the explained or unexplained supernatural, has such a contentious relationship with reality.[13] Existing criticism of the play dismisses its crucial gothic elements as, at most, representative or symbolic of the past.[14] This chapter considers the play's gothicism—its dark European castle setting, its beautiful imprisoned heroine, its melancholic count, and its preoccupation with persecution, suffering, and fear—as a necessary aesthetic and thematic condition for the play's concerns. I argue that these gothic elements are integral to the play's conceptualization of time as it is expressed through the encounter between art and reality, poetry and ideology. The titular castle and its high-culture accouterments are not just a symbol of "Old Europe." Rather, the castle functions primarily as a sanctuary of art meant to freeze time and thus to keep reality at bay, both for the young Jewish woman who has been hidden there and for the count who has both saved and imprisoned her. The tension between the beautiful, static past and the unsightly, dynamic present, however, precludes the possibility of a safe haven, resulting instead in the paradox of the insecure sanctuary. One of the play's most radical innovations in terms of both its utilization and its destabilization of the gothic mode emerges from this paradox: its unusual representation of victimhood.

The driving concern of this chapter—the constellation of art, reality, and time, and its role in producing and deconstructing the interrelated conceptual categories of victim and sanctuary—also animates the stories of one of the most celebrated gothic authors, Edgar Allan Poe (1809–49). Poe has been described as "the maniac of time," and numerous studies have analyzed his stories' seeming obsession with the temporal.[15] What is most compelling about these observations is that they invariably point to a broader theme undergirding what might be described as the chronomania of the protagonist or the narrator. Poe's story "The Masque of the Red Death" (1842) offers an edifying comparison to Goldberg's play not only because it grapples with the role of time as a metonymy of the real and the seeming counterforce to art but also because it engages explicitly with the formative tension undergirding the art/reality dialectic.

I begin by examining the way space and time interact in both texts. The chronotopic structure that governs them relies on a spatiality of inside/outside; a multiple, disjointed temporality engenders the failure of space. After tracing these spatiotemporal disjunctures, I identify time itself as a primary concern in both texts, both of which are centered on beautiful clocks that mediate between art and the real. The clock, as a portal to the real, indicates the permeability of the sanctuary of art. I then consider the implications of these futile fortifications to show that the sanctuary not only fails to preserve life but also can leave one more vulnerable to death. The porousness of sanctuaries and their susceptibility to the forces of time lead to a revision of victimization, an unexpected characteristic in a Hebrew play produced so soon after the Holocaust. Indeed, though the Holocaust would seem to provide an apt, all-too-literal context for the macabre horror of the gothic, Goldberg appropriates gothic motifs to altogether different ends, choosing to expose the complexity underlying the postwar Israeli self-conception. The chapter's final section situates the "porous sanctuary" and its revision of victimhood within the post-Holocaust Israeli cultural context.

In both texts, the gothic setting, a haven enclosed within a stylized edifice, offers potential victims both protection and paralysis by keeping the hideous, destructive reality—marked by the passing of time—just beyond its walls, while preserving art and beauty within. In both texts, however, that seemingly impervious boundary proves to be the greatest illusion of all, as it depends on the passing of time to maintain itself. This disruption of the seeming polarity between life and art unsettles our conceptualization of victimhood. Reading Goldberg's play together with Poe's story provides a new perspective on the ideological quandaries that accompanied and shaped her development as an artist. More broadly, the implications of this argument are ethical: victims are not only victimized, perpetrators are vulnerable to victimization and persecution, and saviors can oppress.

Though my analysis is not intended to make a case for direct influence, it is worth noting that Goldberg was, without a doubt, acquainted with Poe's writing. His poetry and prose had been available in Hebrew translation since the second decade of the twentieth century, and Goldberg's command of English would certainly have allowed her to read those texts that remained untranslated.[16] In an article published in the newspaper La-Merḥav in 1959, Goldberg and several other authors were asked to comment on their writing process. By way of response, she recounts how Poe, in his famous essay "The Philosophy of Composition" (1846), discusses the process of writing "The Raven" only in its external, structural aspect: "But the inner work, which was likely done long beforehand, is not explained at all. The subconscious aspect of his creation was lost for him, and we, the readers, know this better than he himself."[17] Goldberg's stress on the duality of the writing process itself—its external, technical features and its inner, subconscious character—is ironic, given Poe's emphasis in his essay on the idea of "unity of effect." Better conceptualized as what we might call a "disunity of creation," Goldberg's interpretation of Poe's essay in terms of duality can be understood as another facet of the relationship between art and reality, internal and external, past and present. Keenly aware of the limitations of even the most self-conscious authorial act, she leaves room for the ruptures and contradictions that writing can engender, which, as in Poe's poem, create its most resonant effects for readers.

Chronotopic Architectonics and the Failure of Space

Both "The Lady of the Castle" and "The Masque of the Red Death" not only acknowledge a central spatial component in their representation of time but also go so far as to suggest that spatial structures play a role in *controlling* time. However, as the spatial binary itself ultimately fails in Goldberg's play as it does in Poe's story, transgressive temporalities forge a series of impossible but requisite alliances: between the real and the illusory present, between the past of the castle and its exterior counterhistory, and between the futures of the mystical Fourth Kingdom and post-Holocaust Zionism.

In Poe's "The Masque of the Red Death," the plague had "long devastated the country."[18] It prompts the happy Prince Prospero to seclude himself, together with one thousand of his "hale and light-hearted friends," deep within one of his castellated abbeys, where they could pass the days and nights in mirth and pleasure while the Red Death ravaged his dominion beyond the abbey: "A strong and lofty wall girdled it in. This wall had gates of iron."[19] Leaving nothing to chance, the prince's courtiers bring furnaces and hammers and weld the gate's bolts. The narrator describes the colorful scene in the abbey: "There were buffoons, there were improvisatori, there were ballet-dancers, there were musicians, there was Beauty, there was wine. All these and security were within. Without was the 'Red Death.'"[20] The stark contrast he evokes between the inside and the outside, safety and danger, life and death, establishes the binary structure on which the story depends for its dramatic effect.

Oddly, though, the courtiers are as concerned about keeping the revelers *inside* the abbey as they are about keeping the Red Death out: "They resolved to leave means neither of ingress or egress to the sudden impulses of despair or frenzy from within."[21] The narrator asserts, presumably taking on the voice of Prospero himself, that the "external world could take care of itself"; yet the possibility that all "the appliances of pleasure" supplied to the abbey and the security that is so meticulously planned in its enclosure might fail to keep the fortunate *in* haunts the story from its beginning, skewing the seemingly clear duality between inside and outside.[22] Even as the narrator establishes this duality, asserting a sharp contrast in terms of security versus chaos, pleasure versus suffering, and beauty versus hideousness, he casts this clear separation into doubt by suggesting that Prospero's fortunate friends may yet feel "despair or frenzy *from within*" (emphasis mine). This peculiar moment of foresight announces that the possibility of penetration is always already present, sets the tone of ambiguity and reversal that characterizes the rest of the story, and foreshadows the Red Death's murder of all the revelers at the story's horrific ending. The abbey fails in Poe's story: it fails to arrest the inevitable encroachment of violence and death, and it fails even as an expression of one of the most fundamental and definitive structures of human experience, the spatial binary of inside/outside.

This latter failure finds expression in Goldberg's play as well. Grounded in realist concerns and a recognizable postwar reality, "The Lady of the Castle" also relies on a distinctly European geographic and aesthetic milieu. The play opens on a dark and stormy night. Two characters, the Youth Aliyah social worker Dr. Dora Ringel and the librarian Michael Sand, are traveling through an unspecified Eastern European country, Dora in search of orphaned Jewish children to bring back to Israel, and Sand seeking lost or abandoned Jewish books to bring to the National Library in Jerusalem.[23]

Alarmed by the increasing intensity of the storm, they seek shelter in the castle, the only edifice for miles, and the mysterious Count Zabrodsky—formerly the owner and under the postwar communist regime only the custodian of the castle—reluctantly agrees to let them stay until the storm passes.[24] Over the course of the play, the visitors learn that the count has been hiding a nineteen-year-old Jewish girl, Lena, in a secret room. Having fallen in love with her, he has continued hiding her even after the war ended. The play's entire plot unfolds in the castle's grand library, described by Goldberg's stage directions: "Bookcases along the walls. Paintings by old masters and tapestries. One window with heavy curtains. . . . A librarian's ladder by the right bookcase. Above the wall tapestry, between the bookcases, center, an old cuckoo clock."[25] These material details come together to form a well-worn spatiality associated with the gothic.

This familiar setting is a function not only of space but also of a distinctive temporality. As the primary territory of the gothic novel, the castle signifies an intense and readily apparent chronotopy, as Mikhail Bakhtin observes:

> The castle is saturated through and through with a time that is historical in the narrow sense of the word, that is, the time of the historical past. The castle is the place where the lords of the feudal era lived (and consequently also the place of historical figures of the past); the traces of centuries and generations are arranged in it in visible form as various parts of its architecture, in furnishings, weapons, the ancestral portrait gallery, the family archives and in the particular human relationships involving dynastic primacy and the transfer of hereditary rights. And finally legends and traditions animate every corner of the castle and its environs through their constant reminders of past events.[26]

Goldberg's castle is true to form in its visible "traces of centuries and generations," but the *invisible* forces that have penetrated its walls—the external politics and ideologies of the present—have overpowered them. Books, furnishings, and portraits stand, seemingly undisturbed, in their proper place within the castle, while their immaterial referents, the "particular human relationships involving dynastic primacy and the transfer of hereditary rights," have been obliterated. Bakhtin observes that the "somewhat antiquated, museum-like character" of castle time can be balanced through more dynamic forces like "the legend of the castle [and] the link between the castle and its historically conceived, comprehensible setting."[27] Goldberg's castle, however, no longer enjoys this "organic cohesion of spatial and temporal aspects" because the time outside the castle has moved on while the time within has seemingly stayed put, creating a chronotopic disjuncture.²⁸ Impossibly, two incompatible trajectories of time coincide.

Already at the end of World War I, Count Zabrodsky relates, he had recognized himself as living among the dead ("בין המתים הייתי").²⁹ The ancestral castle, a symbol of the social and political structures that had sustained him, catalyzed his spectrality. The eradication of those structures left the castle an empty signifier, transforming him and others like him into ghosts (רוחות רפאים) and draining their lives of meaning: "Without meaning—there can be no life. So I died."³⁰ His postwar metamorphosis results from a collapse of the inside/outside binary not unlike that which transforms Prince Prospero's ball into a massacre and the prince himself into a corpse.

From a perspective decidedly antithetical to Zabrodsky's, Dora, the voice of Zionism in the play, elaborates on this collapse, praising it and deriding the count for his elitist insensitivity to the historical injustices perpetrated by the castle's meticulous preservation of inside/outside: "And those who lived here, who built this wonderful 'culture,' did they have any inkling of what was going on beyond the walls of their estates?" she asks. "Built a culture! And didn't take the trouble to move this culture one meter out of their castles! . . . They used dogs to guard places like these, to keep out intruders!"³¹ Dora's outburst provides a defiant alternative history from the perspective of those outside the castle. Their penetration of the castle has altered its "comprehensible setting," finally transforming the castle into a "museum," a repository of dead culture.³²

Zabrodsky understands that his only hope of rescuing even an illusion of this lost culture and resisting his own mummification as its relic lies in preserving the strict spatial division of inside/outside. As Lena's savior and protector, he constructs a double sanctuary. One is housed within the castle and its trappings of beauty, art, and culture from bygone days. Reminiscent of the beautiful interiority derided by Sa'aroni in his critique of Goldberg, this sanctuary is a bulwark against the ugliness of postwar Europe and its new reigning ideologies positioned squarely against the perceived decadence of the past. Another, more subtle haven is based on a notion of a future-oriented, transcendent "Fourth Kingdom," an alternative reality constituted within the count's and Lena's collective psyche. The illusory worlds he constructs for Lena, whether situated in a lost past or an aspirational, quasimystical future, depend on her habitation within the castle's interior and on the perpetual distance and unattainability of its exterior.

Such disjointed temporalities dominate and reconfigure the notion of space in the play. Although the play in its entirety is set in a single place, the castle's library, Lena's keenest desire relates precisely to overcoming the spatiality that has defined her world for several years. When she realizes, finally, that the war has ended, her first, visceral reaction is to gaze through a window at the moonlit night and to contemplate the manifold sensory experience associated with the outdoors, which has been denied her in the windowless room in the bowels of the castle. "I always dreamt that this moment would come and I would open the window, and touch the leaves and the branches, and the drops would fall on my head from the roof and wet my hair," she recalls. "In my room, down there,—there's no window at all . . . I longed so much—for fresh air! . . . I want air, I want to run, to walk and walk."[33] After Lena decides to leave the castle, she attributes her decision not to anger at Zabrodsky, not to Zionist conviction, and not to Dora's assertion that she can begin life anew, but rather to this single, ardent desire: "I want—fresh air—outside."[34] The same exterior world that drove her into hiding to begin with, the same forests that she traversed to escape certain death at Nazi hands—these continue to signify freedom for Lena.

Her attraction to the outside could be understood as Goldberg's response to the accusation leveled against her by Sa'aroni two decades earlier: "From the room to the museum. She almost doesn't feel life outside these worlds."[35] Yet, as we may expect, in the hands of Goldberg, the spatial division does not correspond so neatly to ideological conviction. Though Lena's decision to leave with Dora and Sand is usually interpreted as a decision to immigrate to Israel, the play subtly suggests that the newly established state, presented as a safe haven for the persecuted, is as permeable as the castle-sanctuary. It is Lena's wish to experience *outside* that drives her decision; but outside does not, as in Sa'aroni's reading, necessarily map onto Zionist space, which signifies for some of Goldberg's characters enclosure more than liberation. Particularly from the perspective of the present-day politics that have created an Israel closed in on itself, armed with walls and weapons to create the most formidable of fortresses against enemies all around, the vulnerability of the boundary separating inside from outside is of ongoing relevance—whether it takes the form of underground tunnels beneath national borders, holes in a barbed-wire fence, or political dissent from within or without. In the context of a sanctuary or safe haven, the inside/outside binary has been utterly destabilized.

The Beautiful Clock as the Portal of the Real

If this most basic spatial category fails, then what can fill the void created by its failure? The answer provided by both texts is time. From the first line of Poe's story, which specifies that the Red Death wrought its fatal horrific suffering in the span of half an hour, the reader is aware of the importance of time. The temporal, in both texts, prevails. It is the only force powerful enough to structure and to destroy as effectively and with as much consequence as the spatial.

Among theories of literary temporality, several stand out as particularly influential: Paul de Man's articulation of simultaneous and extended temporality vis-à-vis symbol and allegory, respectively;[36] Bakhtin's notion of "multitemporality" or "heterochrony," a concept he defines as the temporal parallel of linguistic heteroglossia;[37] and Paul Ricoeur's concept of the reciprocity of narrative and the human experience of time, which rejects both linear chronology and radical achronology to articulate a "deeper experience of time" based on a critique of Heidegger's ideas.[38] De Man understands time in literature to be a function of literary or rhetorical devices, whereas Bakhtin identifies it as a function of its setting, and Ricoeur associates it with character and plot. For all three, a text's temporality engages intensively with language: for de Man it is about the poetics of the romantic text; for Bakhtin this linguistic engagement appears as a function of dialogism; for Ricoeur it is grammatical, emerging in adverbs and adjectives that convey temporality. They all seek to express the experience of time as it emerges from narrative. To this end they account for the role of history, the time "inside" and "outside" and "before" and "after" the world of the text (the time of the reader and the author as well as of the characters), and the experience of reading itself as it is constituted in time.

None of them, however, considers these literary-temporal dynamics as they might pertain to texts whose very subject is time. That is, in analyzing the role that time plays in the progression of plot, in the reader's experience of this development, or in the various ways in which history and other texts contribute to literature, they do not probe those literary texts that explicitly engage with the same questions that drive their theories. My understanding of time not only as a narrative mechanism but also as a subject in these texts proceeds from this gap. Both "The Lady of the Castle" and "The Masque of the Red Death" portray dynamic time—"time passing"—as the measurable manifestation of reality itself, and both subscribe to a correlative of this equation whereby art seems to afford a means of controlling time by freezing it. Art, therefore, functions in both texts as the antithesis of time and, by extension, of reality. In both these texts, the clock, a material objet d'art that measures time but paradoxically fails to control it, actively catalyzes the uneasy, potentially violent encounter of art and life.

References to time generally and to clocks specifically abound in gothic literature. In his study of gothic temporality, Jesse Molesworth distinguishes between "grand scale" historical time and "small scale" clock time, acknowledging the importance of both to gothic temporality.[39] Focusing on the gothic preoccupation with the hour, clocks, and clock time, he argues that it evokes the ritual element of the medievalism that informed eighteenth-century gothic. Having identified a typically gothic "temporal economy in which the hour is prized," he notes that it "is often personified as a supernatural agent capable of action itself."[40] He thus links the specific material manifestation of time—the gothic clock—to the preoccupation with history and the past as it emerges in the gothic narrative's present. The clock, an agent of time, often becomes a formal device in the narrative, actively driving its plot, assuming agency as a character, or coalescing various elements of the setting. This "peculiar temporality of the gothic hour" animates the clock-centered works by Goldberg and Poe.[41]

As we have just seen, though, the true peculiarity in these texts lies not in any singular temporality but rather in multiple, disjointed temporalities that, in both texts, are created and manipulated by clocks: on the one hand, time is an agent of present, dynamic, threatening *becoming*; on the other, it is subject to an arrested, eternal, illusory *being*. The clocks whose ticks and chimes govern both texts provide the passageway between these disparate temporalities and the worlds they represent. The force of their impossible but necessary coexistence perforates the boundaries between the atemporal and the ongoing, the real and the illusory, dangerous places and safe havens.

The features of the abbey's imperial suites in "The Masque of the Red Death," meticulously described by the narrator, have been exhaustively analyzed. Several critics have observed that the design of the abbey's imperial suites, where the grand masked ball is held, resembles a clock's face.[42] Whether or not one accepts this interpretation of the suites' construction—the product of what the narrator calls Prospero's "bizarre" taste—there is no question that time plays a critical role in the atmosphere within the abbey's fortified walls. After describing in vivid detail the layout and design of the richly hued imperial suites, Poe devotes a lengthy paragraph to their crown jewel, the "gigantic clock of ebony," and the "dull, heavy, monotonous clang" of its pendulum. Every hour,

> there came from the brazen lungs of the clock a sound which was clear and loud and deep and exceedingly musical, but of so peculiar a note and emphasis that, at each lapse of an hour, the musicians of the orchestra were constrained to pause, momentarily in their performance.... But when the echoes had fully ceased, a light laughter at once pervaded the assembly; ... and then, after the lapse of sixty minutes, (which embrace three thousand and six hundred seconds of the Time that flies,) there came yet another chiming of the clock, and then were the same disconcert and tremulousness and meditation as before.[43]

Poe mentions the clock's disconcerting power over the revelers twice more: once in passing to emphasize again the pause its chiming brings about in the festivities and the solemnity it imposes on the black velvet chamber in which it stands, and once more at midnight, when it brings the revelry to a standstill as before. This time, however, "there were twelve strokes to be sounded by the bell of the clock; and thus it happened, perhaps, that more of thought crept, with more of time, into the meditations of the thoughtful among those who reveled."[44] The lengthy midnight chiming also, relates the narrator, provides the revelers enough time to notice a masked figure that they had not previously discerned: the gaunt, corpselike, horrific Red Death. The clock is mentioned again after Prince Prospero, having pursued the figure to the black chamber, dies. The crowd of revelers desperately seizes the intruder, "whose tall figure stood erect and motionless within the shadow of the ebony clock."[45] The story's final paragraph establishes with certainty that the intruder is no mere impersonator but is the Red Death personified, and none escapes him: "One by one dropped the revelers in the blood-bedewed halls of their revel, and died each in the despairing posture of his fall. And the life of the ebony clock went out with that of the last of the gay."[46]

The foreboding clock is crucial to the interpretation of "The Masque of the Red Death" as an exemplar of the permeable refuge art offers from life, as William Freedman elegantly argues. The ebony clock represents the "real" world beyond the walls of the castellated abbey: "Situated in the same westernmost room, where the sun will finally set on all efforts to escape it, the clock is the relentlessly paralyzing reminder of 'the Time that flies.'"[47] Despite the best efforts of the revelers to avoid the black chamber, the clock's peals "resound throughout the abbey, arresting every hour the festivities summoned to efface all sense of time."[48] Yet it is the prince himself,

Freedman reminds us, who deliberately included the ebony clock in the intricately conceived design of the marvelous chambers: "Had he wished to truly to exclude all traces of time, decay, and death, to create an aesthetic sanctuary impervious to the mortal world, he could have conjured otherwise."[49] Freedman attributes this seeming paradox to the "artist's dilemma, his apparent recognition that a sanctuary must include—and ultimately master—what it is designed to interdict. . . . Time is outside the world of art it menaces, yet also of it."[50] Certainly the mathematical design of Prospero's suites, their symmetry and harmony, constitute an attempt at mastery. Arguably, even time itself, divided as it is into measured units, suggests a human mastery of what is otherwise a chaotic force. The clock chimes at known, recognized intervals, and despite the temporary terror it incites in the revelers every hour, they await the end of its chiming because they know its intervals exactly.

If Prospero is indeed the precocious artist who intentionally invites the time of reality into the atemporality of art in order to "master" it, what does the story's end suggest? The artist-prince becomes the first victim of this encounter between reality and art, and his guests, lulled into an illusion of security during each sixty-minute stretch between the clock's chimes, are ultimately doomed to the same bloody fate. The figure of the Red Death finds refuge in the clock's great shadow as the desperate revelers finally confront him at the end of the story. The narrator pointedly relates, however, that "the life of the great clock went out with that of the last of the gay," suggesting that the clock is linked not only to the Red Death but also to the life of its victims. Once they are murdered, the clock no longer serves a purpose.

The clock in Poe's story, then, signifies art and the real as possessing disjointed but interdependent temporalities. As the crack in Prospero's fortress of beauty, it allows the Red Death in. But it is also itself an *object* of beauty, an integral component of the fortress of beauty if not its very heart. Intended to measure and master a chaotic force, it encompasses the full spectrum of art—from its attempt to aestheticize and control time to the hourly chiming that demonstrates the impossibility of this project by interrupting and terrifying the guests, reminding them of time's continued movement, and materializing the irresistible presence and force of the real.

At the center of Goldberg's play, too, stands an imposing and mysterious clock weighted with symbolic significance. As a whole, her poetic oeuvre testifies to her preoccupation with clocks and time. The first line of one of her best-known poems, "Oren" (Pine tree), establishes the cuckoo clock as a symbol of the poet's European past: "Here I will not hear the cuckoo's voice / Here the tree will not don a bonnet of snow."[51] The poem, which has been extensively analyzed as exemplary of Goldberg's attachment to her European past even as she helped forge the literary modernism of her Hebrew present, ends with the poet's melancholic acknowledgment that "my roots are in two different landscapes."[52] The cycle that opens her first collection of poems, *Taba'ot ashan* (Smoke rings, 1935), entitled "Ashan ha-zman" (The smoke of time), probes the concept of time and invokes clock imagery. Other poems, such as the cycle "Laila ve-yamim aḥronim" (Night and the last days), "Aḥrey esrim shana" (After twenty years), and "Zman" (Time) attest to the macabre character that Goldberg often ascribes to time. In "The Lady of the Castle," the clock is the castle's centerpiece, the gateway to its alternative temporalities. Just as Prospero's sanctuary must include, incorporate, and master what it has been designed to keep out, so it is in Count Zabrodsky's castle. It, too, represents a sanctuary of culture and art, filled with a vast accumulation of books, paintings, and beautiful objects. As one of these objets d'art, the intricate cuckoo clock immediately captures Sand's eye. The son of a watchmaker, Sand is eager to see the clock in action, but Zabrodsky, eager to avert his attention, deceitfully claims that the clock is broken. Only later do the visitors and the audience learn that the clock activates the secret passage to Lena's hiding place.

The first mention of the clock appears in act 1, during the first debate among Dora, Sand, and Zabrodsky about the aesthetics of "the old" versus the efficacy of the modern. Sand, the librarian, occupies the middle ground between Dora's adamant allegiance to "sunshine and cleanliness" and "a healthy, simple life," on the one hand, and Zabrodsky's longing for the "immeasurably more beautiful" lives that preceded "these modern boxes," on the other. Sand asserts that "this is one of the most beautiful castles I've seen, and I've been through quite a number lately. . . . I can't take my eyes off that clock. It's French, I believe?"[53] Zabrodsky, momentarily caught off guard by Sand's connoisseurship, learns that Sand's father was a watchmaker and that Sand himself loved cuckoo clocks as a child. Regaining his composure, he announces that the clock does not work and offers to show him a different clock in the morning. Later in the same act, Dora announces that it is already ten o'clock, greatly alarming Zabrodsky before she realizes that she has read the time from the broken cuckoo clock. At the end of the act, Dora and Zabrodsky retire, and Sand is left alone in the library. "Now let's have a look at this old clock!" he says to himself, and having discovered the key, he winds the clock—an act that, unbeknownst to him, signals to the hidden Lena that she may emerge from her hiding place through a secret door in the library wall.⁵⁴ Sand thus restores the real and invites Lena *back into time*, an act that parallels the broader event of Dora and Sand's arrival and their eventual extrication of Lena. It is worth noting that, in the years of Lena's hiding, none of the Nazis occupying the castle activated the clock. It is ultimately the modest son of a Jewish watchmaker, not the self-proclaimed purveyors of European culture, whose curiosity compels him to investigate the majestic clock and thus to discover Lena. This fact attests to Sand's status in the play as the intermediary between the beautiful past and the utilitarian present.

Several critics have identified the clock as one of the play's foundational symbols, meant to evoke a lost past. "Both the emissaries from the Land of Israel would like to match the clock of the past to the time of the present," argues Gershon Shaked. "[They] would like to repair the wheel of time that was fractured during the Second World War and to match it to the new needs and the new hopes."⁵⁵ This dualistic interpretation not only conflates Dora and Sand, whose regard of the past is not identical, but also fails to account for the overall complexity of the play's spatiotemporal dynamics. Representatives of the world outside, in this case Dora and Sand, have breached the sanctuary, first when they enter the castle and then, more critically, when they discover Lena thanks to the clock's mechanism. Like Prince Prospero's ebony clock, Count Zabrodsky's cuckoo clock allows the entry of the very force it is designed to forbid.

Why would Zabrodsky leave his sanctuary vulnerable to penetration? Nazi barbarism, like Poe's Red Death, had driven him into isolation in the castle: "When the war broke out," he explains to the others, "I thought I could continue living apart from all those matters, I thought it had nothing to do with me. . . . I closed myself up here, to withdraw from the world, to live out the rest of my days in peace, far from all of them, far from everything."⁵⁶ Nevertheless, as Prospero enables the Red Death to enter so he can face the terrible figure in battle, Zabrodsky allows the Nazis into the castle in order to inform on their activities to the Resistance. The Nazi occupiers, never discovering the clock's function and Lena's hiding place, fail to fully penetrate the sanctuary, but Dora and Sand succeed. Both the count's cuckoo clock and the prince's ebony clock exist in a space otherwise determined to elude time altogether, and both signify the possibility of the failure of this chronotope by allowing destructive exterior forces to penetrate the place of refuge.

In Poe's story, the clock's chiming serves as a chilling reminder to the guests that time cannot be stopped, that nothing can prevent reality from invading even the most exquisitely designed fortresses. Goldberg's play offers a clock that has been manipulated to suggest precisely that humans *can* control time, most obviously in that keeping the clock unwound prevents the cuckoo from chiming the hour and singing its song. Nevertheless, the real finds its way in. Strikingly, the supposedly broken clock signifies the passageway between two disparate temporalities. On one end is a hideout quite literally mired in the exigencies of a past that no longer exists—the war that ended two years earlier. On the other is a present strangely suspended between another extinct past (old Europe) and the dream its extinction has spawned of a future-oriented realm that blurs the very boundary between the dead and the living, echoing Dora's fear that the past exerts a macabre power over the present. In this play, as in Poe's story, the boundary between inside and outside, a fundamental and primary division of space, collapses under the weight of time.

Futile Fortifications: Refuge as Death, Death as Refuge

The spatiotemporal tension encompassed within the clock finds expression in the castle as a whole, with dire implications for its protective function. The library of Goldberg's castle, for the most part a repository of the past, contains a few concessions to modernity. Zabrodsky insists, however, that their presence does nothing to compromise the castle's beauty: "I can introduce an electric kettle and a telephone into this ancient castle—it will bear it. But try to introduce this tapestry or this old bookcase into one of your modern, low-roofed crates—it simply can't be done! It would be ludicrous! Your crate would fall to pieces! . . . These modern lives, all cast in one mould, cannot tolerate beauty."[57] This sentiment links his Eastern European castle to another, famous one. Describing his surroundings in Count Dracula's castle, Jonathan Harker observes, "Unless my senses deceive me, the old centuries had, and have, powers of their own which mere 'modernity' cannot kill."[58] The beautiful past can bear incompatible temporalities and accept the present, but the present is inhospitable to beauty itself and therefore incapable of accommodating the past.

Even Dora does not attempt to refute that the past signifies art, culture, and beauty. To the contrary, her awareness of this signification catalyzes her terror "of being sentimental about this whole vanishing world." In her eyes, the seductions of the past are harbingers of death. "I know that its dangers aren't yet past," she tells Sand. "If you had to deal with children hiding in strange families, in monasteries—you'd see how this 'beauty' still grips them! . . . The dead, with skeleton hands, have fastened on to living children, and are pulling them down to the grave."[59] To Dora's mind, the beauty of art resuscitates the past, allows it to transgress the boundary of its own mortality, and invites it into the present, destabilizing seemingly steadfast temporalities.

While Dora envisions the past as a seductive corpse hungry for the flesh of the living, Zabrodsky blames the present (in the guise of communism's new world order) for the past's violent displacement and for his own annihilation:

> In 1918 the life I loved came to an end. The Empire was gone and what are we with all our titles and castles, without the Empire which was the crown of our existence from the very first? Nothing but ghosts, yes, ghosts! . . . And I—yes, what did I have left to do in such a world? It no longer had any meaning. And without meaning—there can be no life. So I died. . . . Yes, and I continued to eat, drink, sleep, move, but as a matter of fact I was dead—buried in this castle like an Egyptian King embalmed in his pyramid. . . . You asked me before, Madame, whether ghosts haunt this castle. Well, now you see such a one before your very eyes.[60]

Agents of destruction, the ideologies of the present have ravaged the past's beauty. For Zabrodsky, a mystical future offers the only bulwark against their violence, but he readily recognizes that he has already become a casualty of the savagery of the present. Dora, though she considers him a perpetrator rather than a victim, agrees: "He's dead, he's a corpse. That's the truth. He belongs to the world of the dead."[61] On the one hand, the castle is a glorious tomb for the living-dead man Zabrodsky.[62] On the other, it is a sanctuary: an architectural exemplar and safeguard of the beauty that has been lost in the outside world, the hideout that literally saved Lena's life during the war, and the haven from the storm for the Zionist emissaries.

The castle presents a readily apparent contradiction for Lena, as we have seen: its promise of protection is precisely what transforms the castle from her sanctuary to her prison. For Zabrodsky, too, the castle occupies a paradoxical double role, one similar to that of Prince Prospero's imperial suites, which also serve both to protect and to confine the prince and his guests. Both texts vividly portray the unreliability of the very concept of sanctuary and the slippage between what it is intended to do and what it ultimately does. Yet unlike Poe's prince, Goldberg's count readily identifies his sanctuary as also his grave, his castle as also a mausoleum. This awareness impels him to silence the cuckoo clock, the heart of the castle. Time, in his living-dead state, must be controlled, lest it control him. His state itself, however, is also a consequence of his desire to stop the external progression of time within the castle. The play once again positions diverse temporal trajectories at odds not only among themselves but also with the spatiality of the castle.

Given this chronotopic quagmire, Zabrodsky's orientation toward the future vis-à-vis the Fourth Kingdom he promises Lena is unsurprising. Nurturing faith in a future that will never arrive offers his only reprieve from the violence of the present and the irretrievable loss of the past. It also introduces another impossible trajectory into the play's already dissonant temporality, realigning their dynamics. For Zabrodsky, this mythical future offers protection from the aggressions of the present and a glimpse into the vanished past, the only escape from the finality of death. It is rooted in a Christian worldview, based on the Book of Revelation, that Zabrodsky has instilled in Lena, who quotes from it to the puzzled Zionist emissaries: "There will be no living and no dead there, no young and old. There will be a great love there and eternal grandeur, and he that overcometh shall not be hurt of the second death . . . and everything will be as it once was—only different!"[63] Diverging decidedly from Prince Prospero's desire to escape the inevitable future by suspending an artificially perpetuated present, this conviction in a mythical future releases the count's obligation to the real present.

Yet this haven of a perpetually unrealized future, too, proves fragile, when Lena discovers Zabrodsky's elaborate deception. His obsession with the future of the Fourth Kingdom and the glorious European past cannot restrain Lena's longing for *outside*. Even as he has constructed for her a world of illusions sustained by the castle's conflicting temporalities, her dreams center on a sensory present existing beyond its walls: on smelling the rain, feeling the grass, and seeing the moon. All the refinements of her prison cell—books, food, and beautiful dresses—cannot compensate for its stifling interiority and its paralyzed temporality. The almost forcible entry of Dora and Sand into the castle represents its penetration by external forces, exposing the artificiality of Zabrodsky's double sanctuary. The castle is revealed to have been Lena's prison and the dreams of the futural Fourth Kingdom to be fanciful and superfluous in the face of a promising present. Zabrodsky's elaborate chronotopic structure is impossible to sustain.

The play suggests that death itself offers the only truly secure haven. As Zabrodsky explains to Lena after revealing that he has known about the hidden poison in her locket all along, "I said nothing, Lena, because each of us is entitled to a refuge from his fellow man . . . Death."[64] The only true sanctuary is mortality, the only impenetrable boundary the one between life and death. Yet once again, the play denies this macabre resolution as soon as it proposes it. If Zabrodsky recounts the bitterness of his own existence as a ghoulish figure tortuously suspended between life and death, and even as a living-dead man, the reader can only understand that this potential refuge, too, has failed to protect him.

"The Lady of the Castle" and the Revision of Victimization

Perhaps the most paradigmatically gothic moment of the play occurs when Sand activates the clock and inadvertently sends Lena the signal to emerge from her dungeon hideaway, ghostlike and clad in the uniform of the gothic heroine, a white dress. Frightened and vulnerable, she finally believes Dora and Sand's insistence that the war has been over for two years and that she is free to go. However, defying expectations that she will leap at her newfound freedom, she hesitates and considers her options. She can accompany Dora and begin a new life in Israel, or she can stay with Zabrodsky and continue to inhabit the insular world of fantasy and the imagination that he has so carefully crafted and maintained within the castle. Ultimately, though she chooses to leave, she does so neither out of ideological conviction nor out of a feeling of betrayal at Zabrodsky's hands.[65] Most critical for her is her departure from the claustrophobic interior of the castle to the freedom and openness of the outside world, whether Israel or someplace else. The tension between the two poles represented by Dora, the seemingly one-dimensional Zionist ideologue, and Zabrodsky, who mourns the passing of beauty from the world of war and simplistic ideology, remains unresolved. Lena has managed not only to elude the Nazis throughout the war but also to make her own choice afterward. The only certainty regarding her life and her future is that they are now in her hands. Even her destination remains ambiguous: though the play ends with Lena joining Dora, she is uncommitted to Zionism and far from enthusiastic regarding her prospects in Israel.[66]

In Lena, Goldberg has written a different kind of victim, one who does not behave very much like a victim. In the context of 1950s Israel, a country still grappling with its conflicted and paradoxical self-definition in the wake of revelations about the extent of the horrors of the Holocaust, the presentation of such a victim-not-victim—strong, resilient, and autonomous—is unexpected and unusual. Goldberg's paradoxical "strong victim," neither a diasporic weakling nor a courageous hero fighting against all odds, bypasses the stereotype of victimhood in the Israeli collective consciousness in this period.[67] Evident in the postwar ambivalence regarding Holocaust victims, this stereotype supported the young nation's valorization of strength. It conceptualized European Jews as a living reminder of the diasporic powerlessness Zionists renounced, with the exception of the courageous few who had rebelled or resisted.[68] Lena neither succumbs to nor resists her experience as a victim. Rather, in a symbolic act, she changes out of the ethereal white dress of her captivity back to the clothes she wore when she first arrived at the castle, and through a considered leave-taking, she chooses to depart and begin life anew. Equally unswayed by her gratefulness to Zabrodsky for his protection and love, by her incredulity upon discovering that the war has ended, and by Dora's enticing portrait of Israel, she follows only her own desire for outside in making her decision to leave.

Several critics have discussed the play's representation of victimhood as innovative in this context of the Holocaust and, more specifically, of the Zionist Israeli perception of the Holocaust survivor.[69] The play's representation of victims is distinctive not only within its specific historical framework but also as an additional manifestation of Goldberg's use and dismantling of gothic conventions. The gothic, a mode heavily reliant on themes of imprisonment, fear, and victimization of the most blatant and unambiguous sort, lends itself naturally to representations of victims. The suffering heroine of classic British gothic texts—from Isabella in the inaugural gothic novel, Horace Walpole's *The Castle of Otranto* (1764), to the archetypical Adeline, Emily St. Aubert, and Ellena in Ann Radcliffe's novels *The Romance of the Forest* (1791), *The Mysteries of Udolpho* (1794), and *The Italian* (1797)—is pure and innocent. The valiant preservation of her innocence against tremendous odds anchors these lengthy, elaborate narratives. Some scholars have convincingly proposed that the naivete and helplessness of the typical gothic victim-heroine can be read as a subtly subversive performance, but such interpretations do not preclude the prototypical gothic preoccupation with victimization and oppression shaped by the external manifestation of these traits, whether affected or sincere.[70] Gothic persecutors—Walpole's Manfred, Radcliffe's array of Italian villains, Matthew Lewis's Ambrosio in *The Monk* (1796)—while occasionally complex, are driven, at least in some measure, by dark forces.

It is therefore not surprising that some Hebrew writers have turned to the gothic mode to express the victim/perpetrator dynamic in terms of a Western European literary language that transcends the immediate Jewish circumstances of the Holocaust narrative. Aharon Appelfeld, Savyon Liebrecht, Hana Bat-Shahar—all have addressed the Holocaust and its aftermath from within the dark and foreboding territory of gothic, tapping both the victim paradigm and the wellspring of horror and fear that informs it by invoking gothic setting, imagery, and metaphor. "The Lady of the Castle," however, like Jane Austen's *Northanger Abbey* (1817), not only makes use of gothic literature's formulae but also deconstructs them, establishing itself as part of an intertextual web. When Zabrodsky wishes Dora and Sand a pleasant night's sleep, Dora responds by asking, half-jokingly, if the castle is haunted. "Of course," he responds. "All old castles are haunted!"

DORA: Then I'll really have a pleasant sleep! I'll dream about all the English novels I read about as a child. Sand, I'm sure you never read ghost stories! . . .

SAND: I can very well imagine: "And at night, when the clock in the tower struck twelve times, and all the inhabitants of the castle were deep in sleep, there appeared the ghost of the beauteous Lady of the Castle" . . . is that it?

DORA: Exactly! When I was thirteen, those ghosts wouldn't let me shut my eyes at night!

ZABRODSKY: There is nothing fearful about ghosts. . . .

DORA: [*To Sand*] I'll always remember the chill that used to grip me when I read those novels. Ghosts walking through the night; and secret doors opening, and choked voices howling from the cellar . . .

SAND: Naturally! If the castle is haunted by ghosts, it stands to reason that there should be hidden cellars and labyrinths and secret doors in the walls. I'm sure you'll find all these here as well.[71]

Curiously, the English translation omits the phrase that follows Zabrodsky's statement, in the original Hebrew, that there is nothing fearful about ghosts: "Reality is more terrible." In the context of the lighthearted conversation about the conventions of gothic literature, Zabrodsky's statement contrasting ghosts with the terrors of the real world stresses the difference between the explicitly fictional fear produced by the gothic and the horrors of the real. Having been stripped of its significance and transformed into an empty symbol after World War I, the stylized castle has taken on the air of gothic fictionality that distances it from the real, paralleling the operation of gothic literature itself.[72]

In the midst of the conversation about those "English novels" that frightened Dora as a girl, the anxious Zabrodsky curtly denies the existence of hidden dungeons and secret passageways in the castle, cutting short Sand's prescient jesting. The humorous exchange between Dora and Sand parodies the reality soon to be revealed to them. Eventually, the audience learns about Lena, the sole survivor of a murdered family, hidden for years under the noses of the Nazi soldiers who were using the castle as their headquarters. Lena's underground chamber can be opened only from the inside, and a secret sign, the clock's striking ten o'clock, alerts her that she can safely emerge from her hideout to the elaborate castle library. The play's gothic hue deepens upon the revelation that Zabrodsky has kept Lena in her hideout even after the war has ended, never revealing that the war is over because he loves her and wants to prevent her departure. Lena escapes the Nazi threat, but her potential victimization at their hands is transformed, unbeknownst to her, into a genuine one at Zabrodsky's. At the same time, however, she defies this position through the agency she retains over her body and over her life. She not only returns Zabrodsky's romantic feelings but actually initiates intimate relations with him. In an even more defiant assertion of her agency, she secretly wears a poison locket, "a way out."[73]

The intertextual dialogue established with British gothic narratives via ghosts, castles, and secret doors comes to a head in the play's representation of victimization. Goldberg's treatment of this poetics of victimization, however, is more complex than a cursory reading reveals. It exemplifies her simultaneous reliance on and unraveling of a characteristic gothic motif: like the disjointed gothic temporalities that inform the play, the paradox of the victim-not-victim is a formative component of the insecure sanctuary. It forces the reader to confront discomfiting questions about the nature of victimhood and suggests a deeply unsettling ambiguity regarding the spatial dynamics of safety and danger and the past's relationship to the present and the future. These ambiguities, in turn, reflect the mutually informing dialectic of dynamic reality and static art. Such a reading brings us back to Poe's story, as well, in which the privileged victims' relationship to art, intended to stop time and thereby ward off evil, ultimately cannot prevent its entry. Given its instability, the sanctuary inevitably fails to protect those inside, instead transforming them to victims. In Goldberg's play, the penetrability of the sanctuary endangers Lena but ultimately allows her to depart and overcome her victimization.

Yet the same castle that protected her entombs Zabrodsky. Perhaps even more unusual and compelling than Goldberg's paradoxical "strong victim" is her suggestion that Zabrodsky is in some ways himself a victim, a notion that puts the play at odds with the gothic convention of clear boundaries between persecutor and persecuted.[74] Zabrodsky, already a complex character thanks to the dual role he plays as Lena's protector and jailer, is a man whose world has vanished before his very eyes, leaving him hovering in the liminal zone separating life from death. It is a position he occupies with far more nuance than Lena, who is concerned primarily with the conventional sensory and spatial experience of the freedom she can finally enjoy, not with analyzing her years of necessary and unnecessary confinement. Perhaps the result of decades of contemplation, Zabrodsky's eloquence on his world's persecution and, ultimately, its annihilation by communism and by Nazism provides a highly articulate and far-reaching portrait of victimization, one that reverberates beyond the horrors of the gas chambers to a subtler, less corporeal experience.[75] Understood thus, Zabrodsky, whose perpetual mourning for a massacred world suggests a point of identification with Goldberg, is no less than a radical character in the Israel of the late 1950s.

The Nation-Sanctuary and Art

A concern with Jewish national identity underpins the play's events, both in the Zionist grappling with Holocaust victims and survivors and in attitudes toward the Jewish past. In the context of sanctuary, these concerns become even more pressing. There is no doubt that Leah Goldberg supported the Zionist endeavor: she believed in the Jewish right to self-determination and in a national culture rooted in the Hebrew language. Yet, as many scholars have pointed out, her Zionism was not without its qualms and anxieties regarding what she termed "cultural fascism."[76] The myopic perspective attributed in Goldberg's diaries to the irascible Kariv, valorizing ideology and dismissing art, finds expression in "The Lady of the Castle" through Dora. She elicits Zabrodsky's disgust and his most cynical lines in the play: "Do you hear, Lena. . . . You could have been living in this earthly paradise of theirs. You could have wandered with refugee convoys, looked for work, struggled with hunger, filth, ugliness until you dropped . . . and instead you were held captive here."[77] Zabrodsky's scathing portrait, the dark side of Dora's sunny portrayal of Israel, contrasts a questionable freedom, characterized by "filth" and "ugliness," with an attractive captivity nestled among the castle's many material and cultural treasures. In his view, the nation-state that offers political freedom and reentry into reality actually incarcerates spiritually through difficulty and unsightliness. The castle-prison, meanwhile, emancipates one's soul through art and beauty. The illusion, argues Zabrodsky, is not his but theirs, the Zionists', who try to sell Lena an "earthly paradise" that does not really exist, an illusory ideal. Their haven depends no less on artifice and deception than does his own. For Zabrodsky, freedom is not a literal commodity, worthy in its own right. Freedom loses all value without beauty, while beauty is capable of transforming even a jail cell into a kingdom.

The notion of a nation-sanctuary stripped of reverence for culture, and indeed even based on a denial and denigration of this culture's beauty, is eviscerated in Zabrodsky's statement. His dismissal of Dora's nationalism establishes another of the play's disruptions of gothic conventions. Whereas British gothic literature helped create a sense of British national identity by highlighting the foreignness of the figures and forces that threatened its order and homogeneity, in this play Zabrodsky disavows these ideas, inviting a Jewish girl to share his apolitical utopia of art.[78] Though Hanan Hever and others have characterized it as "a Zionist play," "The Lady of the Castle" reflects Goldberg's conflicted Zionism by calling into question the way Hebrew national culture was defining itself.[79]

Clearly, Goldberg is troubled by the notion that a nation must isolate itself from the world to realize its ideological potential. A haven for traumatized refugees cannot sever the art and beauty that can nourish their souls because these were associated with a brutal past. A true sanctuary must lay claim to culture, not relinquish it to violent forces—and this means that a sanctuary's boundaries must, by definition, be penetrable. Goldberg recognizes this principle in her poetic practice itself: she sought sanctuary in writing poetry from a world gone mad. The madness she tried to defy through poetry was, first and foremost, the frenzy of ideologies gone wild, whether those ideologies were literally murderous or intellectually and aesthetically destructive.

In September 1939, Goldberg published an essay, "Al oto ha-noseh atsmo" (On the very same subject), about the poet's role in wartime. In it, she argues provocatively that "the poet is not only allowed to write a love poem in wartime, he *must* do so, because in wartime, too, the value of life is greater than that of murder. It is not simply the right of the poet in terrible times to sing his song to nature, to the flowering trees, to children who know how to laugh, but an *obligation*, the obligation to remind man that he is still a man."[80] This conviction confirms Goldberg's rejection of "mobilized literature" (ספרות מגויסת), to which most of her fellow poets subscribed. Her essay sparked a heated debate among the leading poets of Hebrew modernism: Avraham Shlonsky believed that poets should be silent in the face of war, while Nathan Alterman believed that "literature and poetry could not afford to remain silent in the face of this assault on the spirit of humanity."[81] For Goldberg, however, "a wheat field will forever be better and more beautiful than a barren wilderness (שממה) upon which tanks have passed, even if the goal of those tanks is the most noble."[82] Poetry offers a bulwark of good against the proliferating barbarism of the world. It was not, however, only many of her fellow poets who found fault with this view, but, as Lieblich points out, also Goldberg herself, who admitted in "Ha-omets le-ḥulin" that artists cannot escape their reality.[83] "The Lady of the Castle" can be understood as a representation of her struggle with these contradictory positions. Art, then, offers sanctuary from reality, but like the beautiful castle of her play and the imperial suites of Poe's story, its boundaries must be porous. For Goldberg, *not* writing poetry after Auschwitz would be barbaric.

As evident in both texts, art can create and maintain the conditions for an otherwise impossible heterochrony, in which the past, the present, and the future interact and overpower the fences and walls of seemingly secure spaces. "The Lady of the Castle" reworks multiple gothic devices to enable this heterochrony. It calls on clichéd aesthetic conventions, such as the old castle, the late hour, and the raging storm, but it positions them as accessories to a contemporary debate. It incorporates familiar thematic features, such as the secret door, the hidden girl, and the revelation of her deceitful imprisonment, but it resists presenting her as a helpless victim. Most critically, it represents the diverse, disjointed temporalities that structure these colliding worlds, signified by the great clock, without attempting to integrate or organize them. In reinterpreting these gothic elements, Goldberg's play acknowledges the ambivalence and ambiguity accompanying the development of Hebrew national culture less than a decade after the Holocaust.

As the most catastrophic event in modern Jewish history, the Holocaust made a case for a Jewish national haven even as it demonstrated the fragility of the seemingly civilized sanctuaries of culture and art that preceded it. The harrowing experiences of those subjected to the torments of the Holocaust lend themselves all too well to the terror of the gothic. Goldberg's reconfiguration of the gothic mode in "The Lady of the Castle," however, defies expectations. Instead of merely applying the gothic to the wartime European milieu for which it is so eminently suited, she appropriates it to produce a far more nuanced articulation of her contemporary ideological context and the cultural questions it raised. She offers a platform for questioning the seemingly unassailable and antithetical categories of victim and oppressor at a delicate historical moment for such an investigation. It is a stance in accordance with the complexity and tension underpinning her view of the European past and the Zionist present, and the cultural and ethical implications that these encompassed a mere decade into statehood. Art, seductive and illusory, can serve both life and death; the real, banal and utilitarian, can be just or barbaric. Literature, unlike national homelands but very much like Goldberg's castle and Poe's imperial suites, constructs its boundaries with an eye to their inevitable trespass. As we shall see in the next chapter, though, the construction of national homelands, too, inadvertently incorporates the very mechanism of their susceptibility, leaving them unable to prevent the specters of history from infiltrating their fortifications.

Notes

1. Goldberg, *Yomaney Lea Goldberg*, 318.
2. Moshe Shamir's novel *Be-mo yadav: Pirkey Elik* (*With His Own Hands*), about a quintessential Zionist hero who dies in the war of 1948, opens with the famous line "Elik came from the sea," establishing Elik as a representative of an entirely new, authentic Hebrew culture. This metaphor occupies a central but by now successfully contested spot in the Israeli cultural imagination.
3. For more on the changing attitudes toward translated Hebrew in the Yishuv, see Z. Shavit, "Status of Translated Literature." For a recent study on the role of translation in the development of modern Hebrew poetics, see Jacobs, *Strange Cocktail*; the study opens with an illuminating discussion of the Kariv incident, focusing on his charge that Goldberg was contributing to a "translated nation" at odds with Zionist national culture.

4. Goldberg, *Yomaney Lea Goldberg*, 319.
5. Sa'aroni, "Be-kele ha-intimiyut," 4.
6. These were questions with which Goldberg and others struggled on a personal level, as well. As Yfaat Weiss notes, Goldberg's novel *Letters from an Imaginary Journey* (1937) constitutes "Goldberg's literary attempt to turn her back on Europe and sever all ties with the Berlin she loved so dearly" ("Nothing in My Life," 364).

Today, the concept of a common collective memory among Israeli Jews continues to be challenged by widely varied experiences of immigration, absorption, and cultural, ethnic, and linguistic backgrounds. Yet Israel has deemphasized this diversity to promote a shared collective memory shaped by the traumatic experiences of European Jews, particularly the Holocaust. The perception of Israel as European is informed by a paradox: political Zionism was born in Europe, and the idealistic Zionist "pioneers" (*ḥalutsim*) who established the state were Europeans. Yet as the site of the near annihilation of its Jews, Europe evokes an ambivalent nostalgia.

7. Goldberg's earlier poetic works especially acknowledge her troubled but deep attachment to Europe. See, for example, the collections *Taba'ot ashan* [Smoke rings, 1935], *Shir ba-kfarim* [Songs in the villages, 1942], and *Mi-beyti ha-yashan* [From my old home, 1944]. Her academic studies and translations, too, reflect her attempt to bring Hebrew literature into conversation with European culture. Goldberg helped found the Department of Comparative Literature at the Hebrew University, which she chaired until her death in 1970. Amya Lieblich notes that Goldberg's prolific translations and her academic research and lectures on European literature established her as a representative of European culture in Israel (Lieblich, "Al ba'alat ha-armon," 144). Michael Gluzman writes that though Goldberg expressed her love for the Land of Israel in her poetry, her "close affiliation with European culture [was] perceived as evidence of her lack of commitment to the emerging national culture," rendering her "a liminal figure in a hegemonic coterie" (Gluzman, *Politics of Canonicity*, 64).
8. Known as the "denigration of diaspora" (שלילת הגלות), this phenomenon engendered tensions between Jews and their histories. For more on the denigration of diaspora, see Schweid, "Rejection of Diaspora"; for a critique, see Raz-Karkotzkin, "Galut be-tokh ribonut"; for a critical historical reassessment, see Shapira, "Le-an halkhah shlilat ha-galut."
9. Alter, "Observations," 85. Goldberg's first collection of poetry, *Taba'ot ashan* [Smoke rings, 1935], published the year of her arrival in Palestine, is notable for its depiction of the landscapes and architecture of her past in Christian Europe, including monasteries. Her poetic preoccupation with such spaces attests to her complex identity, informed by both her European past and her Palestinian/Israeli present. This complexity has yielded a wide range of interpretations. For example, Gluzman describes it as an "inability to feel fully at home in either of her homelands" (*Politics of Canonicity*, 63), while Jacobs casts it not as an exilic position of loss but in terms of a generative, translational in-between-ness (*Strange Cocktail*, 120).
10. Weisman, "After All of This," 239. Weisman writes that the concept of the courage for the mundane is useful "for anyone who yearns for the whole and runs into the insulting and at the same time comforting limits of reality; and for anyone addicted to the exalted, the singular, the sublime, and the beautiful, but repelled by the indulgence of decadence or the self-righteousness of ideology" (ibid., 223). The essay argues for "the constant and necessary dialectic of art as such, under all conditions and at all times" (ibid., 225). Weisman specifies that though Goldberg did not mobilize the concept of the courage for the mundane specifically in the context of Nazism, she uses it "as a type of formula or paradigm for any act of self-transcendence or ethical conduct in times of crisis, resonating the one possible response

when a total or totalitarian ideological position gains the upper hand over human culture" (ibid., 235).

11. Adorno, "Cultural Criticism and Society" (1949). Adorno later reconsidered his famous statement in *Negative Dialectics* (1966): "Perennial suffering has as much right to expression as a tortured man has to scream; hence it may have been wrong to say that after Auschwitz you could no longer write poems" (362). Interestingly, his disavowal of his earlier assertion misrepresents the latter: he originally wrote not that it was impossible to write poems after Auschwitz, but that it was *barbaric* to do so.

12. Adorno, "Cultural Criticism and Society," 34.

13. The motif of the beloved woman isolated from modernity is central to several well-known gothic or gothically inflected works, such as Nathaniel Hawthorne's story "Rappaccini's Daughter" (1844), Poe's poem "Annabel Lee" (1849), Charlotte Brontë's novel *Jane Eyre* (1847), and numerous other nineteenth-century texts. Goldberg, a voracious reader and prolific translator, was certainly acquainted with these texts and may well have been influenced by their heroines while writing the play. In a journal entry dated September 29, 1939, she relates having read Charlotte Brontë's *Jane Eyre* (Goldberg, *Yomaney Lea Goldberg*, 267). I am grateful to Adriana X. Jacobs for bringing my attention to this point.

14. See, for example, G. Shaked, "Maḥaze siaḥ," 189, 199; Feingold, "Armon yafe akh lo li-mgurim," 37; Abramson, *Modern Hebrew Drama*, 119; and Dorot, *Nahar lelo gadot*, 99.

15. Weber, "Edgar Poe," 97. For a useful and comprehensive review of the literature on Poe's preoccupation with time, see Zimmerman, "*Allegoria, Chronographia*," 51.

16. For more on Hebrew translations of Poe, see Dykman, "Poe's Poetry." See also the introduction to this study, specifically "Gothic in Hebrew Translation: A Brief Nonhistory."

17. Tsurit, "Sofrim mesaprim al yetsiratam," 6.

18. Poe, "Masque of Red Death," 136.

19. Ibid.

20. Ibid.

21. Ibid.

22. Ibid.

23. Youth Aliyah, or *aliyat ha-no'ar*, is an organization that was established in 1933 to rescue Jewish children, bringing them from continental Europe to Great Britain and Palestine before and during the war. After the war, Youth Aliyah recovered children who had survived the Holocaust from displaced persons camps and elsewhere and relocated them to Israel. The word *aliyah*, literally "ascent," is the official term designating Jewish immigration to Israel.

24. The linguistic dynamics of the play are worth consideration. Though performed in Hebrew, the conversations presumably occur in multiple languages: Dora and Sand speak Hebrew between themselves and an unspecified European language—most likely German, Polish, or Czech—with the others. This implicit linguistic multiplicity brings another dimension of chronotopy to the play, as each language carries within it not only a geographic affiliation but also a historic one, correlating to different phases in the characters' lives.

25. Goldberg, "Lady of the Castle," 247. Unless otherwise noted, all quotations from the play are from the English translation by T. Carmi.

26. Bakhtin, *Dialogic Imagination*, 245–47.

27. Ibid., 246.

28. Ibid.

29. Goldberg, "Ba'alat ha-armon," 36.

30. Ibid., 37; Goldberg, "Lady of the Castle," 267.

31. Goldberg, "Lady of the Castle," 271.
32. Ibid., 270–71.
33. Ibid., 306.
34. Ibid., 312.
35. Sa'aroni, "Be-kele ha-intimiyut," 4.
36. De Man, "Rhetoric of Temporality."
37. Bakhtin develops this concept in his bildungsroman essay; see especially *Speech Genres*, 33–34. Morson and Emerson explain their choice of the word *heterotropy* over the word *multitemporality* because of Bakhtin's intent to parallel the concept to heteroglossia, and also because it stresses variety over plurality (*Mikhail Bakhtin*, 489n12). For more on heterochrony, see Morson and Emerson, *Mikhail Bakhtin*, 368–69, 416–17, 424, 426.
38. Ricoeur, "Narrative Time," 169.
39. Molesworth, "Gothic Time, Sacred Time," 29.
40. Ibid., 36, 39.
41. Ibid., 40.
42. See, for example, Weber, "Edgar Poe," 85; and Zimmerman, "*Allegoria, Chronographia*," 53–54.
43. Poe, "Masque of Red Death," 137–38.
44. Ibid., 139.
45. Ibid., 141.
46. Ibid.
47. W. Freedman, *Porous Sanctuary*, 141.
48. Ibid.
49. Ibid.
50. Ibid., 141–42.
51. Goldberg, *Barak ba-boker*, 39
52. Ibid.
53. Goldberg, "Lady of the Castle," 259, 258, 259–60.
54. Ibid., 274.
55. G. Shaked, "Maḥaze siaḥ," 189.
56. Goldberg, "Lady of the Castle," 269.
57. Ibid., 258.
58. Stoker, *Dracula*, 43.
59. Goldberg, "Lady of the Castle," 274.
60. Ibid., 266–67.
61. Ibid., 296.
62. This living-dead man should be distinguished from *ha-met ha-ḥai*, the living-dead figure made famous by the poet Nathan Alterman, which, as noted in the introduction to this study, became a well-known motif in Hebrew poetry of the twentieth century. Alterman's living dead appears in his poetry at times as an acknowledgment of the force of life over death and at others as a symbol of national sacrifice. For an outline of the development of this figure in Alterman's poetry, see Bartana, "Image of the 'Living-Dead.'" Bartana interprets ha-met ha-ḥai in Alterman's earlier poetry as a signification of "the conjoined force of life and art" and as the "power that overcomes death," offering a compelling counterpoint to the living-dead Zabrodsky as representing the failure of art to triumph over death (Bartana, "Image of the 'Living-Dead,'" 185).

63. Goldberg, "Lady of the Castle," 285.

64. Ibid., 313.

65. Hamutal Bar-Yosef reads Lena's difficult choice to leave behind European culture as a parallel to Goldberg's own "choice" in "Ha-omets le-ḥulin," which in her interpretation relays a far more decisive Goldberg than in Weisman's reading: "Much like Goldberg herself, [Lena] chooses the non-Romantic possibility, representing the choice of life and 'the courage for the mundane'" (Bar-Yosef, *Lea Goldberg*, 255).

66. Upon its premiere in 1959, "The Lady of the Castle" garnered critical praise for lifting Israeli drama out of its self-perceived provincial rut by posing universal questions. More recently, scholars have read it in a more subversive light, asserting its "ideologically incorrect" response to the Holocaust and its less than wholehearted embrace of Zionist ideology. See, for example, Brenner, who argues that the play demonstrates "Goldberg's dissent from the Zionist vision. Instead of predicating the survivor's restoration in the national homeland upon obliteration of the European roots, Goldberg saw post-Holocaust redemption in the establishment of new patterns of Christian-Jewish relationships in the spirit of the Enlightenment" ("Responses to the Holocaust," 5–6). Hever writes about the play in the context of the trauma of the Holocaust, asserting that Goldberg's play criticizes "the lack of the culture in Israel in coping with the grief and the pain of the Holocaust. As such, [Goldberg] pointed to the efforts of Zionism to work toward a quick, raw redemption . . . , which the culture in the state of Israel tied to an intensive teleological narrative of 'from Holocaust to rebirth'" ("Ha-trauma," 266–67). See also Kosh-Zohar, who proposes that the play offers a different perspective on the dynamics between Zionists and Holocaust survivors. She interprets Lena's decision to leave the castle as "a personal decision that has no link to the Zionist vision. This is perhaps the most subversive step of the play, which avoids creating a clear link between Lena the survivor and Zionism in general" (Kosh-Zohar, "Ma haya koreh," 340).

67. For more on Zionist attitudes to the Holocaust from the 1950s to the 1980s and their literary representations, see Brenner, "Responses to the Holocaust," especially 2–4; and Abramson, *Drama and Ideology*, chap. 7, "The Political Uses of the Holocaust."

68. A more recent metamorphosis of the victim position offers another model, a product of a cynical politics situating the Israeli Jew as always already the victim of the Arab world in a grotesque, uninterrupted continuation of what is perceived as the perpetual, centuries-long victimization of Jews at the hands of Christian Europe. This appropriation of the victim position represents a marked departure from the original Israeli ambivalence regarding the victim, whose weakness was at odds with the idealized figure of the "New Jew." For a detailed study of the mobilization of the Holocaust in Israeli national culture, see Zertal, *Israel's Holocaust*.

69. For more on Lena as defying the Israeli stereotype of the Holocaust survivor, see Kosh-Zohar, "Ma haya koreh," especially 337–40. Kosh-Zohar also notes the complex and occasionally deeply problematic regard of Israeli Jews toward Holocaust survivors in the postwar period (ibid., 338n16). At the same time that Holocaust survivors were regarded with disdain because of their supposed passivity, a culture of glorification arose in Israel around tales of heroic Jewish acts in the face of impossible odds during the Holocaust. Hever writes that "Goldberg opposed the distorted mobilization of the Holocaust" in the service of nationalist conceptions of bravery and that her play raises the question of Zionist culpability in Lena's frustration and disappointment on learning that her relations in Palestine never mentioned her to Sand ("Ha-trauma," 270). Kosh-Zohar interprets the scene similarly, noting that this implication of culpability was, in the 1950s, "highly irregular" ("Ma haya koreh," 339).

70. For a valuable outline of the development of scholarship on gender and the gothic, see Smith and Wallace, "Female Gothic." On the interpretation of gothic victim-heroines as subversive, see Hoeveler, *Gothic Feminism*. For more on "gothic feminism," see chap. 2 of this study.

71. Goldberg, "Lady of the Castle," 260.

72. For more on the notion of "safe fictional distancing" as a function of the gothic production of fear, see Hogle, "Hyper-reality," 166.

73. Goldberg, "Lady of the Castle," 288.

74. This characterization is not to deny that gothic villains occasionally suffer hideous punishment for their actions. Ambrosio in Matthew Lewis's notorious novel *The Monk* offers a memorable example.

75. Shaked goes so far as to assert that Zabrodsky is "more a victim of reality than the young woman he imprisoned.... [This] understanding teaches us that the author regards time as a negative force and has in her soul a deep love for the world of the past" ("Maḥaze siaḥ," 198–99). While there is no question that Goldberg revered the culture of the past, her reverence, as we have seen, was tempered not only by her recognition of its violence but also by her own prolific contributions to the creation of Hebrew culture, which was shaped, in Palestine, as notably present centered.

76. Goldberg, *Yomaney Lea Goldberg*, 319. See n. 7 on Lieblich and Gluzman. In *Lea Goldberg, monografya*, Ruebner writes about the play's expressions of *zarut*, otherness or foreignness; see especially 147–49. See also Gordinsky, *Bi-shlosha nofim*; Schachter, *Diasporic Modernisms*; and Jacobs, *Strange Cocktail*.

77. Goldberg, "Lady of the Castle," 301.

78. For more on "the Gothic's successful imagining of a nationalist community," see Wein, *British Identities*, 3. For a study of the depiction of Jews as a counterforce in British gothic literature's shaping of British national identity, see Davison, *Anti-Semitism*.

79. Hever, "Ha-trauma," 270.

80. Goldberg, "Al oto ha-noseh atsmo," 9–10 (emphasis in original).

81. Miron, *From Continuity to Contiguity*, 170.

82. Goldberg, "Al oto ha-noseh atsmo," 9–10. For more on this debate, see Miron, *From Continuity to Contiguity*, 168–70; and U. Shavit, *Lo hakol havalim va-hevel*.

83. Lieblich, "Al ba'alat ha-armon," 141. For more on Goldberg's changing position regarding the responsibility of the artist in the context of her relationship to symbolism and allegory, see Hever, "Ha-trauma," 271.

PART 2
HAUNTED NATION

4

DARK JERUSALEM

Amos Oz's Anxious Literary Cartography between 1948 and 1967

Forty years after the publication of his novel *Mikhael sheli* (*My Michael*, 1968), Amos Oz claimed that its unrelenting narrator, Hana Gonen, haunted him, compelling him to tell her story: "Hana's character took control of me from the inside to such an extent that I began to speak with her tongue and to dream her dreams at night.... She came whence she came, entered me, and wouldn't leave me alone.... I was forced to write the book to get rid of her and return to my life...: far away from Hana Gonen, from her love on its way to dying, and from her gloomy Jerusalem."[1] Kibbutz Hulda, where Oz had been living since his departure from Jerusalem in 1953, allowed him one day a week to devote to his writing, "but before long Hana forced [him] to write her story not only on Thursdays but on all the days of the week."[2] Each night, he would shut himself in his home's tiny bathroom and "write what Hana transcribed to me.... The truth was that I struggled against her with all my might."[3] He recalls their ongoing argument about his role as an author and hers as a character: "You shut up and write," she commanded. "Write what I say and don't get involved."[4] It is a remarkable illustration of writing as exorcism. Possessed by a character who appeared out of thin air and disrupted his life, Oz had no choice but to tell her story. Though he wrote the novel to exorcise her, Hana herself is described in terms of captivity. She, too, is haunted: she turns to Oz to exorcise her own ghosts and to free herself from "the sorrow of her entrapment" in a threatening, claustrophobic Jerusalem.[5]

Oz wrote *My Michael* in the volatile months leading up to the Six-Day War, a period characterized by increased tensions along the border with

Syria, Jordan, and Egypt. Completed mere weeks before the outbreak of war, the novel is set in Jerusalem and narrated from the perspective of Hana, a young woman relating the events of her life in the decade spanning from 1950 to 1960. Oz describes Jerusalem's gothic atmosphere in *My Michael* as beyond his authorial control, "a divided Jerusalem that turned out (שיצאה לי) wintery, gloomy, and threatening."[6] He muses that, had he not finished writing *My Michael* when he did, he would surely have never finished: "Within six weeks [of completing the novel], they blew a ram's horn by the Western Wall and the air was filled with 'Jerusalem of Gold,' which is the opposite of the Jerusalem of Hana and Michael," a city "that no longer exists."[7] The newly united "Jerusalem of Gold," accompanied by the victorious notes of the ram's horn, was not one in which Oz felt comfortable. His unease with the triumphant sensibility that would crystallize weeks after the novel's completion is foreshadowed by the darkness of Hana's city. The greatest threat to her Jerusalem, the novel suggests, is neither the Arab villages that surround it nor its foreboding geography, but rather something that the heroines—both the city and the woman—harbor within: the ambivalence that accompanied 1948. As confirmed by Oz's essay "Ir zara" ("An Alien City," 1968), about his visit to Jerusalem immediately after the war, this ambivalence would grow to explicit doubt in the aftermath of 1967.

In *My Michael*, I argue, 1950s Jerusalem is the conduit to the specter of its most recent conflict, the 1948 war, which presages the violence and moral quagmire to come two decades after the establishment of the state. Drawing from key elements of gothic spatiality, Oz creates a Jerusalem that expresses the anxieties of the first decade of Israeli statehood, exposing their persistence and continued relevance on the eve of the Six-Day War. Over and above the accumulation of history at the city's base, Oz enhances Jerusalem's inherent gothicism to contend with a historical moment formative in his own experience and in Zionist history, a moment that would return in triumph and ambivalence in Israeli culture and historiographic discourse. As in previous chapters, this chapter identifies the gothic operating on two interrelated levels: the gothic aesthetic helps create the conditions for a distinctive engagement with time and history that is, itself, gothic.[8] As chapter 3 showed, time and its accoutrements help shape the gothic engagement with space. By representing time not as an object of the gothic but as its undistilled expression, Oz offers a different engagement with the mode.

In what follows, I identify Hana Gonen's obsessive fear of time in *My Michael* as the driving force of the novel's gothicism. The fear of time, I argue, is translated through her identification with Jerusalem into a broader gothic historicity that evokes fears for Israel's future. Oz's dark city is laced with paranoia, a psychic state related in the novel to a particular mode of engagement with time, and with images and symbols of the past that threaten the fragile stability of the present. The specter of 1948 bides its time within and around Jerusalem, in its hostile landscape, its stony architecture, its fences, boundaries, partitions, and enclosures. Hana Gonen's deteriorating mental state as it relates to the city indicates her increasing susceptibility to its threats, culminating in a violence with which she is complicit and evoking dread and anxiety.

I begin by mapping Oz's representation of the city's divisions and partitions in the context of the paranoia that permeates it. Jerusalem is surrounded by a threatening natural geography, cleaved by war into zones that are forbidden and allowed, and carved into neighborhoods based on residents' ethnicity, religion, and socioeconomic class. These partitions, as we shall see, both breed paranoia and attempt to assuage it. After outlining the city's geopolitical divisions, I turn to the explicitly gothic paradigms of the labyrinth and the crypt to show how the city's spatiality instigates the restless turns of Hana's mind and to examine the tension between enclosure and transgression that characterizes her experience of the city. I then consider Hana's physical movements in this labyrinthine space in terms of gothic flânerie, a revised mode of the Benjaminian paradigm of walking in the city, which encompasses Hana's intimacy with Jerusalem as well as the profound anxiety it evokes in her. These complementary affects lead to Hana's recognition and dread of the monster occupying the center of the labyrinth: time itself, the handmaiden of death, Hana's greatest fear. Jerusalem, for Hana, signifies time: inevitable, omnipotent, relentless, destructive. The sensation of the uncanny that accompanies Hana's paranoid engagement with Jerusalem implicitly points to the cyclical temporality of the city itself, whose histories of conquest and defeat are repeated ad nauseam via their symbolic representatives in the city. Finally, I argue that Jerusalem's temporality as it is expressed in Hana's troubled inner world speaks to a broader conceptualization of Israeli history, whereby 1948 is the latest event to return, to haunt Hana's present, and to herald an uncertain future.

Oz's spectral 1948 complements and contrasts with Shaul Setter's conceptualization of 1948 as a "speculative temporality" in S. Yizhar's oeuvre. Yizhar's "persistent return to 1948," argues Setter, indicates his "refusal of the time of state sovereignty." Yizhar accommodates the dynamic *revenance* of 1948, which is "a time that seems itself to keep returning in different historical moments."⁹ In works clearly not "invested in the present," Yizhar returns to 1948 again and again to confront and engage with it, defying its historical end and suspending it in a perpetual *"yet to begin."*¹⁰ In Oz's novel, on the other hand, the possibility that 1948 has not truly ended is the source of ambivalence and fear. Straddling numerous temporalities (its writing in the 1960s, its action in the 1950s, and its haunting by 1948), *My Michael* addresses anxieties about the present and future; 1948 is the force that returns to rupture the present that tries to resist it. As a primary site of these persistent returns, Hana's Jerusalem indicates, ominously, the ephemerality of sovereignty. Before tracing her anxious explorations of the city's shadowy contours, however, I consider the darkness of Oz's 1950s Jerusalem: as a literal phenomenon, darkness helps historicize power relations in the city; as a metaphorical one, it aids and abets the city's gothic machinations.

City of Many Nights

The Jerusalem of *My Michael*, a topos of uncertainty, is emphatically gothic in its stony buildings and perpetually wintery sky, in the hostile forces encircling the city and lurking just beneath its surface, and in the psychic and spatial transgressions it engenders. But the city is also literally dark. The development of a centralized electric grid in Palestine during the British Mandate period helped delineate a coherent Jewish national space and "civilize" the region by literally enlightening it according to the most technologically sophisticated methods and with the full support of the mandatory authorities.¹¹ The construction of the hydroelectric powerhouse in 1932 according to the grand scale conceptualized by the Jewish engineer Pinhas Rutenberg constituted a central material manifestation of the implementation of the vision of the Balfour Declaration, as Fredrik Meiton has shown.¹² The intimate relation between electric power and political power claimed through nationalist ideology is by no means unique to Israel/Palestine. Observing the significant role of lighting and blackouts in defining English national identity during World War II, Sara Wasson argues that darkness "unsettled people's relationship with their city and capital. Prewar urban illumination had become closely tied to rhetorics of nationhood."¹³ In *My Michael*, frequent references to dim street lanterns, sooty paraffin lamps, power outages, fog, clouds, and shadows underscore Jerusalem's darkness, at odds with the city's official status as the modern capital of a newly sovereign Israel. This darkness, literal and metaphorical, that governs the streets of Jerusalem intensifies the sense of the unknown, contributing to the fear and paranoia that the city induces: "In winter, at night, the buildings of Jerusalem look like gray shapes against a black backcloth. A landscape pregnant with suppressed violence."[14] Darkness creates anxiety in the urban space. Lighting produces a sense of security in the city by distancing it from nature, as Walter Benjamin observes. "The appearance of the street as an *intérieur* in which the phantasmagoria of the flâneur is concentrated is hard to separate from the gas lighting," he notes. "This way of increasing safety in the city made the crowds feel at home in the open streets even at night, and removed the starry sky from the ambience of the big city more effectively than tall buildings had ever done."[15]

In *My Michael*, the city itself is an *intérieur*—not a secure place of dazzling lighting but a claustrophobic space of flickering and broken lamps. Nature conspires with those who would destroy Jewish Jerusalem to reclaim the city. Jerusalem's vulnerable denizens close their windows to ward off the night's shadowy accomplices. The hoodlums who at dusk "make their way to Rehavia from the outskirts of the city to smash her stately street lamps with small, sharp stones," for example, embody the "brooding hills waiting for darkness to fall on the shuttered city."[16] The Palestinian twins Halil and Aziz, whom Hana invites at the end of the novel to raze the city, are similarly aided by darkness: "Night will clutch and veil and swallow them in his folds."[17] Despite and perhaps because of the anxiety it induces, Hana interprets Jerusalem's darkness as one source of her identification with the city. Referring to the conflict between light and darkness that preoccupied the writers of the Haskalah, the Jewish Enlightenment, she admits her preference for darkness, particularly in the summer when "the white light terrorizes Jerusalem [and] puts the city to shame."[18] This observation recalls Rebecca Stern's contention, discussed in chapter 2 of this study, that bright light compromises, exposes, and makes vulnerable gothic heroines, while partial illumination protects them.[19] Conceptualized as an assault, illumination violates the city's inherent darkness.

Night is truly night in Jerusalem, because the street lamps are sparse and their light weak. The feeling of safety that Benjamin attributes to street lighting is diminished, and nature asserts itself. Recalling a nocturnal stroll with Michael, Hana invokes the "nexus between illumination and the nation," in Wasson's words, when she explains the lack of lighting in the city: "We strolled down Isaiah Street toward Geula Street. Sharp stars glittered in the Jerusalem sky. Many of the street lamps of the British Mandate period were destroyed by shell-fire during the War of Independence. In 1950 most of them were still shattered. Shadowy hills showed in the distance at the ends of the streets."[20] Several years later, however, the illumination of the city has not improved. Shortly before the outbreak of the Suez Crisis in 1956, Hana observes that "by five, or a quarter past, darkness reigns. The street lamps are not numerous in Jerusalem. Their light is yellow and feeble."[21] By contrast, Holon, with its well-organized municipal services, is "bright and sun-drenched" not only because of its bright white houses and geographic position by the sea but also because, while Jerusalem reflects Hana's disorganized psyche, Holon is the city associated with Michael—with logic, stability, and order.[22] Epitomizing the Zionist vision of an efficient and organized modern city, Holon is the antithesis of dark, labyrinthine Jerusalem.

Labyrinths, as Fred Botting has shown, constitute "the inverse of proper social space," engendering precisely "the specter of anarchy associated with those darkened spaces cut off from the law."[23] In Jerusalem, a recently reclaimed city, vengeful forces conspire in the darkness. The law that governs the city, however, is not cut off from the darkness but colludes with it. Time polices the streets, establishing its dominion within the city's darkened spaces. Jerusalem's distinctive temporality, characterized in part by a resistance to the politics of the present, corresponds to its resistance to illumination. As such, Oz's Jerusalem literalizes a key feature of the gothic conceptualization of the urban, as articulated by Avril Horner and Sue Zlosnik: "Gothic's uncanny darknesses are not eliminated by the modern city but are the very foundations of its urban subjectivity just as the fear of the fragmentation of the self has been a haunting presence in Gothic narratives."[24] The city's darkness, concealing menacing forces that might destroy it, defines its urban sensibility and parallels Hana's own threatened subjectivity. Signaling the possibility of the radical destabilization of the present, the darkness collaborates with the city's geopolitical fragmentation to create the conditions for paranoia.

Partition and Paranoia

Though Jerusalem is not a city generally conceptualized as gothic, the competing historical claims immediately evident in its multiple divisions contribute, in Oz's novel, to a sense of perpetual vulnerability, instability, and paranoia that accords with the features of more explicitly sinister cities. Writing about London as the quintessential gothic city, Jamieson Ridenhour argues that the city's cultural and economic centrality in the nineteenth century, a product of its imperial endeavors, gives rise to its contradictions: great wealth and abject poverty, industry and crime, polish and filth. These paradoxes signify "the tension between perceptions of the modern and the primitive" that defines the city.[25] The impossibility of stifling or denying the barbaric past elicits profound apprehension at the prospect of its return and disruption of the delicate stability of the present. The anxieties of "the empire's great city" had much to do with the dizzying transformations taking place in the nineteenth century, changes that signaled its status as a leading urban center at the same time as they reflected the cost of such "progress."[26] Violence, penury, grime—scratches in the city's polished veneer spoke to the precariousness of its civilized Victorian propriety. It is London's very imperial achievements and domestic advancements, Ridenhour suggests, that made it vulnerable to the force of a dark past poised to reclaim its territory from a present that merely *performs* civilization.

Though Jerusalem is a very different type of city than London, the presence of the past that Ridenhour identifies with London's gothicism is central in twentieth-century Hebrew writing on Jerusalem.[27] From Shaul Tchernihovsky and S. Y. Agnon to David Shahar, Yehuda Amichai, and Ḥayim Be'er, Jerusalem has attracted authors and poets because of the unparalleled place the city occupies in Jewish history and culture. The expansive critical corpus on modern Hebrew literary representation of Jerusalem proceeds from an understanding of the city, in Jewish eyes, as a site of primordial tension between the terrestrial city and its celestial counterpart. This duality sets the tone for the city's character as a whole, outlining a web of paradoxes, contradictions, and binaries whose tensions lend Jerusalem its disconcerting power: past and present, East and West, Arab and Jew, Sephardi and Ashkenazi, Middle Eastern and European, Judaism and Zionism, myth and reality, memory and forgetting, distance and proximity.[28] Hebrew literature, charged by the city's historical currents, has elevated Jerusalem beyond the conventions of passive setting to the status of a character, depicting it as a prisoner, a lover, a schizophrenic woman, a decapitated corpse, a reincarnation of diaspora Jewry, and more.[29] Such images belie a highly complex set of relations between Jerusalem and its authors and point to the variety of possible interpretations of the city's past ranging from the glorious to the oppressive. What brings together many of these disparate texts, spanning a wide range of political, ideological, social, and historical contexts and relating to different elements of Jerusalem's rich history, is the question of how to contend with the past. As in Ridenhour's London, this anxiety, together with the palpable presence of Jerusalem's history, sets the stage for the paranoia that is a hallmark of the gothic.

The preoccupation with paranoia is a key motif of gothic fiction. The "paranoiac structure" of many gothic texts, as David Punter has argued, removes "the illusory halo of certainty from the so-called 'natural' world."[30] Though generally (and in gothic fiction) understood to mean "unfounded suspicions about a hostile environment," paranoia is a condition that has been exhaustively theorized, primarily through psychoanalytic paradigms.[31] Sigmund Freud defined it primarily on the basis of a repressed homosexual desire, an interpretation that has been criticized for its homophobia.[32] Jacques Lacan did not conceptualize paranoia in terms of "aberration" but rather considered it "structurally crucial to the way that we, as ordinary subjects of bourgeois hegemony, represent ourselves to ourselves."[33] Julia Kristeva identified a specifically "feminine paranoia," which she interpreted through the attraction of both men and women to the cult of the Virgin.[34] Melanie Klein characterized the "paranoid-schizoid position" as rooted in the earliest months of infancy, a period rife with anxieties that give rise to a healthy binary splitting formative in the creation of subjectivity; this splitting can degenerate into a fragmentation that can adversely affect the fragile ego.[35] Despite substantive disagreements among these theorists, they all posit paranoia as a reaction to or expression of subjectivity. In other words, paranoia is a function of the formation and development of one's *self*. The relation to an imagined external antagonist speaks to this process and contributes directly to the psychological instability that, whether envisioned as a healthy part of ego formation or not, contains the potential to destabilize one's psychological equilibrium.

Jerusalem's multiple divisions, as experienced by Hana, can be conceptualized as a geopolitical manifestation of paranoia. In a country barely a decade old, the manifold divisions amplified in Hana's experiences of Jerusalem suggest a fragmentation that defines the city and lends it its character at the same time as it creates a sensation of perpetual instability. As many readings of the novel have acknowledged, there is no question that Hana shares or even reflects her city's sensibilities.[36] Hana's paranoid encounter with the city, however, not only reveals something about her psychological state as an unfulfilled woman; it also exposes the vulnerability of a fissured city precariously poised at a delicate and uncertain political and historical crossroads. The portrait of Jerusalem that emerges at this moment is critical in Oz's imagining—on the eve of 1967—of the city's coming-of-age as a sovereign Jewish entity, resolutely positioned in the present even as forces of partition emanating from 1948 maintain its perpetual instability. Just as Ridenhour's London paid for "progress" with the crime and other violent forces it had to suppress to achieve it, so does Oz's Jerusalem become Israeli both because of and in spite of the competing claims on the city. Where London only performs civilization because it cannot fully eradicate the violence that sustains it, Jerusalem only performs sovereignty because melding its fissures would entail a denial of the very history that defines it. For both cities, anxiety emanates from the threat and abhorrence of the characteristic integral to its being. The split that threatens the cities' subjectivities is what makes them the cities they are. Like Hana, the city is itself paranoid in the face of divisions that perpetually threaten its subjectivity even as they define it.

Hana's Jerusalem is a city recently partitioned by the war preceded and preempted by the partition of Palestine as a whole, resulting in a spatial, geographical expression of the psychological split involved in paranoia. The political division of Jerusalem into Old City and New, East Jerusalem and West, Arab and Jewish, Jordanian and Israeli, is the most readily apparent consequence of the war in the city.[37] Hana's memories of her childhood, which frequently interrupt her narrative, are set in the pre-state period when Jerusalem, still whole, was under British mandatory rule. Hana nostalgically recalls the games she used to play with her neighbors and playmates, the twins Halil and Aziz: "Together we would explore distant streets, prowl through the woods, hungry, panting, teasing Orthodox children, stealing into the woods around St. Simeon's Convent, calling the British policemen names."[38] Though this wistful memory is displaced by violent fantasies of power and disempowerment as the novel progresses, it reminds us of the instability and artifice of political boundaries that make such encounters impossible in the novel's present. United in their disdain for the British and for Orthodox Jewish children, Hana, Halil, and Aziz have free rein to explore, prowl, and steal through the city. The hierarchy of power among them is evident, even in this early memory, in the roles they take on ("I was a princess and they were my bodyguard, I was a conqueror and they my officers, I was an explorer and they my native bearers, a captain and they my crew, a master spy and they my henchmen"), but their relative freedom of movement is a stark contrast to Hana's contemporary reality, in which certain parts of the city are forbidden and closed off, making contact with Palestinian Arabs difficult if not impossible.[39] Two nights before her wedding, Hana has a nightmare in which Michael flees and leaves her alone to be kidnapped by the Arab twins; the most horrific detail of the nightmare is that they allow her to leave but she chooses to stay, attracted despite herself to the promise of their violence. The orientalist overtones of scenes involving the twins have already been attended to.[40] What I want to underscore here is the way Hana's mind figures the encounter with her former neighbors in the political landscape of the 1950s in terms of transgression and, in particular, paranoia—a paranoia in which Hana, an ambivalent victim, both fears and invites the unraveling of established power dynamics.

The only direct contact Hana has with Palestinian Arabs is through the fantasies that constantly reverse the dynamics of power between them. Her paranoia, however, is substantiated by the novel's characterization of Jerusalem in terms of a defenseless heroine at the mercy of "hostile surroundings." Early in the novel, Hana says to Michael, "This isn't a city, . . . it's an illusion. We're crowded in on all sides by the hills—Castel, Mount Scopus, Augusta Victoria, Nebi Samwil, Miss Carey. All of a sudden the city seems very insubstantial."[41] Growing more sinister as the narrative progresses, this notion transforms from a sentiment of insignificance to Hana's feeling that "the Jerusalem hills seem to be plotting some mischief," to the brink of violence: "Villages and suburbs surround Jerusalem in a close circle, like curious bystanders surrounding a wounded woman lying in the road: Nebi Samwil, Shaafat, Sheikh Jarrah, Isawiyeh, Augusta Victoria, Wadi Joz, Silwan, Sur Baher, Beit Safafa. If they clenched their fists the city would be crushed."[42] There is no question that Hana's psychological turmoil and her claustrophobia are symptoms of the deadly boredom and dreary provincialism that afflicted Madame Bovary, to whom she has been convincingly compared.[43] Crucially, though, they also indicate her internalization of the political situation of partition and the geographic vulnerability of Jewish Jerusalem to its surroundings.

That Hana's psychological state responds to and expresses the political upheaval embodied by 1948 and the partition of the city is evident in a postpartum nightmare she has in the hospital. An old Jewish peddler walking through Mandatory Jerusalem during a British-imposed curfew digs a rusty nail into the street, creating a crack that "quickly widened and spread like a railway network in an educational film, where processes are shown speeded up."⁴⁴ Cutting through whole districts and crumbling row after row of buildings, the devastating earthquake splits the city, its religious Jewish residents scrambling to settle on the ruins. The horror of the nightmare is evident not only in its violent concretization of partition but also in its implicit accusation of Jews for initiating and maintaining the chaos, through the archetypal wanderer with the heavy pack and the rusty nail, and the Orthodox boys who "poured in streams silently" toward the ruins. "It was hard to look at them and not be one of them," Hana recalls. "I was one of them."⁴⁵

The political partition, actualized by fences and barbed wire, is the most immediately apparent one, having estranged Jewish and Palestinian Arab elements of the city with significant implications for the contemporary political situation. This primary partition also spatializes additional dimensions of Jewish Jerusalem's forces of otherness. A key locale in the novel is Terra Sancta, a neoclassical building belonging to the Franciscan Church. In 1949, the building became part of a substitute campus for the Hebrew University, as Mount Scopus was cut off from West Jerusalem after the 1948 war. Later, many of the university's courses relocated to the Givat Ram campus, completed in 1958. Others returned to Mount Scopus after the Six-Day War united East and West Jerusalem. An ornate Italian Renaissance–style building of stone and iron capped by a bronze Madonna with outstretched arms "as if she were trying to embrace the whole city," Terra Sancta is evidence of the Christian European presence in Jerusalem's cityscape.⁴⁶ It speaks to the Christian history of Jerusalem at the same time that it embodies the ephemerality of hegemony and the political volatility between Arabs and Jews.

It is this volatility, and its manifestation as concrete evidence of geopolitical partition, that brings Michael Gonen, aspiring geologist, and Hana Greenbaum, romantic student of Hebrew literature, together in the memorable scene of their first encounter, in which Hana trips on the stairs at Terra Sancta and Michael helps her up. A few months later, Hana and Michael's wedding party is held in a lecture room in the Ratisbonne Building, a monastery that, like Terra Sancta, had been used as a temporary locale for university lectures. Reflecting on those days of political uncertainty, Hana recalls examining the faded designs on the high ceiling on the night of their wedding: "With difficulty I could make out various scenes in the life of Christ, from the Nativity to the Crucifixion. I turned my gaze away from the ceiling."⁴⁷ The monastery, built by a Jewish convert to Christianity for the express purpose of converting Jews, bears the traces of forces vying for a claim on the city. The partition of Jerusalem creates the conditions for an intimate encounter with the city's Christian dimension, whose church bells in the Old City form an integral part of the city's soundscape. Furthermore, these two buildings speak to the temporary nature of political power in a city that hosts diverse and competing versions of truth.

The invisible but profoundly experienced rifts among Jerusalem's Jews contribute to Hana's paranoia as much as its Arab and Christian presence, as her nightmare suggests. The city's distinctive groups of Jews are categorized according to familiar classifications of ethnicity, religious observance, and linguistic and cultural background. Though disdainful even of those with whom she identifies—secular European Jews—Hana regards certain groups of Jews with a deep-seated fear and anxiety. Her description of the "Jewish peddlers" of Jerusalem using explicitly antisemitic imagery is most striking in this regard, painting an emphatically gothic portrait:

> There are old peddlers in Jerusalem. . . . An impenetrable, hostile chill envelops them. Old peddlers. Eccentric craftsmen wandering around the city. They are alien. I have known them for years, them and their voices. Already when I was five or six I would shudder from them. I shall write these, too—then perhaps they will stop frightening me at night. . . . *"Gla-zier, gla-zier"*—his voice is hoarse and stark. . . . *"Alte zachen, alte shich"*—a great sack on his shoulder like the burglar in an illustrated children's story. *"Pri-mus stoves"*—a heavy man with a huge, bony skull like the ancient blacksmith. *"Mattresses, mattresses"*—the mattresses resounding in his throat as if they were a lewd slogan. The knife-grinder carries about with him a wooden wheel worked by a treadle. There are no teeth in his mouth. His ears are hairy and protruding. A bat. Old craftsmen and strange peddlers, year after year they float through the streets of Jerusalem untouched by time. As if Jerusalem is a northern ghosts' castle, and they are spirits of rage lying in wait.⁴⁸

Radically different creatures bordering on the supernatural, these Jewish archetypes are frozen in history in the most hideous posture of anti-Jewish European propaganda. They wander with their wares on their back; they are ancient and impervious to time; they are physically repugnant to the point of dehumanization; they are transfigured into the nocturnal creatures that populate the dark side of children's tales, like bats and ghosts. Their presence in Jerusalem allows them to appropriate the city, transforming it into their "ghosts' castle" (טירת-רפאים) for their nefarious purposes, which remain inscrutable and vague. The evil spirits, rooted in the diasporic

Jewish past, lie in wait, but it is not clear *for what*. Nevertheless, Hana's childhood fears have only intensified, and she writes about the "spirits of rage" (רוחות-הזעף) with the explicit intent of exorcising them.⁴⁹

The distinction between Orthodox and secular Jews also plays a role in Hana's paranoid typology of the city's divisions and is emphasized by the fact that Hana and Michael live in one of the city's many Orthodox neighborhoods, among "Ashkenazim with fur hats and Sephardim with striped robes."⁵⁰ The contrast between these locales and Rehavia, the secular, predominantly German Jewish neighborhood that is home to the city's academics and other professionals, is stark: "Tense silence broods in Rehavia, in Saadya Gaon Street, after the sun has set. At a lighted window sits a gray-haired sage at his work. . . . Who could imagine that at the other end of this very street stands the district of Shaarei Hesed, full of barefoot women . . . ? Is it possible that the old man playing tunes on his German typewriter cannot sense them?"⁵¹ The religious women, in Hana's characterization, pose an unspecified threat to the elderly scholar, who is oblivious to this vague danger.

The anxiety evoked by this scene of geographic proximity and cultural distance intensifies, moving from the divisions among groups of people to that between the built and the wild cityscapes: "An ancient grove [creeps] up the slope, clutching at the outermost houses of Rehavia as if about to enfold and smother them in its luxuriant vegetation," while "long-drawn-out, muffled songs rise out of the woods and reach out toward the windowpanes."⁵² Such images, which abound in the novel, convey ominous preparations for an impending attack on Jerusalem. As dusk falls, "at the ends of the streets you can glimpse brooding hills waiting for darkness to fall on the shuttered city."⁵³ The image of elderly German Jews engaged in cultured, enlightened endeavors, visible through windows in their homes while dark, primitive forces lurk outside, biding their time, is a motif. A pianist in Tel Arza practices in preparation for a recital of pieces by Schubert and Chopin. Meanwhile, the tower of Nebi Samwil "stands motionless beyond the border and stares night and day at the elderly pianist who sits innocently at her piano, her stiff back turned to the open window. At night the tower chuckles, the tall, thin tower chuckles as though whispering to himself, 'Chopin and Schubert.'"⁵⁴ Her back to the open window, the woman is in a state of the utmost vulnerability to the phallic Arab tower. Again, Jerusalem stages an unbalanced war between civilization and what in Hana's mind is its antithesis in all its forms: diasporic Jewishness, religious Orthodoxy, uncontained nature, and the Arab presence.

A final, critical division brings us back to Hana's personal experience of the city. Despite the fact that she frequently interrupts her own narrative of her married life to recall episodes from her childhood, the latter remains geographically strictly off limits: "I was born in Kiryat Shmuel, on the edge of Katamon, during the Feast of Succot in 1930. Sometimes I have a strange feeling that a bleak wasteland divides my parents' home from my husband's. I have never revisited the street where I was born."[55] During a walk to the edge of Talbiyeh with her husband and son, she stops short: "I refused to go any further. Like a spoiled child I stamped my foot."[56] As though mirroring the city's political partition, with its fences and no-man's-lands, Hana's Jerusalem contains its own invisible, insurmountable divisions. In the world of her imagination, the mere thought of transgressing them can instigate psychological deterioration, a certainty of harm to come, and, at the same time, its self-destructive invitation. In this temporal manifestation of partition, as in those reflected in the diverse neighborhoods and populace of the city, seemingly clear-cut boundaries fall away to reveal disorder, fragmentation, and uneasy proximity.

The Empty Crypt: Jerusalem as Labyrinth

While Jerusalem's geopolitical divisions provide a sense of the city's history, the distinctly gothic features of its spatiality, evident in the novel's evocation of the labyrinth and the crypt, reveal Hana's acute, existential dread of the city's temporality. The correspondence between the physical space of the labyrinth and the mental structure of characters in gothic literature has established the labyrinth as a convention of gothic fiction. Confusing and convoluted paths constructed around a hidden center resemble the disordered boundaries of the self. Botting has elaborated on the significance of the labyrinth in the conceptualization of subjectivity: simultaneously threatening the loss of subjectivity while promising its recovery, the labyrinth blurs boundaries and entangles the internal and the external.

The labyrinth's disordering of the subject's relation to the world expresses a key characteristic of gothic fiction. As we have seen, darkness plays an important role in this disorganization, which is both physical and psychological. Feminist critics have argued that the labyrinth reflects a decidedly feminine psyche and that its unsettling of the boundaries between the external and the internal represents the anxieties of the maternal.[57] Others emphasize the labyrinth's function as a distinct spatial system. In his reading of Charles Dickens's London as an exemplar of "Urban Gothic," Robert Mighall writes that the labyrinth "provides a model for organizing a dichotomous city, and for suggesting that secrets and mysteries may lurk in its darker recesses."[58] Though the "dichotomous city" in this context is the London of the Industrial Revolution, divided into wealthy and impoverished districts, it is not difficult to envision how this principle of (dis)organization might apply to a Jerusalem subject to multiple divisions. As Hana Wirth-Nesher points out, "labyrinths are frightening in Jerusalem because to abandon direction even temporarily can be dangerous."[59]

The disconcerting power exerted by the labyrinth may lie not in the structure itself but in its secret center and the method of its concealment. Subterranean labyrinths were a feature of the crypts of the early Christian church; the word *crypt*, designating an underground burial chamber or chapel, is derived from the Greek *kruptós*, hidden or secret. In gothic novels such as Matthew Lewis's *The Monk* (1796), set during the Inquisition, crypts often require passage through complex subterranean tunnel systems. The relationship between the crypt and the labyrinth structures gothic spatiality and aids in the conceptualization of key thematic concerns expressed by gothic texts. Jerrold E. Hogle proposes the term *cryptonomy* to describe "a process of crypts supplanting crypts where every attempt to hide a destruction points to a sealing up before it that only reconceals itself."[60] If, as Hogle asserts, the cryptic space is "the central Gothic mystery," then its force is, first and foremost, *temporal*: "The Gothic crypt is the sign of a vanishing past, and to say that is, first, to expose the crypt's past as a series of remnants cut off from clear origins."[61] Revealing only to conceal again, the crypt, like Botting's labyrinth, parallels the workings of the self: "Identity in Gothic novels seems somehow created by the same modes of covering up that form crypts themselves, involving Gothic characters in a paradox of objectives that draws them fearfully away from death only to point them at it."[62] The labyrinth and the crypt illustrate the unstable moorings of the self and its apprehensive engagement with the past.

The link between the physical state of the labyrinth and the mental state of the gothic character calls to mind Hana's psychic disorientation and its relation to the cryptonomy of Jewish Jerusalem. Both, to use Botting's formulation, "reflect the dilemmas and fears of a subject who has lost his sense of knowingness and self-control, no longer master of himself and his world but subjected to other forces, powerful undercurrents hidden beneath the surfaces of mind and world."[63] Hana's frequent references to the discipline of Michael's scholarship, geology, provide the ideal metaphor to structure her narrative according to the "powerful undercurrents" of a labyrinth conceptualized as descending into the earth rather than spreading over its surface. Geology, as filtered through Hana's mind, joins forces with Jerusalem's architectural enclosures to undergird the city's cryptonomy.

Pointing to this contrast between surface and depths as formative in gothic spatiality, Ridenhour argues that "the world we see hides a much more disturbing reality just below its surface."[64] Hana senses this reality keenly: "Strange and frightening at night the thought that Michael studies dark layers in the crust of the earth. As if he's defiling and angering in the night a world that doesn't forgive."[65] Hana's interpretation of Michael's scholarly endeavors draws a direct connection between her own fears and paranoia about her city and the geological processes hidden beneath it. As the study of potentially volatile forces concealed within the earth, geology encompasses developments, often exceedingly slow, that can help delineate the history of the earth itself. The scale of "geologic time" links concealment and the breakdown between inside and outside with temporality. As the object of Hana's anxieties, time visibly saturates the city she encounters and explicitly resists relinquishing its hold. "Can one ever feel at home here in Jerusalem," wonders Hana, "even if one lives here for a century?"[66] A hundred years is but a few days on Jerusalem's geologic time scale.

Even the geological processes that Michael studies, however, occasionally burst forth through the earth's crust in the form of volcanoes or earthquakes. Though it is all too easy to link Hana's fascination with depths as indicative of her own repressed urges and desires, it is critical to acknowledge that these are evident at the very surface of her narrative, readily accessible to her readers. This point is in keeping with gothic fiction more generally, despite the twentieth-century critical preoccupation with reading repression in terms of deeply hidden unconscious desires. Following Eve Sedgwick, Botting observes that "repression and taboos seem very close to the surface of Gothic texts" and are "far from hidden, buried, or repressed."[67] He reminds us that "Freud repeatedly comments on the inaccessibility of repressed material to all but the most careful and painstaking analysis."[68]

In pointing to the labyrinthine construct of Hana's mind as it wanders from fantasy to nightmare to reality, then, I do not intend to repeat the psychoanalytic approaches that others have already proposed.[69] Though this novel invites such interpretation, and though certain psychoanalytic concepts do contribute to a better understanding of its themes, reading it as a gothic novel means also acknowledging the importance of the surface.[70] Rather than psychoanalyze Hana to address her crisis of subjectivity, I want to expose the gothic mechanics of the correspondence between her meandering mind and the sinister yet vulnerable Jerusalem she inhabits. To this end, two critical points of identification intimately related to the figure of the labyrinth emerge from the novel: enclosure, a function of the city's cryptonomy; and the transgression of boundaries that maintain a rigid hold on Jerusalem at the same time as they disorient. In Hana's thoughts about the city, in her emotional engagement with it, and even in her dreams, she consistently stresses these concepts in relation to her obsessive, terrified awareness of time.

Besides its geographic enclosure as a landlocked city surrounded by mountains and desert, Jerusalem is also a city of architectural enclosures and "layers of walls": ramparts encircle the Old City; private courtyards hide residents from prying eyes; gates—some sealed, some open—demarcate points of ingress and egress to and from the city's core.[71] As Wirth-Nesher points out, Hana is unable to engage with Jerusalem's streets and alleys "as part of a visible whole" because these walls block any sense of visual continuity, evoking one of the labyrinth's distinguishing features: it impedes the efforts of those within to visualize its totality and thereby solve the maze.[72] We might recall in this context Donna Haraway's notion of "partial perspective," discussed in chapter 2 of this study. Jerusalem's resistance to visual totality makes Hana feel anxious rather than empowered; possibly a function of her privileged position as an Ashkenazi Israeli Jew, this dread emerges at the prospect of never truly being *of* the city that is her home.

Hana's paranoia sharpens her awareness of the sense of enclosure, to the point that she imagines that the mountains and the Arab villages are collaborating to suffocate the city. Jerusalem's enclosures, however, are more than just figments of Hana's anxious imagination. They are the objective product of distinct cultural and aesthetic sensibilities coupled with geopolitical considerations. It is not only the individual structures that wrap around themselves to conceal their center but also Jerusalem as a whole. Like other historic cities, Jerusalem contains a core of narrow streets and winding alleys not constructed to accommodate modern needs. In the New City, as well as the Old, back alleys and side streets can confound even those most intimate with Jerusalem, while architecture, the city's design, and the natural environment contribute to the sense of enclosure: "Talpiot, a forgotten continent in the south, hidden amid her ever-whispering pine trees.... Beit Hakerem, a solitary hamlet lost beyond the windswept plain, hemmed in by rocky fields. Bayit Vagan, an isolated hill-fort where a violin plays behind windows kept shuttered all day, and at night the jackals howl to the south."[73] Hidden, overshadowed, lost, hemmed-in, isolated, shuttered—these adjectives all point to states that suggest, like the labyrinth itself, both spatial and psychological separation, disorientation, and captivity.

Her familiarity with Jerusalem notwithstanding, Hana is perpetually aware of the city as a repository of secrets rendered inaccessible by its architecture of walls and enclosures, its claustrophobic natural and political geography, and the labyrinthine design of its streets and alleyways. On one of her walks with Michael, she reflects at length on the "overpowering arbitrariness of the intertwining alleys," lingering on the objects that signify time's passing: "Rusting gutters. Ruined walls. A harsh and silent struggle between the stonework and the stubborn vegetation. Waste-plots of rubble and thistles." Her thoughts shift from the material manifestation of time to the city's capacity for concealment:

> And the walls.
> Every quarter, every suburb harbors a hidden kernel surrounded by high walls. Hostile strongholds barred to passers-by. Can one ever feel at home here in Jerusalem, I wonder, even if one lives here for a century? City of enclosed courtyards, her soul sealed up behind bleak walls crowned with jagged glass. There is no Jerusalem. Crumbs have been dropped deliberately to mislead innocent people. I have written "I was born in Jerusalem"; "Jerusalem is my city," this I cannot write. I cannot know what lurks in wait for me in the depths of the Russian Compound, behind the walls of Schneller Barracks, in the monastic lairs of Ein Kerem or in the enclave of the High Commissioner's palace on the Hill of Evil Counsel. This is a brooding city.[74]

This passage, a critical moment in Hana's continually developing understanding of the city, incorporates several key motifs in the novel's representation of Jerusalem, particularly its mazelike streets and alleys and its ruins, rust, and rubble as material signifiers of passing time. Most striking is the way the city's architectural features are imagined in terms of inaccessibility and secret plots: its walls hide, surround, bar, enclose, and seal; mysterious forces mislead and lurk in the depths, lairs, and enclaves of its buildings, courtyards, and districts. It is worth noting that in the original Hebrew, the last line of this passage is more literally rendered—"This is a city gathered into its being" (זוהי עיר אסופה אל תוך נפשה)—emphasizing Jerusalem's wary interiority.[75]

The inaccessible, heavily guarded "hidden kernel" at the heart of every quarter echoes the forbidden hidden kernel of Jerusalem as a whole, the Old City.[76] Even before it became inaccessible to Jews as a consequence of the 1948 war, the Old City was the primary locus of the city's partition, organized and "cleaned up" through tenets of colonial urban planning to accord with the British notion of a historic, religious site, as Nicholas E. Roberts has shown: "Measures such as the prohibition of prostitution, bars, cabarets, and dance halls in the Old City; the designation of certain areas as closed archaeological sites; and the prohibition of major industry and commerce within the city walls were also adopted to create a cleaner and more orderly space that fit with British prejudices about how a holy city should look and operate."[77] The Old City, then, was transformed from the authentic core of a real city—the urban space of the type celebrated by Charles Baudelaire in all its sordidness and splendor—to the idealized, sanitized *idea* of a city. By the same token, this colonial project warded off criminals and other denizens of the monstrous center that are identified with urban labyrinths such as London and Paris. For Hana, it is the inaccessibility of the Old City and not its demographic or mercantile debris that defines it as the city's primary crypt.

Hana seems aware of the cryptonomy at work in her sinister vision. Her sudden assertion that "there is no Jerusalem," that the kernel is, in fact, an illusion, recalls the inaccessibility of the Old City for Jews at this time as well as Hogle's characterization of the crypt at the heart of the labyrinth as "a place of concealment that stands over mere ashes of something not fully present."[78] The essence of Jerusalem in this passage is precisely its concealment, its interiority, its unseen aspects. These aspects, more than "the real" that the city so assiduously works to hide, constitute the power of the cryptic space. The paranoia emanating from Hana's recognition of this cryptonomy recurs throughout the novel: "The convents are surrounded by high walls in the low village of Ein Kerem. Within the walls, too, the pines whisper and whisper. Sinister things are plotting by the blind light of dawn. Plotting as if I were not there to hear them. As if I am not."[79] The intensity of her distress can be attributed as much to an existential uncertainty ("as if I am not") as to conspiracies and "sinister things." The discovery that "there is no Jerusalem," in other words, speaks to the possibility that Hana herself does not exist, that she, like the city, is an illusion, "a sequence of mental veils," to adopt Hogle's image, whose presence has already passed.[80]

At the same time that the city's enclosures and interiorities evoke Hana's crises of subjectivity, she yearns to transgress their boundaries and experience their cryptic cores. Late in the novel, she tells Michael and Yair about the house where Halil and Aziz lived: "Now they surely live in one of the refugee camps. They had a house in the Katamon neighborhood. It was a villa built around an inner courtyard. The house surrounded the yard. It was possible to sit outside and still to be enclosed and concealed. I want to live in a house exactly like that."[81] Fleetingly inviting the political dimension of the present moment into her consciousness by acknowledging the absence of the Arabs who haunt her dreams and by referencing refugee camps, she expresses a longing for the concealment that her neighbors enjoyed: "to sit outside and still to be enclosed and concealed." This yearning for a transgressive subjectivity—to be both inside *and* outside, to be revealed *and* concealed—gestures at the labyrinth's capacity to unsettle the boundaries of space and self.

In Hana's mind, it is a desire implicitly related to power. Upon learning that the twins' house was turned into a pre- and postnatal clinic after 1948, Hana thinks about the demographic shifts in the city in terms of an explicitly gothic temporality that invites time—envisioned as a vengeful past or an apocalyptic future—to disturb the present: "The Germans and the Greeks abandoned the German and Greek colonies. New people moved in to take their places.... That would not be the last battle for Jerusalem.... I too can sense secret forces restlessly scheming, swelling and surging and bursting out through the surface."[82] The mysterious threats that will inevitably transgress to reclaim the city simmer within her own restless psyche as well, but in this passage and in others depicting the violent destruction of Jerusalem, it is not clear whether she is their victim or their perpetrator. This boundary, like those between inside and outside, past and present, concealment and exposure, absence and presence, is perpetually unsettled.

Walking in the Eternal City: The Gothic Flâneuse

Hana's fraught identification with her city is predicated on an amalgamation of intimacy and fear. Her anxiety is based on her perception of estrangement from the city and her vulnerability to its collusion with particular forces: its natural environment, its hostile political entities, its alien Jews, and time itself, which will take back its city sooner or later. At the same time, though, she knows Jerusalem, the city of her birth, intimately. Certain streets and buildings hold special significance in her memory, and she frequently navigates the city's familiar landscape by foot. On her numerous walks, with and without her husband, she observes the changing urban landscape of Jerusalem and the other walkers in its streets to establish her identity as a native Jerusalemite at home in the streets. She also, however, flirts with transgression, performing an empowerment in the streets to fend off the anxiety that assaults her and challenges this identity. The city streets, at once familiar and strangely foreboding, nourish both her fantasies and her fears. As such, Hana's walks in the city give rise to a tense battle between power and vulnerability.

Walter Benjamin identifies the flâneur, the famous walker of the city streets, in Baudelaire's lyrical sketches of Paris and in Edgar Allan Poe's sinister London in "The Man of the Crowd" (1840). The flâneur experiences the city's consumable pleasures as well as the apprehension it evokes. Delineated by the presence of prostitutes and by the monstrous minotaur, his city is described by Benjamin as a labyrinth "whose image has become part of the flâneur's flesh and blood."[83] This conceptualization of the city as labyrinth contains "an image of the minotaur at its center," a creature that embodies "deadly power."[84] Benjamin's flâneur not only traverses the city as a labyrinth but also reflects that labyrinth and its murderous minotaur in his own being. Though the flâneur is usually associated with Baudelaire, whose poetry Benjamin admired, Poe's story contributes an important dimension to the flâneur's relationship to the city and to the crowd, as Benjamin understood it: "To Poe the flâneur was, above all, someone who does not feel comfortable in his own company. That is why he seeks out the crowd; the reason why he hides in it is probably close at hand."[85] In other words, Baudelaire's flâneur is alienated from the crowd he seeks, while Poe's flâneur is alienated from himself. For both, alienation drives the need to consume the sights of the city, suggesting an appropriation of the urban.

At the same time as he consumes, though, the flâneur himself is vulnerable to consumption by the city and an estrangement from the self. The gothic proclivities of the flâneur are located precisely in this vulnerability. Drawn "to the darker side of the metropolis and longing to be annihilated," Wasson points out, the flâneur's pretensions to control over his surroundings capitulate to gothic terror and despair.[86] In this sense, the flâneur is always already a gothic figure, whose attempts at mastery in and of the city indicate his powerlessness, and whose delight in the urban competes with his anxiety. Hana's gothic nightmare, as experienced in the streets of Jerusalem, reflects her helplessness against not only the uncanny returns of time but also the limitations of her gender.

Though Benjamin's flâneur is always a man, critics have long argued that this defining tension between vulnerability and control is not bound by gender. As Wasson and others have shown, the position of the flâneuse, too, is one of ambivalence, "in which a watchful walker surveys and organizes the scene while partially surrendering to it."[87] Hana's gender does not preclude her flânerie; to the contrary, as the subject of her most explicit attempts to exert control over herself and her surroundings, it actually instigates it.[88] It is no coincidence that the two rites of passage of Hana's normative feminine existence—marriage and childbirth—are accompanied by terrifying nightmares about, respectively, an apocalyptic earthquake in Jerusalem and Hana's violent kidnapping by Halil and Aziz through labyrinthine streets and down into a dark, dank cellar. The condition of the maternal itself can be understood as a descent into the labyrinth, as described by Katherine Henry: the "loss of enlightened, rational control and [the] terrifying encounter with [one's] own demons and desires," an experience associated with "anxieties generated by the feminine and the maternal."[89] This association is clearly evident in Hana's constant, sustained emphasis on the femininity of the men who surround her. Her father, she recalls, donned aprons to wash dishes; her husband jokes that he is the one who breastfeeds their son.[90] It is also clear in Hana's efforts to transform herself into a man. As a child, she wished "to grow to be a man and not a woman" and believed that if she played like a boy and read boys' books, "the signs of a boy would appear on my body and I'd no longer be a girl."[91] As a woman, she suddenly decides to cut off all her hair. These attempts to assert control by dictating her own and others' genders can clearly be seen as precursors to what Leslie Fiedler termed "the maternal blackness, imagined by the gothic writer as a prison, a torture chamber."[92] Hana's dark interior landscape resists both its femininity and its interiority, constantly transgressing its own boundaries, unsettling inside and outside, and radically destabilizing the identities of wife and mother to which she might lay claim.[93]

Benjamin considers Baudelaire's Paris a setting that intermingles "the image of woman and the image of death."[94] The feminine counterpart of the flâneur, for Benjamin, is not the flâneuse but the prostitute, "seller and sold in one," who embodies the interplay between death, the city, and consumption.⁹⁵ This paradigm sets drastic limitations on a woman's presence in the public spaces of the city. Though the bourgeois Hana takes care to emphasize that she refrains from intercourse with Michael before their wedding, she is acutely aware of her sexuality in public and does not hesitate to use it to perform empowerment. At bus stops, at gas stations, outside the guard booth at the Schneller Barracks, at the biblical zoo, and in the yard of her apartment, she invites whistles and catcalls but also evokes discomfort and even pain from those on whom she sets her sights. Gender is pliable for Hana: she can resist, detest, and disown being a woman, and she can use her femininity to her advantage when it suits her. Her performance of power in the streets of Jerusalem—whether in a childhood game or in an orientalist adaptation of the persona of the beautiful, adventurous tennis champion Yvonne Azulai—indicates her desperate desire to evade her own subjectivity. Yet the city constantly reminds her of the futility of her efforts and of the uneasy alliance between empowerment and estrangement from herself.

This tension between power and vulnerability is evident in Hana's more innocuous walks through Jerusalem, as well. On the stormy evening of Hana and Michael's chance acquaintanceship at Terra Sancta, they meet again at Café Atara on Ben Yehuda Street. They discuss their families and their childhoods and then go "out into the night."⁹⁶ A demonic cab driver drops them off in an unknown part of town, where, whipped by fierce winds and rain, they wander blindly until they suddenly reach a familiar spot and can proceed toward Hana's apartment: "Michael accompanied me along Melisanda Street, the Street of the Prophets, and then along Strauss Street, where the medical center is. We did not meet a living soul. It was as if the inhabitants had abandoned the city and left it to the two of us. We were lords of the city." She fondly recalls a childhood game called "Princess of the City," in which Halil and Aziz played her submissive subjects. "Sometimes," Hana recalls, "I made them act rebellious subjects, and then I would humble them relentlessly. It was an exquisite thrill."⁹⁷ The momentarily disorienting nocturnal walk through empty city streets triggers her memories of the game that entailed her colonization of the city and her mobilization of the Arab twins to her cause. Once Hana and Michael regain their sense of orientation, she appropriates the city similarly, naming the streets of their trajectory to buttress her claim.

Though Hana bases her ecstatic fantasies of ruling the city on its empty streets, the lack of other walkers—of the crowds associated with the urban experience—underscores not only Hana's vulnerability but also Jerusalem as a different sort of city. Indeed, the only crowd that Hana ever describes in the novel is one that appears in a nightmare she has, in which she loses Michael in a throng in Jericho just before being kidnapped by Halil and Aziz. Though one of the foremost associations with Benjamin's notion of the Baudelairean flâneur is that he is at home in the crowd, Benjamin specifies that the flâneur, "an alienated man," does not feel at home in the metropolis, not even in its crowds. Rather, "he seeks refuge in the crowd."[98] The crowd, "the veil through which the familiar city beckons to the flâneur as phantasmagoria," wards off the city's threats, allowing the flâneur to experience the city despite its hostility.[99] Hana, a flâneuse without a crowd, encounters the city without the protective veil—face-to-face.

Despite the lack of Parisian crowds, Jerusalem does have its walkers, and Hana observes and comments on them. Reflecting on her father's admiration of Jerusalem's famous authors and scholars, she says, "When I was small my father used to point them out to me in the street. . . . And I would see a diminutive old man cautiously feeling his way like a stranger in an unfamiliar city. . . . [They were] troubled and hesitant, as if they were walking down the steep slope of a glacier."[100] Positioning herself as Jerusalem's native, Hana identifies these men's foreignness as the source of their vulnerability. As her psychological disequilibrium intensifies, this foreignness becomes more sinister. Later, she is surprised to encounter Jerusalem's elderly scholars out on the streets. Here, too, she stresses their blindness in the city's radically unfamiliar, vaguely threatening landscape: "Incredibly, in the evening the frail old scholars wander out for a breath of fresh air. They prod the pavement with their sticks like blind wanderers on a snowy steppe. . . . They were strolling arm in arm, as if lending each other support in their hostile surroundings."[101] Whereas the repugnant Jewish peddlers are perfectly at home in Jerusalem's streets partly because they inhabit them "untouched by time," these vulnerable European scholars wander the city's streets emphatically out of place.[102]

As the observer who watches these susceptible strollers, Hana positions herself as someone well acquainted with the city and its potential violence. The encounters between the gothic flâneur and the monsters of the labyrinth have been conceptualized as encounters between those who truly know the city and those who do not. As Ridenhour points out in the context of London, this "is often the apex of the experience of walking in the urban Gothic novel—the sense of anxiety mounts until the walker comes upon a monstrous person or thing who is much more at home in the streets than the walker. These encounters . . . occur precisely because the walker has no true knowledge of his surroundings."[103] In *My Michael*, however, it is Hana's intimacy with the city that threatens to bring her face-to-face with her monstrous adversary, time. The problem is not that she gets lost in the city's labyrinths but that she knows them and senses the danger contained within their unseen, enclosed spaces all too well.

This familiarity, though, does not translate to confidence. Rather, it is shot through with a paranoid sensation of the uncanny and a debilitating fear of impending catastrophe. As we have seen, no crowd offers shelter from the forces that threaten Hana. At most, she is accompanied by her husband and son, whose oblivion to these dark forces does nothing to dispel her anxiety, only increasing her sense of estrangement from her surroundings and herself. Despite her most lucid charting of the city's streets, neighborhoods, and buildings on her strolls in the novel, Jerusalem resists organization, illumination, and intimacy and asserts the inevitable realization of its own secret processes and plots. In gothic works set in labyrinthine London, Ridenhour observes, "the reporting of routes or landmarks does nothing to alleviate the sense of being lost and threatened."[104] Similarly, Wasson notes that wartime London deflects the flâneur's deliberate attempts to classify and organize the city "into narratives over which he has control."[105] This emphasis on the city's ability to resist or succumb to efforts of order and taxonomy applies to Oz's Jerusalem as well. That even Hana's most specific and objective descriptions of the city betray a "patent subjectivity," in Naomi B. Sokoloff's terms, is to be expected if we acknowledge the city's gothicism.[106] Jerusalem is complicit in the ephemerality that terrifies Hana, in the dominion of time evident throughout the city, and, finally, in the inevitable death of everyone in the city.

Hana's perambulations in the city subtly revise Benjamin's conception of Baudelairean flânerie. Rather than emphasizing the city's urbanism and modernism as the source of a tense coexistence of delight and alienation, Hana's gothic flânerie is explicitly preoccupied with the city's mere performance of urbanism. The rapid development of its building and infrastructure, a cornerstone of the realization of the Zionist dream and the establishment of clear boundaries in the new state, provides a thin veneer over the chaos and disorganization that reign. This condition expands, with the novel's end, to include the state as a whole, subject to dark forces and looming disaster.

The disconcerting tension between the city's past and its present finds expression in the battle between Jerusalem's natural and its built topoi. Whether it is "an ancient grove" that threatens "to smother" the houses of Rehavia; "an ancient tree [that forces] its way up between the unevenly laid paving stones . . . clawing the air with pointed talons"; or "brooding hills waiting for darkness to fall on the shuttered city," the city must defend vulnerabilities both within and without.[107] Furthermore, these anxieties are rooted in the temporal and historical characteristics that ensure the ephemerality of the city's development. This preoccupation with time intensifies the gothic sensibilities that Horner and Zlosnik insist are "the very foundations" of the modern city.[108] In Hana's experience of 1950s Jerusalem, a rapidly transforming city both glorified and burdened by its history, these keenly apparent gothic sensibilities express ambivalence regarding the burgeoning national enterprise that would lead Israel from precarious sovereignty to occupation.

Certain sites in the city have a particularly strong effect on Hana, excavating the depths of her memory, generating the sensation of the uncanny, and stoking her fear and despair. On a walk one day, she and Michael pass the outer wall of Schneller Barracks: "Many years ago there was a Syrian orphanage here. The name reminded me of some ancient sadness, the reason for which I could not recall."[109] Years later, she passes the same wall with Yair: "We walk past the heavy iron gates of Schneller Barracks. I have never set foot inside these grim walls. When I was a child the British army was here, and machine guns protruded from the loopholes. Many years ago this fortress was called the Syrian Orphanage, a strange name which threatens me in its own way."[110] Again, she notes the enclosure of the site and its evocation of the uncanny, formerly eliciting sadness and now vague paranoia. This time, her personal memory is laced with an ominous historical one.

Other walks, particularly those that take her to the edges of the city or beyond it altogether, quiet Hana's turbulent psyche. Just as Michael's aunts cannot understand "why [he] lives surrounded by Orthodox people instead of in a civilized neighborhood," so, too, does Hana feel relief at leaving these Orthodox spaces behind for forays into nature that seem benevolently to illuminate all of the city's dark places.[111] Inevitably, though, she recognizes this calm as illusory: "At times I imagine that Jerusalem lies before me with all its hidden places alight. I do not forget that the blue light is a fleeting vision."[112] Hana's walks through the city, whether bathed in temporary sunlight or steeped in gray fog, lead her invariably back to the city's indecipherable crypts and the relentless movement of time they harbor.

Though the bourgeois Hana does not experience the city through the veil of the crowd or sit in cafés to observe passers-by, she embodies the anxious dimension of flânerie that Benjamin identifies in Poe's story. Her flânerie brings her face-to-face with the city's multiple partitions, drives her perambulations in the city's streets, and makes possible her recognition of the city's hidden forces. Above all, Hana's flânerie underscores the extent of her multiple estrangements: from the people to whom she is closest, from herself, and from Jerusalem as a metonymy of Israel itself. The paradigm of flânerie we encounter in *My Michael*, then, deepens the gothic anxieties that to some degree always accompanied the figure, from his manifestation in Baudelaire's marvelous Paris to his darker counterpart in Poe's sinister London. In the gothic context, flânerie breeds an irrepressible dread not only in the experience of isolation but also in the encounter with the "urban subjectivity" that threatens to subsume the flâneuse altogether.

If the labyrinth of Jerusalem structures Hana's meandering subjectivity and paranoid flânerie around her pervasive fear of time as the agent of forgetting and of death, then we might consider, briefly, how the novel represents other places. Two sites act as spatial antitheses to Jerusalem: Holon, the coastal city where Michael's father, Yehezkel, lives; and Nof Harim, the kibbutz on Israel's border with Lebanon, where Hana's brother lives. Where Jerusalem is dark, they are awash in sunlight. Where Jerusalem is a city of enclosures, they are open to sea and sky. Where Jerusalem haunts, oppresses, and possesses, they liberate. Where Jerusalem is weighty and ancient, they are airy and modern. As Yehezkel says, comparing Holon to Jerusalem, "Holon is a new town. It has not been restored to some ancient splendor, but sprang clean and pleasant out of the sands."[113] In design and realization, both Holon and Nof Harim reflect Zionist utopianism.

These self-evident differences in geography and history establish Holon and Nof Harim as antilabyrinthine spaces. Hana makes repeated reference to Holon's well-ordered municipal organization, which fascinates Yair and forms a stark contrast to the tangled vegetation and intertwining alleys of Jerusalem. In Holon, Yair and Yehezkel, grandson and grandfather, would awaken early for a morning stroll through the city's deserted streets. "Yehezkel took pleasure in initiating his grandson into the mysteries of the municipal services," Hana recalls. Yair is intrigued by the city's systems: "the ramifications of the electricity lines from the central transformer, the circuit of the water supply, the headquarters of the fire brigade, and the alarms and hydrants disposed at various points around town, the sanitation department's garbage disposal arrangements, and the network of bus routes. It was a whole new world, with a fascinating logic of its own."[114] Far from the perambulations of the terrified gothic flâneur, these purposeful walks confirm the logic and order that govern Holon's inner workings.

The kibbutz, though not an urban space, is an antilabyrinth because of its commanding presence at the top of a mountain, which allows it to survey its surroundings from above. Jerusalem, haunting and haunted and full of secrets and enclosures and walls that threaten and repel its residents, is unattainable and invisible. Despite these differences, when at the end of the novel Hana finds a respite from the demons of Jerusalem in Nof Harim, she realizes that the city is present there, too. She senses it as she gazes over the border at Arab villages and a lone shepherd. From her vantage point on high, she recognizes the precariousness of her position and its potentially hostile surroundings. The sense of foreboding cultivated by her flânerie in the city follows her beyond its labyrinthine space, a reminder of the fragile stability of Israel as a whole.

The Uncanny Returns of Time

Hana's exploratory forays into the dark reaches of her city and of her mind are activated by the illness that she invites, by restlessness, and, most critically, by fear. Her fear of time structures her terror of death. Permeating her consciousness, it is the impetus behind her writing itself, as she announces in the novel's opening lines. Her vision of Jerusalem through the lens of fear and paranoia yields a city full of dark shadows, unseen terrors within closed courtyards or beneath the earth's crust, battered and bruised buildings and walls. It is time, the most terrible villain of all, that reigns over this landscape. Time is the monstrous minotaur at the center of the labyrinth, the elusive, immaterial, alinear force within the seemingly empty crypt, distorted and distorting. Represented as a shape-shifter, time is both abstract and concrete, both familiar and strange. The uneasy coexistence of these features, together with Hana's frequently expressed conviction that she has experienced certain moments or events in the past, positions her conceptualization of time within the realm of the uncanny.

Unheimlich, for Freud, "applies to everything that was intended to remain secret, hidden away, and has come into the open."[115] Freud underscores that *heimlich* (the familiar, the known) and *unheimlich* (the unfamiliar, the unknown) function not antithetically but rather in tension with one another, to the point that they can merge: "The uncanny is in some ways a species of the familiar."[116] This distressing sense of defamiliarization of formerly familiar concepts generates estrangement: "The frightening element is something that has been repressed and now returns. . . . [This] uncanny element is actually nothing new or strange, but something that was long familiar to the psyche and was estranged from it only through being repressed."[117] Just as the doppelgänger is "an object of terror" because it harks back to "phases in the evolution of the sense of self," so, too, does "the factor of unintended repetition" defamiliarize an event or an object and engender feelings of "helplessness," loss of control, and paranoia.[118] Writing on the gothic unconscious, Botting underscores the crisis of subjectivity instigated by the uncanny: "The uncanny is more than an objectified wish returning from an unconscious identified as a seat of instincts. Instead, in Lacan's terms, the uncanny marks the decomposition of the fantasy underpinning imaginary subjective integrity and the assumption of symbolic consistency: its apprehension discloses, in horror, nothing but a void."[119] The role of the uncanny in exposing and decomposing the artificial wholeness of subjectivity is relevant not only in the context of individuals but also in that of collective entities, such as the nation, whose legitimacy proceeds from claims of wholeness.

Building on Freud's description of the experience of the uncanny as "a human consciousness being usurped by more powerful forces," Wasson suggests that "the uncanny can thus be defined as a crisis of narrative, in that it is fundamentally about feeling in the grip of a narrative governed by an alien intelligence outside one's own conscious control."[120] When we experience the uncanny, we perceive "a malevolent design behind events/an encounter/an object, but we are shut off from knowing that meaning."[121] In *My Michael*, Hana is repeatedly subjected to the feeling that an alien force exerts control over her life, and she spends much mental energy attempting to recuperate it through narrative. As she acknowledges in the novel's first page, she writes to regain control and ultimately to ward off death. Yet she is all too aware of the architect of the "malevolent design" that elicits this sensation of the uncanny: time itself. Time, much like the labyrinth, can disorient and arrogate control. Hana's psychological disintegration occurs not because the source of the uncanny remains a mystery but because it is exposed in all its forms as an invincible, omnipotent foe. Her fantasies of sexual and political empowerment are feeble attempts to assert her subjectivity in the face of its inevitable decomposition. This concept speaks not only to the internal landscape of Hana's mind but also to the political one of divided Jerusalem as a metonymy of Israel and partitioned Palestine. The past, familiar and known though it may be, will inevitably emerge to collapse national fantasies of stability and control.

Time, to Hana's mind, is the agent of forgetting: "to forget means to die."[122] Her fear of death motivates her to write, to resist forgetting, to defy time. It is a lonely battle against a formidable adversary: "Only I refuse to relinquish even one crumb to the claws of cold time."[123] Elsewhere, she conceptualizes time as a dynamic toxin that must be contained: "The movement of abstract time resembles a substance sizzling in a test tube: pure, radiant, and lethal."[124] On occasion, "it seemed as if time were taking on visible features" which she can identify and recognize, only to dissipate once more into an abstract, alien force.[125] This experience of prosopopoeia, a phenomenon which, as Eric Savoy explains, "designates the figure that makes present to the senses something abstract," is central in Hana's engagement with time.[126] Prosopopoeia, argues Savoy, is "the master trope of haunting that is crucial in the discursive production of the other in paranoid Gothic texts."[127] The uncanny sensation prosopopoeia generates for Hana, however, feeds her paranoia, which, as we have seen, expresses her ongoing crisis of self.[128]

Her paranoia points first to her disintegrating subjectivity; her relations with others (and with "the other") are of secondary importance. As such, many of Hana's ruminations are on her highly subjective experience of time, a concept that takes on particular urgency in moments of perceived danger. Walking with Michael before their marriage on a dark and lonely road, she suddenly feels utterly estranged from him, a feeling that triggers a keen sensation of the uncanny: "We were strangers to each other, he and I. For one strange moment, I remember, I was overcome by a sharp feeling that I'm not awake and I'm not in the present. All of this has already happened to me once.... Time ceased to be a measured and equal flow. It split up into several anxious streams. It was in my childhood. Or a dream. Or a frightening story.... When did all this happen before. Someone told me a long time ago that the catastrophe would happen just like this."[129] Of course, that particular catastrophe does not happen, not in the way she imagines. In fact, the symptoms or warning signs of the catastrophe are, themselves, the event. The splitting of time, its uncanny repetitions, her absence from the present—these are the factors that instigate her greatest fears in the novel, and they are themselves the objects of her fear. As the monster within the crypt, time is not trapped like the minotaur but is the panoptic surveyor of the psychic and topographic labyrinth, controlling both Hana and her city. "Time is like a police van patrolling the streets at night, a red light flashing rapidly, the wheels moving slowly by comparison," observes Hana. "Cautiously moving. Slowly. Menacing. Prowling."[130]

Hana conceptualizes time's threats in terms of overt danger and imminent calamity as well as relentless, undifferentiated continuity. "The sameness of the days," which she observes on numerous occasions throughout the novel, finds expression in the structure of her narrative itself. Several chapters begin with the same words as preceding chapters, evoking repetition in both content and form. Versions of the phrase "The dreary sameness of the days" open chapters 28, 29, and 39.[131] "Autumn in Jerusalem" are the first words in chapters 30 and 31.[132] These and other repetitions disorient the reader, much as the uncanny repetition of certain moments throughout the novel disorients Hana, who insists each time, "Again I felt that this isn't, absolutely is not the first time. I've already been here and now."[133] This sense of disorientation, manifested spatially, is one of the defining characteristics of the labyrinth. The labyrinth as the site of ambivalence, confusion, fear, and transgression exposes it, once more, as the link between the spatial and the temporal in the novel. The spatial preoccupations plaguing Hana's mind find broader expression in Jerusalem's temporality.

At the same time that these repetitions work to deny temporal differentiation in Hana's narrative, painting all her days with the same autumnal brush, Hana herself provides specific temporal details about the events she describes. She learns she is pregnant "in June, three months after the wedding"; she gives Michael permission to smoke his pipe in the house "in the middle of May"; she observes their baby recognizing his father for the first time "at the beginning of June"; they take a week's vacation to Holon in the summer of 1955; Michael completes his doctoral thesis "in the spring of 1959, three weeks before Passover."[134] Hana's care in providing the specific month, year, and season of events ranging from the trivial to the significant points to her attempt to exert control over her life by chronicling it. This is even more pronounced when Hana provides the setting of a fantasy in which a Bokharian taxi driver would arrive to pick her up in the guise of her imagined, orientalized double, Yvonne Azulai, "on the seventeenth of August, 1953, at six o'clock in the morning."[135] Time takes her days and years away, instigating her forgetfulness. She writes and fantasizes in order to combat this theft and assert control and ownership over her life: "Were the days all still the same? Days passed without leaving a trace. I owe myself a solemn duty to record in this journal the passing of every day, every hour, for my days are mine and I am at rest."[136] Despite her concerted attempt to reappropriate her days and to control her narrative, this "rest" is a superficial illusion, just like the rusty bowl she observes, which, having hung on a tree branch through years of storms, winds, and curious cats, simply drops to the ground one morning. "I want to write it like this: all those years I saw complete repose in an object in which a hidden inner current was taking place, all those years."[137] Peace—in the bowl, in Hana's psyche, in Jerusalem itself—is an illusion. Lurking just beneath the surface, the dark forces of time and history promise to reassert themselves.

"1948 Will Not Return": Mapping the Nightmare of History

In the essay "Ir zara" ("An Alien City"), published shortly after the Six-Day War, Amos Oz has the ultimate gothic dream. Wandering the streets of conquered East Jerusalem in uniform three days after the war, he not only senses a palpable hostility in the people he encounters but also is unable to join in the breathless celebrations of his victorious compatriots. Recalling his childhood nightmares about uniformed Arabs with semiautomatic weapons coming to his family's street to kill them, he is horrified to realize that he himself has become the murderous figure: "I passed through the streets of East Jerusalem like a man invading a forbidden territory. City of my birth. City of dreams. City that enthralled my forefathers and my people. And I wander its streets armed with a semi-automatic weapon, like one of the figures in my childhood nightmares: an alien in an alien city" (איש זר בעיר זרה).[138] The nightmare has been revealed to be reality, the victim has been transformed into the oppressor, and the past has burst into the superficial and inevitably ephemeral peace of the present.

In some respects, this experience surpasses that of the gothic dream. Oz wakes to find not only that the nightmare is reality (as Eve Sedgwick defines the gothic dream) but also that he himself is responsible for its violence and destruction. In the wake of his descriptions of the horrible stories he heard as a child about the murder of Jewish children, his uncanny experience walking the streets of the city suggests a profound disruption of his subjectivity, one that speaks to a broader unsettling of the conceptualization of the collective Israeli self. The city, he muses, is "mine—and alien. Conquered and hostile. Loyal and inaccessible."[139] Like Hana Gonen's crisis of subjectivity in *My Michael*, Oz's emerges as a direct consequence of his walk through Jerusalem's streets. The end of partition does not eliminate paranoia but only makes it more acute. It does not organize the labyrinth's jumbled boundaries but resists the political boundaries imposed by the Israeli victory. It does not reveal the contents of the crypt by providing a clear sense of historically determined national belonging but intensifies alienation. Utterly unable to feel pleasure, Oz walks through the city's streets isolated from both the ecstatic Israelis and the enraged Palestinians. The Israeli victory of 1967 effected the reunification of the city, the stitching back together of the wound inflicted in 1948. But this victory is revealed, in Oz's postwar visit, to be just another wound—and it, too, will be avenged.

Hana Gonen is dissociated from her present political moment, never identifying with others' nationalistic excitement and anticipation, because she is all too aware of its ephemerality and, therefore, its meaninglessness. To her, history is not an ally that will ultimately collaborate with the Israeli Defense Forces to cinch a final victory and secure the homeland. This is why she inwardly disdains those who, like her neighbor Mr. Glick, excitedly compare the Suez Crisis of 1956 to biblical battles. Rather, history is a function of time, eternal and relentless, omnipotent and heartless. It is invincible, ultimately, because it wields the ultimate weapon: the inevitability of death—the revelation of the emptiness of the crypt.

At the end of the novel, Hana notes the disjuncture between the modernization and development of the city and the quiet but persistent forces of time that make these urban projects ultimately insignificant: "Jerusalem is spreading and developing. Roads. Modern sewers. Public buildings. There are even some spots which convey for an instant an impression of an ordinary city: straight, paved avenues punctuated with public benches." The signifiers of progress, urbanity, and modernity, however, are only temporary in Jerusalem's topography of "spectralized modernity."[140] "If you turn your head," Hana instructs, "you can see in the midst of all the frantic building a rocky field. Olive trees. A barren wilderness. Thick overgrown valleys. Crisscrossing paths worn by the tread of myriad feet. Herds grazing round the newly built Prime Minister's office.... An ancient shepherd frozen on a rock opposite. And all around, the hills. The ruins. The wind in the pine trees. The inhabitants."[141] Beneath this seemingly peaceful modern exterior, the emissaries of time and of the past patiently await their turn to reclaim the city. It is an ominous feeling that Oz himself experiences, uncannily, walking in Jerusalem's streets on the eleventh of June, 1967.

Like Hana, Oz is less preoccupied with his relation to the Palestinian other than he is with the Israeli self. Though *My Michael* was completed just before the Six-Day War and nearly two decades after the establishment of the State of Israel, its representation of the Jerusalem partitioned in 1948 raises precisely the kinds of questions with which Oz would grapple in his postwar essay. How does the war-driven reunification of a damaged Jerusalem affect what it means to be Israeli? How could the wound of 1948 possibly be redressed in a way that would not unsettle national subjectivity from the moment of its very formation? These are questions that induce profound anxieties for those, like Oz, positioned as liberal Zionists. The encounter with the persistent, unavoidable specter of 1948 anticipates the moral dilemma that would begin, for Oz and others, with the occupation of 1967.

When Michael Gonen is called up to serve in the Suez Crisis, he assures the frightened Hana that "1948 will not return."[142] Hana knows, of course, that it is a promise made in vain, since 1948 constantly returns, as evident in the city's streets and its surroundings. Oz's gothic Jerusalem, object of national dreams, city of labyrinths and crypts, agent of the paranoid mind of Hana Gonen, guardian and hostage of time, is the ideal site to host such profound ambivalence. From this chapter's analysis of the spectral presence of 1948 in Jerusalem's gothic cityscape, the next chapter moves to consider how the perpetual return of 1948 would shape the trajectory of Israeli historiography thirty years after the establishment of the state.

Notes

1. Oz, *Mikhael sheli*, 5–6. Citations from the Hebrew edition are my own translation. Though Hana's name is spelled Hannah in Nicholas de Lange's translation of the novel, and though here I cite from Oz's introduction to the Hebrew edition, for the sake of readability and consistency, I spell her name Hana throughout this chapter.
2. Ibid., 6.
3. Ibid., 6–7.
4. Ibid., 7.
5. Ibid., 9.
6. Ibid., 8.
7. Ibid. "Yerushalayim shel zahav" [Jerusalem of gold] was the title of a song written and performed by Naomi Shemer. Before the Six-Day War, the song described a ghostly city with

empty squares, rendering invisible the Arab presence there. After the war unified East and West Jerusalem under Israeli sovereignty, Shemer added a triumphant stanza to describe the city's resurrection, ensuring the song's endurance as the anthem of the victory of 1967. For a critique of the song's "ethnic patriotism," see Yiftachel, "Anu meyahadim otakh."

8. Though Amos Oz is not generally considered to be an author of gothic works, the gothic shapes much of his oeuvre. It is in evidence already in the nocturnal birds, howling jackals, and family secrets of his first collection of short stories, *Artsot ha-tan* (*Where the Jackals Howl*, 1965), where Oz lays the foundation for the dark Jerusalem of *Mikhael sheli*. Robert Alter acknowledges in no uncertain terms Oz's debt to the gothic: "Paranoia is the foundation of gothic fiction, and some of Oz's strongest writing, for all his impulses to historical and social realism, is essentially gothic. In the gothic vision, the world is ultimately inscrutable, a labyrinth of shadowy turns and dark corners from which the uncanny is always ready to spring, whether driven by sexual or murderous impulse or by both. This is more or less the way reality is represented in a good deal of Oz's fiction" (introduction to *The Amos Oz Reader*, xiii).

9. Setter, "Time That Returns," 39.
10. Ibid., 40, 45.
11. For more on the development of the electric grid in Mandatory Palestine, see Meiton, "Radiance."
12. Though Meiton notes that the concession granted to Rutenberg included Jerusalem, Jerusalem had, from the Ottoman period and through 1988, its own Arab electric utility, the Jerusalem District Electric Company, which served Jerusalem's Arabs and Jews (Jabary Salamanca, "Hooked on Electricity," 8). In another essay, Meiton documents the concerted opposition to and protests against Rutenberg and his plan among the Arabs in Palestine (Meiton, "Electrifying Jaffa").
13. Wasson, *Urban Gothic*, 34.
14. Oz, *My Michael*, 14.
15. Benjamin, *Writer of Modern Life*, 81.
16. Oz, *My Michael*, 96.
17. Ibid., 252.
18. Ibid., 17.
19. See Stern, "Gothic Light."
20. Wasson, *Urban Gothic*, 35; Oz, *My Michael*, 22.
21. Oz, *My Michael*, 167.
22. Ibid., 129.
23. Botting, "Power in the Darkness," 272.
24. Horner and Zlosnik, "Strolling in the Dark," 90.
25. Ridenhour, *In Darkest London*, 1.
26. Ibid., x.
27. London and Jerusalem have been linked at least from the time of the Crusades and the birth of the concept of a "New Jerusalem." The Temple Church of the Knights Templar, built in the twelfth century, was a replica of the Church of the Holy Sepulcher. William Blake conceptualized poetically the notion of London as the New Jerusalem, an idealized locale based on the rebuilt Jerusalem as described in the Book of Revelation. His poem "Jerusalem" (1808) is considered the unofficial English national anthem. Finally, the British presence in Palestine from 1917 to 1947 established a political connection between London and Jerusalem that persists in some form to this day. For example, the British ordinance requiring that all buildings

in Mandate Jerusalem be constructed with local limestone was intended to instill a distinctive aesthetic uniformity that accorded with British expectations of the city.

28. Studies on Jerusalem in Hebrew literature abound. Dan Miron presents a thorough, historicized delineation of diverse attitudes toward and representations of Jerusalem in modern Hebrew literature, citing Amos Oz as a later representative of "the debased or dark image of Jerusalem," which he identifies in Yosef Hayim Brenner, Aharon Reuveni, and Dov Kimhi ("Depictions," 253). Nurit Govrin presents a typology of the conventions of Jerusalem and Tel Aviv in Hebrew literature and culture, characterized first and foremost by contrast: Tel Aviv's social, cultural, and geographic openness against Jerusalem's conservative, landlocked sensibility; Tel Aviv's "newness" and modernity against Jerusalem's history and tradition ("Jerusalem and Tel-Aviv"). Though there is no question that this contrast is fundamental in the Israeli imagination, literature set in both cities challenges this neat binary portrait. See also G. Shaked, "Yerushalayim ba-sifrut ha-Ivrit."

29. This dizzying array of images has found expression in centuries of Hebrew literature. In her study tracing depictions of Jerusalem in the Hebrew imagination from the biblical era through medieval Spain to contemporary Israel, DeKoven Ezrahi characterizes the city's boundaries as "the protean demarcations of an imagination informed by and at the same time uncannily liberated from memory" ("Jerusalem as Ground Zero," 222). Differentiating between the city's "symbolic status and the thing itself," she demonstrates the dangers that the accumulation of memory and allegory can activate through a reading of Uri Zvi Greenberg, and she offers Yehuda Amichai as a counterpoint: "This poet of modern Jerusalem provides a nonproprietary return of the Hebrew body to the Hebrew landscape by allowing his imagination to soar freely through, beneath, and on top of the historical and metaphysical detritus of his city" (ibid., 229, 228). The contrast between Greenberg and Amichai in this context emphasizes the way an excess of memory and history can reduce the city to an abstraction. Amichai's balanced integration of the city's historical element with the human, of course, is one of many possible modes of engaging with Jerusalem's history. Between his corporeal poetics of proximity and the distancing allegories of a self-styled "prophet" such as Greenberg, one finds a wide spectrum of possible literary interactions with the variegated history of the city.

30. Punter, *Literature of Terror*, 2:404. For a useful outline of the theorization of paranoia in literary contexts, see Bersani, "Pynchon, Paranoia, and Literature." See also C. Freedman, "Theory of Paranoia"; and Byron and Punter, "Persecution and Paranoia."

31. Bersani, "Pynchon, Paranoia, and Literature," 99.

32. Freud, "Certain Neurotic Mechanisms," 1. For an analysis of Freudian paranoia in the gothic, particularly in gothic monsters, see Halberstam, "Reading Counterclockwise."

33. C. Freedman, "Theory of Paranoia," 17.

34. Kristeva, "Stabat Mater."

35. See M. Klein, "Some Schizoid Mechanisms."

36. For instance, Ben-Dov, "Zohi ir asufa el tokh nafsha"; Sokoloff, "Longing and Belonging"; and Wirth-Nesher, "Modern Jewish Novel."

37. Avner Holtzman draws a parallel between Oz's binary, split representation of Jerusalem in this novel to his early depictions of the kibbutz as orderly and safe within and dangerous but tempting without. See "Karov ve-asur lanu sham," 214. For a historical consideration of Amos Oz's representation of partitioned Jerusalem, see Bar-On, "Oz bi-Yerushalayim ha-ḥatsuya."

38. Oz, *My Michael*, 5–6.
39. Ibid., 5.
40. Elias Khoury situates the Palestinian twins in the context of other representations of voiceless Palestinian characters in Israeli literature, noting that Anton Shammas "was obliged to redraw the twins Khalil and Aziz in *My Michael* as the deaf-mute sons of Surraya Said in his novel *Arabesques*." They are "an archetype of the absent, mute Palestinian" (Khoury, "Rethinking the Nakba," 253, 265). See also Loshitzky, "Orientalist Representations." Upon the publication of the fortieth-anniversary edition of the novel, *Ynet* published an article on the Orientalism of Oz's depiction of the Palestinian twins (Melamed, "Orientalizem ben 40").
41. Oz, *My Michael*, 22.
42. Ibid., 28, 98.
43. Ginsburg, "Madame Bovary bi-Yerushalayim."
44. Oz, *My Michael*, 72.
45. Ibid., 73.
46. Oz, *My Michael*, 19. Recall the critic Y. Sa'aroni's 1935 review of Leah Goldberg's volume of poetry, *Taba'ot ashan* [Smoke rings], discussed in chap. 3 of this study. The "medieval monastery" he identifies with Goldberg's poetry is the basis for his perception that she was failing to acclimate in Palestine, and that her cultural loyalty was "not only to Europe but also to Christianity," in Michael Gluzman's words (Sa'aroni, "Be-kele ha-intimiyut," 4; Gluzman, *Politics of Canonicity*, 64).
47. Oz, *My Michael*, 45.
48. Ibid., 94.
49. Oz, *Mikhael sheli*, 113.
50. Oz, *My Michael*, 95.
51. Ibid. In the 1950s, the Hebrew University of Jerusalem, established in 1918, was one of only two research universities in Israel; the other was the Technion (Israel Institute of Technology), founded in 1916 as a school of engineering and sciences. Bar-Ilan University was established in 1955, Tel Aviv University in 1956, the University of Haifa in 1963, and Ben Gurion University (as the University of the Negev) in 1969. Jerusalem therefore attracted many of the academics and other intellectuals who emigrated from Europe in the first half of the twentieth century.
52. Ibid., 96.
53. Ibid.
54. Ibid.
55. Ibid., 94–95.
56. Ibid., 95.
57. For example, see Henry, "Life-in-Death"; and Kahane, "Maternal Legacy."
58. Mighall, *Victorian Gothic Fiction*, 32.
59. Wirth-Nesher, "Modern Jewish Novel," 103.
60. Hogle, "Restless Labyrinth," 147.
61. Ibid., 146–47.
62. Ibid., 149.
63. Botting, "Power in the Darkness," 264.
64. Ridenhour, *In Darkest London*, 97.
65. Oz, *Mikhael sheli*, 120.

66. Oz, *My Michael*, 97.
67. Botting, "Gothic Production of Unconscious," 18.
68. Ibid.
69. For a study devoted to this approach, see Amir, "Line That Divides."
70. For more on the importance of surfaces in gothic fiction, see Sedgwick, *Coherence of Gothic Conventions*; and Botting, "Gothic Production of Unconscious."
71. Wirth-Nesher, "Modern Jewish Novel," 102.
72. Ibid., 103.
73. Oz, *My Michael*, 95.
74. Ibid., 97–98.
75. Oz, *Mikhael sheli*, 117.
76. Though the human settlement of Jerusalem can be traced back over five millennia, what is known today as the Old City was the product of the Roman emperor Hadrian's efforts to rebuild Jerusalem as a pagan city in the second century CE. The sixteenth century brought the rule of the Ottoman Empire and the construction, under Suleiman the Magnificent, of the Old City's walls. Until 1860, when the new Jewish neighborhood of Mishkenot Sha'ananim was established beyond its walls, the Old City was the whole of Jerusalem. Thereafter, through the end of Ottoman rule in 1917 and into the British Mandate period, new neighborhoods were established primarily to the west of this core to form what came to be known as the New City.
77. N. Roberts, "Dividing Jerusalem," 21.
78. Hogle, "Restless Labyrinth," 146.
79. Oz, *Mikhael sheli*, 100; Oz, *My Michael*, 82.
80. Hogle, "Restless Labyrinth," 149.
81. Oz, *Mikhael sheli*, 255; Oz, *My Michael*, 222.
82. Oz, *My Michael*, 220.
83. Benjamin, *Writer of Modern Life*, 166.
84. Ibid.
85. Ibid., 48. Many critics have commented on the duality of Benjamin's flâneur. Alexandra Warwick, for example, interprets two distinct figures, whom she identifies with Paris and London: "London does not produce the flâneur, the man in easy mastery of his surroundings, but rather his negative double, the person in paranoid relation to his environment. It may be that this is the logical extension of the flâneur, the accomplishment of the short step from glorious individualism to isolation and alienation" ("Lost Cities," 82). She attributes the difference partly to the different architecture in the two cities. Benjamin, though, stresses that these two sensibilities exist simultaneously in the flâneur's experience of the city; they are two sides of the same coin.
86. Wasson, *Urban Gothic*, 32.
87. Ibid., 33.
88. Ben-Dov has compared *My Michael* to novels of flânerie to argue that Hana does not fit the classic flâneur paradigm since she spends so much time in the confines of her drab apartment and not out in the city ("Zohi ir asufa el tokh nafsha," 196). She cites an emphatically aural passage in the novel as evidence that the bedridden Hana experiences the city through its sounds rather than its sights (ibid., 192–93). Yet before and after this chapter, Hana spends much time outside in the city, walking, shopping, and chronicling streets and districts through their historical resonance and their reverberations in her personal memory.

The early days of Hana and Michael's acquaintance, in particular, are spent outside in the city.

89. Henry, "Life-in-Death," 29.
90. Oz, *Mikhael sheli*, 97.
91. Ibid., 17–18, 38.
92. Fiedler, *Love and Death*, 132.
93. More broadly, the women of the novel are frustrated by their limitations as women. Hana, Michael's aunt Jenia, their hysterical neighbor Mrs. Glick—each woman attempts to transgress the limitations of her gender in her own way, and each woman pays a heavy price.
94. *Writer of Modern Life*, 41.
95. Ibid.
96. Oz, *My Michael*, 11.
97. Ibid., 14.
98. *Writer of Modern Life*, 40.
99. Ibid.
100. Oz, *My Michael*, 9.
101. Ibid., 98.
102. Oz, *My Michael*, 94; Oz, *Mikhael sheli*, 113.
103. Ridenhour, *In Darkest London*, 90.
104. Ibid., 84.
105. Wasson, *Urban Gothic*, 51.
106. Sokoloff, "Longing and Belonging," 143.
107. Oz, *My Michael*, 95, 96.
108. Horner and Zlosnik, "Strolling in the Dark," 90.
109. Oz, *My Michael*, 25; Oz, *Mikhael sheli*, 39.
110. Oz, *My Michael*, 146.
111. Ibid., 92.
112. Oz, *My Michael*, 218; Oz, *Mikhael sheli*, 251.
113. Oz, *My Michael*, 131.
114. Oz, *My Michael*, 128; Oz, *Mikhael sheli*, 151–52.
115. Freud, *Uncanny*, 132.
116. Ibid., 134.
117. Ibid., 147–48.
118. Ibid., 143–44.
119. Botting, "Gothic Production of Unconscious," 34.
120. Wasson, *Urban Gothic*, 111.
121. Ibid., 112.
122. Oz, *My Michael*, 53; Oz, *Mikhael sheli*, 68.
123. Oz, *Mikhael sheli*, 82.
124. Oz, *My Michael*, 168; Oz, *Mikhael sheli*, 196.
125. Oz, *My Michael*, 140.
126. Savoy, "Spectres of Abjection," 169.
127. Ibid.
128. For more on the function of prosopopoeia as "the master trope of poetic discourse" and its link to the uncanny and hallucination, see De Man, *Resistance to Theory*, especially 48–51 (48).

129. Oz, *Mikhael sheli*, 42–43. In his English translation, de Lange eliminates the words *anxiety* and *catastrophe* from this passage: time becomes "a series of abrupt rushes" (28–29).
130. Oz, *My Michael*, 101.
131. Ibid., 155, 161, 224.
132. Ibid., 167, 170.
133. Oz, *Mikhael sheli*, 235; see also 42, 158, 222.
134. Oz, *My Michael*, 57, 84, 84, 125, 240.
135. Ibid., 91.
136. Ibid., 90; Oz, *Mikhael sheli*, 109.
137. Oz, *Mikhael sheli*, 121.
138. Oz, "Ir zara," 212.
139. Ibid.
140. Luckhurst, "Contemporary London Gothic," 528.
141. Oz, *My Michael*, 237.
142. Oz, *Mikhael sheli*, 211–12.

5

HISTORIOGRAPHIC PERVERSIONS
Echoes of Otranto *in A. B. Yehoshua's* Mr. Mani

THE GOTHIC CAN PROVIDE THE CONCEPTUAL TOOLS TO contend with a specific historical moment such as 1948 and its spatial, political, and psychological reverberations. As I showed in the previous chapter, the haunting event is a particular manifestation of the broader threat posed by history and time. What about the *representation* of such events? Can the gothic shed light on the ways we narrate and inscribe our histories? To attend to this question, I turn to A. B. Yehoshua's novel *Mar Mani* (*Mr. Mani*, 1990). Madly crisscrossing continents and tunneling backward through time, *Mr. Mani* activates questions about the representation of history, of different paradigms of identity, and of historical and genealogical inheritance. The liberties it takes with novelistic conventions allow *Mr. Mani* to enact, structurally, its thematic interrogation of history and historiography. To level its critique, the novel questions narrative form and content, production and authorship, and underscores the often disrupted dissemination of narrative. *Mr. Mani*'s concern with history and its unstable relationship to narrative emerges through the intergenerational portrait of one family, depicted primarily through the filter of others' narration and in terms of transgression and contamination.

As an acutely historicized mode, the gothic allows authors to represent the ambiguous, complex, and terrifying truth behind seemingly straightforward narratives of family and nation or to question the line between truth and fiction, much as the reader is forced to do upon hearing the highly subjective, emphatically one-sided stories each teller tells in *Mr. Mani*. The questions of genealogy, dark secrets, and genetic inheritance that animate *Mr. Mani* are central to the gothic, and they transform the novel's obsession with history into an undeniably gothic obsession. The anxieties of the present, suggests Yehoshua, can be traced directly back to the transgressions of the past. The Mani family's "story," riddled with ambiguity, reflecting or reflected by other stories like the proliferating mirrors in the novel's Jerusalem section, challenges the conventions of narrative and historical continuity. In this context, the narration of history itself is exposed as a violation. Enacting a necessary transgression, historical narration oversteps its bounds and takes its captives, performing itself through the description of the Mani men who themselves cross multiple boundaries, geographical, political, ideological, and sexual. Ultimately, the novel is less preoccupied with the content of the histories themselves and more with how they have been told: who writes them, how, and for whom; how they are disseminated; and how they fail or succeed. It is the *process* of historical representation, as it emerges in the narrative expression of history, that dictates the chronotopic labyrinths of Yehoshua's novel. Acting out the very transgressions and instabilities it depicts, the novel crosses the line between history and fiction, adapts the gothic and parodies it, critiques nationalist historiography and seems to accept it.

The plot of *Mr. Mani*, anchored by an original sin revealed in the novel's final pages, shares key elements with that of the work considered to be the first gothic novel, an exemplar of the mode, Horace Walpole's *The Castle of Otranto* (1764). I begin this chapter with a discussion of the debates on history and historiography that provided the backdrop to the publication of both *Otranto* and *Mr. Mani*. Drawing from the extensive scholarship on *Otranto*'s engagement with history, I argue that the gothic preoccupation with historiography evident in Walpole's novella similarly informs *Mr. Mani*. First demonstrating how *Mr. Mani*'s distinctive composition and multivalent narration of history support this claim structurally, I then examine its thematization of history. Questions of inheritance—genetic, ideological, moral—lead to an analysis of the novel's transgressions, particularly its consequential "original sin."

The filial dynamics and questions of inheritance, genealogy, and bloodlines that animate *Mr. Mani*'s plot are central to the gothic as a mode, and especially relevant to *Otranto*. Reading the two texts together, I underscore Yehoshua's engagement with questions about the nature and role of narrative in history, of filial and national continuities and bequests, of masculinity, sexuality, and transgression. The gothic devices and themes that abound in *Mr. Mani* undergird its depiction of the contamination of genealogies both filial and national, eliciting the maintenance or dismantling of historiographic paradigms. These devices include the novel's imagery of labyrinths, mirrors, doubles; its repeated invocation of imprisonment and death; its spatial and temporal displacements; its various disruptions, confusions, and ambiguities; and its fixation on blood and genetic corruption. Recognizing *Mr. Mani*'s gothicism brings to the fore its subtle but persistent engagement with questions regarding the Jew's role on history's stage. Does he write his story or is he written by it? Is he the victim of history or its most elusive subject? And how do defilement and transgression dictate the undulating path of his past?

Gothic Historiography: The Invitation of the Repressed

As we have seen, the centrality of the past is a key characteristic of the gothic. Critics have emphasized the past in gothic literature not only as history but also as the processes and conditions accompanying its *construction* as history, including dissemination, narration, and textuality. The most pertinent point to make in this regard in the context of the texts at hand is that the past and its representation, history and historiography, are not the same thing. The gothic's development "as a way of conceptualizing the present as the legacy of a mythologized past, a way . . . of imagining history," suggests that the gothic is not just a literary mode preoccupied with the past but also a historiographic method.[1] Working to delegitimize accepted historiographic conventions even as it makes use of them, the gothic may rely on material objects, on official or unofficial modes of communication, on revenants and other supernatural figures, or on some combination of these in its representation and transmission of history. The adversarial relationship between the gothic and history is ambivalent at best. The gothic may well express fears that the past will invade the present, but it also acts as the vehicle for precisely these invasions. The gothic invites the repressed to return, despite and perhaps because of the terror they elicit.

The Castle of Otranto has become an archetype of gothic literary historiography. Studies of its historicity have analyzed the material and the textual aspects of the novella and considered their alignment with or resistance to particular historiographic approaches associated with narrative, allegory, antiquarianism, and, later, archaeology. Various interpretations insist on different modes of historicity in the novel, but all agree that the past plays a central role in the novel as in the gothic more broadly. Engaging with Horace Walpole as a "Gothic historian," as Toni Wein characterizes him, some studies trace the representation of contemporary English history in *Otranto*.[2]

Others, like Sean Silver, have defined "Gothic historiography" through *Otranto*'s engagement with history and, more broadly, "the writing of English history as Gothic history."[3] This approach draws attention less to the parallels between the novel and specific events in English history and more to *Otranto* as a paradigm of eighteenth-century "Gothic historiography" more broadly. Thus, as Silver demonstrates, by the middle of the eighteenth century, "amateur and professional historians alike turned to the Gothic as the opportunity for all sorts of cultural narratives" that had been stifled by the previously dominant "exemplary model of history" (i.e., "history as the story of great men").[4] Gothic historiography, by invoking the past amid the present and foregrounding their tension, points to "the act of violence that the official history obscures."[5] It is not the past itself, and not even just the past's emergence in the present, that characterizes "the Gothic way of telling history."[6] Rather, it is the conflicting ways of *writing* the past that are at stake. As Jonathan Dent argues, the promotion of an overarching national historical consciousness like that espoused by Hume's *History of England* is antithetical to the gothic approach to the past, which emphasizes the historically conditioned nature of existence. A gothic text like *Otranto*, suggests Dent, offers not an alternative historiographic mode but rather "an imaginative protest against rational, reductive historiographic techniques." As such, it acknowledges the significance of "the glimmers of a multifarious past" glossed over by histories like Hume's: "Emerging out of the conceptual anarchy of eighteenth-century historiography, the Gothic highlights the need for a more flexible, elastic method of writing the past; one that can more effectively accommodate imagination, violence and contingency."[7] Official history stifles violence, and the gothic aims to recover and recognize it. The violence disinterred by the gothic is not only the event that has been occluded by the official history but also the violence enacted by the official history itself in this act of occlusion. The gothic exposes the violent event behind the sanitizing narrative of "exemplary" or official history, and it also reveals the continual reenactment of this violence through officially sanctioned historiography.

In the briefest terms, the plot of *The Castle of Otranto* concerns the tyrannous Manfred, the illegitimate ruler of Otranto, whose son, Conrad, has been killed on the day Conrad is to marry Isabella. A series of supernatural omens suggests that Conrad's death marks the fulfillment of "an ancient prophecy" that promises "that the castle and lordship of Otranto should pass from the present family, whenever the real owner should be grown too large to inhabit it."[8] Terrified at this prospect, Manfred decides to divorce his own wife and marry Isabella, his son's intended wife, to produce an heir; she flees through labyrinthine passageways beneath the old castle that lead her finally to the safety of a church. Furiously pursuing her, Manfred mistakes his own daughter, Matilda, for Isabella and murders her. A peasant, Theodore, is finally revealed as the true heir of Otranto. Though his true love had been Matilda, he marries Isabella and takes ownership of Otranto. The political order has been restored, but the resolution of Theodore's marriage is presented as a means for him to "forever indulge the melancholy that had taken possession of his soul."[9]

The tension between the political resolution and personal discontent at the end of *Otranto* finds expression in Yehoshua's novel in altered form. At the end of the first (chronologically last) conversation in *Mr. Mani*, the young woman Hagar Shiloh gives birth to another Mani. Her widowed mother develops a relationship with the baby's paternal grandfather, Gavriel Mani. The elusive Mr. Mani insists that the road through Hebron, which he takes to the kibbutz where Hagar and her mother live, is perfectly safe. When a rock is thrown at his car, he reluctantly acknowledges the danger, "even though he felt drawn to that route."[10] The unconventional family that has formed—the unwed Hagar, her son, her widowed mother, and Gavriel Mani—suggests domestic tranquility, but the political order contextualizing it is far from stable. Like *Otranto*, *Mr. Mani* is centered on a family secret and the specters of illegitimacy and incest. It traces the story of the Mani family in reverse chronology, through the perspectives of diverse interlocutors, across Europe and Asia, to arrive at an originary darkness that rivals and in some respects surpasses that of *Otranto*. Though Yehoshua invokes the gothic in a very different spatiotemporal context than Walpole, both are writing in the context of transformations of the conceptualization and articulation of history that emerged in the wake of important political events in the England and Israel of their time. The gothic is amenable to such processes, leading readers to the cobwebbed corners of a past they may prefer to leave undisturbed.

The Castle of Otranto emerges in the wake of the Seven Years' War (1756–63), in which the British defeat of France altered the balance of power in Europe and established Britain's supremacy as a world power. The British victory intensified the conceptualization of British nationhood but simultaneously posed challenges to it: as the British empire expanded to include non-Protestant territories in Canada and Asia, notions of Britishness became increasingly unstable.[11] In addition to the external threats to national cohesion, domestic disagreements about monarchical power characterized this period. Horace Walpole's grandfather had been an important Whig politician and a proponent of the 1688–89 Glorious Revolution and the constitutional monarchy that was its outcome. His father, also a Whig, was the first British prime minister. Like them, Horace served as a Whig member of parliament and was vocally supportive of a strong parliamentary monarchy and against monarchical absolutism, a stance that several critics have identified in allegorical readings of *Otranto*.[12]

The debates regarding the power of the monarchy habitually invoked the Magna Carta and other documents as a basis for historical legitimacy, distressing Walpole "as both a Whig and an antiquary," as Crystal B. Lake notes.[13] Antiquaries considered material objects and ancient manuscripts to be artifacts indispensable for an empirical understanding of the past, positioning antiquarianism as a bulwark against the subjective foibles of text-based historiographies. Critics have interpreted *Otranto*'s preoccupation with objects explicitly in terms of Walpole's antiquarianism and on that basis have identified historiographic practices for which the text seems to advocate. Ruth Mack argues that Walpole's text theorizes the transition from the strictly text-based Enlightenment historiographic practice that reigned until the late eighteenth century to one based on objects. This new emphasis on artifacts heralded the nineteenth-century rise of archaeology as a field.[14]

While Mack's interpretation emphasizes Walpole's lack of interest in historical veracity, others, like Lake, insist on his "real historical knowledge" as the basis of *Otranto*'s broader critique.[15] Ultimately, Lake argues, *Otranto*'s allusions to historical source materials only emphasize the extent to which these have become "playthings of politicians ... easily misinterpreted, forgotten, or forged," finally emerging as "literary productions."[16] She concludes that, for Walpole, "who saw medieval manuscripts as evidentiary strongholds against tyranny, the antiquarian abuse of such sources for the benefit of the monarchy had poisoned the water in the archive."[17] It is precisely Walpole's esteem for the archive that causes him to lament its strategic manipulation in the interest of a distressing politics.

Whether Walpole lost faith in antiquarianism as a viable historiographic practice or not, there is no doubt that the representation of the past and the relationship between historical fact and fiction are matters at the center of *Otranto*.

The particular circumstances of *Otranto*'s publication speak to this centrality. Walpole first published the novel in 1764, under the guise of a pseudonym, William Marshal. In his preface to this first edition, he claims to have translated the text, a discovered medieval manuscript, from "the purest Italian." In this preface, Walpole assumes Marshal's persona, offering explanations of the manuscript's provenance, its date, its language, and the aims of its purported author. The assertion that the first edition was a translation of a discovered manuscript successfully duped even discerning readers. After the novel's positive reception, Walpole confessed his authorship in the new preface of the 1765 edition. This second edition, revealed as Walpole's own creation, met a cooler reception. In it, Walpole explains his motivation in composing *Otranto* as "an attempt to blend the two kinds of romance, the ancient and the modern."[18] Along with his decision to add the subtitle "A Gothic Story," this declaration transforms the second edition of the text to no less than "a manifesto for a new kind of writing," as E. J. Clery observes in her introduction to the text.[19] Walpole himself devotes a good portion of the preface to the second edition to a patriotic defense of Shakespeare—occasioned by Voltaire's critique of Shakespeare—announcing Shakespeare as his model and establishing himself as part of a continuum of a distinctly English literature.

The circumstances and reception of *Otranto*'s publication illustrate the tense interplay between fiction and history. Though the first edition, like subsequent ones, presented the text as fiction, its fictiveness was framed within an antiquarian act of historically relevant discovery. When the text was disguised as a relic from a past age, it offered readers a window to the past, reassuring them of the wide gap between their civilized contemporary reality and the terrifying one depicted in the novel. Walpole's confession of his authorship in the second edition, and his decision to label *Otranto* "A Gothic Story," confirmed it as *fiction* first and foremost, replacing the comfortable distance between antiquarian translator and ancient text with the proximity between author and contemporary text—in his words, "an attempt to blend" the past and present through literature. Whereas the first edition was presented to readers as a historical artifact, the second was a revealed as a product of their own age—an age clearly capable of imagining and representing violence and terror, despite its civilized, seemingly stable veneer.

As I have noted, several studies have traced the characters and plot of *Otranto* to the real-life personages and historical events that contextualized its writing and publication, and to Walpole's own historical sensibility.[20] They have analyzed *Otranto* in light of political debates in Walpole's England regarding the monarchy, the constitution, and the shifting social landscape and its effects on English law and custom.[21] For some readers, the story advocates against illegitimate succession, while for others it issues a scathing critique against the institution of the monarchy altogether.[22] This multiplicity of possible analyses of the past's function in the politics of the present is characteristic of the gothic. The dizzying plurality of interpretations of the novel's engagement with history and contemporary English politics; the first preface with its claims of historical authority and authenticity; the second preface, which confessed historical forgery and offered the novella as politically and culturally relevant fiction—all these factors converged in a tense moment in English political history.[23] Taken together with Walpole's antiquarian proclivities and his commitment to the material-historical basis for limited monarchical power, these circumstances make *The Castle of Otranto* fertile ground for a broader investigation of gothic historiography. It is critical to emphasize that Walpole did not dispute the historical method that some antiquarians invoked in defense of unchecked monarchical powers. To the contrary, as we have seen, the exploitation of the archive by politically savvy antiquarians dismayed him because of his commitment to historical manuscripts as truth. This faith in historical source material is directly relevant to the context of the writing and publication of *Mr. Mani*.

Though Yehoshua's novel was not published in its entirety until 1990, Yehoshua began writing it years earlier. Arnold Band traces its "original concept" to 1983–84 and the writing of its third section, published in March 1986 in the journal *Politika*, to 1984–85. Yehoshua resumed work on *Mr. Mani* two years later, after writing the novel *Molkho*.[24] The beginning of that decade in Israel saw the advent of the Israeli New History, a sweeping historiographic reassessment of the 1948 war.[25] This "historiographic revolution," in Benny Morris's words, was heralded by the publication of a handful of initially controversial historical studies that set about revising heretofore unquestioned aspects of the 1948 war, such as the question of whether Palestinians were expelled from their villages or simply left in the chaos of impending war, whether the British supported a Palestinian state or a Jewish one, and whether it was the Arabs or the Jews who obstructed attempts at conciliation following the war.[26] Led by Morris, Ilan Pappé, Avi Shlaim, and others, the Israeli New Historians revised Israeli history on the basis of the most established of historiographic conventions. The archive figured prominently in their work: in the early 1980s, they gained access to a vast trove of documents that had been sealed in accordance with Israel's Archives Law and its thirty-year rule, a relic of the British colonial presence in Palestine. Morris writes that the access to newly available documents meant that "for the first time historians have been able to write studies of the period on the basis of a large collection of contemporary source material."[27] The studies they published based on these documents dramatically transformed the way Israelis engaged with their own history and particularly with what the New History reinscribed as the founding myths of Israel.

In other words, the New Historians' methods were old, but the history they yielded was new. It constituted a radical revision of the Jewish Israeli narrative of the 1948 war that, for three decades, had nourished a comforting self-conception of Israeli innocence, bravery, and victimization. The New Historians refuted the narrative that had operated in the collective Israeli psyche less than a generation after the 1948 war. This "historiographic earthquake," asserts Morris, not only undermined previously held assumptions but also led to "the significant expansion of the realm of the permissible in Israeli historiographic discourse."[28]

Writing in 1988 about this watershed moment in Israeli historiography, Morris proposes a neat binary paradigm to explain the difference between the New Historians and their predecessors. He is particularly critical of previous historians' lack of empirical rigor: the "Old History was written largely on the basis of interviews and memoirs, and at best it made use of select batches of documents, many of them censored, such as those from the IDF Archive."[29] Morris points to their personal proximity to the historical events they narrate as a factor that compromises their objectivity, but he considers their inability to access the archives the key weakness of their studies. The paucity of documents referenced by the so-called Old Historians, according to Morris, invalidates their historiography. Indeed, he questions its status as historiography altogether: "Israel's Old Historiography was in a sense merely a 'prehistory,' not academic historiography at all. Much of it, indeed, was written by politicians, . . . and was not based on repositories of contemporary documentation (as all good history must be)."[30] In Morris's eyes, the New Historians alone could produce "good history"—rigorous, objective, and unbiased historical studies based on empirical evidence in the form of archival material. It is not only the Old Historians whose historical seriousness Morris doubts, however. He also dismisses those historians who work with the same declassified documents as the New Historians but arrive at conclusions that support different political inclinations.[31] Here, then, we encounter an Israeli parallel to the antiquarian abuses lamented by Walpole: archival material, despite its claim of empiricism and historical truth, is always in danger of becoming a "plaything of politicians."

The publication of these studies in Israel and the painful, protracted public discourse they instigated began in the same decade as the Israeli invasion of Lebanon, the first Israeli war to garner popular opposition and protest since the establishment of the state, and a flash point in *Mr. Mani*. The questions of history and historiography that obsessively circulate through the novel were clearly influenced by these developments and the increasing public awareness in Israel of the violability of the most widely held historical truths. Much as eighteenth-century England grappled with the incorporation of its history into newly forming notions of "Englishness," leaving its mark in the gothic mechanics and theme of *Otranto*, so did the revision of the Israeli historical narrative upend comfortable notions of Israeliness. For Yehoshua, the fragility and changeability of the narrative representation of the past is grounded in the public discourse of his present. Like *Otranto*, *Mr. Mani* is preoccupied with the highly ambiguous relationship between fiction and historical fact. This fixation is evident in the novel's narrative structure, its thematizations of history, and its destabilization of the concept of historical origin through transgression generally and incest specifically.

Structures of History-Telling

As authors of fiction, both Walpole and Yehoshua express the relations between the past and the present less through an investigation of the past event itself and more through a consideration of how the story of the past is told. "*Otranto* does not attempt to rationally and realistically chronicle a given historical period," Dent points out. "It is more concerned with the way in which the past comes to be narrativized and structured."[32] Something akin to this "fetishization of the process of narrative," in Fiona Robertson's words, characterizes *Mr. Mani*.[33] From the novel's first pages, it is clear that we are dealing with no ordinary narrative apparatus. The novel opens with a table of contents, entitled "The Order of the Conversations," that lists five conversations, including the year and place of their occurrence as well as the corresponding page number in the book. The first conversation takes place in 1982, and subsequent conversations move backward in time until the fifth, which takes place in 1848. The next page lists all the "Conversation partners" and includes their occupations and the dates of their births and deaths. Each of the five conversations opens by indicating the setting, this time adding the exact date and even the time of each conversation. The title page is followed by a brief, factual biography of each of the conversation partners. These sections are italicized in their entirety, setting them apart visually. These biographies invariably end with the following bizarre announcement about one of the conversation partners: "His [or her] half of the conversation is missing." Presented as metatextual materials that grant the narrative historical authenticity, these sections perform a function similar to that of the "discovered manuscript" device employed by Walpole in the first edition of *Otranto*. As the reader is encouraged to accept William Marshal's classification of *Otranto* as an authentic historical manuscript on the basis of the first preface of *Otranto*, so, too, are Yehoshua's readers compelled to accept his narrator's authority in these metatextual sections, on the basis of their authoritative tone, plentiful empirical historical data, and a structural separation from the obviously subjective conversation sections.

The central function of these metatextual sections is to ground the conversations within a seemingly impartial narrative. The tone of the narrator in the sections preceding and following each conversation ("The Conversation Partners" and "Biographical Supplements") offers a thread of coherence and continuity from one conversation to the next. Whereas the conversations themselves vary wildly in narrative voice and in the language the characters presumably speak, the sections framing them offer a consistent narrative presence. This narrator's authoritative, omniscient, and distant comportment, even when he narrates exceedingly violent and painful events, suggests historical objectivity.

At the same time, however, the narrator subtly subverts his own uncompromising subjectivity. The "Conversation Partners" section of the second conversation, for example, on Egon Bruner, reads thus: "Twenty-two years old. Born in 1922 on an estate near Flansburg, in the north German district of Schleswig-Holstein, to Werner Sauchon and Mariette Bruner. Admiral

Werner Sauchon (b. 1861) was one of the most highly lauded German officers in the First World War, in which he served with special distinction in the great Baltic Sea battles of 1914. In 1916 he and his wife Andrea lost their only son Egon on the Western Front, in the trenches of Verdun."[34] Andrea's biography details the same events thus: "With the outbreak of the world war, Egon was called to the colors and sent to the Western Front after a short period of basic training. He was only twenty when he was killed. His death affected Andrea more severely than it did her husband, who was involved in fighting the war, in which he served with great merit and won the highest decorations."[35] Both sections report facts and strike an almost encyclopedic tone through incomplete sentences ("Born in 1922"), dates and other details enclosed in parenthesis, and the bolding of names. However, the subtle shifts in emphasis and tone—such the observation that Egon "was only twenty when he was killed" in Andrea's biography—suggest that the narrator does, in fact, have some emotional investment in these characters and their plights. The official history contains affective shades of gray. Yehoshua elasticizes these seemingly rigid biographies in other ways, as well. Rather than adhering to the year specified, these historical sections must also deviate from their own timelines to refer to past and future events. For example, the second conversation takes place in 1944, but "The Conversation Partners" section preceding it refers to World War I and the Treaty of Versailles; the "Biographical Supplements" section refers to the 1982 Israeli invasion of Lebanon. Interspersed with affect and the intrusions of other times and places, these moments of official historical narratives can function only by evoking others.

The conversations in *Mr. Mani*, it turns out, are actually not conversations at all but lengthy, detailed monologues. Each "conversation" is followed by a section titled "Biographical Supplements," which informs the reader of the fate of the conversation partner, reprising the ostensibly disinterested tone of the biographies that precede the conversations. By contrast, the speakers in the "conversations" themselves are passionate, eloquent (sometimes overly so), even desperate to convince their "partners" or auditors of their version of events. Though each conversation is centered on a personal, individual experience, it is also rooted in a collective historical experience: the Lebanon War, the German occupation of Crete during World War II, the British Mandate of Palestine starting in 1918, the birth pangs of political Zionism in Europe at the turn of the nineteenth century, and the rumblings of revolutions and uprisings of 1848 that presaged the downfall of feudalism and empire and the rise of nationalism. Though the conversations themselves engage with these events from a highly subjective perspective, the structure of the novel compels the reader to relate their narratives to these dates and their historical significance. Yehoshua, then, presents us with a personal narrative entangled with and framed within a historical one. In *Mr. Mani*, the personal is history, and history is personal.

Unlike the narrator of the metatextual sections, the speakers in the conversations are highly emotional. They are frequently critical of their auditors, domineering in their dialogue, and determined to tell their story in its entirety and in their own way. The stories they tell often contradict the official histories with which they are associated, subverting the continuity suggested by the biographical sections that bookend them. Egon Bruner's description of his decidedly unheroic experience after barely surviving his parachute jump does not align with the narrative, mentioned by the biographer, of "the daring conquest of Crete." Lieutenant Ivor Stephen Horowitz's report on espionage reveals a spy whose motivations confound the British. Efrayim Shapiro's account of the Zionist Congress in Basel strips away the veneer of ideological conviction to reveal carousing delegates and a sickly Herzl whose pulse disappears.[36] The conversations, which comprise the bulk of the novel, emerge from those gray areas that interrupt the objectivity of the biographies' official histories. Egon Bruner speaks for all five speakers when he scolds his conversation partner for questioning him: "Look here, Grandmother, this is *my* story."[37] The implication is that his grandmother is acquainted with the official history and on that basis tries to correct or question his account, an act he resists because his personal experience adds a new dimension to the official narrative.

Yet it would be wrong to claim that the conversations merely "fill in the blanks" of the biographical information, as we might imagine that personal oral histories flesh out archival records. After all, Yehoshua could have simply produced five monologues rather than five one-sided conversations; doing so would have eliminated the interrupted sentences, the digressions, ellipses, and frustrations that accompany oral conversation. Of course, these are the very factors that emphasize the subjectivity of the "conversation" narratives. Critically, the conversation structure subverts itself no less than do the biographical elements. The reader can access only one of the two sides of the conversation and can only deduce what the missing side contributes. The only explanation the narrator provides for the one-sided conversations is that the other side is "missing," a claim that consolidates the historiographic nature of the narrative and points to the inherent incompleteness of historical accounts. The missing conversation half contributes to an antiquarian sensibility: by compelling us to rely on the existing half, this structure literalizes the materiality of narrative and underscores our tendency to fetishize it. As in the first edition of *Otranto*, presented as a discovered manuscript, the telling of history consciously announces itself as a substitute for the past, an accumulation of fragments that depends on a reader who can collect and interpret them—despite the missing pieces, and despite the hidden origin.

This relates to another paradigm for the conceptualization of historical narrative in *Mr. Mani*, the labyrinth. "What the cryptic maze produces most," argues Jerrold E. Hogle, "is the drive of narrative itself, narrative emerging from other narratives as new fabrications try and fail to fill the blanks in the old ones. Here lies the Gothic penchant for stories-within-stories-within-stories."[38] One narrative gives birth to another, each one attempting to resolve the unresolvable riddle at the heart of the maze, until finally the narrative arrives at its origin, only to discover that it also contains the seeds of its own dissolution.

Like the missing conversation halves, multiple examples of failed communication in the novel suggest structural fragmentation. The result of textual tampering or loss, they lead to misunderstanding and anxiety. The first conversation opens with Hagar's insistence that she called her mother and left a message with a kibbutz volunteer, which her worried mother never received. In the second conversation, Egon explains his extended silence to his hurt grandmother, who has flown from northern Germany to Crete to deliver personally a military transfer order that he ultimately destroys. In the fourth conversation, Efrayim Shapiro learns from his father that the telegraph Efrayim claims to have composed—"We are well. Will start home after Yom Kippur"—was altered and truncated to read, enigmatically, "We are happy," greatly concerning his father.[39]

Such failures of transmission are characteristic of gothic novels, which deploy, as Cannon Schmitt observes, "as both a theme and a narrative device, indecipherable, illegible, or unspeakable words."[40] This "breakdown of communication between genders and classes" in gothic literature, he argues, is a mode of "estrangement" that parallels the uneasy relationship that modernity has with its own feudal past.[41] In none of these examples of failed intergenerational communication in *Mr. Mani* can the reader be certain that the speakers are telling their auditors the truth; each one contains the possibility of mendaciousness and unreliability. In each case, the text involved—a message, a military communiqué, a telegram—has the capacity to shed light on or change the course of events but instead creates distrust, ambiguity, and fear. Again, the novel problematizes the fetishization of narrative by presenting texts as material historical fragments subject to interference.

Yehoshua offers readers two historiographic paradigms: one that seems objective, positivist, dry, and factual and one that seems subjective, passionate, one-sided, and affective. Both of these paradigms, though, expose and trespass their own limitations. The singular "official history" encompasses multiple histories; meanwhile, the personal narratives, despite their pronounced subjectivity, depend on and are shaped by official history, even as they resist or contradict it. Dates and names presented in the context of their personal rather than collective relevance carry for the reader accumulated historical associations that transform the signifier into the signified, such as "Oświęcim," the Polish name for Auschwitz, and 1897, the eventful year of Ivor Horowitz's birth.[42] In *Mr. Mani*, narrative itself becomes a substitute for the past.

Reading *Mr. Mani* as an unidealized Sephardic Jewish history, Arnold Band argues that it "is by no means a historical novel; on the contrary, it is an antihistorical novel in that it is an attempt to undo Jewish historiography of the past century."[43] The novel's distinctive reverse chronology, he asserts, is designed to shatter "any possible sense of continuum" and subvert assumptions of Zionist and Jewish history: "Our normative comprehension of meaningful historical sequence is subverted; our reading is actually archaeological, since we are led to dig from the present through successive layers to the lowest, initial level."[44] Similarly, Gershon Shaked writes that *Mr. Mani* is a "historical novel, based on an anti-historical methodology."[45] While there is no doubt that the narrative's reverse chronology is disorienting, is it as subversive as it seems? The novel maintains chronological order, causality, and continuity—in reverse. Rather than "shatter" a sense of historical sequence, it flips it, calling attention to the retrospective nature of historiography itself. As such, it is more concerned with exposing and exploring the mechanics of historical narrative than with undermining them. In this light, Band's likening of the experience of reading *Mr. Mani* to archaeology is relevant beyond the temporal sense he indicates. Archaeology's emphasis on artifacts suggests a privileging of materiality that, in the context of historiography, we may connect to archive-based historiographic practice such as that espoused by antiquarianism or by the Israeli New Historians. Like the New Historians, Yehoshua does not radically revise traditional methodologies in *Mr. Mani*; like them, he mobilizes these methodologies to new, unexpected ends.

Whether or not we accept the overall temporal organization of the novel as relatively conservative, there is no question that other structural elements are unusual. For example, despite the retroactive linear chronology, there is at the same time something cyclical encoded in the plot's mysterious Manis, its deaths, its births, and its transgressions.[46] Beyond the plot's simultaneously linear and cyclical temporal organization lie additional structural idiosyncrasies, such as its dialogic or, more accurately, monologic construction, and its insistence on labeling these narratives "conversations" and then enigmatically proclaiming half of each conversation to be "missing." Even if the reader had access to the missing half of the conversations, it is immediately evident in all five that the speakers whose stories we have monopolize the conversations, whereas their auditors—always their elders or other authority figures—are captives in a gothic drama. All the speakers beseech their auditors, in varying degrees of intensity, to allow them to tell their stories, to hear them out, to avoid jumping to conclusions. These disruptions in the monologue indicate the presence of the conversation partner while emphasizing the absence of his or her narrative. The partner is present but absent, a specter haunting the speaker's narrative. The one-sided conversations offer the most readily apparent example of incomplete communication, but as we have seen, the novel also includes truncated telegrams, undelivered notes, and destroyed military communiqués. These interrupted and incomplete narratives point to the complex relationship between telling a story and "telling history" in *Mr. Mani*, leading to the same question as *Otranto*: How does narrative function as both method and subject?

Thematizations of History in *Mr. Mani*

Many readers have understood *Mr. Mani* as, on some level, a subversive Sephardic Jewish history.[47] Like the gothic narratives whose representations of the past challenge the rational and teleological historiography associated with the Enlightenment, Yehoshua's novel entangles the reader in the weblike trajectories of the Mani family and its interlocutors to contest historiographic narratives that present Jewish and Israeli histories as linear, univocal, and transparently causational. Though *Mr. Mani* does establish an absent Sephardi story within the Israeli narrative, this is no facile attempt to replace one official history with another. Yehoshua demonstrates how the Manis' story—or one of its many versions—spills far beyond the geographic, cultural, and ideological boundaries of Israel. Further, though the Manis' "Sephardi story" is perhaps the most readily apparent manifestation of Yehoshua's preoccupation with history and historiography in the novel, it is by no means the only one. Each of the five conversations confronts the question of history thematically, in the context of a particular historical event or development.

In the first conversation, Hagar follows the suicidal Judge Gavriel Mani through an unfamiliar Jerusalem, seeking "the true inner heart" of the city.[48] She discovers facets of the city that were foreign to her—an Orthodox Jewish neighborhood, an Arab hospital, an old cemetery far below the Mount of Olives, with a Mani grave dating to the nineteenth century, that is "not a place tourists get to."[49] Convinced that he has met Hagar before, Mani subjects her to a "family interrogation," asking about her parents and specifically wondering "if there weren't some Jerusalemites among them."[50] When she mentions the book she has seen in his home on historic Jerusalem neighborhoods, Hagar elicits Mani's enthusiasm and learns about the Kerem Avraham house he inherited from his great-grandfather, who ran a gynecological clinic for Arabs and Jews there. This conversation sees the transformation of Hagar from a visitor to someone more intimately acquainted with the city's "true heart," its historic diversity. It also establishes the history of Jerusalem itself as interwoven with that of the Manis.

The second conversation takes up the study of history itself as a central theme.[51] Its interpretation vis-à-vis contemporary events motivates the German soldier Egon Bruner to tell his story. Egon, having requested that his grandmother send him a text on ancient Greek history, recalls his studies of this subject with his tutor Gustav Koch: "He was the first to call for casting the rusty anchor of German history back into that sea you see down there, because there, he used to say, was the warm, true, blue womb of the German genius."[52] Egon interprets this connection between Greece and Germany, realized finally in the German occupation of Crete, as the opportunity "*to exit from history* by hook or by crook, if not forward then backward."[53] Walking through the ruins of the Labyrinth at Knossos, Egon feels that he has guessed Hitler's secret motivation: "The Führer was obeying old

Gustav Koch's imperative to look for that most ancient source at which, Grandmother, I, Private Egon Bruner, had arrived all by myself, the first German arrow to be shot from that great bow."[54] Mani's astonishing assertion to Egon—that he had "cancelled" his Jewishness—proves irresistible to Egon, who wonders "for the sake of Germany and the Germans, . . . if one couldn't return to the starting point and become *simply human again*, a new man who can cancel the scab of history that sticks to us like ugly dandruff and put the dark, moldy rooms full of worm-eaten books, the faded oil paintings, the grotesque sculptures, behind him for the sunlit aperture."[55] Knossos and ancient Greek civilization represent the purity of origin unhindered by invented identities and even by the materiality of history—books, paintings, sculptures.[56] To exit history means to reject the corruption and artifice that create the wound of "identity," which festers beneath the "scab of history."

In the third conversation, Yosef Mani risks his life to advocate for the opposite of this idea: that identity is the key to *entering* history. In exchange for the British documents he smuggles, he demands to deliver speeches to Arab villagers, reading them an Arabic translation of the Balfour Declaration and entreating them to define themselves: "'Who are ye? Awake, before it is too late and the world is changed beyond recognition! Get ye an identity, and be quick!' . . . 'All over the world people now have identities, and we Jews are on our way, and you had better have an identity or else!'"[57] As his impassioned plea nearly costs him his life, it comes as no great surprise that his son will reject this sensibility in the second conversation, preferring to dissociate from matters of identity and history.

The fourth conversation's comical portrayal of the 1899 Zionist Congress deflates the gravitas of this historic event. Efrayim describes his sister Linka's "scandalous" black dress, the men hanging over her, the sickly Theodor Herzl himself, whose alarming "vanished pulse" gives way to laughter "as if he had simply played a prank on all the doctors."[58] It is not Basel but Jerusalem, not the newly designed flag for the Jewish State but the Western Wall, that encompasses "a last stop of history. . . . It is perhaps the ultimate dam, built to hold back the Jews in their restless proclivity to return to their past."[59] In Efrayim's narrative, Herzl is pitifully weak and destined to die young; though Zionist ideology fosters hope for the future, the Zionist Congress is a rowdy, opportunistic circus. Jerusalem, by contrast, is the "stone womb that is the mother of us all," both the origin and the end of Jewishness and Jewish history.[60]

Efrayim does not stay in Palestine, however. His return from Palestine to "the black waters of the Vistula," near an estate abutting a Polish forest and the future site of Auschwitz, is one of the novel's most distinctly gothic passages:

> You once told us a story about the dead . . . at the Resurrection, the Christians would rise from their graves where they were, but we Jews would crawl through underground caverns and come out in the Land of Israel . . . which is just what I've been doing these past few days, but in the opposite direction—from there to here—cavern-crawling and turning over in many graves—as though traveling not upon the globe but deep beneath its surface . . . from tunnel to tunnel and from one remote station to another—each time the same flicker of gas lamps and the same onrush of blackness, and then the same total nothing—and wherever you looked in the foggy distance, our flour mills standing like titans—talk of resurrection![61]

Evoking standard gothic imagery—subterranean labyrinths, darkness, graves, fog, giants—Efrayim's description of the journey that culminates in his return to his beloved native Poland reverses the Zionist vision of return to Zion and suggests a countermythology to the Land of Israel mythos of a land flowing with milk and honey. Emphatically macabre, the description foreshadows his homeland's transformation to the most notorious of mass Jewish graves. At the same time, it sketches a route, from Palestine back to Poland, that is convoluted, dark, and regressive. Though it presents a stark contrast to the Shapiros' well-organized itinerary of trains and ships *to* Palestine, that straightforward trajectory, too, is shrouded in gothic mystery by dint of the siblings' confinement in Palestine by Dr. Mani, "our captor, that oriental gynecologist."[62]

The final conversation returns explicitly to the question of identity and its role in history. Yosef Mani is obsessed with Jews "who did not yet know that they were Jews or had completely forgotten it."[63] Together with the British consul, he had attempted to remind them. His father, Avraham Mani, comments that "the consul, like all Englishmen, looked upon us Jews not as creatures of flesh and blood but as purely literary heroes who had stepped out of the pages of the Old Testament and would step back into those of the New at the Last Judgment, and who meanwhile must be kept from entering another story by mistake."[64] That "other story" might be the story of Jewish national consciousness, still half a century away from its political expression. It might be a story of coexistence in a diverse Jerusalem, or it might simply be a disengagement from politics and history.

Avraham Mani understands Yosef's idée fixe about returning Muslims to their forgotten Jewishness as a direct threat to his marriage and to the continuity of his family: "It was then that I first understood . . . that he was in the grips of a notion more important to him than his own marriage—of an *idée fixe*, as the French say, that mattered to him more than having seed."[65] It is here, in the originary conversation—in the lowest stratum, to reprise the archaeological metaphor—that the filial and the political intersect, that the question of identity has implications for the future of the family. In Avraham's mind, Yosef's homosexual relations with the young Arab men of Jerusalem are intertwined with his political idée fixe. Both his politics and his sexuality are transgressive and prevent him from fulfilling his obligation to his family. Both undergird Avraham's likely murder of his own son and the incest he commits to ensure the continuity of the Mani line. The transgressions multiply, converging as a gothic wail whose reverberations echo through each of the earlier conversations' articulations of history and identity.

The Artifice of Origin and the Rise of the House of Mani

As we have seen, several studies have established the link between the gothic and the formation of Englishness, or what today we would call an English national identity. In a statement that might well be applicable to twentieth-century Israel, Diane Long Hoeveler, writing about British gothic dramas, observes that in "a nation struggling to consolidate land it had only recently claimed, as well as land it was claiming abroad on a tenuous basis at best, the political guilt and social anxiety must have been intense. At the same time that the national borders were viewed as precarious and diffuse, so were the psychic ones."[66] The gothic disinterred buried corpses and unleashed wronged specters to speak for those whom nationalist endeavors had silenced. The text of *Otranto*, however, is also amenable to a very different interpretation. Reading *Otranto* through Julia Kristeva's notion of abjection, for example, Robert Miles suggests that "the story allegorizes the foundering of the emergent nation's attempt at identity, with its 'imaginary' unity crumbling back into its component parts."[67] *Otranto* can thus be read as either subversive or complicit with nationalism.

The point, however, is not to ascertain whether *Otranto* reinforces the nation but rather to recognize the gothic representation of "historically specific material that was part and parcel of the construction of the Nation, with what was thrown down, in order for the Nation to be built up."⁶⁸ The thematic concern of the gothic is thus linked to its preoccupation with pure national identity, argues Miles: "The recurrent Gothic interest in fakes, faking, and plagiarism, belongs to the nationalist trajectory of the Gothic."⁶⁹ Texts may express the tension between "fakery" and authenticity structurally and thematically to reflect the paradox of national identity, which bases claims of authenticity on artful historical constructions.

The most significant factor destabilizing the Mani narrative is the "fakery" revealed at its origin: the novel's exposure of false filial purity, of corrupt blood, and, by extension, of the artifice of the nation itself.⁷⁰ This fakery is revealed, at the novel's conclusion, to be based on incest, forbidden for Jews in Leviticus 18. The melodramatic scene that exposes the dark secret at the heart of the Mani family constitutes the novel's most typically gothic tableau and the most explicit instance of adulteration in a novel brimming with corruption, impurity, and transgression. The existing critical landscape of the novel reads the incest scene either as an intertextual allusion to the biblical story of Judah and Tamar or as evidence of Yehoshua's engagement with Freudian and Lacanian thought.⁷¹ In this novel that not only opens itself up to alternate interpretations but emphatically invites them, the gothic is well positioned to offer a compelling additional interpretive stratum to these critical layers.

In gothic texts, the sins of the fathers are figured, literally, as fragments, "traces that suggest an absence as they supplement each other to begin a series of substitution where one script of death takes over from another to establish an illusion of genealogy," in Hogle's vivid formulation.⁷² The diverting of these traces results in what Hogle calls a Gothic cryptonomy, which produces "a perpetual dissolution of identity."⁷³ In *The Castle of Otranto*, the "perpetual dissolution of identity" is linked to the illusion of genealogy, revealed through the acknowledgment of Manfred's illegitimacy and his willingness to commit incest and murder to maintain the pretense of legitimacy. These factors, in turn, expose the inadequacies of histories and their telling, and at the same time establish narrative as the only means of (re)establishing legitimacy. *Mr. Mani*, on the other hand, deals with a similar set of "traces"—incest, murder, and other transgressions—within its own gothic cryptonomy, but to different ends.

The key gothic tableau that seals *Mr. Mani* and reveals, finally, the secret at the heart of the family is composed of a dying rabbi, who has been rendered speechless by a stroke, lying helplessly in an inn in Athens, forced to listen to the narrative of Avraham Mani, who reveals to him in a lengthy, detailed monologue the truth about his grandson: that he is actually his *son*, the product of an incestuous encounter between Avraham and his dead son's young wife, intended to save the Mani line from extinction.[74] The dead son's ambiguous sexual orientation, his intimate friendship with the Arab men of Jerusalem, his lack of interest in his wife, and his obsession with a nativist idée fixe may, the novel suggests, have even driven Avraham to murder him. The passage evokes an intense gothic sensibility through macabre imagery and a marked emphasis on mirrors and seemingly supernatural doubles:

> I began to strip off my clothes, until I was standing naked in that frozen room, in that locked, vestigial house, facing a looking-glass that was facing a looking-glass.... He was turning among the old graves on the Mount of Olives, he was icy and shredding, his blood was ebbing from him, his flesh was ebbing and being eaten away, and as I drew him back into myself his seed flew through the darkness like a snowflake and was swallowed inside me until we were one again, I was he and he was me—and then, by solemn virtue of his betrothal in Beirut and of his holy matrimony in Jerusalem, he rose, and went into the next room, and ... possessed his bride to beget his grandson, and died once more.
> And died once more, Rabbi Shabbetai, do you hear me?[75]

A month after his son's death and his own transgression, Mani goes to the graveyard to consecrate the tombstone: "And when the 'Lord, Full of Mercy' was sung opposite the yellow walls of that drear city while a raw winter wind cut to the bone, I felt most certain ... that I had succeeded in preventing any future disgrace.... The world would have its Manis after all."[76] Avraham Mani directs his confession to the dying Rabbi Heddaya and his wife, Flora Molkho, because he blames them for the narrowly averted catastrophe of the end of the Mani line. Though he had hoped to marry Doña Flora, she had spurned him and instead wed the elderly rabbi, a man incapable of having children. Avraham Mani's relations with his son's wife, Tamara, are as much a function of his desire to maintain the Mani line as to avenge his humiliation, as Tamara is Doña Flora's doppelgänger, "but thirty years younger.... A most wondrous apparition."[77] For Avraham Mani, her uncanny resemblance to Doña Flora makes her the ideal vehicle to reassert his masculinity and save the Mani line from extinction. It also intensifies his misdeed, as he considers Doña Flora "the one woman he ever loved, half a mother and half an older sister," with whom he imagines the "great transgression" to have occurred.[78]

The shocking revelation that emerges from Avraham Mani's triumphant confession reconstitutes the action driving *The Castle of Otranto*. Manfred is determined to safeguard his ill-begotten castle and estate at Otranto by marrying his only son, Conrad, to Isabella, the daughter of the marquis of Vicenza, later revealed to be the rightful inheritor of the Otranto estate. Conrad is killed by supernatural forces in the beginning of the novel just before the nuptials, spinning Manfred into a frenzied state. The only way to ensure that Otranto remains in Manfred's family, he decides, is for him to take his son's intended, Isabella, for himself so as to produce an heir. "Isabella, since I cannot give you my son, I offer you myself," he announces. "Heavens," cries the stunned Isabella, "What do I hear? You, my lord! You! My father in law! The father of Conrad!" Isabella, who initially believes that "grief had disordered Manfred's understanding," is "half-dead with fright and horror," and flees through the locked castle, lit only by tremulous moonlight, until she discovers a subterraneous passage leading to a nearby church.[79]

The similarities in Yehoshua's key scene to *Otranto*'s plot are striking. A desperate father wants to ensure the continuation of his bloodline; rendered irrational by the murder of the son that constituted his only hope (and, in both texts, whose "manliness was in doubt"), he determines to take his son's place by taking his daughter-in-law for himself and producing the longed-for heir.[80] As in *Otranto*, which stresses Conrad's femininity as a factor in his father's attempt to take his place in impregnating the young daughter-in-law, so, too, does *Mr. Mani*'s fifth conversation portray Yosef Mani's homosexual relations with Jerusalem's Arab men as similarly motivating his father's assumption of Yosef's marital obligations. Moreover, in both texts, the father is directly or indirectly responsible for his son's murder. However, while incest in *Otranto* and in other gothic novels is forcible—that is, it is both rape and incest—in *Mr. Mani* it is consensual. In fact, the incest in *Otranto* is not actually realized, while in *Mr. Mani* it is. Compounding the gothicism of the scene, Yehoshua raises the murdered Yosef Mani from his grave, incorporating him into his father's body to impregnate his widowed bride and killing him a second time after the deed is done. In Avraham Mani's narration, incest is a joint venture that mingles the appropriate with the illegitimate and the conception of new life with death.

Both *Otranto* and *Mr. Mani* contain the threat or actualization of sexual transgressions, symbolic or literal; both also relate these transgressive sexual acts to imagined doppelgängers. In *Otranto*, Manfred terrorizes his intended daughter-in-law, ultimately plunging a dagger into his own daughter—enacting a symbolic incest—in a case of mistaken identity. *Mr. Mani* narrates a proliferation of incestuous acts. The crucial origin scene that sets the tone for the Mani genealogy, in which Avraham Mani impregnates his dead son's wife, is complicated by Tamara's uncanny resemblance to Doña Flora. "One passage through life had not been enough for so charming a visage, and so it had come back a second time," observes Avraham Mani.[81] The fourth conversation all but explicitly reveals the incestuous relationship between the Shapiro siblings, Linka and Efrayim, though its surface concern is with the adulterous love between the married Dr. Mani and Linka. The third conversation deals more with political transgressions than sexual ones, describing a Turkish spy for the British as "Mani's double from over the lines."[82] Egon Bruner, the speaker of the second conversation, was conceived as a replacement for his parents' dead son. Because of their advanced age, they had to enlist another woman to conceive and give birth to him, and he calls the woman who raised him "Grandmother." An instant before her death, she momentarily thinks that the British fighter pilot who downs her plane looks like Egon. In the first conversation, Hagar dons Judge Mani's dead grandmother's embroidered nightgown when she spends the night at his apartment. Meanwhile, her own mother develops a romantic relationship with Judge Mani after Hagar's baby is born. Judge Mani himself is certain that he has seen Hagar somewhere before. What lies behind the novel's fulfilled and unfulfilled transgressions, mostly sexual in nature? What is the relationship between doubles, doppelgängers, uncanny resemblances, and sexual transgression, and what does this relationship contribute to the novel's understanding of history and historiography?

Sexual transgression is a defining feature of gothic literature, and incest in particular has been the subject of much scholarly scrutiny. A fundamental paradox characterizes incest, as Maggie Kilgour has observed: "At the same time as it opposes the needs of modern society, [incest] is also an exaggerated form of the relations they require, a parody of the modern introverted nuclear family."[83] This contradiction recalls what Shira Stav, writing about father-daughter relations, has characterized as an "incest trap," whereby both the taboo of incest and its breach operate to maintain patriarchal social structures.[84] Similarly, but beyond fathers and daughters, Paul Baines describes the incest depicted in another Walpole text, *The Mysterious Mother*, as "stimulated by the very domestic scene it violates," since the mother seduces the son who resembles his dead father.[85]

Incestuous sexuality is linked to uncanny resemblance more broadly, as Jill Campbell posits. Female bodies, she argues, are either spectral in their uncanny resemblance to other (absent) women or hyperphysical and present always in the context of wombs or childbirth. These possibilities lead to her to identify "two ontologies of the body" in Walpole's writing, one highly physical and material, the other spectral and immaterial.[86] The question of the body is relevant in Yehoshua's novel, as well, which emphasizes childbirth, labor, infant death, fatally incompatible blood types, maternal weakness and illness, and of course the final morbid insemination of Yosef Mani's young wife by her dead husband via the body of Avraham Mani.[87] In *The Mysterious Mother*, Campbell points out, the countess desires her son when she sees him as the image of his father, "the strict resemblance of a recently-departed body; the body that is the doomed object of incestuous designs is characterized not by its hypermateriality but by the uncanniness with which it evokes the spectral recollection of a lost spouse."[88] As in *Otranto*, spectral bodies in *The Mysterious Mother* "have a way of stepping out of their frames," becoming physicalized through their uncanny resemblance to others. The incest in *Otranto*, asserts Campbell, occurs not only because Isabella is Manfred's intended daughter-in-law but also because the text presents her relations with Manfred and his wife Hippolita as one between a daughter and her parents.[89] The "dual ontology" that emerges from *Mr. Mani* is based on relations that were but are no more, and relations that could have been but were not. The incest or symbolic incest, in each case, mirrors another, unrealized relationship. The material body evokes the spectral body of another, and it is this evocation that allows incestuous desire to take hold.

How does incest relate to history? In a Foucauldian interpretation of the family as inherently incestuous, Ruth Perry underscores "the psychosexual meaning" of gothic historicity and the way it shapes filial ties and political inheritance. The gothic expression of

> the significance of the past to the meaning of the present ... is an essential aspect of incestuous threats and incestuous longings. Gothic remains invoke—and telescope—the history of a society as an analogue to that of an individual.... The gothic suggests that no one can create himself sui generis, ignoring his real genealogy, trying to be his own heir. No man can jump generations to create a new line, to father himself. No one can pervert the rightful succession, usurping another man's place or another generation's place. The meaning of the present can only be made out in terms of the past; the crimes of the past will be solved, will see the light of day, will be

acknowledged.... Incest implies the violation of genealogical principles and hence the short-circuiting of true succession and the perversion of history."⁹⁰

This interpretation is ultimately political. Where incest represents an attempt to subvert, defy, and rewrite filial and collective histories, gothic novels offer resolutions that resist this attempt. As Perry argues, "the way lineage always triumphs, usurpers are punished and rightful heirs reinstated... these genealogical inevitabilities must be read in part as a literary wish-fulfillment response to accelerating geographical and class mobility."⁹¹ Gothic works represent incest to signify a disruption of the "natural" social order, then work to restore this order.

Mr. Mani offers no such resolutions. To the contrary, it portrays an incestuous origin in which Avraham Mani attempts precisely "to be his own heir"—and succeeds. As Band has noted, that the Mani family story is inaugurated by this transgression suggests a critique of the concept of purity claimed through categories such as *Sfaradi tahor*, pure Sephardi. Rather than resolve or repress corruption and contamination, the novel highlights the complex histories to which they give rise. In *Mr. Mani*, there is no real "assertion of the genealogical imperative," in Perry's words.⁹² The novel begins where the historical narrative leaves off, with the continuation of the line through the birth of Roni Mani in 1983.

Nevertheless, death reigns. Each generation of Mani men inherits suicidal tendencies and carries death close; in the second conversation, Egon Bruner repeatedly refers to Yosef Mani as a ghost. Further, the relatively peaceful birth of Roni Mani and the continuation of the Mani line has as its backdrop war. Roni's maternal grandfather has died long before his birth in the 1967 Six-Day War, his father was on leave from the 1982 war when Roni was conceived, and his grandfather draws gunfire from an Arab village when he visits the kibbutz where Roni is being raised. War marks his past, present, and future. The significant role of Hagar's father, "our dead hero, who exists more than any of us in a single photograph," confirms the dominant role that war and death play in families, suggesting an explicit link between the filial and the national.⁹³

The ambiguities of *Mr. Mani* point less to an alternative historical narrative than to the inevitable ambiguity accompanying narrative in general. As in other gothic novels, continuity is disrupted, identities are revealed to have been false, and origins are discovered to have been deceptive. However, *Mr. Mani* reaches no resolution. The final conversation ends with two words, "Yes ... No ... ," their ellipses suggesting that the cycle of ambiguity is bound to continue as we spiral ever further back in time. There is no neat recitation of the "real" lineage or inheritance of the Mani family, no repositioning of the narrative threads, no ordering of the chaos.

Mr. Mani's resistance to the historical closure that typifies other gothic plots of incest shapes the role of narrative in the novel. Addressing the linguistic and narrative complexities emerging from acts of sexual transgression in *The Mysterious Mother*, Baines focuses on the discomfort and unease that the characters experience when attempting to speak about their acts. He relates this unease to the "link between paternity and authorship," urging for "the realization of the play as a collective document," not just psychobiography but "a more public kind of textual genealogy."[94] The fifth conversation in *Mr. Mani* centers on Avraham Mani's confession to his speechless rabbi; the rabbi's inability to speak literalizes the absent voices of the auditors in the previous four conversations. On the other hand, those conversation partners who do speak do so almost too eloquently. Not only do they feel no discomfort while speaking—and this includes Avraham Mani in the fifth conversation—but they also insist on telling the story, even if it means they must force it on their auditors. Indeed, it is the auditors, silent and submissive, who feel discomfort on hearing these stories, especially in the final conversation involving the confession of incest. Narrative itself is revealed as a tool of power and transgresses its own boundaries at the hands of these tenacious speakers. It is not telling stories that produces discomfort but listening to them, just as it is not writing histories but silently and passively consuming them that creates anxiety.

The matter of paternity factors into this narrative equation. Besides the incest that ensured that the world would have its Manis, the fact that the Mani line is patrilineal leaves various opportunities for genealogical trickery, as the mother's connection to the child, unlike the father's, is ascertained at the moment of birth. The novel portrays this phenomenon in an explicit and emphatically material manner—for example, in the descriptions of childbirth at Dr. Mani's Jerusalem clinic. In the second conversation, Egon Bruner observes that Efrayim Mani looks "like one of us"—that is, Aryan—suggesting genealogical interference like that which brought Egon himself into the world and into his own family's genealogy.[95] The notion of the author as paternal figure or sire of his text in relation to this narrative dynamic suggests that fragmentation and uncertainty are inherent components of storytelling, seeming to cast doubt on the author's authority. Yet the lack of discomfort in narrating transgressive acts, indeed the tone of triumph—"the world would have its Manis!"—together with the unbridled enthusiasm of the speakers to tell their stories in their own way and in their own time, suggest ownership and a firm grip on narrative on the part of the speakers as well as the author himself—even as they acknowledge that ambiguity is always at its foundation. If the novel is a "collective document," then readers must take stock of their own role as shapers of narrative through its consumption. Similarly, the designation of the missing conversation half matters, because it helps determine the way the stories are told. This multiplicity of narratives and of their shapers suggests that authorial paternity is never singular. It relies on the various speakers and readers, the seemingly objective narrator tying them together, and of course the author, Yehoshua himself, who had his own complex relationship with his father.[96]

Incest, to reprise Perry's phrasing, allows and signifies the "perversion of history." Early gothic novels like *Otranto* restore genealogy to its "appropriate" trajectory, preventing incest from hijacking it. We have already acknowledged that incest confirms filial ties through their very distortion, defamiliarizing and modifying existing relations to reassert them, ultimately confirming their validity. Despite its taboo status, incest does not radically revise family relations but rather works within their existing structure. This is one reason that some scholars read the gothic as reactionary and conservative, even as other characteristics of the mode point to its revolutionary potential. Regardless of which political reading one finds most convincing, it is clear that incest in gothic narratives mediates between the filial and history, genealogy and historiography. The dark secret at the foundation of the Manis' genealogy and the psychological echoes that emerge with each new generation suggest that history, as Egon Bruner observes, "is a scab," attempting to protect the painful wound throbbing beneath it and destined always to leave a scar. In the Israeli context of the writing of *Mr. Mani* in the 1980s, reading the novel thus can help historicize the novel itself and clarify the outsize role that historiography and the question of narrating history had taken on in the collective Israeli consciousness and public discourse in that decade. The 1980s in Israel saw a public reluctant and even hostile to the scab's lifting and the revelation of the wound beneath it. Ultimately, the renewed confrontation with the wound of 1948 urged Israelis to think in new ways not only about their past but also about the way it had been shaped, represented, narrated, and perceived. *Mr. Mani* reflects these critical confrontations with historiography by highlighting ambiguities of paternity and authorship and exposing the steep price the maintenance of historical continuity can exact.[97]

Narrative Disruptions and the Revision of Power

Though most critics agree that *Mr. Mani* disrupts conventional histories, whether in the form of ethnic-cultural mythologies, nationalist ideologies, or generational continuities, there is no consensus regarding what *Mr. Mani* offers instead: An alternative Sephardi history? A critique of nationalist ideology? An affirmation of Zionism as the telos of Jewish history? A psychoanalytic treatment of identity? Whichever interpretation one finds most compelling, the novel invites us to reevaluate our conception not only of Jewish and Israeli histories but also of historiographic practice more broadly.

How do these notions of history and historiography tie into the experience and representation of victimization? How can we outline the power relations in historiographic practice? The illumination of overshadowed narratives, suggests the novel, creates its own victims. Telling the story imbues the speaker with power; listening requires relinquishing that power. The novel directs our attention to the paradigm of the victims of historiography, of the violence of the narrative of history rather than of its concrete events. If we return for a moment to the two texts at hand, then we recall that one of the primary differences between their representations of incest is that in *Otranto* the threat of incest provokes Isabella's terror and her flight from the castle, while in *Mr. Mani* the perpetrator stays with his son's wife up to the moment she gives birth to his son, apparently without her objection. In fact, the text suggests that she herself has been frustrated by her husband's lack of ability or desire to consummate their marriage. Her father-in-law's advances seem more like a desperate last resort than a threat, suggesting that, like the biblical Tamar, she has some say in the unfolding of events. In any case, she is no terrified Isabella.

In the very structure of its narrative, *Mr. Mani* offers a set of relations capable of upending our understanding of power and powerlessness altogether by rejecting the paradigm of victims and victors usually understood to structure historiography. Defying the conventions of authority, the novel gives voice to the younger of the two conversation partners and denies it to his or her elder, who becomes, as we have noted, a literally captive audience.

Though the auditors do participate in the conversation, their interjections and responses are acknowledged but not transcribed; their presence is represented as an absence. Moreover, the novel casts them as figures who may have accomplished tremendous feats but who, in the moment of narration, are to various degrees passive, inconsequential, physically reduced, or incapable of defending themselves against various accusations leveled by the speakers. Just as the auditors are captives despite—and perhaps because of—their position of authority, so do the speakers themselves straddle the subject positions of both victor and victim, occupying both and neither at once: a confident young woman who lost her father to war, a cowardly German soldier whose existence was intended to compensate for his half-brother's death in battle, a loquacious Jewish British colonel affecting indifference to his colleagues' genteel antisemitism, a Polish Jew whose comical depiction of the Zionist Congress contrasts starkly with his tragic eventual death at Auschwitz, and a man who impregnates the young doppelgänger of the woman who rejected him.

The fact that we do not tell or write histories in a vacuum, that narrative requires consumers and interpreters, means that historiography is always filtered hierarchically. *Mr. Mani* complicates this notion: by promoting disappointing sons and daughters to independent thought and action and demoting great colonels and rabbis to speechlessness, it demonstrates the fluidity of roles within inherently violent hierarchies of power and weakness. While the auditors in *Mr. Mani* are violated by the narrative that denies them a voice, the speakers are both empowered and made vulnerable by it, constantly having to plea, defend themselves, and assert themselves in the face of incredulity, impatience, and resistance to their stories. Narrative is a knife that cuts both ways. The representation of its orality in the novel, however, reminds us that it signifies a social relation. Much as incest confirms the very filial structure it seems to defy, so does the violent silencing of the conversation partners confirm that this is a dialogue and not a monologue. In other words, the missing conversation halves serve as a constant reminder of the dialogism of each section, even as they evoke an authoritarian univocality—a forceful representation of the mechanics of historiography.

The complex and highly detailed geographical biographies at the basis of Yehoshua's disruptive narratives, which trace the characters' movements across the Mediterranean region and Eastern Europe, establish a ghostly Jewish cartography that, like the conversations themselves, is composed as much of absence and disappearance as it is of presence. Jerusalem is the spectral anchor for the novel as a whole, wintery in affect even in the summer. Each conversation, save the second, establishes a spatial pairing between a shadowy, mysterious Jerusalem and another place: in the first, with secular Israel (signified both by the kibbutz and Tel Aviv); in the third, with colonial Britain; in the fourth, with Poland; in the fifth, with Salonika. It is no coincidence that the only conversation in which Jerusalem is not central is also the only one whose speaker is a non-Jew. For Egon Bruner, the "womb" of German (and thus world) civilization is not stony Jerusalem but cerulean Greece.

The novel stresses Jerusalem's uncanniness as much as it emphasizes that of the characters traversing and inhabiting the city—the cryptonomy of Jerusalem mirrors the Labyrinth at Knossos, just as its "stone womb" mirrors the "blue womb of the Mediterranean."[98] The uncanniness of Jerusalem in this novel is accentuated by Yehoshua's gothic imagery, as, for example, the black goats that revisit each conversation like a sinister omen. Lying in a hospital room in East Jerusalem, Hagar Shiloh watches a wave of black goats approaching in the desert landscape visible from her window. In Jerusalem in 1918, recounts Sergeant Shapiro, "a shepherdless herd of black goats came charging out of a lane in such a dark frenzy that they might have been a pack of devils looking for the Archfiend himself." In the final conversation, Avraham Mani tells Doña Flora that his son had his throat cut in Jerusalem like "a black goat in the dead of night.... He was butchered like a black sheep."[99] The black goat, the city's satanic mascot, signifies the unknown, the unfamiliar, the jarring, and in several cases heralds violence. As we saw in the previous chapter, this dark aesthetic, forcefully taken up by Amos Oz, is one factor shaping Jerusalem's gothic cityscape. In the next chapter, we remain in Jerusalem, now as the site of history's most literal haunting.

Notes

1. Silver, "Politics of Gothic Historiography," 3.
2. Wein, *British Identities*, 52, 54.
3. Silver, "Politics of Gothic Historiography," 3.
4. Ibid., 7.
5. Ibid., 11.
6. Ibid., 3.

7. Dent, "Contested Pasts," 31.
8. Walpole, *Castle of Otranto*, 17.
9. Ibid., 115.
10. Yehoshua, *Mr. Mani*, 69. All quotations are from this English translation of the novel unless otherwise noted.
11. For more on the relation between the rise of the gothic and the consolidation of British nationhood, see Wein, *British Identities*; and Edwards, "British Gothic Nationhood."
12. One historical incident in particular has attracted attention from critics. In 1763, the radical journalist and politician John Wilkes was charged with libel and presented a "general warrant" over his attack of a speech by King George III. As the legality of the warrant was questionable, the incident sparked debates about the limited power of the monarchy and about liberties granted by the constitution. Walpole, as a member of the House of Commons, supported Wilkes but became discouraged enough by his conviction and by other political developments, including the removal of his cousin Henry Seymour Conway from the king's court, to decide to withdraw from politics altogether. See Samson, "Politics Gothicized"; Wein, *British Identities*; and Lake, "Bloody Records."
13. Lake, "Bloody Records," 507.
14. Mack, "Horace Walpole," 370.
15. Lake, "Bloody Records," 490.
16. Ibid., 491, 511.
17. Ibid., 511.
18. Walpole, *Castle of Otranto*, 8.
19. Clery, introduction to *Castle of Otranto*, xii.
20. In addition to the studies by Dent, Lake, and Mack, cited above, see also Price, "Ancient Liberties."
21. For example, Bird, "Treason and Imagination"; Hoeveler, "Gothic Drama"; Miles, "Europhobia"; Edwards, "British Gothic Nationhood"; and Wein, *British Identities*, especially chap. 2, "When Everything New Is Old Again: Horace Walpole's Heroic Bequests," 49–69.
22. Ruth Perry argues that a key concern of gothic writers is defending the established but embattled process of legitimate succession ("Incest"). Bird insists that gothic is more concerned with scrutinizing the very notion of legitimacy itself, often in order to challenge it. He reads *Otranto* as a "genuinely seditious" text that articulates "genuine hostility to the contemporary monarchy," and he cites Walpole's political activities against what he considered the abuses of King George III's government (Bird, "Treason and Imagination," 192).
23. For detailed accounts of the political context of the writing and publication of *Otranto*, see Samson, "Politics Gothicized"; Wein, *British Identities*, 49–69; Mowl, *Horace Walpole*; Ketton-Cremer, *Horace Walpole*, 198–203; and Dole, "Three Tyrants," 26–35.
24. Band, "Archaeology," 234.
25. In his introduction to a 2007 collection of essays on the New History, Morris reflects on the narrow focus on 1948 that characterized the earlier discussions of the New History in Israel, acknowledging that, though rethinking 1948 was central to the New History, it was part of broader historical and sociological revisions taking place. Morris, introduction to *Making Israel*, 7.
26. Morris, "New Historiography," 1.
27. Ibid., 14.
28. Morris, introduction to *Making Israel*, 3.

29. Morris, "New Historiography," 14.
30. Morris, introduction to *Making Israel*, 5.
31. Derek Penslar elaborates on this notion. See "Innovation and Revisionism," 138.
32. Dent, "Contested Pasts," 25.
33. Robertson, *Legitimate Histories*, 86.
34. Yehoshua, *Mr. Mani*, 77.
35. Ibid., 79.
36. Ibid., 80.
37. Ibid., 91.
38. Hogle, "Restless Labyrinth," 152.
39. Yehoshua, *Mr. Mani*, 266.
40. Schmitt, "Introduction: Gothic Fictions," 12.
41. Ibid., 2.
42. Yehoshua, *Mr. Mani*, 283.
43. Band, "Archaeology," 237.
44. Ibid.
45. G. Shaked, "Shorashim," 132.
46. Nurith Gertz has acknowledged this duality. She analyzes the second conversation in *Mr. Mani* to argue that it encompasses an ongoing, irresolvable tension between two contradictory, mutually exclusive modes of history: "deterministic" history, concerned with cycles of wars, races, and nations; and "calm," humanistic history. She contextualizes her reading in her identification of a pattern in Yehoshua's fiction, whereby characters trapped in a perpetually repeating cycle attempt in vain to construct "a different history," a linear historical narrative that will usher them to a meaningful future ("Historiya aḥeret," 311). Framing her investigation within the broader context of Israeli literature, she thematizes the novel's engagement with history to conclude that the characters in the second conversation both succeed and fail in their rebellion against the deterministic history to which they—and Yehoshua himself—are beholden.
47. For example, see Band, "Archaeology"; Balaban, *Mar Molkho*; Ramras-Rauch, "Yehoshua"; and Oz, "Ha-tanur ve-ha-reḥem."
48. Yehoshua, *Mr. Mani*, 21.
49. Ibid., 54.
50. Ibid., 31.
51. For a thorough analysis of the thematization of history in the second conversation, see Gertz, "Historiya aḥeret."
52. Yehoshua, *Mr. Mani*, 88.
53. Ibid., 93 (emphasis in original).
54. Ibid., 95.
55. Ibid., 128.
56. Egon's understanding of Greek culture as the antidote to the artifice of identity evokes the fascination with Greco-Roman culture in late nineteenth-century Hebrew poetry, typified by Shaul Tchernihovsky's famous poem "Le-nokhaḥ pesel Apolo" ["Before a Statue of Apollo," 1899], in which the poet rejects the rabbinic tradition associated with the exilic past and yearns instead for a God who reflects the Hebraic affinity to Hellenistic culture. The poem promotes the broader ideological call for a present-based Hebrew or new Jew as the embodiment of Hebrew national revival. Contemporary Hebrew poetry continues to engage

with Hellenism in different ways. Shimon Adaf's *Ha-monolog shel Ikarus* [Icarus's monologue, 1997] rewrites the Icarus myth in the autobiographical context of the poet's childhood. The personal and individual nature of these poems is balanced by their broader relevance; as Dorit Lemberger has argued, Adaf engages in a "linguistic adaptation of mythic elements that coalesce with Israeli reality, transforming it into embodiments of universal themes" ("Contacts and Discontinuities," 338).

57. Yehoshua, *Mr. Mani*, 189–90.
58. Ibid., 224, 225.
59. Ibid., 265–66.
60. Ibid., 265.
61. Ibid., 208, 209.
62. Ibid., 264.
63. Ibid., 325.
64. Ibid., 325–26.
65. Ibid., 324–26.
66. Hoeveler, "Gothic Drama," 172.
67. Miles, "Abjection, Nationalism, and the Gothic," 205.
68. Ibid., 208.
69. Ibid., 209.
70. Arnold Band points to the novel's construction of an alternative Sephardi historical narrative as encompassing a critique not only of the European-Jewish historiography that excludes Sephardim and provides the foundation for Zionist ideology, but also of the concept of the Sfaradi tahor, or "pure Sephardi." See Band, "Archaeology."
71. For example, Yael Feldman argues that two models inform Yehoshua's novel, the Oedipal and the biblical; Anne Golomb Hoffman considers the question of history in *Mr. Mani* in light of feminist theory and psychoanalysis; Arnold Band discusses the novel's "Freudian modalities" ("Archaeology," 234); Avraham Balaban offers a psychoanalytic interpretation of the Mani family. See Feldman, "Ḥazara le-be-reshit"; Hoffman, "Womb of Culture"; and Balaban, *Mar Molkho*.
72. Hogle, "Restless Labyrinth," 153.
73. Ibid., 161–62.
74. The prohibition of sexual relations between a daughter-in-law and a father-in-law in Leviticus 18:15 holds even when the father-in-law acts as his dead son's surrogate, notwithstanding some interpretations of the story of Judah and Tamar (Gen. 38) that suggest its suspension in such cases (see Milgrom, *Leviticus 17–22*, 1544–55). In *Mr. Mani*, Avraham Mani's narration of his own intercourse with Tamara clearly indicates that he himself considers it to be "sinful" (Yehoshua, *Mr. Mani*, 355). Though he acts, like Judah, in the place of his dead son, he himself may have murdered his son. Further, Avraham's transgression is multiplied because of his conflation of Tamara with Doña Flora, the maternal object of his unrequited love since childhood.
75. Yehoshua, *Mr. Mani*, 354–55.
76. Ibid., 357.
77. Ibid., 323.
78. Ibid., 354, 355.
79. Walpole, *Castle of Otranto*, 24–25.
80. Yehoshua, *Mr. Mani*, 354.

81. Ibid., 323.
82. Ibid., 188.
83. Kilgour, *Rise of Gothic Novel*, 12.
84. Stav, "Avot u-vanot." Stav proposes that incest is a fundamental force in Hebrew and Israeli culture. She has examined it chiefly (though not solely) in sublimated, symbolic, or metaphoric form and has considered its role in diverse cultural paradigms: as a model for gendered power relations and the sustenance of patriarchal social structures ("Avot u-vanot," "'Kri'a"); as manifested linguistically and thematically in the relations among Hebrew poetic texts ("Giluy [arayot] ve-kisuy ba-lashon"); and, in its violent literal execution, as an extreme expression of "the patriarchal social logic reflected in capitalistic western society" ("Parashat Frizl," 286).
85. Baines, "Theatre of Monstrous Guilt," 293.
86. Campbell, "I Am No Giant," 243.
87. Hagar Shiloh's baby brother died from their parents' incompatible blood types; Dr. Mani also had two children who died from incompatible blood types, and indeed one of his medical interests involved this condition (Yehoshua, *Mr. Mani*, 7, 230).

The novel's preoccupation with birth and death, with the womb and the tomb, has been the subject of several studies that have focused on the Mani gynecological clinic in Jerusalem, a hall of mirrors that serves Arab and Jewish women alike. The Swedish midwife who runs the clinic almost singlehandedly is worth closer consideration. A former pilgrim who can feel a birthing woman's contractions before she herself can do so, "the amazing Swede" performs strange rituals during women's labor, "as if fending off an evil spirit" (ibid., 255). Efrayim Shapiro explicitly describes her as a vampire, recalling a labor he witnessed in which the midwife thrust "her head toward the womb as if to lap up the blood that was dripping from it" (ibid.). Though she does not actually drink the woman's blood, he "could have sworn that the Swedish Brunhild took all the pain upon herself," further implying her supernatural affiliation, whether as a sorceress, a vampire, or a Christ-figure (ibid.).

88. Campbell, "I Am No Giant," 247.
89. Ibid., 250, 252.
90. Perry, "Incest," 268–69.
91. Ibid., 271.
92. Ibid.
93. Yehoshua, *Mr. Mani*, 68.
94. Baines, "Theatre of Monstrous Guilt," 299, 306. George Haggerty and Jill Campbell both read incest in the context of homosexuality (Haggerty later changed his position on this issue). Haggerty links the difficulties of what he thinks is Walpole's own unresolved homosexuality to the sexual transgressions suggested by the text. See Haggerty, "Literature and Homosexuality"; and Campbell, "I Am No Giant." It is also noteworthy that *Mr. Mani* explicitly associates the incest scene of the fifth conversation with Yosef Mani's own homosexuality.
95. Yehoshua, *Mr. Mani*, 99.
96. The question of paternity is relevant to Arnold Band's reading of the novel through Yehoshua's complex relationship with his own father and the more accomplished authorial trajectory charted by the son. Nancy Berg considers paternity in *Mr. Mani* within a broader analysis of the subject in Hebrew literature. In light of Yehoshua's dedication of *Mr. Mani* to his father, these interpretations are particularly resonant. See Band, "Archaeology"; and Berg, "Paternity and Patrimony."

97. It is not only Jewish and Israeli historical narratives but also Jewish and Hebrew literatures that have been beholden to illusions of continuity. In his important 2010 study, *From Continuity to Contiguity*, Dan Miron aims to emancipate Jewish literary criticism and historiography from the shackles of continuity, arguing for a Jewish "literary complex" as an alternate model that acknowledges and engages with literary disjunctures and disparities. Reading Hebrew literature contiguously, as Miron proposes, helps disrupt supposedly organic continuities.

98. Yehoshua, *Mr. Mani*, 265, 115.

99. Ibid., 162, 318.

6

A SÉANCE FOR THE SELF

Memory, Nonmemory, and the Reorientation of History in Almog Behar and Toni Morrison

As I have shown in this study thus far, the gothic provides a means for an anxious or ambivalent confrontation with the past and its representation. The authors we have encountered have called on the gothic to expose the limits of conventional historiographic practice, to offer alternative histories, and to reframe our understanding of the present by looking to the past. With these poetic strategies in mind, I now look to the elision of Arab culture and the Arabic language from the Israeli narrative of the past, considering it side by side with the present absence of the African American story in American history.

In this context, it is no coincidence that cultural and academic discourse about Palestine frequently draws on the lexicon of ghosts and haunting to refer to Palestinian cultural and territorial dispossession. Maps that erase Palestinian villages and replace Arabic place-names with Hebrew yield a "haunted geography," artists invoke haunting to represent "the spectral spaces of the occupation" in elaborate exhibits, and the Nakba itself seeps into Jewish Israeli fiction in the form of "the haunting mark of the muted ghost" and "the ghosts of catastrophe."[1] Magazines and newspapers participate in this hauntology as well, in articles with titles such as "The Twin Ghosts of Slavery and the Nakba" and "In Palestine, Memory Is a Living, Haunting Thing."[2] While ghosts and haunting provide apt metaphors for historical trauma in general, the ongoing denial of Palestinian sovereignty and the erasure of the Palestinian presence in Israel are conditions particularly amenable to spectrality. Israel/Palestine harbors other ghosts as well. Brimming with diverse places and languages that were suppressed in the name of nationalist ideology, Israel/Palestine is a thoroughly haunted landscape. For some of its Jewish specters, the narrative of Palestinian loss and dispossession is especially resonant—not because their own stories claim equivalence in suffering and violence but because of a shared, if largely unacknowledged, cultural and historical sensibility.

This chapter brings together Almog Behar's Hebrew story "Ana min al-Yahoud" ("I'm One of the Jews," 2005) and Toni Morrison's historical American novel *Beloved* (1987). In both, I argue, haunting disrupts the power relations dictated by the narration and content of official histories, thereby articulating new modes of memory and forgetting and revising the conventions of victimhood. The national narrative of the United States, like that of Israel, has engendered its own specters. American gothic literature, preoccupied with race, history, and violence in its exposure of the dark currents underlying American history and nationhood, offers a productive if unconventional comparative framework for Mizrahi efforts at the recovery and reconstruction of silences and gaps in Israeli history and historiography.[3] Though it goes without saying, I do not mean to suggest an equivalence between the trauma of slavery in the United States and the oppression of Jews from Arab lands in Israel. Further, there is no question that these authors contend with a fundamentally different set of power relations. Morrison is a black woman in a society that continues to systemically privilege whites and men. Behar, though he may be marginalized as a Mizrahi, is an Israeli Jew and therefore identified with hegemonic power structures in Israel. Nonetheless, certain similarities in the representation of these histories warrant comparison, as Ranen Omer-Sherman has suggested by evoking W. E. B. DuBois's "double consciousness" of black Americans in the context of Mizrahim in Israel.[4] The comparison between *Beloved* and "Ana min al-Yahoud," however, is compelling not only because of similarities in the experiences of blacks in America and Mizrahim in Israel. It also offers new hermeneutic strategies for both texts, centered on their depiction of the subjugated self transformed, through haunting, to an active agent of history and its articulation.

Giving voice to characters previously absent or mute, *Beloved*, one of the most important works of twentieth-century American literature, redresses the incompleteness of literary representations of American history, a story, in Avery Gordon's words, "about haunting and about the crucial way it mediates between institution and person"—between slavery and slaves.[5] To be sure, other texts had addressed slavery and racism in America.

Morrison's novel, however, provides a platform for her characters to speak in their own voices, from their own perspectives, and on their own terms.

The characters' narrative autonomy and the new historical perspective it offers imbue *Beloved* with a weighty responsibility. This gravitas, confirmed by the Nobel Prize awarded its author six years after its publication, can perhaps help explain why so many readers and critics initially resisted reading it as a ghost story whose most natural milieu is the gothic.[6] The hostility to the figure of the ghost ranged from lamentations of Morrison's adaptation of what was seen as a ridiculous trope to concerted efforts to deny that the ghost is actually a ghost.[7] As any student of the gothic knows, though, its popular allure does not belie its serious concerns, and further, whether or not a specter is truly a specter is beside the point. *Beloved*'s haunting does no less than structure Morrison's novel, which aims to recover and communicate a history whose violence is known but not adequately represented. As such, the novel is not conceivable without its ghost, who mediates between Morrison's main concerns: narrative and storytelling, history and historiography, and memory and forgetting. It is this matrix and not merely the presence of the ghost, whether literal or allegorical, that ensured that eventually the novel's characterization as gothic would prevail in the critical and popular sensibilities.[8] Moreover, as the horrors of slavery are not a product of the literary imagination but documented historical facts, novels like *Beloved* navigate an ambivalent territory that undercuts the distinction between the "reality" of history and the "fantasy" of gothic fiction.[9]

Behar, too, conjures ghosts in the story that brought him to literary prominence in Israel, "Ana min al-Yahoud." The story tells of an unnamed protagonist who finds himself to have suddenly acquired the Iraqi Arabic accent of his deceased grandfather. The condition spreads to affect others around him, beginning with Mizraḥim and eventually infecting European Jews, as well, all of whom suddenly begin speaking accented Hebrew. While the gradual appearance of diversely accented Hebrews suggests a disintegration of national cohesion (or its illusion), the story focuses on the particular experience of the narrator.[10] His haunting is not only metaphoric but also literal: the grandfather's specter visits him, speaks to him, and speaks through him. By contrast, the narrator finds no common language in which to communicate with the Palestinian ghosts he encounters in the streets of Jerusalem, with whom he desperately wants to engage. It is an explicitly political story that directly confronts the known-unknown secret of the Zionist dispossession of Arab culture.

Like Morrison's novel, Behar's story negotiates matters of historiographic violence, of memory and forgetting, and of language and storytelling through the haunting ghost. For both authors, the conventional articulation of the past is a prison from which the characters, ostensibly free, must liberate themselves. The ghosts in their texts offer one way out of this prison, clearly signifying the eruption of the suppressed past in the present and calling for the supplementation of existing histories with those that have been underacknowledged or invisible. As Morrison's novel forces a confrontation with the specter of slavery that has defined American history, so, too, does Behar's story bring to light the specter of occupation and cultural dispossession to reshape the conceptualization of the Israeli past. It is not just the haunting ghosts that identify these narratives as gothic, but the invocation of these ghosts to engage with these questions of history and its representation.

Though written in a critical vein from the ethnic and racial margins of their societies, both *Beloved* and "Ana min al-Yahoud" were immediately recognized as significant additions to their respective national literatures. Morrison's novel was nominated for the National Book Award and won a Pulitzer Prize, while Behar, a young Mizrahi author, won the prestigious *Haaretz* short-story competition for his story. These authors, in terms of their impact on and visibility in their societies, are anything but transparent specters. Their protagonists, however, have been rejected forcefully by their nations' historical narratives and find themselves grappling with ghosts that haunt the black or Mizrahi self in exceedingly material ways.

Depicting transgenerational spectral visitations that amount to a self-haunting, these texts shift the focus from one on the struggle between the victim and oppressor to one on a more nuanced struggle *within* the victim as a collective self. As such, their ghosts draw attention not only to the wrongs committed by hegemonic forces but also to the painful choices their victims have made in response to these wrongs, casting the central tension as one that emerges within one's self. Consequentially, both authors choose to portray their characters primarily through their own subjective field rather than the one afforded through their relations with powerful policing forces that disempower and marginalize them. The haunting by and of the self brings the marginalized characters into focus on their own terms, rather than locking them into the dialectic dictated by oppression.

This autospectrality forces the haunted characters to confront forgetting and the limitations of memory and to devise alternative engagements with the past: for Morrison, in the form of "rememory" and "disremembering," and for Behar, in the rejection of "nonmemory." These terms in and of themselves exemplify the way language, too, undergoes revision to accommodate the ghosts and to formulate a poetics of spectrality: for Morrison, through the ghost's acquisition of language, through the haunting by the forgotten African language, and through the hallucinatory language narrating the experience of the Middle Passage; and for Behar, through the persistence of accents in Hebrew and through an increasingly diverse array of Hebrews that culminates in the reappropriation of the language as sacred. For both, it is, finally, the inability of language—the only language the protagonists have—to adequately express loss that haunts as persistently as any specter. The hauntings in these texts operate according to gothic conventions, drawing on the return of repressed histories and an anxiety regarding the relations between self and other, victim and oppressor. However, the ghosts in both texts do more than bring the past to light. They prompt the characters to revise the practice of remembering, historical recovery, and narration, thus acknowledging their agency within an alternative narrative not by exorcising their ghosts but by inviting them and making space for them in the world of the living.

Haunted Selves: Revising Victimization

The symbolic significance of the ghost is in some ways so deeply embedded in our cultural sensibilities that any formal theorization can seem extraneous. Ghosts and their haunting signify the past intruding on the present. The repressed return to reveal a secret, complete unfinished business, or exact revenge for injustice. The basis for these seemingly self-evident significations is developed in Freud's 1919 essay on the uncanny, in which he posits that trauma evokes a compulsive repetition and return, rendering the domestic unhomely, *unheimlich*, and the familiar unfamiliar. For Freud, "among those things that are felt to be frightening there must be one group in which it can be shown that the frightening element is something that has been repressed and now returns. This species of the frightening would then constitute the uncanny," a phenomenon best exemplified by "anything to do with death, dead bodies, revenants, spirits and ghosts."[11] Though of course the emergence of British gothic literature in the eighteenth century, and of ghost stories and folk legends more broadly, predate and prefigure Freud, his essay on the uncanny has paved the way for twentieth-century theorizations indicating the ghost's orientation as a political entity (or nonentity).[12] Using the uncanny to structure his analysis of the haunting in *Beloved*, for example, Homi Bhabha writes that the "unhomely moment relates the traumatic ambivalences of a personal, psychic history to the wider disjunctions of political existence."[13] Mediating between the personal and the political, the gothic uncanny invokes the figure of the ghost to navigate the territory of the nation and history as well as of the psyche. Besides its status as simultaneously designating presence and absence, the present and the past, the specter not only haunts but also "is haunted by the culture which produced it," as Andrew Smith notes.[14] In other words, the culture the ghost invades has always already invaded it, having created the conditions that the specter must protest, and indeed makes its protest necessary.

Elaborating on the theorization of haunting as fundamentally historical, Jacques Derrida asserts that its historicity makes haunting necessary. Despite the political specificity of his analysis, which considers the future of Marxist social and ideological projects in the wake of the dissolution of the Soviet Union, his ideas about spectrality are broadly applicable, as he himself demonstrates in his extended analysis of *Hamlet* as well as in his assertion that "haunting belongs to the structure of every hegemony."[15] The ghost, for Derrida, is a necessary interlocutor "in the name of justice." His essay is a call to action—"learning to live"—that requires conjuration because it "can happen only between life and death. Neither in life nor in death *alone*." We must therefore "learn to live with ghosts, in the upkeep, the conversation, the company, or the companionship, in the commerce without commerce of ghosts. To live otherwise, and ... more justly.... And this being-with specters would also be, not only but also, a *politics* of memory, of inheritance, and of generations."[16] The disjointed temporality effected by the ghost is related to the multiple generations affected by it: a ghost need not be one who is already dead but can be one who is not yet born. Haunting, therefore, entails a political and ethical responsibility not only to remember the past but also to contribute to a more just future.

Avery Gordon, too, figures haunting's relation to history as one of its key features. Like Derrida, she interprets the ghost's presence not only as an invitation to historical restoration of suppressed narratives of social violence but also as an invitation to action. The identification of the ghost as something other than other is integral to her theorization of haunting:

> The ghost has its own desires, so to speak, which figure the whole complicated sociality of a determining formation that seems inoperative (like slavery) or

invisible (like racially gendered capitalism) but that is nonetheless alive and enforced. But the force of the ghost's desire is not just negative, not just the haunting and staged words, marks, or gestures of domination and injury. *The ghost is not other or alterity as such, ever.* It is (like Beloved) pregnant with unfulfilled possibility, with the something to be done that the wavering present is demanding. This something to be done is not a return to the past but a reckoning with its repression in the present, a reckoning with that which we have lost, but never had.[17]

Erupting from the past, the ghost fixes its gaze on the present and the future. Most critically, the ghost is figured not only in its relation to oppression but also in its autonomous desires and needs, which indicate its subjectivity as encompassing but also moving *beyond* victimization.

Despite such critical paradigms that complicate the power dynamics of haunting, a focus on the gothic's replication of hegemonic power relations still structures the discourse of gothic haunting. There is much of value in the widely accepted position that, in Eric Savoy's words, "the entire tradition of American gothic can be conceptualized as the attempt to invoke . . . the specter of Otherness that haunts the house of national narrative."[18] This late twentieth-century conceptualization of "the entire tradition" in terms of self and other, however, discounts the significant shift in perspective and structure undertaken by key American gothic texts that invoke alterity and, at the same time, dismantle the dyad of self/other altogether. In the American context, the other is not only the haunter but also the haunted, not only a ghost but also a self.

Writing insightfully about "the ghostly presence of the Palestinian tragedy at the heart of the Jewish Israeli Zionist narrative," Gil Hochberg is similarly reluctant to release Palestinian Arabs and Israeli Jews from the separatist conventions she otherwise resists.[19] She asserts, in 2012, that "we are still awaiting a full-fledged Hebrew 'ghostly narrative' in which a Palestinian ghost emerges out of the ruins, laying open his or her accusations."[20] Coming seven years after the publication of Behar's celebrated story, this statement elides the Palestinian ghosts with whom his narrator tries in vain to communicate, a failure that is a consequence not of the Palestinians' muteness but rather, as we shall see, of the narrator's linguistic "disremembering." The assumption that it is always the Palestinian other who, uninvited, haunts the Jewish Israeli self with "gestures of domination or injury" does not acknowledge the specters in plain sight. It also disregards points of contact that destabilize this binary of self and other, such as the one Behar recognizes between Arab Jews and Palestinian Arabs—something to which the gothic, which bends and ruptures the boundaries of identity, is highly amenable.

As I have tried to show throughout this study, when the villainized or disempowered themselves author gothic texts, the gothic literary and historiographic paradigm necessarily undergoes a shift, requiring a modified theorization. To this end, recent studies on postcolonial gothic have developed diverse interpretive strategies that trace precisely this shift from the use of the gothic to demonize and suppress otherness, to its adaptation to address the ambivalence or unacknowledged guilt instigated by colonial and imperial projects, to its appropriation in the service of historical revision. This evolution, as Cynthia Sugars and Gerry Turcotte note, has made the gothic "a way to insist on, rather than deny, a colonial history."[21] Though I identify an affinity between the theoretical interventions embedded in the postcolonial gothic and my own analysis, and though Israel and the United States are both settler societies, my concern here is not to argue for or against their designation as colonial or postcolonial. More compelling, to my mind, is the way these two texts adapt and reshape the gothic not only to force forgetful nations to acknowledge their past but also to confront the forgetfulness of those who have, themselves, been written out of history.

The hauntings we encounter in Morrison and Behar, I argue, convey a relation to the past beyond the claustrophobic and limited binary structure of victim and oppressor, beyond even the notion of "a horrific 'alternate' history," in Savoy's words.[22] In these narratives, the boundaries separating the haunter and the haunted, the self and the other, are eroded. Silence, injustice, and erasure conjure transgenerational specters who cannot abide them *to haunt versions of themselves*, and not, as may be expected, those who have persecuted them. This conjuration disrupts both exclusionary historiographic narratives and their well-intentioned revisions, which consign disenfranchised characters to eternal victimhood and powerlessness by positioning them always within existing power structures (black/white, Mizraḥi/Ashkenazi) rather than independently of them.

The transgenerational haunting that features in both the texts at hand unravels these divisions. Conceptualizing the haunted subject as a passive, unwitting receptacle for the staging of parental secrets that have nothing to do with his or her own lived experience, Nicolas Abraham's theory of transgenerational haunting expands and radically revises Freudian theories of psychopathology: "Here symptoms do not spring from the individual's own life experience but from someone else's psychic conflicts, traumas, or secrets."[23] Likening the phantom to a ventriloquist, Abraham insists that its appearance is unrelated to the return of repressed psychic material since what is at stake is not the haunted subject's secrets but those of the haunting parent: "In no way can the subject relate to the phantom as his or her own repressed experience, not even as an experience by incorporation."[24] Elaborating on this theory, Maria Torok stresses that the "phantom is alien to the subject who harbors it."[25] It is easy to see how the hauntings we encounter in Morrison's novel and Behar's story diverge from such a model. In these texts, ghosts resemble mirrors more than ventriloquists; the haunted subjects recognize their ghosts, identify with them, and glimpse themselves within their haunting presence, therein finding recourse to engage with their own secrets and silence.

Furthermore, their trajectory is not a linear one in which children inherit their parents' memories but circular: a daughter haunts a mother; a grandson is urged to relay his story to his parents. The circular, transgenerational dynamic of these hauntings indicates traumas they experienced personally as well as broader historical ones they did not, both of which affect them profoundly. The transgenerational hauntings in both texts illuminate the characters' exclusion from the national story. At the same time, though, they point to their willed forgetting of cultural and corporeal violence suffered over the course of generations. Morrison's Sethe, a runaway slave who murders her own infant rather than turning her over to slavery, contends first with an invisible specter who aggressively haunts her house and then with the physicalized apparition of her murdered child, who joins her household as a young woman named Beloved, gently destructive and starved for maternal affection. Behar's narrator's speech is suddenly accosted by the Iraqi Arabic accent of his departed grandfather Anwar, whose presence becomes increasingly tangible as the story progresses. As the Hebrew of his friends and acquaintances undergoes a similar transformation, the specters multiply, but his parents' Hebrew remains staunchly unaffected. The haunting in Behar's story is not just a nuclear family affair. As the narrator walks the streets of Jerusalem, he encounters entire neighborhoods that are suddenly occupied by the ghosts of Palestinians who might have been—specters from a past that never came to pass. The ghosts who haunt these texts are not, like Abraham's phantom, parents. They include a child, a grandparent, and a collective clamor of "the black and angry dead" and vanished Palestinian Arabs.[26]

Both texts' primary hauntings, by Beloved and Grandfather Anwar, emphasize the generational continuity of their histories of oppression. Both focus on how this inheritance might create the conditions for an otherwise impossible intergenerational communication through haunting, and thus effect change. As such, the figure of the oppressor shrinks to near obsolescence in *Beloved* and is flattened to caricature in Behar's story. The black ghost haunts the black mother, not the slave master who drove her to do the unthinkable. The Arab grandfather haunts the Arab grandson, not a representative of the Ashkenazi political and cultural elite whose policies denigrated his culture. Though both texts depict scenes of violence in the encounter with the representatives of hegemony, they are primarily preoccupied with the characters' internal struggle and its family dynamics, and not the struggle between victim and oppressor. Haunting signifies neither the guilt of the oppressors nor a restitution of historical wrongs but rather the black or Arab Jewish subject's coming to terms with remembering or forgetting them.

Sethe's encounter with the horrific Schoolteacher, who comes to take her back to Sweet Home under the auspices of the Fugitive Slave Law of 1850, is critical in that it spurs Sethe's infanticide. The specificities of Schoolteacher, however, hardly matter. He is an archetype of the cruel slave master, justifying his brutality with books and science that dehumanize black people. Sethe's interactions with Beloved, on the other hand, reveal the pain of her experience in all its complexity, beginning with the impulse that drives her to protect through murder and continuing throughout the novel in Beloved's fierce and all-encompassing possession of her. As Teresa A. Goddu points out, unlike other American gothic texts about slavery, such as Hannah Crafts's *The Bondwoman's Narrative, Beloved* is not a story that "transfers the slave's terror of possession to the master."[27] What is at stake here is not only or even mostly the indictment of Sethe's former masters but, first and foremost, her role as a mother and a daughter.[28]

In Behar's story, the police proliferate as if in a Kafkaesque nightmare, prompting the narrator initially to defend himself against their accusations. He searches for his ever-vanishing identity card to prove his Jewish nationality, explains that his accent is not Palestinian but Iraqi, suggests that the police officer himself might be Mizraḥi, and finally offers to call his Ashkenazi friends to vouch for his Jewishness with their unaccented Hebrew—all to no avail. As the story progresses, the Arabic accent that initially invades the narrator becomes a full-blown possession: "And thus my voice was replaced by my grandfather's voice.... And suddenly that beautiful voice, which had been entirely in my past, started coming out of me and not as a beggar and not asking for crumbs, but truly my voice, my voice strong and clear."[29] Even as his subjectivity is interlaced with his grandfather's, it remains distinctly independent. Furthermore, the possession is multidirectional: "And my grandfather would speak to me, asking me in my voice whether there is any end to this story." Over and above the narrator's dealings with the police, his engagements with his grandfather and with his parents dictate the story's primary concerns with the denial, forgetting, and interment of one's own past. As in *Beloved*, the encounter with those who police the hegemony in "Ana min al-Yahoud" is critical for the development of the plot and for the broader concerns of the story. In both texts, however, it is the protagonists' engagement with the ghosts who haunt them, familial representatives of the haunted subject's past, that illuminates their complex experiences of self.

Whereas the conventions of ghost stories dictate that specters return in order to communicate something to another person, in both Morrison's novel and Behar's story the boundaries of the self mingle with those of the haunting ghost. Beyond the motif of spectral possession, in which the ghost's subjectivity hijacks that of the living person, these texts speak to an intimate identification with the ghost that reveals dimensions of the protagonists' self. As the revenant of Sethe's murdered child, Beloved forces her to acknowledge her past and her present, exploiting Sethe's guilt and sorrow to merge their selves and possess her completely: "I am Beloved and she is mine.... I am not separate from her ... Sethe's is the face that left me ... it is the face I lost she is my face smiling at me doing it at last a hot thing now we can join a hot thing."[30] The primal memory undergoes a subtle and ambiguous shift in perspective in the following chapter, which continues to repudiate a singular identity: "Beloved You are my sister You are my daughter You are my face; you are me ... You are mine You are mine You are mine."[31] The unstable boundary between identification ("You are me") and possession ("You are mine") is exposed by these disorienting passages. Further, the spectral Beloved is not only a manifestation of the infant her mother murdered. She also represents Sethe's annihilation of her own genealogy as a desperate attempt to escape slavery. Sethe would have killed her other children, too, if she had had the chance, to ensure their permanent exit from that grotesque narrative. When Beloved returns, Sethe comes back to herself, so to speak, and reenters the matrilineal history the novel offers as one of several supplements to "official" history.

One of the novel's most disconcerting passages, thematically and poetically, best conveys this intertwined subjectivity: the phantasmagoric chapter on the Middle Passage. Depicting the journey on the slave ship through jarring, fragmentary prose, the chapter brings together the consciousness of Beloved, of Sethe, and of Sethe's mother, whom she hardly knew and who was lynched when Sethe was a girl. In this convergence of experience and inherited memory, the boundaries of Sethe's imagination and her memory give way to those of Beloved and upend the conventions of haunter and haunted. Though the events charting this haunting are dictated by the historical facts of slavery, the force that breathes life into the narrative is Sethe's engagement with her ghost and, through her, with herself.

Behar's hero has never met the grandfather who haunts him, as he died before his birth, yet he immediately recognizes the ghost. The grandfather's invasion of the narrator's Hebrew in the form of a heavy Iraqi Arabic accent anticipates the narrator's fantastic encounter with the Palestinian Arabs who inhabited the city "the way they had been before the 1948 War, as if there had never been a 1948 War." This additional dimension of his haunting is instigated by his reaction to his grandfather's return. In effect, it makes him receptive to the possibility of his own haunting in the streets of Jerusalem, emphasizing a particular facet of his multifarious historical narrative. Rather than imagine the journey that brought his grandfather to Israel, or conjure up an Iraq with its Jews restored, however, he summons a vision of an alternative history of Palestine in which he himself, unable to communicate in Arabic, has no place. Instead of situating himself as the victim denied his rightful place in the Israeli narrative or robbed of his Iraqi homeland—both legitimate critical stances that have been taken up by Mizraḥi authors such as Sami Mikhael, Shimon Ballas, Eli Amir, and others—he directs his vision to the oppression of bygone Palestinian Arabs. Even as he links his own persecution by the police to that of Palestinians, ultimately he imagines himself *out* of history altogether. The grandfather's return, then, triggers the grandson's investigation of the spectrality of his own presence in Israel/Palestine. The narrator engenders his own ghost and activates his own haunting. Like Sethe, he makes no attempt to exorcise the specter, instead making room for its presence/absence in his world and recalibrating his vision of his personal and collective past accordingly.

In *Beloved*, the ghost forces Sethe to confront her terrible past. As we shall see in the following section, her memory of it compels the reader to acknowledge the dark interior landscape of slavery as an integral component of American history writ large. In "Ana min al-Yahoud," the ghost points to the cultural dispossession of Mizraḥi Jews not only in the Israeli denigration of their past but also in the denial of their cultural kinship with Palestinian Arabs and of points of intersection in their alternative histories. The challenges introduced by these hauntings notwithstanding, both bypass the paradigms of victim and oppressor that continue to structure the stories of those who would leave them behind in favor of a more autonomous subjectivity, while providing a basis for the investigation of the insufficiently acknowledged dark corners of these histories.

History, Memory, and the Thematization of Haunting

There is no doubt that the hauntings in these texts call attention to "the histories that 'History' neglects," as Jonathan Dent calls them.[32] Beyond this task, their characters also modify the practice of remembering, historical recovery, and narration to affirm their agency. By inviting their ghosts and making room for them among the living, they establish themselves as autonomous subjects in an alternative narrative.

The designation of *Beloved* as a historical text that provides an alternative or a supplement to official American historiography has been exhaustively addressed, and its status as such is perhaps no more clearly illustrated than in Morrison's adaptation in the novel of a historical figure and event. While editing the eclectic historical text *The Black Book*, a compendium of newspaper clippings, photographs, slavery bills of sale, and other historical documents and artifacts, Morrison came across an abolitionist account of the story of the escaped slave Margaret Garner, who, in 1856, chose to murder her three-year-old child rather than allow her to return to slavery. Giving voice to Garner's narrative through Sethe not only foregrounds her perspective but also allows Morrison to tell her story through haunting rather through "history" and thus to provide, as Gordon puts it, "all the reasons why the reasons are never quite enough."[33] These reasons are conspicuously absent even from the best-known accounts of slavery, the slave narratives. In her essay "The Site of Memory," Morrison analyzes the generic characteristics of the slave narrative, specifically their desire to "drop a veil" over the most horrific details of slavery to make them more "palatable" to their white readers.³⁴ Morrison sees her task as a black twentieth-century author "to rip that veil" to expose the slave's "interior life."³⁵ On the basis of the intertextual relationship between *The Black Book* and *Beloved*, some critics have read *Beloved* as a complement to the slave narrative and a revision of its generic limitations. As such, as Marilyn Sanders Mobley argues, "history becomes both theme and narrative process" in *Beloved*.³⁶

Morrison's intervention, which links the personal, individual act of violence to the broader, systematic violence institutionalized by slavery, includes both the redress of "black exclusion from the national memory" and "a strategic recentering of American history in the lives of the historically dispossessed," in the words of Deborah H. Barnes and Caroline Rody, respectively.³⁷ In other words, *Beloved* is concerned not only with restoring slavery to the national memory but also with foregrounding the subjective struggle of those most profoundly affected by it: to disown the past, or to possess it. Though the novel works against amnesia both thematically and formally, it neither wholeheartedly embraces memory nor flatly rejects forgetfulness. After all, as Kimberly Chabot Davis puts it, "a historical memory also has its costs."³⁸ This tension constitutes a central preoccupation of the novel, encompassed in Beloved's relationship with Sethe. Executing what David Lawrence calls "a precarious balancing act between the danger of forgetting a past that should not be forgotten and of remembering a past that threatens to engulf the present," the novel must devise new modes of engagement with that past.³⁹

Behar, whose literary and scholarly oeuvres in many ways work to redress historical omissions and erasures, has also spoken about the relationship between literary and historical representations of the past. In an interview, he said, "History gives us a very partial story that is connected to a particular national age; literature is an alternative to that history. I think that for many minority or colonized communities, literature sometimes comes before history, by telling the story anew after a long repression or silencing of memory."⁴⁰ For Behar, as for Morrison, literature offers access to the stories that official history suppresses. For both authors, the suppression itself is a violent act. The violence that "Ana min al-Yahoud" invokes has left its mark not only on the narrator and on the Jerusalem cityscape but also on Israeli history. Behar, who is himself of mixed Iraqi Jewish and Turkish Jewish origin, summons the ghost of the Iraqi Jewish grandfather as a bridge between the narrator's own willful amnesia about his past and the broader national erasure of the Palestinian Nakba. Engaging with his grandfather's ghost, confronting his own Iraqi accent, restores the grandson's memory of two interrelated histories that have been stifled, rewritten, or marginalized by the Zionist narrative: the Arab Jewish immigration to and absorption in Israel, and the Palestinian Nakba of 1948.

In juxtaposing these victims of Zionist historiographic practice and making a claim for certain correlations in their experience, Behar contributes to a process of historical revision already well underway. Ella Shohat is perhaps the most prolific and visible scholar to have called for cooperation between Mizraḥim and Palestinians in Israel against a national entity dominated by European Jews. Shohat has repeatedly urged recognition of the "affinity and analogy" in the experiences of Palestinians and Mizraḥim vis-à-vis the Zionist establishment in Israel.[41] Explicitly alluding to the opening lines of *The Communist Manifesto*, itself the primary referent for Derrida's spectrality, she characterizes the relations between Ashkenazi Jews and Arab Jews and non-Jews in gothic terms: "A spectre haunts European Zionism, the spectre that all of its victims—Palestinians, Sephardim (as well as critical Ashkenazim, in and outside Israel, stigmatized as 'self-hating' malcontents)—will perceive the linked analogies between their oppressions."[42] Shohat and others work to expose these "linked analogies" by pointing to a shared experience of oppression.[43]

Authors and poets, too, have participated in similarly restorative work by depicting the complexity and richness of the Arab Jewish past and, in some cases, acknowledging points of intersection with Palestinian Arabs.[44] Yet such a stance is still well beyond the mainstream in Israeli academic circles, as attested by the fact that so many of the scholars and cultural figures who espouse it, including Shohat herself, live and work in the United States. Shohat's call for Mizraḥi-Palestinian cooperation is indeed radical relative to mainstream Israeli sensibilities, in part because her ideas are also based on a recognition of a common Arab cultural foundation that precedes Zionism. Nevertheless, her call to action is activated primarily through the conceptualization of a shared Mizraḥi and Palestinian victimhood at the hands of Zionist ideology. Behar's story, then, participates in extant restorative efforts but also offers something different. Bridging the Arab Jewish past directly to the Palestinian past, and acknowledging the shared victimization of Arab Jews and non-Jews, it nonetheless grants its Mizraḥi subject a measure of responsibility for telling his story, or for allowing it to be erased. The double haunting—by Grandfather Anwar and by the Palestinian ghosts—mediates between the forgetful young Israeli (and his equally forgetful society) and the two acts of historical violence in which he is entangled.

Both texts indict the limitations of memory. The ghosts' presence forces the haunted characters to confront forgetting and to devise alternative engagements with the past. These "distortions of memory," in Bhabha's words, can be roused to positive effect "when historical visibility has faded."[45] Beloved embodies Morrison's concept of "rememory" (both a verb and a noun), mobilized against the act of "disremembering," while Behar's narrator grapples with the layers of "nonmemory" under which he has buried his grandfather. Rememory, disremembering, and nonmemory differ from conventional memory and forgetting, signifying processes that are both deeply individual and definitively collective. Despite the ghosts' clearly defined individual subjectivities, they also speak to the collective grappling with the African American and Arab Jewish past.

Morrison's elusive concept of rememory, and how it differs from memory, has challenged scholars. The prefix *re-*, which suggests a repetition, points to the function of rememory not simply as a recovery but rather as a recovery that can be experienced communally and not only individually—a *shared* memory that transcends the conventional temporality of memory. The *re* in rememory designates a repetition among different members of a community rather than repetition within an individual consciousness. Indicating, in Rody's words, "the interconnectedness of minds, past and present," rememory is the key to the novel's function as "communal epic" and its realization of collective memory."[46] The recognition of rememory as haunting, as Gordon shows, clarifies this link between the individual and the collective: "In this moment of enchantment when you are remembering something in the world, or something in the world is remembering you, you are not alone or hallucinating or making something out of nothing but your own unconscious thoughts. You have bumped into somebody else's memory; you have encountered haunting and the picture of it the ghost imprints."[47] Rememory, then, involves the imagination, transcends individual experience, makes possible transgenerational connections. As such, it bends time, juxtaposing impossible recollections of a slave ship in the Middle Passage (a historical moment preceding Sethe's own birth) with Sethe's infanticide and later the haunting of 124 Bluestone Road. The transgression of temporal boundaries through the spectral figure of Beloved exemplifies the work of rememory. It allows Morrison's novel to assert an African American story that relies on its narration and its bequest for its existence.

Before I look more closely at the function of rememory in the texts, I want to briefly consider Marianne Hirsch's well-known conceptualization of postmemory. Hirsch theorized postmemory to account for the inherited but not personally experienced traumatic memories of the Holocaust by the second generation of Holocaust survivors. Like rememory, postmemory is "a *structure* of inter- and trans-generational transmission of traumatic knowledge and experience."[48] Despite a shared preoccupation with inheritance, though, these two modes of memory should be distinguished. Postmemory entails transmission through "stories, images, and behaviors" to those who did not actually experience trauma. The traumatic experiences of the previous generation "were transmitted to them so deeply and affectively as to *seem* to constitute memories in their own right."[49] Postmemory depends on transmission, even through absence or silence, that creates a "memory," whereas rememory is invoked through forgetting and the ghost who returns to indict forgetfulness. The evocative refrain that ends the novel and that seems to contradict its purpose, "This is not a story to pass on," points to transmission as both necessary and impossible—hence the haunting.[50] Sethe "worked hard to remember as close to nothing as was safe," notes the narrator early in the novel.[51] Even after Beloved appears, Sethe resists her as an embodiment of memory: "To Sethe, the future was a matter of keeping the past at bay."[52] Despite her daughter Denver's wish to hear stories about her past, Sethe keeps quiet, determined to bequeath her the peace of a blank slate. Critically, the silence at home is matched by a broader silence. Denver has no recourse to the "broadly available public images and narratives" that make postmemory possible.[53] As a historiographic intervention, *Beloved* indicates the absence of such narratives on both an individual and a collective scale. Rememory emerges from and in spite of the dearth of stories and images that are passed on, both individually and collectively. Haunting takes the place of transmission.

The contemporary Jerusalem of Behar's story is characterized by the absence, erasure, and denial of painful memories. As far as we know, the narrator's parents do not transmit their experience as first-generation Arab Jews in Israel except in the form of triumphant scenes of overcoming their Arabness. When the narrator tries in vain to throw his grandfather's accent away "in one of the public trash cans," he recalls how his mother had softened the Arabic pronunciation of Hebrew in her childhood.[54] As the plague of haunting accents spreads, his parents' Hebrew, alone, remains insistently unchanged. They repeatedly warn their son that his new accent imperils his status in Israeli society, and they insist to the police that they have no idea how he acquired this foreign accent: "My parents stood staunchly against me and against the plague, remembering the years of effort they had invested to acquire their clean accent." The parents' silence pulls the son one generation further back in time to investigate the meaning of his new accent.

Defying the trajectory of inherited memory, his grandfather suggests that the narrator transmit his newly remembered narrative to his parents: "And why don't you show them your story, perhaps that way they will wake up, said my grandfather from the dead, almost making me swear an oath." The ghost of Grandfather Anwar instigates his grandson's self-reflection and his confrontation with his own silence, which he attributes to his nonmemory, a concept that parallels another of Morrison's neologisms: to *disremember*. The unusual term "nonmemory" (*i-zikaron*, אי-זיכרון) is distinct from "forgetting" (שכחה): to forget, one must first know or experience something. Nonmemory points to an absence, a lacuna, that would seem to absolve its bearer of responsibility. Both concepts suggest passivity (a memory escapes *you*). Behar's use of nonmemory, however, suggests that it is an active choice and therefore signifies an abdication from responsibility: "And a stranger who didn't know me would have thought that I was a loyal grandson, and would not have known how much I had piled nonmemory on memory over the years, and would not have guessed how much my memory had blurred and how many times, how many, many times, I had not made the connection to my grandfather on my lips." The grandson's agency is indisputable, and he accepts responsibility for disremembering, implying that his act of piling "non-memory on memory over the years" amounts to a conscious and active process of forgetting. The "dybbuk" haunting the grandson, and soon thereafter his friends and acquaintances, speaks in an accent that is "foreign from the distance of two generations of forgetting," but its new proximity and intimacy have been catalyzed by the acknowledgment of responsibility effected by the recognition of years of nonmemory.

A Yiddish word used also in Hebrew, *dybbuk* is derived from the Hebrew root ד-ב-ק, denoting "adhere," in reference to spiritual possession. Widely associated with S. Ansky's famous play "The Dybbuk, or Between Two Worlds" (1914–19), the term predates it by centuries. As Joachim Neugroschel notes, *dybbuk* is one of several words used in Hebrew (such as רוח, spirit, or שד, demon) to designate "the undead entity that takes over a human being."⁵⁵ Neugroschel points out that, while early representations of dybbuk possession and exorcism were less bound to the Judaic nuances of such experiences (he provides an example of a mid-seventeenth-century story whose influences may be pagan in origin), such representations "seem to have become more 'Jewish' through the centuries" and "appear to rely almost entirely on Jewish religious customs."⁵⁶ Though derived originally from non-Jewish sources, then, over time the dybbuk took on explicitly Judaic characteristics and became a central component of Eastern European Jewish folklore, distinct from the ghosts and ghouls populating British gothic literature. Behar's only use of it in this story speaks to the dybbuk's Jewish associations, since it refers only to the Jews who take on their ancestors' accents and not to the Palestinian ghosts in the story. Indeed, he uses the term not to refer to the story's ghosts at all but rather to point to the haunting accents that afflict the Jewish characters—the accents that "adhere" to them despite all efforts to discard them.

Recognizing that his cultivated forgetting has, in a sense, invited the stubbornly clinging accent, the grandson acknowledges his role in the drama of nonmemory. It is a lonely place, this i-zikaron (in Hebrew, the term is homophonous with "an island of memory"), where he defies his parents and the normative cultural milieu into which they have fully integrated.⁵⁷ Multiple islands of memory emerge in the story, invoking accents from Germany to Ukraine and across North Africa and the Middle East. But the ones that make the authorities anxious are those attesting to the Arab Jewish past, "creating concern that the country would be filled with Arabs, many, many Arabs." At stake is the collective rememory of the Arabness that was always already part of Israeli society.

Addressing the phenomenon of people remembering events they did not experience, Ashraf Rushdy relates rememory to a version of Freud's "primal scene." He redefines Freud's concept as a key event whose significance becomes apparent only through a secondary key event, "when by a preconscious association the primal scene is recalled."⁵⁸ Tracing the shared narrative of Sethe and Paul D—back in her life after an eighteen-year absence—from 124 Bluestone Road back to Sweet Home, he argues that the network of primal scenes "accentuates the deferral of narrative origins further and further back, until only slavery stands alone as cause and curse."⁵⁹ But slavery does not begin at Sweet Home. The same interconnectedness that Rushdy identifies as integral to the mechanics of rememory as they unite the individual experiences of Sethe and Paul D apply to the chilling chapter on the Middle Passage. Impressionistic and devoid of punctuation, the chapter disorients the reader, destabilizing narrative perspective through a narrator that might be an anonymous African woman, Beloved, Sethe, or, it would seem, all three, to demonstrate their intertwinement and the destabilization of boundaries of time and subjectivity:

> the woman is there with the face I want the face that is mine . . . if I had the teeth of the man who died on my face I would bite the circle around her neck bite it away I know she does not like it . . . the woman with my face is in the sea . . . I want her face . . . I cannot lose her again . . . she goes in the water with my face . . . my face is coming I have to have it I am looking for the join I am loving my face so much my dark face is close to me I want to join . . . I come out of blue water . . . I am not dead . . . she is my face smiling at me doing it at last a hot thing now we can join.[60]

The sea where the slave ship sails and where corpses are discarded blurs into the river from which Beloved arises to join Sethe again. The circle around the neck signifies the iron circle around slaves' necks and echoes the circles associated with Sethe's almost unknown mother (who was branded with a circle and a cross, and who was lynched). Most striking, though, is the face that is both Sethe's and Beloved's—the site of the "join." Melding the subjectivities and experiences of an unknown mother and daughter, it locates the point of origin not in the *already-being* of the plantation but in the *becoming* of the slave ship. That moment of transformation from human to slave, the movement from Africa to America—this is the memory transmitted through silence, which begets more silence. As rememory, it is the experience that brings together three generations of women across the border between life and death, between forgotten languages and silence, between the past and the present.

The significance of the liminal finds similarly forceful expression in the relationship between Behar's narrator and his grandfather. Upon conversing with his grandson, the specter issues its lament: "Why is this history of mine mixed up with yours. . . . You are the generation for which we waited so that there would be no difference between its past and the past of its teachers, because our past was already very painful and we remained in the desert for the birds of prey to eat us for your sake, so that you would not remember me, so that you would not be hurting like me." The story's evocation of the desert alludes to *dor midbar*, the generation of Israelites prohibited from entering the Land of Israel and doomed to perish in the desert. In the eyes of the Labor establishment during the early decades of statehood, the first generation of Mizraḥi immigrants were, as Lital Levy notes, "a *dor midbar* hopelessly mired in their Diasporic mentality, . . . whereas their children might still be redeemable."⁶¹ The narrator's grandfather, however, modifies the concept of dor midbar by suggesting that he himself accepted his role therein, choosing to perish in the desert. This narrative of sacrifice makes way for the grandfather's recollection of his demise: "I did not meet my death in Jerusalem, nor in the city of my birth, but rather in the desert between them, a great desert of silence." His death in the "desert of silence" suggests that the birds of prey that consumed him and the others of his generation signify the cultivated silence of a transgenerational disremembering. The interment of the grandfather's story in the desert sands is sealed by the determined eradication of his accent in the next generation and by the willful nonmemory of the following one. The grandfather, however, implicates himself in this forgetting: "We remained in the desert . . . for your sake, so that you would not remember me." Pointing to the desert, the ultimate liminal space, as the site of his death, the grandfather's ghost suggests that the point of origin of the haunted grandson's travails is, as in *Beloved*, in the transitional space and moment: between Iraq and Israel, between cultural at-home-ness and alienation, between Arabic and Hebrew.⁶²

It is not the desert, though, that creates the conditions for rememory's merging of diverse experiences. In fact, even as other characters are haunted by their own myriad accents, our narrator's alienation sets him apart. Rather, it is the scene of his walk through the streets of Jerusalem after his initial interrogation that offers the possibility of interconnectedness. As he walks down the street, suddenly the movie theater disappears, the streets revert to their Arabic names, and the houses and the people all become Arab: "not only construction workers, not only street cleaners and renovators"—in other words, not the working-class Arabs that have become a familiar part of the Jewish Israeli space, but a full and thriving human landscape, "and they were the way they had been before the 1948 War, as if there had never been a 1948 War. I see them and they are strolling in the yards among the fruit trees and picking fruit as though the newspapers had not told them that the trees would wither, that the land would be filled with refugees." In this haunted memory of a past that might have been, "it was as though time had gone through another history, a different history, and I remembered that I had asked my mother why we talked history so much, enough history, we've had enough of history, because this history binds me, leaving nothing inside me, and also nothing inside you. And really, we have become so fixed in our history, and extinguished, but here for a moment history has followed a different trajectory." Here, then, thinks the hopeful narrator, is an opportunity to right historical and historiographic wrongs, to challenge the rigid authority of newspapers and books. This rememory that allows him to interact with the specters of bygone Palestinians, to cross from the broken present into another past, seems to offer a redemptive possibility. But all his efforts to communicate with the specters fail—not because they are specters and he is not, not because they are in the past and he is in the present, not even because they do not exist and he does. Rather, he fails because they cannot understand his halting Arabic.

This moment reveals the true nature of this inherited historical trauma, the trauma he shares with his grandfather: the relinquishing of history, language, even accent, and the severing of communication and identification. The event that is not represented but that spectrally occupies the text through these Palestinian ghosts is, of course, the Nakba. The flash point is neither only the broad cultural loss and dispossession experienced by Arab Jews nor only the grandson's willful forgetting of it, but also the collective trauma of Palestinian Arabs in 1948. Michael Rothberg's conceptualization of "multidirectional memory" seems to refer to precisely the kind of dialogue the story forges among these traumatic events. Working against the idea of "competitive memory," which he describes as "a struggle for recognition in which there can only be winners and losers," Rothberg suggests that we acknowledge "the interaction of different historical memories."[63] Multidirectional memory offers a conceptualization of memory "as subject to ongoing negotiation, cross-referencing, and borrowing; as productive and not privative."[64]

This notion, while potentially illuminating, can be unnerving to those who feel that such negotiations only pull their particular narrative further into historical obsolescence. Regarding Behar's story, the applicability of multidirectional memory is limited for a different reason. Behar moves beyond it by suggesting that the story of Mizrahi cultural dispossession and of the Nakba are not separate historical narratives that might be fruitfully brought into dialogue but rather are *already* intimately related. Just as the grandson had not "made the connection to [his] grandfather on [his] lips," so too had he not made the connection to the Palestinian Arabs on his streets. The story, on the other hand, illuminates this connection forcefully. Rejecting nonmemory, the grandson opts instead to reflect on the primal scene at the base of his inherited memory: not his grandfather's departure from Iraq or arrival in Israel, but the Nakba; not the violent scenes of war and dispossession that did happen, but peace and prosperity that did not. He thus conjures an alternative history, a 1948 that knew no Nakba. Forging circular connections between the past and the present, he not only *allows* the ghosts to transgress the temporal boundary between the past and the present, as ghosts do, but also *invites* the haunted across these lines. Both *Beloved* and "Ana min al-Yahoud" focus on tracing their immediate transgenerational hauntings (by Beloved and Grandfather Anwar) further back. Connecting their individual experience of violence to the broader historical experiences that precede them by generations, the texts summon and expose events their characters did not undergo personally, the Middle Passage and the Nakba, shameful open secrets within the American and Israeli national stories.

As such, the accent, the corporeal manifestation of the grandfather's visitation, is configured as a historical restoration, just as the ghostly Palestinians in the streets are restored to their rightful place, and much as Beloved herself is restored in her mother's house and in her arms. Yet all these historical restorations are partial. The accent does not reappropriate the Arabic, Yiddish, or other language but rather only indicates the traces these languages leave on "pure" Hebrew. The return of Palestinian Arabs to the streets of Jerusalem is ephemeral, and Beloved eventually departs. Though none of these hauntings resolve the historical wrongs they address, they suggest that historical restoration is an ongoing, perpetual process.

Significantly, both authors implicate their protagonists, foregrounding their role in the broader disremembering of history while at the same time contextualizing it empathetically. Neither Morrison nor Behar allows readers to lose sight of the complex positioning that urges their characters, on the one hand, to forget painful things in order to reassert control of their lives and redefine themselves as something other than victims, and on the other, to remember these things in the name of historical justice. Moreover, these spectral visitations demonstrate that haunting is more than the eruption of suppressed memories. It also works to displace nonmemory—active forgetting—through rememory. Critically, the agency at the center of both nonmemory and rememory empowers its practitioners. Both texts hold their characters responsible for their disremembering, pointing to their obligation to remember and to transmit their stories and thus positioning them as something other than victims. Finally, this practice of memory restores characters to an inherited transgenerational history, empowering them to "rip the veil" from seemingly stable national stories to expose the darkness beneath.

"This Is Not a Story to Pass On": Language, Silence, and Narrating the Past

The need to coin new terms to account for the unconventional processes of memory and forgetfulness in both texts exemplifies the way language undergoes revision to accommodate ghosts and to formulate a spectral poetics. Both *Beloved* and "Ana min al-Yahoud" show that language acquisition can be a politically charged process, one that can document and even activate the obliteration of past places and experiences. In both texts, characters must reclaim the very language that has alienated or subjugated them, the only language they have, by revising its sounds or its meaning, to articulate their story and to establish its legitimacy. In this context, twin phantoms haunt these narratives persistently: the loss of one language, and the inability of the language that remains to adequately express loss. Both texts seek a way to express the disremembered not only despite but also *through* these limitations of language.

Morrison's lecture at her Nobel Prize ceremony addresses the abuse, neglect, and power of language. Well aware that language is susceptible to usurpation by violent forces, she nevertheless insists that only language offers resistance against such manipulations and their dire consequences: "The systematic looting of language can be recognized by the tendency of its users to forgo its nuanced, complex, mid-wifery properties for menace and subjugation. . . . [Whether] it is the malign language of law-without-ethics, or language designed for the estrangement of minorities, hiding its racist plunder in its literary cheek—it must be rejected, altered, and exposed. It is the language that drinks blood, laps vulnerabilities, tucks its fascist boots under crinolines of respectability and patriotism."[65] Despite this brutal transformation of language from a midwife bringing new ideas into the world to a bloodthirsty vampire, however, Morrison, in the name of the subjugated, refuses to relinquish responsibility for its fate. In the words of the wise woman whose story she tells in the lecture, "when language dies, out of carelessness, disuse, indifference and absence of esteem, or killed by fiat, not only she herself, but all users and makers are accountable for its demise."[66] Morrison empowers the disenfranchised through language, through the ability to tell stories and the necessity of storytelling. Language is potent not because it can relay facts but rather because it can gesture beyond their limits: "Language can never live up to life once and for all. Nor should it. Language can never 'pin down' slavery, genocide, war. Nor should it yearn for the arrogance to be able to do so. Its force, its felicity is in its reach toward the ineffable."[67]

That ghosts inhabit "the interstices of the visible and the invisible," in Gordon's words, makes them able emissaries of the ineffable.[68] But their ability to speak and to be heard is at least as important in the act of haunting. Derrida's most urgent advice to his readers is that they "speak to the specter."[69] When we encounter spirits, we must learn "how to let them speak or how to give them back speech, even if it is in oneself, in the other, in the other in oneself: they are always *there*, specters, even if they do not exist, even if they are no longer, even if they are not yet."[70] Ghosts not only inhabit the spaces between the seen and unseen, the visible and invisible; they also haunt the interstice between silence and speech. By inviting the specter to speak, and by listening to the specter tell untold stories, we can breach the fortress defending the unsayable, even if language can never accurately represent it.

The characters in *Beloved* recall and narrate a story that defies language. If the common currency of rememory is not utterance but vision, then telling a story becomes an act rife with complications. "How can I say things that are pictures," wonders Beloved before opening the floodgates of rememory of the slave ship.[71] It is a language disorienting for its lack of punctuation, expressing the chaos that heralds the creation of a new world order defined by slavery: "In the beginning I could see her.... In the beginning the women are away from the men and the men are away from the women storms rock us and mix the men into the women and the women into the men."[72] Certain literary features signal the encounter of language with the unsayable: the lack of punctuation over the course of several chapters, new words (rememory, disremember) coined to designate experiences for which existing language is inadequate, the jarring typography that marks certain passages. Similarly, when Sethe tries to articulate her story using reason, to explain why she killed Beloved, she sounds absurd despite the simple truth of her words: "If I hadn't killed her she would have died and that is something I could not bear to happen to her."[73]

This challenge posed by the disjuncture between language and story is compounded by the loss of the original African language. The story itself survives, but Sethe and others must find alternative ways to access it.

Nan, the almost-forgotten wet nurse at Sweet Home, "used different words. Words Sethe understood then but could neither recall nor repeat now.... What Nan told her she had forgotten, along with the language she told it in. The same language her ma'am spoke, and which would never come back.... [She] was picking meaning out of a code she no longer understood."[74] Not only the lost African language but also the cryptic speech of the dead poses challenges of comprehension and articulation in the novel. Speaking a language incomprehensible to the living, the dead nonetheless insist on being heard. When Stamp Paid approaches 124 Bluestone Road, he hears "a conflagration of hasty voices—loud, urgent, all speaking at once so he could not make out what they were talking about or to whom. The speech wasn't nonsensical, exactly, nor was it tongues. But something was wrong with the order of the words and he couldn't describe or cipher it to save his life."[75] Stamp Paid knows all too well that "the undecipherable language clamoring around the house was the mumbling of the black and angry dead."[76] Again and again we are told that the cacophony of voices "that ringed 124 like a noose" is "recognizable but undecipherable to Stamp Paid."[77] By contrast with the outspoken—if incomprehensible—dead, the women in the house are silent, characterized by their "unspeakable thoughts, unspoken."[78] The dead speak a language that no one can understand, while the living fall silent because their stories are unspeakable. Language fails.

And yet, critically, the indecipherability of language is also conceptualized in *Beloved* as a mode of resistance. Throughout the novel, Morrison demonstrates how the same language used to rationalize the dehumanization of human beings can be appropriated by those subjugated people. Those same "gelded workhorses whose neigh and whinny could not be translated into a language responsible humans spoke" deliberately unsettle the master's language, modifying it not only to make it undecipherable to the master but also to tell the truth.[79] Paul D recalls how, in a chain gang, he and his fellow prisoners assigned new meanings to language as a mode of survival: "With a sledge hammer in his hands and Hi Man's lead, the men got through. They sang it out and beat it up, garbling the words so they could not be understood; tricking the words so their syllables yielded up other meanings."[80] The sledgehammer the prisoners wield by command of the three white men is reconceptualized, in their minds, as a tool that helps them break language and remake it to avenge their helplessness and to tell untold stories. It is "the key, the code, the sound that broke the back of words" that finally emancipates Sethe from the clutches of an angry ghost and restores her ownership of her own past.[81] Language, ill-equipped to tell the stories of slavery, must be actively appropriated and revised, its words assigned new meanings, so that it can begin to express the unsayable. On a broader scale, this is the task that Morrison achieves in the novel as a whole through Beloved's haunting: the indecipherability of "the black and angry dead" becomes the story itself. The exposure of the limits of language, and the integration of the incomprehensible and the unspeakable into the American story—this is what Morrison achieves by inviting us to "speak with the specter."

As we have seen, the question of language underpins the hauntings in Behar's story, as well. The motivating factor in both texts is telling the story, restoring and recollecting the narrative that has been forgotten. Like Morrison, Behar thematizes these acts through facets of language and narration. Language not only communicates past events but also is the very subject of those events: through terminology and accent, language tells a story even before it begins to narrate. In the wake of erasure, denial, or forgetting of language, silence speaks. Most critically, language can be co-opted and reappropriated through the alteration of syntax, cadence, and diction, a subversive act that makes the restoration of language, itself, the subject of Behar's story.

Initially, the narrator is eager to assert his Jewish identity to the suspicious policemen who question him and, it seems, to the reader. Trying to de-Arabize his newly accented pronunciation, he lists the unwritten rules intended to maintain the "purity" of Israeli Hebrew by denying its association with Arabic, the language of the enemy: "to soften the ʿayyin," "to soften the ḥet and make it a khaf," "to distance the tsaddi from the samekh . . . to get out of that Iraqi quf."[82] But the tone of his defense becomes increasingly ironic. By the time the policemen begin to search him for weapons, his diction speaks for itself. Terms like חגורת נפץ (ḥagorat nefets, explosive belt), חפץ חשוד (ḥefets ḥashud, suspicious object), and, later, מחסום (maḥsom, barrier) and מתקן הכליאה (mitkan ha-kli'a, military holding facility) are familiar to Israelis for whom the threat of terrorism has been normalized.[83] They are associated with a broader rhetoric citing terror as justification for ever-increasing surveillance of and restrictions on Palestinians. Though the Iraqi Arabic accent differs from the Palestinian Arab accent, the narrator is subjected to the same searches as suspected terrorists on its basis, exposing the authorities' conflation of Arab Jews and of Palestinian non-Jews. At the same time, he appropriates this conflation, identifying with

Palestinians—who are always already suspects—and engendering the crimes of which he is suspected: "And really, during the time when I left my body to them explosive belts began to be born on my heart, swelling and refusing to be defused, thundering and thundering. But as they were not made of steel or gunpowder they succeeded in evading the mechanical detectors." Like Sethe, who commits a horrific act to prevent her children's return to slavery, so does Behar's narrator nourish the "explosive belt" born upon his heart, in identification with the stereotyped Palestinian enemy he is suspected of being, forcing the reader to negotiate a new type of ethical framework. The presence of Arabic, even only as an accent on Hebrew, instigates the discourse and praxis of terror and security, which, in turn, help produce the conditions for the very violence they try to thwart.

The narrator's identification with Palestinian Arabs is not, however, limited to the policemen's inability to distinguish between a Palestinian accent and an Iraqi accent in Hebrew. Though he initially denies any commonality with Palestinians, explaining to the police in vain that their accents differ, he comes to embrace it. Walking through the haunted streets of a Jerusalem with its pre-1948 Palestinians returned, he is eager to connect with the specters: "I hoped that I would be able to tell them how much I had read about the writer and educator Khalil al Sakakini, and how much I wanted to make friends with his grandchildren, and I would walk among them, approaching their yards." As it turns out, however, his hobbling Arabic is not only inadequate for purposes of communication but also suggestive of mockery rather than respect:

> I do not succeed in mingling with them because all I have at my disposal is Hebrew with an Arabic accent and my Arabic, which doesn't come from my home but from the army, is suddenly mute, strangled from my throat, cursing itself without uttering a word, hanging in the suffocating air of the refuges of my soul, hiding from family members behind the shutters of Hebrew. And all the time, when I tried to speak to them in the small, halting vocabulary of the Arabic I knew, what came out was Hebrew with an Arabic accent, until they thought that I was ridiculing them, and had my accent not been so Iraqi, had it not been for that, they would have been certain that I was making fun of them.

Despite his intentions, he cannot "speak to the specters"—not because of their spectrality but because of his lost language. The narrator's Arabic is not *his*—it comes from the army, not from home, and therefore is imbued with an ideological purpose at odds with his desire to befriend the Palestinians. In any case, even this malnourished Arabic eludes him, hiding behind his accented Hebrew. Far from forging a bond with the Palestinians he considers "family members," his accent offends them and alienates him, pointing to the absence of Arabic.

The diverse accents referenced in this story—Arabic, Yiddish, Ladino, Ukrainian, German—point to similar losses. These other languages, repressed by Zionist ideology in the name of a homogeneous national culture anchored by Hebrew, haunt Hebrew in this story not to replace it but rather to activate memory and counter the ideologically sanctioned, cultivated silence of unaccented Hebrew. This willful silence of "Hebrew as it should be spoken, with no accent," designates a broader, collective disremembering or nonmemory, one that encompasses the expansive geographic and linguistic swath homogenized in the name of Israeliness.[84] Behar's thematic focus on Arabic in the story, a choice that speaks to the author's own biography, allows him to address the consequences of the nationalist appropriation of Hebrew not only for the Jews who were encouraged to forget their other languages, but also for the Palestinians who had been disremembered even by those who were, culturally, linguistically, and ethnically, "family members."

What is left if the languages of the past are irrevocably lost? Morrison's characters "break the back" of the only language they have left to possess it and compel it to tell their stories. Behar's narrator, too, finally claims Hebrew as his, but he does so differently. Throughout the story, he draws from biblical and rabbinic Hebrew, as well as from various registers of modern Hebrew.[85] For example, his syllabification of the word בר-חוב (bar-ḥov, in the street), instead of the standard ברחוב (ba-reḥov), follows the grammar of biblical Hebrew rather than modern.[86] His use of the *nitpa'el* construction in verbs such as נשתכחה (nishtak'ḥa, was forgotten) instead of the *nif'al* (נשכחה, nishkeḥa), on the other hand, is Mishnaic in origin.[87] The unusual and distinctly biblical phrase אם לא תיטיב שאת (im lo teitiv set, if thou doest not well) appears twice at the story's end.[88] Though the Hebrew language, even in its modern Israeli form, is by definition rooted in these texts, Behar's story evokes them in unusual contexts and juxtapositions, calling attention to the different historical periods and forms of the language. Behar pieces together a Hebrew whose history is suddenly visible, a Hebrew that is rich in its diasporic heritage and distinctly Judaic—the "traditional, multilayered, polyphonic Hebrew of the liturgical, poetic, and mystical traditions of Sepharad," in Levy's words.[89] As Behar has put it, "the language remembers God."[90]

It is unlikely that most contemporary readers of modern Hebrew, particularly secular readers, could identify the textual origin of these terms and phrases. At most, they may strike all but the most erudite readers as archaic in a general sense. In the modern Hebrew reader, this method of destabilization produces, as Levy observes, "an uncanniness of confronting the distantly familiar unknown."[91] This lack of familiarity (or distant familiarity) with the antecedents of Hebrew is another loss that Behar's story underscores, another manifestation of the Israeli divestment from the Jewish past. Behar's confrontation with this loss recalls precisely the concern expressed by Gershom Scholem in his letter to Franz Rosenzweig, discussed in the first chapter of this study: that the Zionist effort to modernize Hebrew by repressing its religious aspect would inevitably result in a "ghostly" language, posing an "uncanny" threat to the national Jewish endeavor.[92] By inviting the repressed elements back into a Hebrew that cannot quite accommodate them, Behar's story highlights the estrangement of the diasporic and the Judaic from the national language.

The story's concern with language, then, is two pronged. While the plot is concerned with lost or silenced Arabic, the language effectuates the spectral presence of what Levy terms "other Hebrews."[93] This dual absence of "other Hebrews" and of Arabic is the consequence of the same act of cultural dispossession. Yet the thematization of the loss of Arabic is what catalyzes the narrator's defiant reclamation of desecularized Hebrew, which reaches its apex at the story's disconcerting end. This Hebrew itself, presented not only with an Arabic accent but also with its historical diversity allowed to unsettle normative Israeli Hebrew, is the story the narrator recovers—and the story is his only form of resistance. Having lost Arabic, he turns to a multifarious Hebrew to tell the story that finally breaks the silence of nonmemory. The story—which indicts his parents directly for the shame that robbed him of his inheritance—is his weapon against nonmemory:

> And the language that became my language commands me to pour my soul out in it . . . we'll disguise ourselves as another language, absent. And this is really the same story that returns again and again. So many stories I have, mother, father, a person has so many stories, the same story he tries to tell each time with slightly different words, each time trying to resolve from a different time the same irresolvable story, and don't you also recognize your story, your silence nevertheless told me a little. Now I've tried to tell the story with the Arabic accent, but what came out of it, look where we're meeting. Take, read my story, mother father, read all my stories that I hid from you for many years, you too are the same exile, the same silence, the same alienation between heart

and body and between thought and speech, perhaps you will know how the plot will be resolved.[94]

Hebrew becomes his coconspirator, collaborating with him in a linguistic masquerade to conjure the absent language, while his parents' narrative of loss is evident only in their profound silence. The narrator chooses, instead, to make his Hebrew speak its loss. The language of the story *becomes* the story—of the reclamation of past places, languages, and linguistic praxis, a counter to the Israeli nonmemory of diasporic Jewish histories. Herein lies the story's gothicism: it not only tells the tale of the loss of Arabic but also resists that loss *in the telling*, by inviting Arab ghosts to haunt it, by invoking the Hebrew pasts in unconventional linguistic juxtapositions to disrupt its normative present, by adulterating the unaccented Hebrew narrative.

At the end of the story, Behar's narrator, pleased to note that "the streets of Jerusalem were changing" and that only his parents resisted the transformation, reveals that he had started to write his stories "in Arabic letters." The department heads he expects to shock, however, only laugh: "Let him write like that. Let him write stories that only he can read, his parents or his children will not read them and our children will not fall into the danger and, if he applies, we will give him all the government prizes for Arabic literature without having read a word in his books." This passage evokes the specter of Samir Naqqash, the sole Iraqi Jewish author to continue writing in Arabic even after his reluctant immigration to Israel. Upon his death in 2004, Naqqash was eulogized as "a tragic hero" whose complex Arabic works were accessible only to a handful of admiring readers.[95] Though he was awarded the Prime Minister's Prize for Arabic Literature and recognized by celebrated authors outside Israel, such as the Egyptian Nobel laureate Naguib Mahfouz, his insistence on writing in Arabic limited his audience and prevented his rise to literary prominence. Similarly, Behar's narrator writes his stories "in Arabic letters" and then resorts to silence: "And everything is the voice of my silences, my silences are many, many silenced words." However, finally reclaiming the Hebrew language through "poems of opposition to Hebrew in Hebrew," he evades historical oblivion. His use of "accented Hebrew" calls attention to the violence in which Hebrew has been implicated even if it cannot undo its effects.

The Future of the Past

"Slavery is the family secret of America," writes Ashraf Rushdy, not because it is inaccessible or unknown, but "in the sense that it haunts the peripheries of the national imaginary . . . , the partially hidden phantom of a past that needs to be revised in order to be revered."[96] Similarly accessible and known, the Israeli "family secret" of Mizraḥi oppression is linked in this story to that known/unknown secret of the Palestinian Nakba, both through their role in the creation of an Israeli national collective and in the common Arab cultural foundation of its subjects. The "family" that guards this secret is the nation as well as the narrator's nuclear family, his parents, who insist he had no connection to his deceased grandfather. The emphasis in Behar's story, as in Morrison's novel, is on the characters' unconventional, radical modes of empowerment and self-assertion in the face of violence and suppression. Much as Morrison's characters are "generative and creative change-agents" rather than only "victims of hegemonic agency and control," in Barnes's words, so, too, does Behar's narrator indicate a Mizraḥi subjectivity that resists primary classification as a victim of Zionist praxis.[97] He does so by acknowledging Mizraḥi nonmemory as a phenomenon enabling hegemonic Zionist forces, and haunting as a face-to-face confrontation with the forgotten past. The confrontation is frightening, but it is desired, at least for a time. These ghosts have been welcomed, and their hosts accommodate and engage with them. Forging a spectral poetics to tell the story of the disremembered past from the perspective of the historically disempowered, these narratives not only disinter and revise buried histories but also force a reevaluation of the practices of memory and of forgetting themselves.

Finally, both texts end on a similar note of ambivalence. "This is not a story to pass on," asserts Morrison's narrator ambiguously, while Behar's narrator laments the failure of his Arabic-accented story to get through to his parents. The personal and historical anguish both texts recall defy resolution. Engaging with the past through specters, though, reconfigures history with an eye to the future: "haunting, unlike trauma, is distinctive for producing a something-to-be-done," as Gordon asserts.[98] Haunting is a call to action—to confront the family secret, to rememory, to tell the story, to pass it on.

Notes

1. Busbridge, "On Haunted Geography"; "Artist of the Month," *This Week in Palestine*; Hochberg, "Poetics of Haunting"; J. Roberts, *Contested Land, Contested Memory*. The Nakba (catastrophe) is the Arabic term used to refer to the Arab defeat in the 1948 war and to its consequences, Palestinian dispossession and exile from Palestine.

2. Somerson, "Twin Ghosts"; Shulman, "In Palestine."
3. The term *Mizraḥi*, literally "Eastern" in Hebrew, refers to Israeli Jews descended from North Africa and the Middle East. Mizraḥim, the majority of whom immigrated to Israel after the establishment of Israel in a series of state-sponsored "rescue operations" in the 1950s and 1960s, come from an Arabic cultural background that they were encouraged to disown in Israel, as Arabic is associated with the Palestinians and the "Arab enemy" supporting their territorial claims. The result of this strongly encouraged abandonment of Arabic cultural affiliation is that, after only a generation, few Mizraḥim could speak Arabic or identify with the Arab culture of their parents and grandparents.
4. Omer-Sherman, "Jewish and Muslim Identities," 445. Mizraḥim themselves have identified with the oppression of African Americans in the United States. Mizraḥi activists formed the Israeli Black Panthers movement in 1971 on the basis of this identification.
5. Gordon, *Ghostly Matters*, 142.
6. Leslie Fiedler sees no contradiction between the gothic and serious literature. He asserts that American literature is especially amenable to the gothic, the mode best equipped to express the horrors underpinning American history: "Of all the fiction of the West, our own is most deeply influenced by the gothic, is almost essentially a gothic one.... Until the gothic had been discovered, the serious American novel could not begin" (Fiedler, *Love and Death*, 142–43). He ascribes this appeal to "certain special guilts [that] awaited projection in the gothic form" in the United States: the genocide of Native Americans and the disgrace of slavery (ibid., 143).
7. Goddu notes that reviewers of *Beloved* "seem uneasy affiliating Toni Morrison with the gothic.... Associated with the sensational, the formulaic, and the popular, the gothic is seen to lack seriousness of purpose and connection to actual experience" (*Gothic America*, 187n15). Elizabeth B. House devotes an entire essay to arguing that the ghost in *Beloved* is not a ghost but an escaped slave (House, "Toni Morrison's Ghost").
8. Studies on the gothicism of *Beloved* abound. Maisha Wester, in *African-American Gothic*, devotes an entire chapter to *Beloved*, the only text to warrant its own chapter in her study. See also Bryant, "*Soul Has Bandaged Moments*"; Goldner, "Other(ed) Ghosts"; Hamilton, "Revisions, Rememories and Exorcisms"; Moglen, "Redeeming History"; and Rody, "Toni Morrison's *Beloved*." The discussion of *Beloved*'s gothicism is not limited to the critical milieu of the novel itself or even to that of American literature. For example, Smith's essay on "Hauntings," included in the *Routledge Companion to Gothic*, cites *Beloved* as an example of a gothic ghost story (Smith, "Hauntings").
9. Several critics have noted the blurred line between the harrowing facts of slavery and the gothic fiction that narrates it, which reorients our conception of the gothic. Goddu notes that "everyday realities of slavery are already coded in Gothic terms" and cites American texts that present "the Gothic as a realistic mode" ("American Gothic," 65). Goldner echoes this sentiment, asserting that "*Beloved* defines the gothic as the real" in its portrayal of a fully materialized ghost and in its haunting as an event accepted as possible by all the African American characters ("Other[ed] Ghosts," 72).
10. Questions of accent and pronunciation have been key factors in the development of Israeli Hebrew as a unified and unifying national language in the twentieth century, as Miryam Segal has shown. See Segal, *New Sound*.
11. Freud, *Uncanny*, 147. The fact that "so-called educated people have officially ceased to believe that the dead can become visible as spirits" provides the element of repression that is necessary for the return to be considered uncanny (ibid., 149). Freud distinguishes between

the uncanny in literature and the uncanny in real life, arguing that if the text accepts demons, ghosts, and other supernatural entities as possible "within its literary reality," then "such figures forfeit any uncanny quality that might otherwise attach to them" (ibid., 156). This does not mean, however, that literature cannot portray such figures as uncanny: "Not so, however, if the writer has to all appearances taken up his stance on the ground of common reality. By doing so he adopts all the conditions that apply to the emergence of a sense of the uncanny in normal experience; whatever has an uncanny effect in real life has the same in literature" (ibid., 156–57).

12. The introduction of this study offers a brief sketch of what has come to be known as "the Spectral Turn," a period, beginning in the 1990s, of increased interest in the theoretical possibilities of ghosts and haunting within the humanities and social sciences.

13. Bhabha, "World and the Home," 144.

14. Smith, "Hauntings," 147.

15. Derrida, *Specters of Marx*, 46.

16. Ibid., xvii–xviii.

17. Gordon, *Ghostly Matters*, 183 (emphasis mine, parentheses hers).

18. Savoy, "Face of the Tenant," 13–14.

19. Hochberg, "Poetics of Haunting," 56.

20. Ibid., 66.

21. Sugars and Turcotte, *Unsettled Remains*, xvii. Revisionist theorizations of the gothic in the context of settler societies and colonial, imperial, and postcolonial configurations are numerous. A 2003 issue of *Gothic Studies* titled "Postcolonial Gothic" includes a thorough and thoughtful introduction to the topic and attests to growing interest in the intersection of gothic and postcolonial studies (Hughes and Smith, "Introduction"). Several book-length studies and essay collections on the subject have appeared recently, complementing scores of articles: Rudd, *Postcolonial Gothic Fictions*; Tabish, *Gothic, Postcolonialism and Otherness*; Ng, *Interrogating Interstices*; Smith and Hughes, *Empire and the Gothic*; Sugars and Turcotte, *Unsettled Remains*.

22. Savoy, "Face of the Tenant," 7.

23. Abraham and Torok, *Shell and the Kernel*, 166.

24. Ibid., 175.

25. Ibid., 181.

26. T. Morrison, *Beloved*, 188.

27. Goddu, "American Gothic," 65.

28. The familial dynamics brought to light in *Beloved*, particularly as they are figured in the mother-daughter bond, have spurred a substantial body of critical literature. See, for example, Wester's chapter on *Beloved* in *African American Gothic*, "'Murdered by Piece-Meal': The Destruction of African American Family in *Beloved*," 185–214; Budick, "Absence, Loss, and Space"; Horvitz, "Nameless Ghosts"; Offutt Mathieson, "Memory and Mother Love"; Heller, "Reconstructing Kin"; and Rushdy, "Daughters Signifyin(g) History."

29. Behar, "Ana min al-Yahoud" [English translation]. All citations are from the unpaginated English translation unless otherwise noted; citations from the original Hebrew refer to the page number of the original Hebrew text.

30. T. Morrison, *Beloved*, 200–203.

31. Ibid., 206.

32. Dent, "Contested Pasts," 25.

33. Gordon, *Ghostly Matters*, 142.

34. T. Morrison, "Site of Memory," 90–91.
35. Ibid., 91.
36. Mobley, "Different Remembering," 190. Mobley observes that the circular, meandering temporality of *Beloved* defies the linear teleology of slave narratives and "challenges the Western notion of linear time that informs American history and the slave narratives" (ibid., 190, 192). Cynthia S. Hamilton takes this point further, arguing that *Beloved* constitutes Morrison's attempt to "escape from the limitations of the traditional slave narrative" by imbuing it with the psychological power of the gothic (Hamilton, "Revisions, Rememories and Exorcisms," 431).
37. Barnes, "Myth, Metaphor, and Memory," 20; Rody, "Toni Morrison's *Beloved*," 94.
38. K. Davis, "Postmodern Blackness," 250.
39. Lawrence, "Fleshly Ghost," 200.
40. Behar, "Language We Inherit."
41. Shohat, "Sephardim in Israel," 33. Other scholars working in a similar vein include the sociologist and critical theorist Yehuda Shenhav, the anthropologist Smadar Lavie, and the poet and political scientist Sami Shalom Chetrit. Literature has been an especially fertile field of inquiry in indicating cultural and linguistic affinities between Arabic and Hebrew. See, for example, Brenner, *Inextricably Bonded*; Hochberg, *In Spite of Partition*; and Levy, *Poetic Trespass*.
42. Shohat, "Sephardim in Israel," 32. Karl Marx and Friedrich Engels famously begin their 1848 *Manifesto* thus: "A spectre is haunting Europe—the spectre of communism. All the powers of old Europe have entered into a holy alliance to exorcise this spectre" (Marx and Engels, *Manifesto*, 14).
43. Strategic political action on the basis of these commonalities has been limited. Levy notes that "although one can find expressions of solidarity and activism linking Mizraḥim and Palestinians from the earliest years of statehood, they remained marginal and never developed into a popular movement" (*Poetic Trespass*, 7). Massad points to the 1980s as an era of increased solidarity between Mizraḥim and Palestinians, as evident, for example, in Mizraḥi prominence in the Committee for Israeli-Palestinian Dialogue created in 1986 (Massad, "Zionism's Internal Others").
44. For example, Eli Amir and Sami Mikhael, both Iraqi Jewish authors who arrived in Israel just after the establishment of the state, have written about the experience of Jews in Iraq, and of the ambivalence experienced by Iraqi Jews vis-à-vis their encounter with European Israelis. Ronit Matalon, a Jewish Hebrew author of Egyptian origin, has addressed the irony of Mizraḥi Jewish subjugation of Palestinian Arabs in her novels and short stories. The Hebrew poets Erez Bitton and Sami Shalom Chetrit, both of Moroccan Jewish origin, have written prolifically about their intimate identification with the Arabic culture that has been suppressed in Israel.
45. Bhabha, "World and the Home," 153.
46. Rody, "Toni Morrison's *Beloved*," 102.
47. Gordon, *Ghostly Matters*, 166.
48. Hirsch, "Generation of Postmemory," 106.
49. Ibid., 106–7.
50. T. Morrison, *Beloved*, 260. This statement has bedeviled Morrison's critics. Given the book's preoccupation with individual and collective memory, and its status as a supplementary history, it makes sense to interpret it as ironic, as most have. Others have characterized the statement as a "chilling" suggestion that the project of rememory the book sets out to

accomplish is doomed to failure (Budick, "Absence, Loss, and Space," 117). Several have pointed to the double entendre of the phrase *to pass on* as meaning both to transmit and to decline.

51. T. Morrison, *Beloved*, 5.
52. Ibid., 40.
53. Hirsch, "Generation of Postmemory," 112.
54. Behar, "Ana min al-Yahoud" [in Hebrew], 55.
55. Neugroschel, *Dybbuk and Yiddish Imagination*, xvi.
56. Ibid., xvii.
57. I wish to thank Ilana Szobel for bringing my attention to this point. Behar, "Ana min al-Yahoud" [in Hebrew], 59.
58. Rushdy, "Rememory: Primal Scenes," 303.
59. Ibid., 318.
60. T. Morrison, *Beloved*, 200–203.
61. Levy, *Poetic Trespass*, 273. Levy also calls attention to Behar's reappropriation of the canonical 1912 poem by H. N. Bialik, "Metey midbar" ["The Desert Dead"]. Also see Omer-Sherman, "Jewish and Muslim Identities."
62. For more on the desert in Jewish and Israeli thought, see Zerubavel, *Desert in the Promised Land*; Grumberg, "Zionist Places"; Omer-Sherman, *Israel in Exile*; Pardes, *Biography of Ancient Israel*; Gurevitch, "Double Site of Israel."
63. Rothberg, *Multidirectional Memory*, 13.
64. Ibid.
65. T. Morrison, "Toni Morrison—Nobel Lecture."
66. Ibid.
67. Ibid.
68. Gordon, *Ghostly Matters*, 24.
69. Derrida, *Specters of Marx*, 11.
70. Ibid., 221.
71. T. Morrison, *Beloved*, 200.
72. Ibid., 201.
73. Ibid., 190.
74. Ibid., 58–59.
75. Ibid., 164.
76. Ibid., 188.
77. Ibid., 174, 189.
78. Ibid., 189.
79. Ibid., 118–19.
80. Ibid., 101.
81. Ibid., 248.
82. Behar, "Ana min al-Yahoud" [in Hebrew], 55. Vivian Eden's English translation adds linguistic terminology not present in the Hebrew original to convey the differences in the pronunciation of these letters in spoken Israeli Hebrew and in Arabic or Arabic-accented Hebrew.
83. Ibid., 57, 60, 64.
84. Ibid., 56.
85. Following Evelyn Nien-Ming Ch'ien's theorization of "weird English," Levy refers to this idiosyncratic use of language as "weird Hebrew" (*Poetic Trespass*, 270). Her reading

of Behar's story focuses on his cultivation of "linguistic excess" as a means to rebel "against both the loss of Arabic and the flattening of modern Hebrew" (ibid.).

86. Behar, "Ana min al-Yahoud" [in Hebrew], 55.
87. Ibid., 58.
88. Ibid., 64.
89. Levy, *Poetic Trespass*, 271.
90. Behar, "Language We Inherit."
91. Levy, *Poetic Trespass*, 270.
92. See n. 39 in chap. 1 of this study.
93. Levy, *Poetic Trespass*, 272.
94. Behar, "Ana min al-Yahoud" [in Hebrew], 64.
95. Livneh, "Exiled from Babylon."
96. Rushdy, *Remembering Generations*, 2.
97. Barnes, "Myth, Metaphor, and Memory," 20.
98. Gordon, *Ghostly Matters*, 8.

CODA: "HERE ARE OUR MONSTERS"

Hebrew Horror from the Political to Pop

THE "ABOUT" PAGE ON THE VAMPIRE TLV FACEBOOK page reads: "Vampire TLV is a Live Action Role Playing (LARP) platform in Tel Aviv. In the game, the characters play vampires that control Tel Aviv and its surroundings. The games take place in different and special sites. The atmosphere is gothic and electrifying and will take you straight to a fantasy world, putting your imagination in a frenzy ☺."[1] The "Vampire TLV Masquerade Ball" held on February 16, 2017, attracted 103 guests from the Vampire TLV community. "Gothic Night," which took place on June 17, 2017, at the Potion Bar on Tel Aviv's Allenby Street, capped three nights of festivities and promised to be "dark and intoxicating, an evening entirely dedicated to the dark gothic scene." On Saturday, September 30, the night following the Yom Kippur fast, the same venue hosted "A Black Sabbath," an event that coyly refers to the holy Sabbath and the Day of Atonement as the basis for a raucous "gothic" celebration anticipating Halloween: "Naughty vampires, sullen witches, and hungry werewolves. After they asked for atonement, we're setting out in a storm of celebration, because the blood is fresh and the flesh is pure ☺ Come to drink and celebrate because October 31 is still far away." Other events listed on the Facebook page at the time of writing include "Goth Night II" at the Potion Bar, advertised in ornate lettering intertwined with skulls, coffins, and crosses; and part seven of the LARP game, entitled "Katarina's Wine Cellar."[2]

In the new millennium, Hebrew gothic is alive and well. Its presence is palpable in Israeli popular culture: social media collectives, literature, film, and television brim with the undead and other supernatural creatures returning to terrify or seduce their eager consumers. Some of these cultural products are obviously inspired by their globally successful American and European forebears, such as, for example, Anne Rice's vampire novels, the *Twilight* films, and the television series *Buffy the Vampire Slayer* and *True Blood*. Others are more invested in specifically Israeli concerns, rewriting key concepts and themes to accord with Jewish Israeli culture and charting narratives dictated by the Israeli political and social reality. There is no doubt that this proliferation of zombies, vampires, and associated accoutrements on page and screen are part of an international trend. This broader trend itself is usually interpreted as evidence of cultural anxiety in various forms or, conversely, may be understood as fulfilling a lighthearted desire for the pleasures the gothic so masterfully produces.[3] A broad survey of the Israeli manifestation of contemporary popular gothic suggests that it is motivated by both politics and pleasure, with some texts overtly engaging with the political moment and others defiantly asserting their right to disengage from it.

Like the literature examined in this study, contemporary gothic cultural texts in Israel do not work toward a common political or ideological goal; no single motivation drives their production and consumption. Despite their heterogeneity, however, they do share two points of divergence from the novels and stories analyzed thus far in *Hebrew Gothic*. They are less preoccupied with the past than with the present, and almost without exception, their gothic visions deploy comedy in all its forms, a characteristic not often associated with the gothic. Whereas the texts examined in previous chapters are weighted down with gravitas, the mostly visual popular cultural products as a rule make use of the comic in various modes: camp, parody, and black humor appear prominently. Humor shapes these texts' articulation of the violence of the present and of the uneven dynamics of power, whether understood in terms of callous interpersonal relations, of nonpolitical crime, or of a state of perpetual occupation and war. As an age-old mechanism for confronting modernity and what Ruth Wisse terms "the paradoxes of Jewish life," humor affords these texts one way of engaging with the specificity of their situation.[4] On the other hand, in some of these texts, humor invites viewers to enjoy themselves. When a seductive vampire begins lip-synching a popular song, we may laugh simply for the pleasure of laughing.

In this concluding section of my study, I turn to the pervasiveness of the gothic in contemporary Hebrew popular culture, particularly in Israeli visual culture, to consider how this popular manifestation of gothic functions differently than its counterpart in Hebrew belles lettres. I aim not to arrive at a resolution or closure of the matter of gothic in Hebrew culture but rather to draw attention to this increasingly prevalent Israeli phenomenon of "postmillennial" popular Hebrew gothic culture, and to lay the groundwork for new avenues of investigation.[5]

* * *

Adaptations of the gothic and of related genres and modes have earned a place in Israel's cultural landscape. Popular fiction in Israel has seen increasing recourse to the fantastic, mostly expressed by the development of a robust science-fiction culture.[6] The Israeli Society for Science Fiction and Fantasy recently celebrated twenty years since its establishment, and Israel regularly hosts several science fiction and fantasy festivals and conventions, such as ICon and Olamot. Fan organizations and dedicated publications have helped develop a distinctly Israeli science-fiction scene in literature and film, supporting local authors, artists, and filmmakers. In addition to science-fictional reconceptualizations of the gothic, the familiar manifestations of the undead have been haunting the pages of popular fiction in Israel since the early aughts. Gal Amir's vampire novel *Laila adom* (Red night), published in 2003, garnered positive reviews in all the major newspapers, including two in the prestigious *Haaretz* literary supplement. Nine years later, another Hebrew vampire novel, Vered Tochterman's *Dam kaḥol* (Blue blood, 2012), was heralded in the same *Haaretz* literary supplement as the "first Hebrew vampire novel."[7] Both novels are distinctly Israeli in their setting, characters, and plot. Amir's novel is set in the Galilee, in Northern Israel, where a cursed yeshiva student has been transformed into a vampire; Tochterman's novel unfolds in hipster Tel Aviv, where a brokenhearted young woman is introduced by her gay roommate to a mysterious agency that offers erotic encounters with vampires in exchange for blood. Both are concerned with specific dimensions of the contemporary domestic Israeli milieu—masculinity, criminal violence, relationships.

Bolstering these Israeli popular-literary forays into the gothic is a wave of translations of original gothic texts, which had languished beyond the realm of acceptability for a century. As we saw in the introduction to this study, for decades the only classically gothic author to be translated to Hebrew was Edgar Allan Poe. In the 1980s—a decade of profound change in Israeli society politically, culturally, and socially—the translation of classical gothic works finally began in earnest. Mary Shelley's *Frankenstein* (1818) was first translated in 1983 and has seen at least five different translations in total. Bram Stoker's *Dracula* (1897) was translated in 1984, with at least two translations and three editions to date. Even those foundational gothic texts considered less prestigious have finally found expression in Hebrew: Horace Walpole's *The Castle of Otranto* (1764) is available in two different Hebrew translations (from 2014 and 2017), and Ann Radcliffe's *The Romance of the Forest* (1791) and *The Mysteries of Udolpho* (1794) have both been translated (2012 and 2017, respectively). Some of these translations are published by small, specialized presses, such as Sial, which specializes in science fiction and fantasy; others are published by prominent Israeli presses. For example, the 1996 edition of *Frankenstein*, translated by Dalit Lev, was published by Keter, and the 2017 edition of *Otranto*, translated by Yonatan Dayan, was published by Resling.

It is in visual culture, however, that contemporary gothic truly thrives in Israel. Though there is no such thing as "Gothic cinema," as Misha Kavka observes, there is "something peculiarly visual about the Gothic," owing to the prominence of spectacle in gothic narrative.[8] The slippage between gothic and horror in popular and scholarly discourse derives from their shared "visual codes," the bequest of the literary gothic, consisting of familiar images such as crumbling castles and moonlit skies.[9] Horror films both recycle these familiar visual codes and recast them in contemporary form, spanning the spectrum from nuanced social and political commentary to spine-tingling, adrenaline-induced thrills. As such, horror films are an important contemporary, popular incarnation of the gothic mode, hosting key gothic literary tropes such as the production of terror, the cultivation and representation of paranoia, and the evocation of the uncanny. Film noir offers another cinematic adaptation of the elements of literary gothic, in its jarring camera angles and ubiquitous shadows as well as its treatment of themes such as deception, estrangement, and dread.[10]

Several Israeli art house films in the gothic vein have been produced to great critical success in recent years—for example, the film noir–influenced *Mistor* (*Shelter*, Eran Riklis, 2017), about a Mossad agent charged with protecting a Lebanese collaborator; *Goldberg ve-Eisenberg* (*Goldberg and Eisenberg*, Oren Carmi, 2013), an urban psychological thriller whose dark humor owes a debt to the Coen brothers; and *Tikkun* (Avishai Sivan, 2016), a tightly controlled, imagistic black-and-white film about an Orthodox yeshiva student who is brought to life after having been dead for forty minutes. The dark wave in Israeli cinema, though, has been dominated over the past decade less by auteur cinema than by over-the-top horror. Since 2010, at least nine such horror films have been released in Israel, ranging from camp (*Mesuvag ḥarig*/*Freak Out*, Boaz Armoni, 2016) to slasher films (*Kalevet*/*Rabies*, Aharon Keshales and Navot Papushado, 2010), psychological thrillers

(*Mi mefaḥed mi-ha-ze'ev ha-ra*/*Big Bad Wolves*, Keshales and Papushado, 2013), and classic zombie tales (*JeruZalem*, Doron and Yoav Paz, 2015; and *Basar totaḥim*/*Cannon Fodder*, Eitan Gafni, 2013). This veritable wave of "Hebrew Horror" films is the most immediately apparent evidence of the popular Israeli engagement with the gothic and its legacy.

Unsurprisingly, critics, scholars, and filmmakers have focused on interpreting or presenting these films as political commentary or its antithesis, escapism. Yonatan Sagiv reads Israeli horror films as unequivocally political, depicting "dread, pain and anxiety as an inherent part of Israeli-Jewish existence while ambivalently portraying Palestinians, either as the harbingers of such violence or alternatively as its ultimate victims."[11] Neta Alexander points to *Big Bad Wolves* and *Rabies* (as well as other violent films not categorized as horror) to illustrate the emergence of what she terms the "New Violence" movement in Israeli cinema. The excessive violence of such films, she argues, is a symptom "of much deeper social and national anxieties and concerns."[12] As such, these films offer "a radical way to think about the interrelation between aesthetics and politics by . . . turning the occupation and the militarization of Israeli society into the subtext rather than the text."[13] Thus, though the "New Violence" films do not promote explicit political agendas, they engage indirectly with Israeli social and political apprehensions. Danny Sagal, reviewing *Rabies* in 2013, notes "the absence of vampire Nazis, zombie Palestinians and other predictable scenarios" in the few Israeli horror films produced up to then, including *Rabies*.[14] He attributes the wave of seemingly apolitical "Hebrew Horror" films to young filmmakers' fatigue regarding the seriousness of the predominant subjects of Israeli cinema, the Holocaust and the Israel/Palestine conflict.

Among the horror films produced in Israel since 2013, some bring to the fore the political concerns that Sagal detects between the lines in *Rabies*, deploying precisely the "predictable" figures that he anticipates. Others resist these political impulses defiantly. Though the imagery in some of these films is anything but subtle, they maintain the ambiguity typical of gothic texts more broadly, often lending themselves to interpretations supporting antithetical positions on the Israeli ideological spectrum. The critical responses sometimes align with the ideas expressed by the filmmakers themselves and sometimes diverge from them. What they share is a desire to articulate a relationship between serious political content and a "light" form of comedic horror, through denial or affirmation. This is the primary tension they express, though its valence is interpreted differently even by viewers of the same film.¹⁵

A case in point is the slasher horror-comedy *Freak Out*. A nervous, bespectacled soldier is left alone on a bleak, remote army base in hostile territory when his comrades abandon him for a night on the town. His paranoia, aided by sweeping exterior shots contrasted with the narrow, claustrophobic interiors, intensifies. Finally, gore abounds when he is ambushed in the night. In the "Director's Statement" included in the film's press notes, Boaz Armoni enumerates some of the issues the film purportedly deals with, including the military experience in Israel, inter-Jewish ethnic divisions, and the Israeli relation to "the Other": "Our behavior is driven by fear," he observes, "an artificial fear that often prevents us from seeing our flaws." His summation indicates the tension that characterizes most, if not all, the horror films produced in Israel: "*Freak Out* is a movie that contains substantial social criticism. But above all it is a movie that the audience will enjoy to watch."¹⁶ He repeatedly makes the point that the film "is meant to be entertaining in every aspect—from the humoristic gags to the blood-spilling" and that it "does not take itself too seriously," self-consciously disassociating from "Israeli cinema that contains so many 'important' and 'serious' films."¹⁷ It is unlikely that a Hollywood director would feel compelled to defend a comparable American film as merely entertaining. Though there is no doubt that fun and humor are primary motivators of his film, Armoni, like other Israeli filmmakers, uses the director's statement as an opportunity to legitimize his film by insisting that it is more than just fun.

Some viewers found it difficult to reconcile these traits, expressing disappointment at the lack of an explicit political message, and even outraged accusations of racism.¹⁸ For others, the film offers a refreshing expression of the general state of fear and paranoia that pervades contemporary Israel, a country whose policies vis-à-vis the Palestinians have pushed it farther to the political right and led to increasing isolation by the international community. For these viewers, the film and others like it offer not resolution or commentary but atmosphere. "This is the greatness of the genre films," writes one reviewer: "a critical preoccupation with explosive social issues through light entertainment, instead of an oppressive and repetitive discussion."¹⁹

Big Bad Wolves, perhaps the greatest commercial success of the wave of Hebrew horror films, also mingles comedy with horror, winning the admiration of Quentin Tarantino, a fact breathlessly reported by the Israeli media. A revenge thriller, it relates the kidnap and torture of a religious studies teacher suspected of assaulting and murdering young girls. Israeli reviews of the film were mainly positive, acknowledging its subversive nature. "Since this is an Israeli film," writes a reviewer in *Haaretz*, "its sadism cannot be separated from its setting, and the horrors described have social, cultural, historical, and mainly political implications."[20] Internationally, too, the film was a success, drawing enthusiastic attention at the 2013 Tribeca Film Festival and other prestigious international screenings. Nevertheless, some critics lamented "the wasted potential of the film's political possibilities."[21] In their press notes, the directors write that Israeli "existential anxiety" about persecution and victimhood and "a historical craving for vengeance create an ideal breeding ground for extreme actions and subsequent reactions."[22] Most reviewers did identify a subtle critical commentary in the exceedingly violent film. Others found it lacking, particularly given the directors' statement. They express a preference for an "explosive and unavoidable political message" issued through "powerful, thought-provoking drama"—in other words, for *another* film, one that is more serious than funny, more about the political conflict than about a serial killer.[23] In the *New York Times* review, Manohla Dargis wisely dismisses the directors' claims in the press notes. "Nice try, guys," she quips, before dryly asking, "Is there a point?"[24]

Some directors have defiantly resisted the impulse to politicize their horror films, announcing their intent to make "popcorn films" for sheer pleasure. The zombie movie *JeruZalem* is about American tourists in Jerusalem who find themselves trapped in the Old City as a horde of zombies and assorted demons descend. Employing a "found footage" conceit to play with fact and fiction, it recalls the "discovered manuscript" of classic gothic narratives like Horace Walpole's *The Castle of Otranto*. The prologue, a short 8 mm reel purportedly dating back to 1972, establishes a faux historical frame for the plot about to unfold, while the Google Glass perspective of the rest of the film suggests seemingly raw material, updating the conceit to the twenty-first century. Shot on a relatively low budget, it nevertheless won distribution in Europe and Asia, represented Israel at various international film festivals, and was released in the United States on Netflix. Though the directors contend that "we didn't have anything political to say to the world," some critics see it differently.[25] It "is hard not to read it as . . . a sharp commentary on the current Israel's self-destructive policies. Zombies are but a metaphor for what will take place should the so-called Israeli-Palestinian conflict not be resolved," insists the film scholar Olga Gershenson in the *Forward*.[26] She observes that the twisted cars, bloodied appendages, and rubble that are a result of the zombie apocalypse and the opening of the gate of hell are not unfamiliar to viewers of more realistic, explicitly political Israeli films—or TV news programs.

The tagline of another zombie film, *Cannon Fodder*, is "There's a new conflict in the Middle East." Despite its overtly political structure—its setting on the Lebanese border, its evocation of refugees, its identification of Hezbollah as the zombie adversaries—its director, too, refuses to identify a political stance with the film, insisting that "everyone should interpret it in their own way."[27] And they have: some view it as right-wing propaganda—heroic IDF soldiers fending off Arab zombies—while others see it as critiquing precisely this perception of Palestinians and calling for the rehumanization of the other. Pleased with the antithetical political interpretations the film sparked, Eitan Gafni claims that his goal was "just to make a fun movie that people will enjoy. A good popcorn movie."[28] In a similar vein, the writer and director William Blesch, asked whether the vampires in his upcoming film *Requiem for the Night* represent anything Israeli or Jewish, responds sardonically that "it's a vampire story. About vampires."[29] The filmmakers themselves are well aware of the tendency not only of their viewers at home but also of those abroad to expect their films to address politics explicitly or implicitly, by *not* making a political statement. In other words, audiences demand that such horror films offer either "realgothik" representations of political violence or escapism from it.[30]

Though film dominates contemporary gothic popular culture in Israel, television is also emerging as a considerable force, and it turns out to be no less amenable to a wide, even global, audience. The smash tween vampire television series *Ḥatsuya* (Split, dir. Shai Kapon, 2009–12), about a schoolgirl who discovers she is half-vampire and half-human, was an international success—at its height, in 2010, over seven million viewers had watched it. It was distributed in seventy-eight countries, including Italy, Portugal, Brazil, and Vietnam, and was dubbed into numerous languages.[31] Its unabashed imitation of American vampire enterprises like *Buffy the Vampire Slayer* and the *Twilight* films irritated the few critics who deigned to review it, who felt it ought to attend to the Israeli milieu.[32]

A more recent Israeli vampire television series for adults, *Juda*, received the lion's share of a 200 million NIS (just under $57 million) budget for original television series from the production company HOT.³³ The visually sophisticated *Juda* is strategically positioned with an eye to the international market, which has already proved its interest in Israeli television through successful adaptations of original Israeli series. The Showtime series *Homeland*, based on the Israeli *Ḥatufim*, and HBO's *In Treatment*, based on the Israeli *Be-tipul*, among others, have situated Israeli television within the influential American market, motivating Israeli production companies to invest in promising television series. Mere weeks after its April 27, 2017, premier, *Juda*'s first episodes were available for view, in full, on YouTube, and a lively Facebook page keeps fans involved between episodes. The show won the Bloggers' Prize for Best International Series at the 2017 Series Mania television awards show in Paris, signaling its broad appeal. In early 2019, the American television network Hulu acquired the series and announced its impending United States premiere; meanwhile, the Paris-based media company Banijay Group has, in partnership with an as-yet-undisclosed American studio, acquired the remake rights.³⁴ A glossy, expensive production clearly influenced by American predecessors like *True Blood*, *Juda* is distinctive, not least because of its Jewish-centered plot. Even the reviewer of the prestigious *Haaretz* newspaper was cautiously enthusiastic, labelling it "high-quality blue-and-white trash TV" with potential.³⁵

Juda offers a compelling case study of the characteristics distinguishing contemporary Israeli gothic from the Hebrew gothic texts examined throughout this study: namely, it balances lighthearted humor with gruesome violence, and its firm entrenchment in the present turns to the past only as a prop. Of all the adaptations of the undead discussed thus far, *Juda* engages in the most deliberate confrontation with gothic conventions, and it does so neither by merely localizing its vampire to the Israeli context nor by ignoring his Israeliness altogether. Not content with appropriation or adaptation, *Juda* adds an entirely new chapter to the conventions of vampire lore, thus offering an original narrative of reconciliation of the Jew and the vampire.

By the second episode, viewers know that the hapless Juda is a petty criminal with aspirations. Having travelled to Romania to gamble, he encounters a beautiful femme fatale, a vampire who poses as a prostitute. Her bite initiates his eight-day-long transformation into a vampire; Jewish vampires, we later learn, do not immediately transform like non-Jews. The redheaded temptress, meanwhile, falls ill, a consequence of drinking forbidden Jewish blood, recalling the fate of Agnon's vampire in "The Lady and the Peddler," who cannot ingest her Jewish victim's icy blood. In this case, however, Jewish blood is forbidden not merely because it is different—and it *is* different, in smell and taste. It is forbidden because of a pseudo-kabbalistic myth that foretells a vampire apocalypse, the destruction of the forces of darkness at the hands of a supervampire—a Jewish vampire. Thus, Juda's Jewishness is not just a matter of local color, nor is it used to diffuse the antisemitism that was historically so closely tied to the association of Jews with vampires, as discussed in chapter 1 of this study. To the contrary, in interviews and media appearances, the series creator and lead actor, Tsiyon Baruch, has repeatedly mentioned that he wanted to create the first Jewish vampire, giving no indication that he is aware of the centuries-long association of vampires with Jews.[36]

Juda's vampire does not become a vampire like all others, but he also does not turn the tale on its head, in the manner of Agnon. Instead, the Jew gets to join in on the vampiric fun, with special privileges owing to his difference. Should a Jewish vampire be allowed to mature, we learn, his power becomes so great as to render him invincible. "He is not like us. He has all our strengths, and none of our weaknesses. . . . He is not like us. Daylight, holy water, and the cross do not affect him," a Romanian guardian warns the vampires in his care. Taking the notion of Jewish difference to an empowering extreme, the show also manipulates the popular history of vampire lore by presenting the non-Jewish vampires as the victims of the Jewish one, and the Jewish vampire as the emissary of God himself, sent to eradicate the forces of darkness. The Christian vampires' anti-Jewish sentiment is a consequence of the Jew's empowerment and his essential goodness.

Juda's modification of established historical links associating Jews and vampires is one of its defining characteristics. To examine this revision more closely, I want to turn to a crucial scene from the second episode. In this episode, Juda, unaware of what has befallen him, begins to feel the symptoms of his transformation. Starved yet unable to consume food or drink, suddenly preternaturally powerful, and stimulated by the sight of blood, he is kidnapped and taken to a mysterious rabbi who explains everything. Juda finds himself in a space best described, like other settings in the show, as goth-kitsch Judaica. Ornate menorahs and candelabras with dripping candles, a carved grandfather clock, and dark shadows set the tone. The skeptical and suspicious Juda listens to the rabbi explain his symptoms: "There are those who call it *arpad*, vampire, *nosferatu* in German. In our history, it's called *motmindam*," a fictional amalgamation of the Hebrew words for death, sex, and blood. He reveals an old tome with a silver engraved Star of David on the cover—a pseudosacred text. After he opens it to a section entitled "Motmindam," the camera shifts to show the page, with its ornamental Hebrew lettering and an illustration of this alternative tale of the creation of the world: a black silhouette of a man hovering over a sea of undulating human bodies, behind him a large Star of David.

Having constructed a pseudomythology, the episode turns to the construction of a pseudohistory. The scene shifts to a bizarre animated sequence illustrating the rabbi's narration of a Holocaust-era tale of a nine-year-old Jewish boy, Żadek, fleeing from Nazis in a Transylvanian forest, to be saved by two figures with glowing red eyes, none other than Count Dracula himself and his son. Forbidden from drinking his Jewish blood, they take him under their protection. When the Nazis discover Żadek and murder him, Dracula's son bites him, distraught at the thought of losing his friend. To transform a Jew into a vampire, however, is to invite the final death of all vampires. At the edge of the forest and the outskirts of a concentration camp, Dracula's son embraces Żadek, then plunges a dagger into his heart, whispering, "Forgive me, my brother, but I had no other choice." The black, white, and gray color palette of this scene is disrupted by a few striking exceptions that recall the girl's red coat in *Schindler's List*, certainly not an accidental reference: the red eyes of Dracula and his son; red blood; and the yellow star that Żadek, as a Jew in Nazi territory, wears. The use of motion graphics in lieu of a more fluid animation technique produces a jarring visual affect and makes clear that verisimilitude is not the main concern. The past occupies a realm that is clearly distinguishable and separate from the present. The sequence cuts back to the rabbi, who completes the tragic tale, and Juda, who listens solemnly and after a long pause, says impatiently, "Nice story. I'll buy the book. Can you open the door for me?"

This moment breaks the tension of the animated sequence, which is, after all, set in the decidedly not funny Holocaust and lasts almost four full minutes (16:00–19:50). It complements the comedy underlying the parodic pseudokabbalah scene, with its fake *Zohar* and fabricated creation story. Any temptation viewers may have to read something into these fictive worlds is challenged by their presentations as elaborate props. The decor of the rabbi's abode finds a parallel in that of another distinctive space in the series: the home of the ancient patriarch of the Romanian vampire family. Shrouded in mist and smoke, the centerpiece of that unhomey home is a stone throne decorated with skulls—the ultimate example of vampire kitsch. The vampire siblings who visit him take a modern elevator in a sleek hotel to get there, but they emerge on a secret floor that seems to exist on another temporal plane.

The past, in all these scenes, is subject to a kitschy commodification, whether it is the past on which religious belief and myth are founded, the past of vampire folktales, or the *real* past of the Holocaust. The show's visual and comedic effects work to diminish the significance of the past as a force influencing the present, parodying and caricaturing its power. History is invoked not to be challenged, revised, grappled with, or feared. Like the dripping candles and the grinning skulls, it is no more than a static artifact. It is Juda's present that compels viewers, and the future—which he, as a Jewish vampire, will shape—that is at stake. Juda's humorous refusal to engage with these faux histories enhances the viewer's capacity to identify with him, to welcome the monster. Viewers of these films and series fear not a past that might invade and shatter an illusion of stability but rather the events of the present itself, depicted as always already unstable. Comedy, in *Juda* as in the tsunami of Hebrew horror films, is a driving force of this engagement with the monsters of the present.

It is only recently that critics of the gothic have started to take humor seriously. Critical studies of the gothic since David Punter's foundational *Literature of Terror* have tended to view the mode as preoccupied with trauma, crisis, and anxiety—states that define the Hebrew literary gothic examined by this study as a whole. While these approaches have been instrumental for understanding the mode, recent studies have shown that the gothic is not only and not always grave but also highly amenable to comedy. Humor, it turns out, does not present a deviation or perversion of the mode but has always informed it. Avril Horner and Sue Zlosnik reject the division of gothic into "serious" and "comic," proposing instead a range of comic effects underpinning gothic texts. This juxtaposition of solemnity and humor indicates an important but underdiscussed aspect of the uncanny. The same repressed thoughts that Freud identifies with jokes may manifest as "the object of uncanny feelings," notes the philosopher Noël Carroll, suggesting that "the road to comic laughter and the road to feelings of uncanniness are unaccountably the same."[37] Whereas the gothic exposure of the world's disconcerting uncanniness is typically associated with terror, it can just as well elicit laughter, signaling a "celebratory embrace of Gothic instability," in Horner and Zlosnik's words.[38]

As such, the comic helps readers negotiate terrains of terror and violence that might otherwise overwhelm, states easily identifiable in the contemporary Israeli reality of occupation, militarization, and constant fear of political violence. "Comic gothic moments," argue Horner and Zlosnik, "invite a conscious, self-reflexive engagement with the Gothic mode that sets up a different kind of contract between the reader and the text, offering a measure of detachment from scenes of pain and suffering that would be disturbing in a different Gothic context."[39] In short, "comic Gothic helps to make the modern condition more livable."[40] Humor, understood thus, works precisely against the charge of escapism that is leveled at so many of these contemporary gothic Israeli works: it functions not to escape the difficult reality but to confront it and cope with it. The sense of perpetual instability brought on by repeatedly failed attempts at peacemaking in Israel/Palestine has created the conditions for such strategies.

Working from a similar impulse to dismantle the seemingly obligatory seriousness of the gothic, Catherine Spooner identifies the phenomenon she terms "post-millennial happy Gothic." In contrast to the predominant conceptualization of the gothic "as almost universally gloomy and miserable, or even scary and horrid," in the twenty-first century, gothic texts increasingly incorporate "positively inclined emotions or moods that are unexpected in conventional Gothic critical discourse," according to Spooner.[41] The recognition that the gothic can be lighthearted, playful, funny, and fun indicates not "an eschewal of politics or of historical context" but rather a rejection of the view that gothic must always explicitly address trauma and anxiety to be gothic.[42] The comic moments and celebratory mood of "happy Gothic" can reveal as much about our culture as more "serious" expressions.

The monstrous undead are apt vehicles for happy gothic: they are monsters, but they are also (or used to be) human and thus perfectly, disconcertingly uncanny. First-wave gothic works do not necessarily include the monstrous undead that populate gothic popular culture in Israel and elsewhere, yet these creatures are perhaps the most prevalent signifiers of the gothic since the turn of the millennium. Since the 1980s, their popularity has grown exponentially, as Spooner notes: "In post-millennial culture monsters have become virtually synonymous with Gothic in popular identification."[43] Besides subsuming the gothic mode itself, monsters have also undergone a transformation in the popular imagination. Formerly a signifier of radical alterity, the monster has become normalized and familiar. To help clarify this transformation, Spooner calls on Jacques Derrida's observation about the domestication of monsters: "One cannot say 'here are our monsters' without immediately turning the monsters into pets."[44] In effect, the monster loses its monstrosity, becoming identifiable and eliciting fondness, or, conversely, normalizing the monstrous. Spooner interprets the monster's domestication in postmillennial gothic partly as a consequence of its representation in popular culture as possessing "a comic sensibility" that makes it "a comic *subject* rather than object."[45] Whereas the monster we laugh *at* preserves difference and distance, the monster we can laugh *with* is a monster with whom we can, at some level, identify.

In many of these Israeli productions, the lines between the monster and the self are blurred, and laughing at the monster entails laughing at the self. It is not difficult to imagine how a nation whose governmental policies have made it into a pariah, a monster in itself, might seek relief from such a designation through laughter—whether to reaffirm its own humanity or to assert a critical distance between the self and the violence with which it is associated. Yet popular gothic culture in Israel is so diverse and so variegated that I offer this interpretation only as a starting point; I invite others to pick up where my observations leave off.

In interviews, reviews, and online comments, critics, viewers, and even the authors of popular gothic cultural texts in Israel negotiate a tension between political interpretations and critiques, between a serious message, on the one hand, and pleasure, on the other. We ask of these cultural products whether they say something about politics: Do they critique? Disavow? Confirm? Ignore? But this is the wrong question to pose. The question is not whether a film is political enough, whether it is obligated to be political, whether it is "escapist"—for good or for bad. It is disingenuous to entertain the idea that any cultural text in Israel can escape the political. Indeed, even the attempt to escape the political is in itself a political stance. Rather than engaging in tiresome and unproductive debates about the political merits or lacks of a given text, we might be better served by asking, Why monsters? Why monsters who are funny? The answer brings us back to Derrida: putting our monsters on-screen, facing them, and laughing with them, or watching them laugh with others, is an act of domestication. In the Israeli case, this domestication operates in two senses. It is a domestication of the horror or other popular gothic genres, in popular culture associated primarily with the United States and secondarily with Europe, and therefore indicates Israel's eagerness to participate on the stage of global popular culture. It also signifies a domestication of the monstrous, inviting the monster into our world, engaging with it. Nevertheless, normalizing the monster does not make it no longer a monster. Whether the monster is conceptualized as the self or the other, its potential for violence is never absolutely extinguished.

We end, then, appropriately, on an ambivalent note. Hebrew horror, fully mired in the present, announces its monsters, finally, but it is not clear yet to what end: hospitality, which entails engaging with the monster as a human, or domestication, which merely tames wild beasts? It is still early to tell. Either way, one thing is clear: the monsters are there to stay.

Notes

1. Vampire TLV, "About," Facebook. Page content no longer available. All translations from the Hebrew in this source are mine.
2. Ibid.
3. Catherine Spooner traces the persistence of "the anxiety model" in gothic studies and offers several alternatives. Her approach to contemporary gothic proposes that, while the anxiety model provides a useful context for the interpretation of many gothic texts, it leads critics to overlook "products and artefacts that do not seem remotely anxious or traumatized" yet "revel in their Gothicness" (*Post-millennial Gothic*, 17). See Spooner, *Post-millennial Gothic*, 11–17.
4. Wisse, *No Joke*, 28. For more on Jewish humor as "serious business," see Dauber, *Jewish Comedy*, xi.
5. *Postmillennial gothic* is Spooner's phrase, from her book of the same title.
6. Mary Shelley's *Frankenstein* (1818) is generally acknowledged as a key progenitor of science fiction. Botting notes that *Frankenstein* is "one of the Romantic works that impressed the writer most influential in the science fictional reformulation of Gothic strategies, H. G. Wells," who identified "terror and horror as forces encroaching on the present from the future rather than the past" (Botting, *Gothic*, 162–63).
7. Herzog, "Dam kaḥol."
8. Kavka, "Gothic on Screen," 209.
9. Ibid., 210. Spooner notes that gothic "and horror are overlapping genres and distinguishing between them can be difficult.... Nevertheless, if 'Gothic' is defined as a 'literature of terror,' as it is by Punter in his seminal 1980 work, then these distinctions dissolve" (*Post-millennial Gothic*, 28n1). Kavka's essay calls for the invention of a gothic film genre as distinctive from horror and related cinematic genres with which it is often conflated. The main difference between gothic film and horror film, for Kavka, is in what viewers see and what is withheld: "There is, in other words, a world of difference between not being able to see something that remains shadowed or off-screen (the Gothic), on the one hand, and being able to see something terrifying placed before our very eyes but from which we want to avert our gaze (horror), on the other. The horror genre, in contrast to the Gothic, demands that we see—not that we always answer the demand" (Kavka, "Gothic on Screen," 227). In horror, we

are invited to see, but we try not to, while in gothic, the object of our fear is withheld from our field of vision. The key to both, as Spooner suggests, is their evocation of terror.

10. The key features of film noir—mysterious characters, melancholic atmosphere, settings swathed in darkness and shadows, plots punctuated by murder and death—owe a debt to the literary gothic. Arguing that film noir's influence on "films of the female-centered Gothic" helps situate gothic cinema "between *film noir* and horror," Kavka nevertheless insists on acknowledging gothic and film noir as distinct modes ("Gothic on Screen," 219, 214). David Fine has written on German film during the Weimar period as the source of gothicism in American film noir; see Fine, "Film Noir and Gothic."

11. Sagiv, "Israel, Palestine and Zombies," 11.
12. Alexander, "Body in Every Cellar," 7.
13. Ibid., 4.
14. Sagal, review of *Rabies/Kalevet*, 420.
15. Recent scholarship on horror cinema has insightfully investigated the relationship between horror films and national anxieties. See, for example, Lowenstein, *Shocking Representations*; and Blake, *Wounds of Nations*. Acknowledging the important contributions of such studies, Spooner laments the broader persistence of "the anxiety model" in contemporary gothic studies and in popular media accounts, in which "nuances are often overlooked" in the rush to assign significance and utility to mass culture (*Post-millennial Gothic*, 14).
16. FREAK OUT Press Kit, "Director's Statement."
17. Ibid.
18. Duvdevani, "*Mesuvag ḥarig.*"
19. O. Shamir, "*Mesuvag ḥarig.*"
20. U. Klein, "Mi mefaḥed mi-ha-ze'ev ha-ra."
21. Cheshire, "Big Bad Wolves."
22. Keshales and Papushado, Final Press Notes.
23. Cheshire, "Big Bad Wolves."
24. Dargis, "Trail of Vicious Killer."
25. Donahue, "It's the Talmud."
26. Gershenson, "Zombie Armageddon."
27. Caplan, "Israel's First Zombie Movie."
28. Ibid.
29. Gray, "'Big Bad' Israeli Film."
30. The term *realgothik* was first used by Laura Doyle in *Freedom's Empire* and again by Maisha Wester in *African American Gothic*; while neither explicitly defines it, both use the term to designate actual historical events and experiences characterized by the thematic, aesthetic, and affective features of gothic literature.
31. "TET TV Channel."
32. Duvdevani, "Arpadim bli shinayim."
33. "HOT hishika eser sdarot makor."
34. Keslassy, "Hulu Acquires."
35. Shlomovitz, "*Juda.*"
36. For more on this association, see, for example, Davison, *Anti-Semitism*; Robinson, "Novel Anti-Semitisms"; and chap. 1 of this study.
37. Carroll, "Horror and Humor," 146. Carroll offers a compelling theorization of the natural and "intimate relation of affinity between horror and humor" (ibid., 146–47). To this

end, he calls on the vocabulary of the gothic ("depression, paranoia, and dread," 147; "the violation, problematization, and transgression of our categories, norms, and concepts," 152) and cites nineteenth-century gothic literary works by Horace Walpole, Mary Shelley, Joseph Sheridan LeFanu, and others. He does not, however, distinguish the horror genre from gothic.

38. Horner and Zlosnik, "Comic Gothic," 327.

39. Ibid., 330.

40. Ibid., 332. For more on comedy, especially in the form of parody, and the gothic, see Horner and Zlosnik. *Gothic and Comic Turn.*

41. Spooner, *Post-millennial Gothic*, 3.

42. Ibid., 16.

43. Ibid., 121.

44. Derrida, "Some Statements and Truisms," 80.

45. Spooner, *Post-millennial Gothic*, 124.

BIBLIOGRAPHY

Abraham, Nicolas, and Maria Torok. *The Shell and the Kernel: Renewals of Psychoanalysis.* Translated and edited by Nicholas T. Rand. Chicago: University of Chicago Press, 1994.
Abramson, Glenda. *Drama and Ideology in Modern Israel.* Cambridge: Cambridge University Press, 1998.
———. *Modern Hebrew Drama.* New York: St. Martin's, 1979.
Adorno, Theodor W. "Cultural Criticism and Society." In *Prisms*, translated by Shierry Weber Nicholsen and Samuel Weber, 19–34. Cambridge, MA: MIT Press, 1983.
———. *Negative Dialectics.* Translated by E. B. Ashton. New York: Continuum, 1973.
Agnon, S. Y. "Ha-adonit ve-ha-rokhel" ["The Lady and the Peddler"]. In *Samukh ve-nir'eh*, 75–83. Jerusalem: Schocken, 1998.
———. "The Lady and the Peddler." In *A Book That Was Lost and Other Stories*, edited by Alan Mintz and Anne Golomb Hoffman, translated by Robert Alter, 198–210. New York: Schocken, 1995.
———. "Meḥolat ha-mavet" ["The Dance of Death"]. In *Elu ve-elu*, 290–93. Jerusalem: Schocken, 1998.
Ahmed, Sara. *Cultural Politics of Emotion.* Edinburgh: Edinburgh University Press, 2014.
Aldana Reyes, Xavier. "Gothic Affect: An Alternative Approach to Critical Models of the Contemporary Gothic." In *New Directions in 21st-Century Gothic: The Gothic Compass*, edited by Lorna Piatti-Farnell and Donna Lee Brien, 11–23. New York: Routledge, 2015.
Alexander, Neta. "A Body in Every Cellar: The 'New Violence' Movement in Israeli Cinema." *Jewish Film and New Media* 4, no. 1 (2016): 4–24.
Alter, Robert. Introduction to *The Amos Oz Reader*, edited by Nitza Ben-Dov, ix–xv. Boston: Houghton Mifflin Harcourt, 2009.
———. *The Invention of Hebrew Prose: Modern Fiction and the Language of Realism.* Seattle: University of Washington Press, 1988.
———. "Observations: On Leah Goldberg and S. Y. Agnon." *Commentary*, May 1, 1970.
Amir, Dana. "The Line That Divides Sleeping from Waking: The Malignant Interaction between the Emergent Principal and the Continuous Principal in *My Michael* by Amos Oz." In *On the Lyricism of the Mind: Psychoanalysis and Literature*, 69–75. New York: Routledge, 2016.
Anderson, G. K. "Popular Survivals of the Wandering Jew in England." In Hasan-Rokem and Dundes, *Wandering Jew*, 76–104.
Anolik, Ruth Bienstock. "The Absent Mother: Negotiations of Maternal Presence in the Gothic Mode." In *The Literary Mother: Essays on Representations of Maternity and Child Care*, edited by Susan C. Staub, 95–116. Jefferson, NC: McFarland, 2007.
Arata, Stephen. "The Occidental Tourist: Dracula and the Anxiety of Reverse Colonization." *Victorian Studies* 33, no. 4 (1990): 621–45.
Arbel, Michal. "Ha-ktiva ke-matseva: Romantika ve-historyosofia bi-sipurav shel S. Y. Agnon" [Writing as gravestone: Romanticism and historiosophy in the stories of S. Y. Agnon]. *Mi-kan* 2 (2001): 65–94.

Arpali, Boaz. "Ha-met ve-ha-re'aya" [The dead and his wife]. In *Avotot shel ḥoshekh*, 29–50. Tel Aviv: Hakibbutz Hameuchad, 1982–83.

Austen, Jane. *Northanger Abbey*. New York: Modern Library, 1995.

Baer, Elizabeth R. *The Golem Redux: From Prague to Post-Holocaust Fiction*. Detroit: Wayne State University Press, 2012.

Baines, Paul. "'This Theatre of Monstrous Guilt': Horace Walpole and the Drama of Incest." *Studies in Eighteenth-Century Culture* 28, no. 1 (1999): 287–309.

Bakhtin, Mikhail. *The Dialogic Imagination: Four Essays*. Edited by Michael Holquist. Translated by Caryl Emerson and Michael Holquist. Austin: University of Texas Press, 1982.

———. *Speech Genres and Other Late Essays*. Edited by Caryl Emerson and Michael Holquist. Translated by Vern W. McGee. Austin: University of Texas Press, 1986.

Balaban, Avraham. *Mar Molkho: Iyun ba-romanim Mar Mani ve-Molkho me-et A. B. Yehoshua* [Mar Molkho: A study of the novels *Mr. Mani* and *Molkho* by A. B. Yehoshua]. Tel Aviv: Hakibbutz Hameuchad, 1992.

Band, Arnold J. "Agnon's Synthetic Shtetl." In Katz, *Shtetl: New Evaluations*, 233–42.

———. "*Mar Mani*: The Archaeology of Self-Deception." *Prooftexts* 12, no. 3 (1992): 231–44.

———. *Nostalgia and Nightmare: A Study in the Fiction of S. Y. Agnon*. Berkeley: University of California Press, 1968.

———. "Refractions of the Blood Libel in Modern Literature." In *Memory and History in Christianity and Judaism*, edited by Michael A. Signer, 113–33. Notre Dame, IN: University of Notre Dame Press, 2001.

Barnes, Deborah H. "Myth, Metaphor, and Memory in Toni Morrison's Reconstructed South." *Studies in the Literary Imagination* 31, no. 2 (1998): 17–35.

Baron, Dvora. "Atsbanut" [Nervousness], *Ha-zman*, January 2, 1912, 2–3.

———. *The First Day and Other Stories*. Translated and edited by Chana Kronfeld and Naomi Seidman. Berkeley: University of California Press, 2001.

———. "Hitparets..." ["Erupt..."], *Ha-zman*, April 9, 1907, 1–2.

———. "Shifra." [In Hebrew.] In *Ha-kol ha-aḥer: Siporet nashim Ivrit* [The other voice: Hebrew women's fiction], edited by Lili Ratok, 181–86. Tel Aviv: Hakibbutz Hameuchad, 1994.

———. "Shifra." In *First Day*, 99–108.

———. "Shifra." In *Sipurim*. Tel Aviv: Davar, 1926, 61–70.

Bar-On, Mordechai. "Oz bi-Yerushalayim ha-ḥatsuya" [Oz in divided Jerusalem]. *Yisrael: Ktav et le-ḥeker ha-Tsiyonut u-medinat Yisrael, historya, tarbut, ḥevra* 7 (2004/05): 41–72.

Bartana, Ortsion. "The Image of the 'Living-Dead' in Nathan Alterman's Poetry: From Archetype to National Symbol." *Israel Affairs* 20, no. 2 (2014): 182–94.

Bartov, Omer. *The Voice of Your Brother's Blood: Buczacz, Biography of a Town*. New York: Simon and Schuster, 2017.

Bar-Yosef, Hamutal. *Lea Goldberg*. Jerusalem: Shazar Center, 2012.

Barzilai, Maya. *Golem: Modern Wars and Their Monsters*. New York: New York University Press, 2016.

———. "S. Y. Agnon's German Consecration and the 'Miracle' of Hebrew Letters." *Prooftexts* 33, no. 1 (2013): 48–75.

Becker, Suzanne. *Gothic Forms of Feminine Fiction*. Manchester: Manchester University Press, 1999.

Behar, Almog. "Ana min al-Yahoud." In *Ana min al-Yahoud*, 55–64. Tel Aviv: Babel, 2008.
———. "Ana min al-Yahoud [I'm One of the Jews]." Translated by Vivian Eden. Accessed May 4, 2018. https://almogbehar.wordpress.com/english/.
———. "The Language We Inherit Is Not One: A Conversation with Almog Behar." Interview by Shoshana Olidort. *Los Angeles Review of Books*, May 1, 2017. https://lareviewofbooks.org/article/the-language-we-inherit-is-not-one-a-conversation-with-almog-behar/.
Ben-Dov, Nitza, ed. *Ba-kivun ha-negdi*. Tel Aviv: Hakibbutz Hameuchad, 1995.
———. "Biblical Allusion in Agnon's 'Dance of Death': A Study in Intertextual Dissonance." *Modern Judaism* 7, no. 3 (1987): 271–86.
———. "Poland as a 'Promised Land' in Agnon's *Tales of Poland*." In *Polish and Hebrew Literature and National Identity*, edited by Alina Molisak and Shoshana Ronen, 98–105. Warsaw: Elipsa, 2010.
———. "'Zohi ir asufa el tokh nafsha': Yerushalayim shel Amos Oz be-Mikhael Sheli" [This is a city gathered unto itself: Amos Oz's Jerusalem in *My Michael*]. *Kivunim ḥadashim* 19 (2008): 188–97.
Benjamin, Walter. *The Writer of Modern Life: Essays on Charles Baudelaire*. Edited by Michael W. Jennings. Translated by Howard Eiland, Edmund Jephcott, Rodney Livingston, and Harry Zohn. Cambridge, MA: Harvard University Press, 2006.
Berg, Nancy E. "The Politics of Paternity and Patrimony." *Shofar* 24, no. 3 (2006): 100–114.
Bersani, Leo. "Pynchon, Paranoia, and Literature." *Representations* 25 (1989): 99–118.
Bhabha, Homi. "The World and the Home." *Social Text* 31/32 (1992): 141–53.
Biale, David. *Blood and Belief: The Circulation of a Symbol between Jews and Christians*. Berkeley: University of California Press, 2007.
———. *Gershom Scholem: Kabbalah and Counter-history*. Cambridge, MA: Harvard University Press, 1982.
Bialik, Ḥayim Naḥman. "Shiratenu ha-tse'ira." In *Kol kitvey Ḥayim Naḥman Bialik*, 230–35. Tel Aviv: Dvir, 1954.
Bird, B. "Treason and Imagination: The Anxiety of Legitimacy in the Subject of the 1760s." *Romanticism* 12, no. 3 (2006): 189–99.
Blake, Linnie. *The Wounds of Nations: Horror Cinema, Historical Trauma and National Identity*. Oxford: Oxford University Press, 2012.
Botting, Fred. *Gothic*. London: Routledge, 1996.
———. "The Gothic Production of the Unconscious." In Byron and Punter, *Spectral Readings*, 11–36.
———. "Power in the Darkness: Heterotopias, Literature and Gothic Labyrinths." *Genre* 26, no. 2–3 (1993): 253–82.
Botting, Fred, and Dale Townshend, eds. *Gothic: Critical Concepts in Literary and Cultural Studies*. London: Routledge, 2004.
Boyarin, Daniel. *Unheroic Conduct: The Rise of Heterosexuality and the Invention of the Jewish Man*. Berkeley: University of California Press, 1997.
Brenner, Naomi. *Lingering Bilingualism: Modern Hebrew and Yiddish Literatures in Contact*. Syracuse: Syracuse University Press, 2016.
Brenner, Rachel Feldhay. "'Ideologically Incorrect' Responses to the Holocaust by Three Israeli Women Writers." *CLCWeb: Comparative Literature and Culture* 11, no. 1 (2009). https://docs.lib.purdue.edu/cgi/viewcontent.cgi?article=1421&context=clcweb.
———. *Inextricably Bonded: Israeli Arab and Jewish Writers Revisioning Culture*. Madison: University of Wisconsin Press, 2003.

Bryant, Cedric Gael. "'The Soul Has Bandaged Moments': Reading the African American Gothic in Wright's 'Big Boy Leaves Home,' Morrison's *Beloved*, and Gomez's *Gilda*." *African American Review* 39, no. 4 (2005): 541–53.

Budick, Emily Miller. "Absence, Loss, and the Space of History in Toni Morrison's *Beloved*." *Arizona Quarterly* 48, no. 2 (1992): 117–38.

Busbridge, Rachel. "On Haunted Geography: Writing Nation and Contesting Claims in the Ghost Village of Lifta." *Interventions* 17, no. 4 (2015): 469–87.

Byron, Glennis, ed. *Globalgothic*. Manchester: Manchester University Press, 2013.

Byron, Glennis, and David Punter. "Persecution and Paranoia." In *The Gothic*, edited by Glennis Byron and David Punter, 273–77. Oxford: Blackwell, 2004.

———, eds. *Spectral Readings: Towards a Gothic Geography*. New York: St. Martin's, 1999.

Byron, Glennis, and Dale Townshend, eds. *The Gothic World*. New York: Routledge, 2014.

Campbell, Jill. "'I Am No Giant': Horace Walpole, Heterosexual Incest, and Love among Men." *The Eighteenth Century* 39, no. 3 (1998): 238–60.

Caplan, B. "Israel's First Zombie Movie, *Cannon Fodder*: 'We Tried to Piss Everyone Off.'" *Miami New Times*, October 22, 2013. http://www.miaminewtimes.com/arts/israels-first-zombie-movie-cannon-fodder-we-tried-to-piss-everyone-off-6488693.

Carroll, Noël. "Horror and Humor." *Journal of Aesthetics and Art Criticism* 57, no. 2 (1999): 145–60.

Cheshire, Godfrey. "Big Bad Wolves." RogerEbert.com. January 17, 2014. http://www.rogerebert.com/reviews/big-bad-wolves-2014.

Clery, E. J. Introduction to *The Castle of Otranto: A Gothic Story*, by Horace Walpole, vii–xxxiii. Oxford: Oxford University Press, 1996.

Cohen, Yisrael. *Ya'akov Shtainberg: Ha-ish vi-yetsirato* [Ya'akov Shteinberg: The man and his works]. Tel Aviv: Dvir, 1972.

Copjec, Joan. "Vampires, Breast-Feeding, and Anxiety." *October* 58 (1991): 25–43.

Cutter, William. "Ghostly Hebrew, Ghastly Speech: Scholem to Rosenzweig, 1926." *Prooftexts* 10, no. 3 (1990): 413–33.

Cvetkovich, Ann. *Mixed Feelings: Feminism, Mass Culture, and Victorian Sensationalism*. New Brunswick: Rutgers University Press, 1992.

Dargis, Manohla. "On the Trail of a Vicious Killer, Eagerly Licking Their Chops." *New York Times*, January 16, 2014. https://www.nytimes.com/2014/01/17/movies/big-bad-wolves-an-israeli-thriller-about-a-manhunt.html?mcubz=2&_r=0.

Dauber, Jeremy Asher. *In the Demon's Bedroom: Yiddish Literature and the Early Modern*. New Haven: Yale University Press, 2010.

———. *Jewish Comedy: A Serious History*. London: W. W. Norton, 2017.

Davis, Colin. "État présent: Hauntologies, Spectres, and Phantoms." In Pilar Blanco and Peeren, *Spectralities Reader*, 53–60.

Davis, Kimberly Chabot. "'Postmodern Blackness': Toni Morrison's *Beloved* and the End of History." *Twentieth Century Literature* 44, no. 2 (1998): 242–60.

Davison, Carol Margaret. *Anti-Semitism and British Gothic Literature*. New York: Palgrave Macmillan, 2004.

———. *Gothic Literature 1764–1824*. Cardiff: University of Wales Press, 2009.

DeKoven Ezrahi, Sidra. "Agnon Before and After." *Prooftexts* 2, no. 1 (1982): 78–94.

———. "Revisioning the Past: The Changing Legacy of the Holocaust in Hebrew Literature." *Salmagundi* 68/69 (1985): 245–70.

———. "The Shtetl and Its Afterlife: Agnon in Jerusalem." *AJS Review* 4, no. 1 (2017): 133–54.
———. "S. Y. Agnon's Jerusalem: Before and after 1948." *Jewish Social Studies* 18, no. 3 (2012): 136–52.
———. "'To What Shall I Compare You?' Jerusalem as Ground Zero of the Hebrew Imagination." *PMLA* 122, no. 1 (2007): 220–34.
De Man, Paul. *The Resistance to Theory*. Minneapolis: University of Minnesota Press, 1986.
———. "The Rhetoric of Temporality." In *Blindness and Insight: Essays in the Rhetoric of Contemporary Criticism*, 187–228. Minneapolis: University of Minnesota Press, 1983.
Dent, Jonathan. "Contested Pasts: David Hume, Horace Walpole and the Emergence of Gothic Fiction." *Gothic Studies* 14, no. 1 (2012): 21–33.
Derrida, Jacques. "Some Statements and Truisms about Neologisms, Newisms, Positisms, Parasitisms, and Other Small Seismisms." In *The States of Theory*, edited by D. Carroll, 63–94. New York: Columbia University Press, 1989.
———. *Specters of Marx: The State of the Debt, the Work of Mourning and the New International*. Translated by Peggy Kamuf. New York: Routledge, 2006.
Dolan, Elizabeth A. *Seeing Suffering in Women's Literature of the Romantic Era*. Farnham, UK: Ashgate, 2008.
Dole, Carole M. "Three Tyrants in *The Castle of Otranto*." *ELN* 26 (1988): 26–35.
Donahue, Laurie. "It's the Talmud—with Zombies!—in New Israeli Horror Film." *Times of Israel*, August 28, 2015. http://www.timesofisrael.com/its-the-talmud-with-zombies-in-new-israeli-horror-film/.
Dorot, Ruth. *Nahar lelo gadot: Zman ve-simbolizem be-ba'alat ha-armon le-Lea Goldberg ve-ba-tsiyur ha-moderni* [A river without banks: Time and symbolism in "The Lady of the Castle" by Leah Goldberg and in modern painting]. Ariel: Ariel University, 2013.
Doyle, Laura. *Freedom's Empire: Race and the Rise of the Novel in Atlantic Modernity, 1640–1940*. Durham, NC: Duke University Press, 2008.
Dundes, Alan, ed. *The Blood Libel Legend: A Casebook in Anti-Semitic Folklore*. Madison: University of Wisconsin Press, 1991.
Duvdevani, Shmulik. "Arpadim bli shinayim" [Vampires without teeth]. *Ynet*, May 31, 2009. http://www.ynet.co.il/articles/0,7340,L-3722325,00.html.
———. "*Mesuvag ḥarig*: Eyma tsahalit bli basis" [*Freak Out*: A baseless IDF threat]. *Ynet*, October 21, 2015. http://www.ynet.co.il/articles/0,7340,L-4714007,00.html.
Dykman, Aminadav A. "Poe's Poetry in Israel (and Russia)." *Poe Studies* 33, no. 1–2 (2000): 33–40.
Edelmann, R. "Ahasuerus, the Wandering Jew: Origin and Background." In Hasan-Rokem and Dundes, *Wandering Jew*, 1–10.
Edwards, Justin D. "British Gothic Nationhood, 1760–1830." In Byron and Townshend, *Gothic World*, 51–61.
———. *Gothic Canada: Reading the Spectre of a National Literature*. Edmonton: University of Alberta, 2005.
Ellis, Kate Ferguson. *The Contested Castle: Gothic Novels and the Subversion of Domestic Ideology*. Urbana: University of Illinois Press, 1989.
Ellis, Markman. *The History of Gothic Fiction*. Edinburgh: Edinburgh University Press, 2000.
Elstein, Yoav, and Avidov Lipsker. "The Homogeneous Series in the Literature of the Jewish People: A Thematological Methodology." In *Thematics Reconsidered: Essays in Honor of Horst S. Daemmrich*, edited by Frank Trommler, 87–116. Amsterdam: Rodopi, 1995.

Eshel, Amir. *Futurity: Contemporary Literature and the Quest for the Past*. Chicago: University of Chicago Press, 2013.
Ewence, Hannah. "Blurring the Boundaries of Difference: Dracula, the Empire, and 'the Jew.'" *Jewish Culture and History* 12, no. 1–2 (2010): 213–22.
Feingold, Ben-Ami. "Armon yafe akh lo li-mgurim" [A beautiful castle but not for habitation]. *Moznayim* 59, no. 1–2 (May–June 1985): 35–38.
Feldman, Yael. "Ḥazara le-be-reshit" [Back to the beginning]. In Ben-Dov, *Ba-kivun ha-negdi*, 204–22.
Fiedler, Leslie A. *Love and Death in the American Novel*. New York: Stein and Day, 1960.
Fine, David. "Film Noir and the Gothic." In *A Companion to American Gothic*, edited by C. L. Crow, 475–87. Oxford: Wiley, 2013.
Foucault, Michel. *The Birth of the Clinic*. New York: Routledge, 1989.
———. *History of Madness*. New York: Routledge, 2006.
FREAK OUT Press Kit. "Director's Statement." Accessed May 20, 2018. https://jfilmbox.org/film/michelle-pose/jzbwo1i1e6id3edxk-ai43jxhon36s/?download_press_kit.
Freedman, Carl. "Towards a Theory of Paranoia: The Science Fiction of Philip K. Dick." *Science Fiction Studies* 11, no. 1 (1984) 15–24.
Freedman, William. *The Porous Sanctuary: Art and Anxiety in Poe's Short Fiction*. New York: Peter Lang, 2002.
Freud, Sigmund. "Certain Neurotic Mechanisms in Jealousy, Paranoia and Homosexuality." *International Journal of Psycho-analysis* 4 (1923): 1–10.
———. "The Uncanny." New York: Penguin Books, 2003.
Gamer, Michael. *Romanticism and the Gothic: Genre, Reception, and Canon Formation*. New York: Cambridge University Press, 2000.
Gardenour, Brenda. "The Biology of Blood-Lust: Medieval Medicine, Theology, and the Vampire Jew." *Film and History: An Interdisciplinary Journal of Film and Television Studies* 41, no. 2 (2011): 51–63.
Gelbin, Cathy S. *The Golem Returns: From German Romantic Literature to Global Jewish Culture, 1808–2008*. Ann Arbor: University of Michigan Press, 2011.
Gelder, Ken. *Reading the Vampire*. London: Routledge, 1994.
Gershenson, Olga. "Is Zombie Armageddon a Metaphor for Mideast Conflict?" *Forward*, August 13, 2015. http://forward.com/culture/film-tv/318482/z-is-for-zombie-a-new-metaphor-for-the-israeli-palestinian-conflict/?attribution=author-article-listing-2-headline.
Gertz, Nurith. "Historiya aḥeret" [A different history]. In Ben-Dov, *Ba-kivun ha-negdi*, 309–21.
Gilman, Sander. *The Jew's Body*. New York: Routledge, 1991.
Ginsburg, Michal Peled. "Madame Bovary bi-Yerushalayim." *Zehuyot* 3 (2013): 33–44.
Gluzman, Michael. *The Politics of Canonicity: Lines of Resistance in Modernist Hebrew Poetry*. Palo Alto: Stanford University Press, 2003.
Goddu, Teresa A. "American Gothic." In Spooner and McEvoy, *Routledge Companion*, 63–72.
———. *Gothic America: Narrative, History, and Nation*. New York: Columbia University Press, 1997.
———. "Vampire Gothic." *American Literary History* 11, no. 1 (1999): 125–41.
Goldberg, Leah. "Al oto ha-noseh atsmo" [On the very same subject]. *Ha-shomer ha-tsa'ir*, September 8, 1939, 9–10.

———. "Ba'alat ha-armon: Epizoda dramatit be-shalosh ma'arkhot" [The lady of the castle]. Merhavia: Sifriyat Poalim, 1956.
———. *Barak ba-boker* [Lightening in the morning]. Merhavia: Sifriyat Poalim, 1957.
———. "Ha-omets le-ḥulin" [The courage for the mundane]. In *Ha-omets le-ḥulin: Beḥinot ve-ta'amim be-sifruteynu ha-ḥadasha*, 165–70. Tel Aviv: Sifriyat Poalim, 1976.
———. *Mi-beyti ha-yashan* [From my old home]. Merhavia: Sifriyat Poalim, 1944.
———. *Shir ba-kfarim* [Songs in the villages]. Tel Aviv: Dfus Ha-Nakdan, 1942.
———. *Taba'ot ashan* [Smoke rings]. Tel Aviv: Yachdav, 1935.
———. "The Lady of the Castle." Translated by T. Carmi. Jerusalem: Institute for the Translation of Hebrew Literature, 1974.
———. *Yomaney Lea Goldberg* [The diaries of Leah Goldberg]. Edited by Rachel Aharoni and Aryeh Aharoni. Bnei Brak: Sifriyat Poalim-Hakibbutz Hameuchad, 2006.
Goldner, Ellen J. "Other(ed) Ghosts: Gothicism and the Bonds of Reason in Melville, Chesnutt, and Morrison." *Melus* 24, no. 1 (1999): 59–83.
Goodwin, Sarah McKim Webster. *Kitsch and Culture: The Dance of Death in Nineteenth-Century Literature and Graphic Arts*. New York: Garland, 1988.
Gordinsky, Natasha. *Bi-shlosha nofim: Yetsirata ha-mukdemet shel Lea Goldberg* [In three landscapes: Leah Goldberg's early writings]. Jerusalem: Hebrew University Magnes Press, 2016.
Gordon, Avery F. *Ghostly Matters: Haunting and the Sociological Imagination*. Minneapolis: University of Minnesota Press, 2008.
Gorton, Kristyn. "Theorizing Emotion and Affect: Feminist Engagements." *Feminist Theory* 8, no. 3 (2007): 333–48.
Govrin, Nurit. *Ha-maḥatsit ha-rishona: Dvora Baron—ḥayeha vi-yetsirata* [The first half: Dvora Baron—her life and works]. Jerusalem: Mossad Bialik, 1988.
———. "Jerusalem and Tel-Aviv as Metaphors in Hebrew Literature." *Modern Hebrew Literature* 2 (1989): 23–27.
———. *Telishut ve-hithadshut: Ha-siporet ha-Ivrit ba-gola u-ve-Erets-Yisrael be-reshit ha-me'a ha-esrim* [Rootlessness and renewal: Hebrew fiction in the diaspora and in the Land of Israel in the early twentieth century]. Tel Aviv: Ministry of Defense, 1985.
Gray, Julie. "'Big Bad' Israeli Film." *Huffpost*, July 2, 2014. http://www.huffingtonpost.com/julie-gray/big-bad-israeli-film_b_5539860.html.
Green, Kenneth Hart. "What S. Y. Agnon Taught Gershom Scholem About Jewish History." In *Encountering the Medieval in Modern Jewish Thought*, edited by James A. Diamond and Aaron W. Hughes, 153–76. Leiden: Brill, 2012.
Greenberg, Uri Zvi. "Ze'ev Jabotinsky bi-sfirat ha-shir" [Ze'ev Jabotinsky in the sphere of the poem]. In *Mi-shirey Edgar Alan Po* [From the poems of Edgar Allan Poe], translated by Ze'ev Jabotinsky, 11–14. Haifa: Renaissance Publishing House, 1964.
Gregg, Melissa, and Gregory J. Seigworth. "An Inventory of Shimmers." In *The Affect Theory Reader*, edited by Melissa Gregg and Gregory J. Seigworth, 1–25. Durham: Duke University Press, 2010.
Grumberg, Karen. "Zionist Places against the Desert Wilderness." In *Place and Ideology in Contemporary Hebrew Literature*, 26–75. Syracuse: Syracuse University Press, 2011.
Gurevitch, Zali. "The Double Site of Israel." In *Grasping Land: Space and Place in Contemporary Israeli Discourse and Experience*, edited by Eyal Ben-Ari and Yoram Bilu, 203–16. Albany: State University of New York Press, 1997.

Haggerty, George E. *Gothic Fiction/Gothic Form*. University Park: Pennsylvania State University Press, 1989.

———. "Literature and Homosexuality in the Late Eighteenth Century: Walpole, Beckford, and Lewis." *Studies in the Novel* 18, no. 4 (1986): 341–52.

———. *Queer Gothic*. Urbana: University of Illinois Press, 2006.

Halberstam, Judith. "Reading Counterclockwise: Paranoid Gothic or Gothic Paranoia?" In *Skin Shows: Gothic Horror and the Technology of Monsters*, 107–37. Durham: Duke University Press, 1995.

———. "Technologies of Monstrosity: Bram Stoker's *Dracula*." *Victorian Studies* 36, no. 3 (1993): 333–52.

Halkin, Hillel. *Jabotinsky: A Life*. New Haven: Yale University Press, 2014.

Halkin, Simon. *Mavo le-sifrut Ivrit* [Introduction to Hebrew literature]. Jerusalem: Mifal ha-shikhpul, 1958.

Hamilton, Cynthia S. "Revisions, Rememories and Exorcisms: Toni Morrison and the Slave Narrative." *Journal of American Studies* 30, no. 3 (1996): 429–45.

Haraway, Donna. "The Persistence of Vision." In *The Visual Culture Reader*, edited by Nicholas Mirzoeff, 677–84. New York: Routledge, 1998.

Hasan-Rokem, Galit, and Alan Dundes, eds. *The Wandering Jew: Essays in the Interpretation of a Christian Legend*. Bloomington: Indiana University Press, 1986.

Heller, Dana. "Reconstructing Kin: Family, History, and Narrative in Toni Morrison's *Beloved*." *College Literature* 21, no. 2 (1994): 105–17.

Henry, Katherine. "Life-in-Death: The Monstrous Female and the Gothic Labyrinth in *Aliens* and 'Ligeia.'" In *Horrifying Sex: Essays on Sexual Difference in Gothic Literature*, edited by Ruth Bienstock Anolik, 27–39. Jefferson, NC: McFarland, 2007.

Herzog, Omri. "'Dam kaḥol': Ha-arpadim ha-yehudim" [Blue blood: The Jewish vampires]. *Haaretz*, September 12, 2012. http://www.haaretz.co.il/literature/prose/1.1821201.

Hever, Hanan. "Hai ha-ḥai u-met ha-met" [The living lives and the dead is dead]. *Siman Kriah* 19 (1986): 188–92.

———. "Ha-trauma shel ba'alat ha-armon" [The trauma of the lady of the castle]. *Tarbits* 17, no. 2 (2011/12): 265–73.

———. *Moledet ha-mavet yafa: Estetika ve-politika be-shirat Uri Tsvi Grinberg* [The homeland of death is beautiful: Aesthetics and politics in the poetry of Uri Zvi Greenberg]. Tel Aviv: Am Oved, 2004.

———. *Suddenly, the Sight of War: Violence and Nationalism in Hebrew Poetry in the 1940s*. Palo Alto: Stanford University Press, 2016.

Hilu, Alon. *Aḥuzat Dajani*. Tel Aviv: Yedioth Ahronoth and Chemed, 2008.

———. "Alon Hilu Recommends the Best Books on Israel and Palestine in Art." Five Books. March 5, 2010. http://fivebooks.com/interview/alon-hilu-on-israel-and-palestine-in-art/.

———. *The House of Rajani*. Translated by Evan Fallenberg. London: Harvill Secker, 2010.

Hirsch, Marianne. "The Generation of Postmemory." *Poetics Today* 29, no. 1 (2008): 103–28.

Hochberg, Gil. *In Spite of Partition: Jews, Arabs, and the Limits of Separatist Imagination*. Princeton: Princeton University Press, 2007.

———. "A Poetics of Haunting: From Yizhar's Hirbeh to Yehoshua's Ruins to Koren's Crypts." *Jewish Social Studies* 18, no. 3 (2012): 55–69.

Hoeveler, Diane Long. "Charlotte Dacre's Zofloya: The Gothic Demonization of the Jew." In *The Jews and British Romanticism: Politics Religion, Culture*, edited by Sheila A. Spector, 165–78. New York: Palgrave Macmillan, 2005.

———. "Gothic Drama as Nationalistic Catharsis." *Wordsworth Circle* 31, no. 3 (2000): 169–72.

———. *Gothic Feminism: The Professionalization of Gender from Charlotte Smith to the Brontës*. University Park: Pennsylvania State University Press, 2010.

Hoffman, Anne Golomb. "The Womb of Culture: Fictions of Identity and Their Undoing in Yehoshua's *Mar Mani*." *Prooftexts* 12, no. 3 (1992): 245–63.

Hogle, Jerrold E. "Hyper-reality and the Gothic Affect." *English Language Notes* 48, no. 1 (2010): 163–76.

———. "The Restless Labyrinth: Cryptonomy in the Gothic Novel." In Botting and Townshend, *Gothic*, 145–66.

Holtzman, Avner. "Karov ve-asur lanu sham: Yerushalayim ha-ḥatsuya bi-r'i ha-sifrut ha-Yisraelit" [Close and forbidden: Divided Jerusalem in the mirror of Israeli literature]. *Yerushalayim ha-ḥatsuya, 1948–1967*, edited by Avi Bareli, 202–23. Jerusalem: Yad Yitsḥak Ben-Tsvi, 1994.

Horner, Avril, and Sue Zlosnik. "Comic Gothic." In Punter, *New Companion to the Gothic*, 321–34.

———. *Gothic and the Comic Turn*. New York: Palgrave Macmillan, 2005.

———. "Strolling in the Dark: Gothic Flânerie in Djuna Barnes's Nightwood." In *Gothic Modernisms*, edited by Andrew Smith and Jeff Wallace, 78–94. New York: Palgrave Macmillan, 2001.

Horvitz, Deborah. "Nameless Ghosts: Possession and Dispossession in *Beloved*." *Studies in American Fiction* 17, no. 2 (1989): 157–67.

House, Elizabeth B. "Toni Morrison's Ghost: The Beloved Is Not Beloved." *Studies in American Fiction* 18, no. 1 (1990): 17–26.

Howells, Coral Ann. *Love, Mystery and Misery: Feeling in Gothic Fiction*. London: Bloomsbury, 2013.

Hughes, William, and Andrew Smith. "Introduction: Defining the Relationships between Gothic and the Postcolonial." *Gothic Studies* 5, no. 2 (2003): 1–6.

———. *Queering the Gothic*. Manchester: Manchester University Press, 2009.

Hume, Robert D. "Gothic versus Romantic: A Revaluation of the Gothic Novel." *Publications of the Modern Language Association of America* 84 (1969): 282–90.

Jabary Salamanca, Omar. "Hooked on Electricity: The Charged Political Economy of Electrification in the Palestinian West Bank." Paper presented at the symposium "Political Economy and Economy of the Political" at Brown University, Providence, RI, February 2014.

Jabotinsky, Vladimir. *Vladimir Jabotinsky's Story of My Life*. Detroit: Wayne State University Press, 2016.

Jacobs, Adriana X. *Strange Cocktail: Translation and the Making of Modern Hebrew Poetry*. Ann Arbor: University of Michigan Press, 2018.

Jaffee, Martin S. "The Victim Community in Myth and History: Holocaust Ritual, the Question of Palestine, and the Rhetoric of Christian Witness." *Journal of Ecumenical Studies* 28, no. 2 (1991): 223–38.

Jay, Martin. "The Disenchantment of the Eye: Surrealism and the Crisis of Ocularcentrism." *Visual Anthropology Review* 7 (1991): 15–38.

———. *Downcast Eyes: The Denigration of Vision in Twentieth-Century French Thought.* Berkeley: University of California Press, 1993.

———. "The Rise of Hermeneutics and the Crisis of Ocularcentrism." *Poetics Today* 9, no. 2 (1988): 307–26.

Jelen, Sheila. "All Writers Are Jews, All Jews Are Men: Dvora Baron and the Literature of 'The Uprooted.'" In Jelen and Pinsker, *Hebrew, Gender, and Modernity*, 189–200.

———. *Intimations of Difference: Dvora Baron in the Modern Hebrew Renaissance.* Syracuse: Syracuse University Press, 2007.

Jelen, Sheila, and Shachar Pinsker, eds. *Hebrew, Gender, and Modernity: Critical Responses to Dvora Baron's Fiction.* Bethesda: University Press of Maryland, 2007.

Johnson, Hannah. *Blood Libel: The Ritual Murder Accusation at the Limit of Jewish History.* Ann Arbor: University of Michigan Press, 2012.

Kahane, Claire. "Gothic Mirrors and Feminine Identity." *Centennial Review* 24, no. 1 (1980): 43–64.

———. "The Maternal Legacy: The Grotesque Tradition in Flannery O'Connor's Female Gothic." In *The Female Gothic*, edited by Juliann E. Fleenor, 242–56. Fountain Valley, CA: Eden, 1983.

Katsman, Roman. *Literature, History, Choice: The Principle of Alternative History in Literature (S. Y. Agnon, the City with All That Is Therein).* Newcastle upon Tyne: Cambridge Scholars Publishing, 2013.

Katz, Stephen T., ed. *The Shtetl: New Evaluations.* New York: New York University Press, 2009.

Kavka, Misha. "The Gothic on Screen." In *The Cambridge Companion to Gothic Fiction*, edited by Jerrold E. Hogle, 209–28. Cambridge: Cambridge University Press, 2002.

Keshales, Aharon, and Navot Papushado. Final press notes for *Big Bad Wolves*. Accessed May 20, 2018. http://www.magpictures.com/resources/presskits/bigbadwolves/BIGBADWOLVESfinalnotes.doc.

Keslassy, Elsa. "Hulu Acquires Israeli Vampire Series 'Juda' and U.S. Remake Rights Sold by Banijay." *Variety*, February 4, 2019. https://variety.com/2019/tv/news/hulu-israeli-series-juda-us-remake-rights-banijay-1203127485/.

Ketton-Cremer, Robert Wyndham. *Horace Walpole: A Biography.* Ithaca, NY: Cornell University Press, 1966.

Khair, Tabish. *The Gothic, Postcolonialism and Otherness.* New York: Palgrave Macmillan, 2009.

Khoury, Elias. "Rethinking the Nakba." *Critical Inquiry* 38, no. 2 (2012): 250–66.

Kilgour, Maggie. *The Rise of the Gothic Novel.* New York: Routledge, 2013.

Klein, Melanie. "Notes on Some Schizoid Mechanisms." In *Object Relations Theory and Practice: An Introduction*, edited by David E. Scharff, 136–55. New York: Rowman and Littlefield, 2005.

———. *The Psycho-analysis of Children.* Translated by Alix Strachey. London: Hogarth, 1932.

Klein, Uri. "'Mi mefaḥed mi-ha-ze'ev ha-ra' matsdik et ha-tsipiyot ha-gvohot" [*Big Bad Wolves* justifies the high expectations]. *Haaretz*, August 14, 2013. http://www.haaretz.co.il/gallery/cinema/movie-reviews/.premium-1.2097499.

Komem, Aharon. "The Use of Setting in Jacob Steinberg's Short Stories." *Scripta Hierosolymitana* 27 (1978): 174–91.

Kosh-Zohar, Talila. "Ma haya koreh le-'ba'alat ha-armon' be-Erets-Yisrael?" [What would have happened to "the lady of the castle" in the Land of Israel?]. *Ha-ḥinukh ve-svivo* 12 (2007/08): 331–41.

Kotlerman, Ber. "'And His Heart a Precious Violin': The Musical Layering of S. Y. Agnon's Yiddish Story 'Toytntants.'" *Jewish Social Studies* 18, no. 1(2001): 127–44.

Kotlerman, Boris. "Historical Time and Space in S. Y. Agnon's *Sipure Polin*." In *Agnon and Germany: The Presence of the German World in the Writings of S. Y. Agnon*, edited by Hans-Jürgen Becker and Hillel Weiss, 361–74. Tel Aviv: Bar-Ilan University Press, 2010.

Kristeva, Julia. *Melanie Klein*. Vol. 2. Translated by Ross Guberman. New York: Columbia University Press, 2001.

———. "Stabat Mater." *Poetics Today* 6, no. 1/2 (1985): 133–52.

Kronfeld, Chana, and Naomi Seidman. Introduction to *The First Day and Other Stories*, by Dvora Baron, xv–xxv. Berkeley: University of California Press, 2001.

Kurzweil, Baruch. "The Lady and the Peddler." In *Masot al sipurey Shai Agnon* [Essays on the stories of S. Y. Agnon], 123–29. Jerusalem: Schocken, 1966.

———. "Mahuta shel simḥat aniyim" [The essence of joy of the poor]. In Shamir and Luz, *Ha-poema ha-modernistit bi-yetsirat Alterman*, 125–45.

Lacan, Jacques. *The Psychoses: The Seminar of Jacques Lacan*. Bk. 3, 1955–56. Edited by Jacques-Alain Miller. Translated by Russell Grigg. London: Routledge, 1993.

Lake, Crystal B. "Bloody Records: Manuscripts and Politics in The Castle of Otranto." *Modern Philology* 110, no. 4 (2013): 489–512.

Laor, Dan. "Agnon and Buber: The Story of a Friendship, or The Rise and Fall of the 'Corpus Hasidicum.'" In *Martin Buber: A Contemporary Perspective*, edited by Paul Mendes-Flohr, 48–86. Syracuse: Syracuse University Press, 2002.

———. "Did Agnon Write about the Holocaust?" *Yad Vashem Studies* 22 (1992): 17–63.

———. "Ha-im katav Agnon al ha-Shoa?" [Did Agnon write about the Holocaust?]. In *Shai Agnon: Hebetim ḥadashim*, 60–97. Tel Aviv: Sifriyat Poalim, 1995.

———. *Ḥayey Agnon* [S. Y. Agnon: A biography]. Jerusalem: Schocken, 1998.

Lawrence, David. "Fleshly Ghost and Ghostly Flesh: The Word and the Body in *Beloved*." *Studies in American Fiction* 19, no. 2 (1991): 189–201.

Lemberger, Dorit. "Contacts and Discontinuities: Changing Aspects in Shimon Adaf's Work." *Hebrew Studies* 55 (2014): 330–54.

Lessard, Bruno. "Gothic Affect: Digitally Haunted Houses and the Production of Affect-Value." In Pilar Blanco and Peeren, *Popular Ghosts*, 213–24.

Levy, Lital. *Poetic Trespass: Writing between Hebrew and Arabic in Israel/Palestine*. Princeton: Princeton University Press, 2014.

Levy, Lital, and Allison Schachter. "Jewish Literature/World Literature: Between the Local and the Transnational." *PMLA* 130, no. 1 (2015): 92–109.

Leys, Ruth. "The Turn to Affect: A Critique." *Critical Inquiry* 37, no. 3 (2011): 434–72.

Liberles, Robert. *Salo Wittmayer Baron: Architect of Jewish History*. New York: New York University Press, 1995.

Lieblich, Amia. "Al 'ba'alat ha-armon' me'et Lea Goldberg: Pirkey biografya" [On Leah Goldberg's "The Lady of the Castle": Chapters of a biography]. *Alpayim* 13 (1996): 135–53.

Livneh, Neri. "Exiled from Babylon." *Haaretz*, August 5, 2004.

Loshitzky, Yosefa. "Orientalist Representations: Palestinians and Arabs in Some Postcolonial Film and Literature." In *Cultural Encounters: Representing Otherness*, edited by Elizabeth Hallam and Brian Street, 51–71. London: Routledge, 2000.

Lowenstein, Adam. *Shocking Representations: Historical Trauma, National Cinema, and the Modern Horror Film*. New York: Columbia University Press, 2005.

Löwy, Michael, and Robert Sayre. *Romanticism against the Tide of Modernity*. Durham: Duke University Press, 2001.

Lubin, Orly. "Tidbits from Nehama's Kitchen: Alternative Nationalism in Dvora Baron's *The Exiles*." In Jelen and Pinsker, *Hebrew, Gender, and Modernity*, 91–104.

Luckhurst, Roger. "The Contemporary London Gothic and the Limits of the 'Spectral Turn.'" *Textual Practice* 16, no. 3 (2002): 527–46.

Mack, Ruth. "Horace Walpole and the Objects of Literary History." *ELH* 75, no. 2 (2008): 367–87.

Marx, Karl, and Friedrich Engels. *Manifesto of the Communist Party*. Marxists Internet Archive. 2010. https://www.marxists.org/archive/marx/works/download/pdf/Manifesto.pdf. Originally published February 1848.

Massad, Joseph. "Zionism's Internal Others: Israel and the Oriental Jews." *Journal of Palestine Studies* 25, no. 4 (1996): 53–68.

Massumi, Brian. "Pleasures of Philosophy." Translator's foreword to *A Thousand Plateaus: Capitalism and Schizophrenia*, by Gilles Deleuze and Felix Guattari, ix–xv. London: University of Minnesota Press, 1987.

Meiton, Fredrik. "Electrifying Jaffa: Boundary-Work and the Origins of the Arab-Israeli Conflict." *Past and Present* 231 (2016): 201–36.

———. "The Radiance of the Jewish National Home: Technocapitalism, Electrification, and the Making of Modern Palestine." *Comparative Studies in Society and History* 57, no. 4 (2015): 975–1006.

Melamed, Ariana. "Orientalizem ben 40" [Orientalism turns 40]. *Ynet*, April 15, 2008. http://www.ynet.co.il/articles/0,7340,L-3532077,00.html.

Mighall, Robert. *A Geography of Victorian Gothic Fiction: Mapping History's Nightmares*. Oxford: Oxford University Press, 2003.

Miles, Robert. "Abjection, Nationalism, and the Gothic." In Botting and Townshend, *Gothic*, 192–211.

———. "Europhobia: The Catholic Other in Horace Walpole and Charles Maturin." In *European Gothic: A Spirited Exchange, 1760–1960*, edited by Avril Horner, 84–103. Manchester: Manchester University Press, 2002.

Milgrom, Jacob. *Leviticus 17–22: A New Translation with Introduction and Commentary*. Anchor Bible 3A. New York: Doubleday, 2000.

Mintz, Alan. "'I Am Building a City': On Agnon's Buczacz Tales." Foreword to *A City in Its Fullness*, by S. Y. Agnon, edited by Alan Mintz and Jeffrey Saks, xv–xxxi. New Milford, CT: Toby, 2016.

———. *Translating Israel: Contemporary Hebrew Literature and Its Reception in America*. Syracuse: Syracuse University Press, 2001.

Miron, Dan. "Depictions in Modern Hebrew Literature." In *City of the Great King: Jerusalem from David to the Present*, edited by Nitza Rosovsky, 241–87. Cambridge, MA: Harvard University Press, 1996.

———. "The Endless Cycle: The Poetic World of Dvora Baron." In Jelen and Pinsker, *Hebrew, Gender, and Modernity*, 17–31.

———. *From Continuity to Contiguity: Toward a New Jewish Literary Thinking*. Palo Alto: Stanford University Press, 2010.

———. "Ha-met ve-ha-re'aya: Al shirat ha-ahava shel Nathan Alterman" [The dead and his wife: On Nathan Alterman's love poetry]. In Shamir and Luz, *Ha-poema ha-modernistit bi-yetsirat Alterman*, 91–108.

———. *The Image of the Shtetl and Other Studies of Modern Jewish Literary Imagination.* Syracuse: Syracuse University Press, 2000.

Mobley, Marilyn Sanders. "A Different Remembering: Memory, History, and Meaning in Toni Morrison's *Beloved.*" In *Modern Critical Views: Toni Morrison,* edited by Harold Bloom, 189–99. New York: Chelsea, 1990.

Moers, Ellen. "Female Gothic." In Botting and Townshend, *Gothic,* 123–44.

———. *Literary Women.* Oxford: Oxford University Press, 1976.

Moglen, Helene. "Redeeming History: Toni Morrison's *Beloved.*" *Cultural Critique* 24 (1993): 17–40.

Mohanty, Chandra Talpade. "Under Western Eyes: Feminist Scholarship and Colonial Discourses." *Boundary 2* 12/13 (1984): 333–58.

Molesworth, Jesse. "Gothic Time, Sacred Time." *Modern Language Quarterly* 75, no. 1 (2014): 29–55.

Morris, Benny. Introduction to Morris, *Making Israel,* 1–10.

———, ed. *Making Israel.* Ann Arbor: University of Michigan Press, 2007.

———. "The New Historiography: Israel Confronts Its Past." In Morris, *Making Israel,* 11–28.

Morrison, Paul. "Enclosed in Openness: Northanger Abbey and the Domestic Carceral." *Texas Studies in Literature and Language* 33, no. 1 (1991): 1–23.

Morrison, Toni. *Beloved.* New York: Penguin Books, 2000.

———. "The Site of Memory." In *Inventing the Truth: The Art and Craft of Memoir,* edited by William Zinsser, 83–102. New York: Houghton Mifflin, 1995.

———. "Toni Morrison—Nobel Lecture." NobelPrize.org. Accessed January 27, 2017. http://www.nobelprize.org/nobel_prizes/literature/laureates/1993/morrison-lecture.html. Lecture originally given December 7, 1993.

Morson, Gary Saul, and Caryl Emerson. *Mikhail Bakhtin: Creation of a Prosaics.* Palo Alto: Stanford University Press, 1990.

Mowl, Timothy. *Horace Walpole: The Great Outsider.* London: Faber and Faber, 2014.

Mulvey-Roberts, Marie. *Dangerous Bodies: Historicising the Gothic Corporeal.* Manchester: Manchester University Press, 2016.

Naveh, Hana. "Politika shel hashtaka: Mashma'uto shel ha-ivaron be-sipuro shel Ya'akov Shtainberg 'Ha-iveret'" [A politics of silencing: The significance of blindness in Ya'akov Shteinberg's Ha-iveret]. In *Sefer Yisrael Levin—kovets meḥkarim ba-sifrut ha-Ivrit le-doroteyha,* edited by Reuben Tsur and Tova Rosen, 143–68. Tel Aviv: Katz Center, 1995.

Neugroschel, Joachim. *The Dybbuk and the Yiddish Imagination: A Haunted Reader.* Syracuse: Syracuse University Press, 2000.

Ng, Andrew Hock-soon. *Interrogating Interstices: Gothic Aesthetics in Postcolonial Asian and Asian American Literature.* Bern: Peter Lang, 2007.

Nicolaisen, W. F. H. "The Past as Place: Names, Stories, and the Remembered Self." *Folklore* 102, no. 1 (1991): 3–15.

O'Brien, Darren. *The Pinnacle of Hatred: The Blood Libel and the Jews.* Jerusalem: Hebrew University Magnes Press, 2011.

Offutt Mathieson, Barbara. "Memory and Mother Love in Morrison's *Beloved.*" *American Imago* 47, no. 1 (1990): 1–21.

Omer-Sherman, Ranen. *Israel in Exile: Jewish Writing and the Desert.* Urbana: University of Illinois Press, 2006.

———. "Paradoxes of Jewish and Muslim Identities in Israeli Short Stories." *Peace Review* 22, no. 4 (2010): 440–52.

Ophir, Adi. "The Identity of the Victims and the Victims of Identity: A Critique of Zionist Ideology for a Post-Zionist Age." In *Mapping Jewish Identities*, edited by Laurence J. Silberstein, 174–200. New York: New York University Press, 2000.

Oppenheimer, Yohai. "Gilgulav shel degem ha-met ha-ḥai be-shirat milḥemet ha-atsma'ut" [The evolution of the living-dead in the poetry of the War of Independence]. In *Ha-zkhut ha-gdola lomar lo: Shira politit bi-Yisrael*, 81–102. Jerusalem: Magnes Press, 2003.

Oz, Amos. "Ha-tanur ve-ha-reḥem" [The oven and the womb]. In Ben-Dov, *Ba-kivun ha-negdi*, 348–52.

———. "Ir zara." In *Be-or ha-tkhelet ha-aza*, 209–12. Jerusalem: Keter, 1990.

———. *Mikhael sheli*. Jerusalem: Keter, 2008.

———. *My Michael*. Translated by Nicholas de Lange. New York: Harcourt, 2005.

Pardes, Ilana. *The Biography of Ancient Israel: National Narratives in the Desert*. Berkeley: University of California Press, 2000.

Penslar, Derek Jonathan. "Innovation and Revisionism in Israeli Historiography." *History and Memory* 7, no. 1 (1995): 125–46.

Perry, Ruth. "Incest as the Meaning of the Gothic Novel." *Eighteenth Century* 39, no. 3 (1998): 261–78.

Pilar Blanco, María del, and Esther Peeren. "Introduction." In Pilar Blanco and Peeren, *Popular Ghosts*, ix–xxiv.

———. "Introduction: Conceptualizing Spectralities." In Pilar Blanco and Peeren, *Spectralities Reader*, 1–27.

———, eds. *Popular Ghosts: The Haunted Spaces of Everyday Culture*. New York: Continuum, 2010.

———, eds. *The Spectralities Reader: Ghosts and Haunting in Contemporary Cultural Theory*. New York: Bloomsbury, 2013.

———. "The Spectral Turn/Introduction." In Pilar Blanco and Peeren, *Spectralities Reader*, 31–36.

Pinsker, Leo. "Auto-emancipation." Translated by D. S. Blondheim. New York: Masada, 1935.

Pinsker, Shachar. "Unraveling the Yarn: Intertextuality, Gender, and Cultural Critique in Dvora Baron's Fiction." In Jelen and Pinsker, *Hebrew, Gender, and Modernity*, 145–65.

Poe, Edgar Allan. "The Masque of the Red Death." In *Selected Tales*, 136–41. Oxford: Oxford University Press, 1980.

———. "The Philosophy of Composition." *Graham's Magazine* 28, no. 4 (1846): 163–67.

Price, Fiona. "Ancient Liberties? Rewriting the Historical Novel: Thomas Leland, Horace Walpole and Clara Reeve." *Journal for Eighteenth-Century Studies* 34 (2011): 19–38.

Punter, David. "Introduction: Of Apparitions." In Byron and Punter, *Spectral Readings*, 1–8.

———. *The Literature of Terror*. Vol. 1, *The Gothic Tradition*. New York: Routledge, 2014.

———. *The Literature of Terror*. Vol. 2, *The Modern Gothic*. New York: Routledge, 2014.

———, ed. *A New Companion to the Gothic*. Oxford: Wiley-Blackwell, 2012.

Radcliffe, Ann. *The Mysteries of Udolpho*. Oxford: Oxford University Press, 2008.

———. *The Romance of the Forest*. Oxford: Oxford University Press, 2009.

Ragussis, Michael. *Figures of Conversion: "The Jewish Question" and English National Identity*. Durham: Duke University Press, 1995.

Ramras-Rauch, Gila. "A. B. Yehoshua and the Sephardic Experience." *World Literature Today* 65, no. 1 (1991): 8–13.

Raz-Krakotzkin, Amnon. "Galut be-tokh ribonut: Le-bikoret shlilat ha-galut ba-tarbut ha-Yisra'elit" [Exile in the midst of sovereignty: Toward a critique of *shlilat ha-galut* in Israeli culture]. Pts. 1 and 2. *Teorya u-vikoret* 4 (1993): 23–55; 5 (1994): 113–32.

Ricoeur, Paul. "Narrative Time." *Critical Inquiry* 7, no. 1 (1980): 169–90.

Ridenhour, Jamieson. *In Darkest London: The Gothic Cityscape in Victorian Literature*. Lanham, MD: Scarecrow Press, 2013.

Roberts, Jo. *Contested Land, Contested Memory: Israel's Jews and Arabs and the Ghosts of Catastrophe*. Toronto: Dundurn, 2013.

Roberts, Nicholas E. "Dividing Jerusalem: British Urban Planning in the Holy City. *Journal of Palestine Studies* 42, no. 4 (2013): 7–26.

Robertson, Fiona. *Legitimate Histories: Scott, Gothic, and the Authorities of Fiction*. Oxford: Clarendon Press, 1994.

Robinson, Sara Libby. *Blood Will Tell: Vampires as Political Metaphors before World War I*. Boston: Academic Studies Press, 2011.

———. "Novel Anti-Semitisms: Vampiric Reflections of the Jew in Britain, 1875–1914." In *Jewish Studies in Violence: A Collection of Essays*, edited by Roberta Rosenberg Farber and Simcha Fishbane, 143–54. Lanham, MD: University Press of America, 2007.

Rody, Caroline. "Toni Morrison's *Beloved*: History, 'Rememory,' and a 'Clamor for a Kiss.'" *American Literary History* 7, no. 1 (1995): 92–119.

Roshwald, Miriam. *Ghetto, Shtetl, or Polis? The Jewish Community in the Writings of Karl Emil Franzos, Sholom Aleichem, and Shemuel Yosef Agnon*. Rockville, MD: Wildside, 1997.

Roskies, David G., and Naomi Diamant. *Holocaust Literature: A History and Guide*. Waltham, MA: University Press of New England, 2012.

Rothberg, Michael. *Multidirectional Memory: Remembering the Holocaust in the Age of Decolonization*. Palo Alto: Stanford University Press, 2009.

Rovner, Adam L. *In the Shadow of Zion: Promised Lands before Israel*. New York: New York University Press, 2014.

Rudd, Alison. *Postcolonial Gothic Fictions from the Caribbean, Canada, Australia and New Zealand*. Cardiff: University of Wales Press, 2010.

Ruebner, Tuvia. *Lea Goldberg, monografya* [Leah Goldberg, a monograph]. Tel Aviv: Sifriyat Poalim, 1980.

Rushdy, Ashraf H. A. "Daughters Signifyin(g) History: The Example of Toni Morrison's *Beloved*." *American Literature* 64, no. 3 (1992): 567–97.

———. *Remembering Generations: Race and Family in Contemporary African-American Fiction*. Chapel Hill: University of North Carolina Press, 2001.

———. "'Rememory': Primal Scenes and Constructions in Toni Morrison's Novels." *Contemporary Literature* 31, no. 3 (1990): 300–323.

Sa'aroni, Y. [Y. Sin]. "Be-kele ha-intimiyut" [In the prison of intimacy]. *Ha-boker*, October 25, 1935, 4.

Sadan, Dov. *Al Shai Agnon* [On S. Y. Agnon]. Tel Aviv: Hakibbutz Hameuchad, 1967.

Sagal, Danny. Review of *Rabies/Kalevet*. *Science Fiction Film and Television* 6, no. 3 (2013): 420–22.

Sagiv, Yonatan. "Israel, Palestine and Zombies." *Middle East in London* 13, no. 1 (December 2016–January 2017): 10–11.

Samson, John. "Politics Gothicized: The Conway Incident and *The Castle of Otranto*." *Eighteenth-Century Life* 10, no. 3 (1986): 145–58.

Savoy, Eric. "The Face of the Tenant: A Theory of American Gothic." In *American Gothic: New Interventions in a National Narrative*, edited by Robert K. Martin and Eric Savoy, 3–19. Iowa City: University of Iowa Press, 1998.

———. "Spectres of Abjection: The Queer Subject of James's 'The Jolly Corner.'" In Byron and Punter, *Spectral Readings*, 161–76.

Schachter, Allison. *Diasporic Modernisms: Hebrew and Yiddish Literature in the Twentieth Century.* Oxford: Oxford University Press, 2012.

Schmitt, Cannon. "Introduction: Gothic Fictions and English Nationality." In *Alien Nation: Nineteenth-Century Gothic Fictions and English Nationality*, 1–20. Philadelphia: University of Pennsylvania Press, 1997.

Scholem, Gershom. "A Confession Regarding Our Language (Gershom Scholem to Franz Rosenzweig, December 26, 1926)." Translated by Alexander Gelley. In Cutter, "Ghostly Hebrew, Ghastly Speech," 431–32.

———. "Reflections on S. Y. Agnon." *Commentary* 44, no. 6 (1967): 59–66.

Schweid, Eliezer. "The Rejection of the Diaspora in Zionist Thought: Two Approaches." *Journal of Israeli History* 5, no. 1 (1984): 43–70.

Sedgwick, Eve. *The Coherence of Gothic Conventions.* New York: Methuen, 1986.

Segal, Miryam. *A New Sound in Hebrew Poetry: Poetics, Politics, Accent.* Bloomington: Indiana University Press, 2010.

Segev, Tom. *The Seventh Million: The Israelis and the Holocaust.* New York: Picador, 2000.

Seidman, Naomi. "Gender and the Disintegration of the Shtetl in Modern Hebrew and Yiddish Literature." In Katz, *Shtetl: New Evaluations*, 193–210.

———. *A Marriage Made in Heaven: The Sexual Politics of Hebrew and Yiddish.* Berkeley: University of California Press, 1997.

Setter, Shaul. "The Time That Returns: Speculative Temporality in S. Yizhar's 1948." *Jewish Social Studies* 18, no. 3 (2012): 38–54.

Shaham, Haya. "Bein mithizatsya le-demithizatsya: Al aspekt eḥad bi-klitat ha-motiv ha-met-ha-ḥai ha-Altermani ba-shira ha-tse'ira bi-shnot ha-arba'im ve-reshit shnot ha-ḥamishim" [Between mythicization and demythicization: On one aspect of Alterman's living-dead]. *Dapim le-meḥkar be-sifrut* 5/6 (1989): 153–66.

Shaked, Gershon. "Maḥaze siaḥ: 'Ba'alat ha-armon' me-et Lea Goldberg" [A dialogic play: 'The Lady of the Castle' by Leah Goldberg]. In *Al sipurim u-maḥazot*, 187–200. Jerusalem: Keter, 1992.

———. *Omanut ha-sipur shel Agnon* [The narrative art of S. Y. Agnon]. Merhavia: Sifriyat Poalim, 1973.

———. *Shmuel Yosef Agnon: A Revolutionary Traditionalist.* New York: New York University Press, 1989.

———. "Shorashim" [Roots]. In Ben-Dov, *Ba-kivun ha-negdi*, 132–38.

———. "Yerushalayim ba-sifrut ha-Ivrit" [Jerusalem in Hebrew literature]. *Mada'ey ha-yahadut* 38 (1997–98): 15–32.

Shaked, Malka. "What Dances in Agnon's 'Dance of Death.'" In *History and Literature: New Readings of Jewish Texts in Honor of Arnold J. Band*, edited by William Cutter and David C. Jacobson, 161–70. Providence: Program in Judaic Studies, Brown University, 2002.

Shamir, Moshe. *Be-mo yadav: Pirkey Elik* [With his own hands: The chronicles of Elik]. Merhavia: Sifriyat Poalim, 1967.

Shamir, Oron. "'Mesuvag ḥarig': Mikrokosmus shel ha-ḥevra" [*Freak Out*: A microcosm of society]. *Akhbar ha-ir*, October 15, 2015. http://www.mouse.co.il/movies/reviews/1.3260320.

Shamir, Ziva. "Ha-met ha-ḥai: Gilguleyha shel dmut ha-met ha-ḥai bi-yetsirat Alterman" [The living-dead: The evolution of the figure of the living-dead in Alterman's work]. *Gag* 14 (2006): 67–72.

———. "Isha Ivriya mi yeda ḥayayikh? Ha-folklor ha-yehudi ve-hishtakfuyotav be-sipurav shel Yod Shtainberg 'Ha-iveret' ve-'Bat-Yisrael'" [O, Hebrew woman, who knows your life? Folklore and pseudofolklore in Y. Shteinberg's short stories "Ha-iveret" and "Bat-Yisrael"]. *Jerusalem Studies in Jewish Folklore* 21 (2001): 63–89.

Shamir, Ziva, and Zvi Luz, eds. *Ha-poema ha-modernistit bi-yetsirat Alterman* [The modernist poem in Alterman's work]. Ramat Gan: Bar Ilan University Press, 1991.

Shapira, Anita. "The Holocaust: Private Memories, Public Memory." *Jewish Social Studies* 4, no. 2 (1998): 40–58.

———. "Le-an halkhah shlilat ha-galut" [Where has the negation of diaspora gone]. *Alpayim* 25 (2003): 9–54.

Shapiro, James. *Shakespeare and the Jews*. New York: Columbia University Press, 1996.

Shavit, Uzi. *Lo hakol havalim va-hevel: Ha-ḥayim al kav ha-kets al-pi Alterman* [Not all is vanity: Life on the edge according to Alterman]. Tel Aviv: Hakibbutz Hameuchad, 2007.

Shavit, Zohar. "The Status of Translated Literature in the Creation of Hebrew Literature in Pre-state Israel (the Yishuv Period)." *Meta* 43, no. 1 (1998): 46–53.

Shenhar, Aliza. "Motivim amamiyim be-Ḥupat Dodim le-Shai Agnon" [Folk motifs in S. Y. Agnon's 'Ḥupat Dodim']. In *Meḥkarey Yerushalayim be-folklor Yehudi*, edited by Tamar Alexander and Galit Hasan-Rokem, 27–62. Jerusalem: Magnes Press, 1973.

Sherwin, Byron L. *The Golem Legend: Origins and Implications*. Lanham, MD: University Press of America, 1985.

Shlomovitz, Netanel. "*Juda*: Eikh nir'eh Tsiyon Barukh be-tor arpad?" [*Juda*: How does Tsiyon Barukh look as a vampire?"]. *Haaretz*, April 29, 2017. http://www.haaretz.co.il/gallery/television/.premium-1.4053838.

Shohat, Ella. "The Invention of the Mizrahim." *Journal of Palestine Studies* 29, no. 1 (1999): 5–20.

———. "Sephardim in Israel: Zionism from the Standpoint of its Jewish Victims." *Social Text* 19/20 (1988): 1–35.

Shteinberg, Ya'akov. "Di Blinde." *Der Fraind*, April 5, 1912, 3, and April 7, 1912, 2.

———. "Ha-iveret" [The blind woman]. In *Shene Sipurim*, 11–27. Jerusalem: Ha-histadrut ha-Tsiyonit ha-olamit, 1973–74.

———. "Ha-iveret." In *Sipurim*, vol. 1, 186–94. Jerusalem and Berlin: Moriah and Dvir, 1923.

Shulman, David. "In Palestine, Memory Is a Living, Haunting Thing." *The Wire*, December 27, 2015. https://thewire.in/18083/in-palestine-memory-is-a-living-haunting-thing/.

Silver, Sean. "The Politics of Gothic Historiography, 1660–1800." In Byron and Townshend, *Gothic World*, 3–14.

Smith, Andrew. "Hauntings." In Spooner and McEvoy, *Routledge Companion*, 147–54.

Smith, Andrew, and William Hughes, eds. *Empire and the Gothic: The Politics of Genre*. New York: Palgrave Macmillan, 2002.

Smith, Andrew, and Diana Wallace, eds. "The Female Gothic: Then and Now." *Gothic Studies* 6, no. 1 (2004): 1–7.

Sokoloff, Naomi B. "Longing and Belonging: Jerusalem in Fiction as Setting and as Mindset." *Hebrew Studies* 24 (1983): 137–49.

Somerson, Wendy Elisheva. "The Twin Ghosts of Slavery and the Nakba: The Roots That Connect Ferguson and Palestine." *Tikkun*, January 23, 2015. http://www.tikkun.org/nextgen/the-twin-ghosts-of-slavery-and-the-nakba-the-roots-that-connect-ferguson-and-palestine.

Spooner, Catherine. *Contemporary Gothic*. London: Reaktion, 2006.

———. *Post-millennial Gothic: Comedy, Romance and the Rise of Happy Gothic*. London: Bloomsbury, 2017.

Spooner, Catherine, and Emma McEvoy, eds. *The Routledge Companion to the Gothic*. New York: Routledge, 2007.

Stav, Shira. "Avot u-vanot: Ha-milkud shel giluy ha-arayot" [Fathers and daughters: The incest trap]. *Teorya u-vikoret* 37 (2010): 69–95.

———. "Giluy [arayot] ve-kisuy ba-lashon: Bialik, Wallach, Wieselthier" [Incest and intertext: Bialik, Wallach, Wieselthier]. *Israel Studies in Language and Society* 10, no. 2 (2017): 156–74.

———. "'Kri'a': Brakha Seri ve-ha-seder ha-insestuali" ["Tear": Bracha Serri and the incestuous order]. *Teorya u-vikoret* 48 (2017): 59–80.

———. "Parashat Frizl: Giluy arayot be-merḥav mithi" [The Frizl affair: Incest in a mythical and capitalist space]. In *Kapitalizem u-migdar: Sugiyot feministiyot be-tarbut ha-shuk* [Gender and capitalism: Feminist encounters with market cultures], edited by Orna Coussin, Ronna Brayr-Garb, Dana Olmert, and Yofi Tirosh, 285–304. Jerusalem: Van Leer Institute, 2017.

Stern, Rebecca F. "Gothic Light: Vision and Visibility in the Victorian Novel." *South Central Review* 11, no. 4 (1994): 26–39.

Stoker, Bram. *Dracula*. New York: Penguin Books, 2011.

Sugars, Cynthia, and Gerry Turcotte, eds. *Unsettled Remains: Canadian Literature and the Postcolonial Gothic*. Waterloo, ON: Wilfrid Laurier University Press, 2009.

Tabish, Khair. *The Gothic, Postcolonialism and Otherness: Ghosts from Elsewhere*. New York: Springer, 2009.

TCH. "TET TV Channel Has Begun Shooting 'Split' Series." [In Russian.] August 18, 2011. https://ru.tsn.ua/glamur/events/telekanal-tet-nachal-semki-seriala-split.html.

Tel Aviv Times. "HOT hishika eser sdarot makor ḥadashot be-alut kolelet shel 200 milyon shekel" [HOT launched ten original series at a total cost of 200 million shekels]. September 20, 2016. http://www.tel-avivtimes.com/culture/television/16913.html.

This Week in Palestine. "Artist of the Month: Bashir Makhoul." No. 177 (January 2013). http://archive.thisweekinpalestine.com/details.php?catid=11&id=3931&edid=214.

Tsurit, A. "Sofrim mesaprim al yetsiratam" [Authors talk about their creation]. *La-Merḥav*, May 8, 1959, 6.

Udel, Miriam. *Never Better! The Modern Jewish Picaresque*. Ann Arbor: University of Michigan Press, 2016.

Vampire TLV. "About." Facebook. Accessed May 2, 2018. https://www.facebook.com/pg/Vampire.TLV/about/?ref=page_internal.

Walpole, Horace. *The Castle of Otranto: A Gothic Story*. Oxford: Oxford University Press, 1996.

Warwick, Alexandra. "Lost Cities: London's Apocalypse." In Byron and Punter, *Spectral Readings*, 73–87.

Wasson, Sarah. *Urban Gothic of the Second World War: Dark London*. New York: Palgrave Macmillan, 2010.

Weber, Jean-Paul. "Edgar Poe or the Theme of the Clock." In *Poe: A Collection of Critical Essays*, edited by Robert Regan, 79–97. Englewood Cliffs, NJ: Prentice, 1967.
Wein, Toni. *British Identities, Heroic Nationalisms, and the Gothic Novel, 1764–1824*. New York: Palgrave Macmillan, 2002.
Weisman, Anat. "After All of This, I Will Have to Muster All of My 'Courage for the Mundane': On Leah Goldberg's Paradigmatic Temperament." *Prooftexts* 33, no. 2 (2014): 222–50.
Weiss, Hillel. "The Presence of the Holocaust in Agnon's Writings." In *Agnon and Germany: The Presence of the German World in the Writings of S. Y. Agnon*, edited by Hans-Jürgen Becker and Hillel Weiss, 427–50. Ramat Gan, Israel: Bar-Ilan University Press, 2010.
Weiss, Vered. "Generic Hybridity, or Mediating Modes of Writing: Agnon's Magical Realistic and Gothic National Narration." *Symbolism: An International Annual of Critical Aesthetics* 12–13 (2013): 69–90.
Weiss, Yfaat. "'Nothing in My Life Has Been Lost': Lea Goldberg Revisits Her German Experience." *Leo Baeck Institute Year Book* 54 (2009): 357–77.
Werses, Shmuel. "Bein metsiyut historit le-te'ur sipuri: Bein Yehudim le-Polanim be-kitvey S. Y. Agnon" [Between historical reality and literary description: Between Jews and Poles in the works of S. Y. Agnon]. *Gilad* 11 (1989): 109–60.
Wester, Maisha. *African American Gothic: Screams from Shadowed Places*. New York: Palgrave Macmillan, 2012.
Williams, Anne. *Art of Darkness: A Poetics of Gothic*. Chicago: University of Chicago Press, 1995.
Wirth-Nesher, Hana. "The Modern Jewish Novel and the City: Franz Kafka, Henry Roth, and Amos Oz." *Modern Fiction Studies* 24, no. 1 (1978): 91–109.
Wisse, Ruth R. *No Joke: Making Jewish Humor*. Princeton: Princeton University Press, 2013.
Wolkstein, Oded. "Ani omer lakhem she-ani met! Masa al Edgar Alan Po" [I'm telling you I'm dead! An essay on Edgar Allan Poe].Tel Aviv: Resling, 2016.
Wolstenholme, Susan. *Gothic (Re)Visions: Writing Women as Readers*. Albany: State University of New York Press, 1993.
Yehoshua, A. B. *Mar Mani*. Tel Aviv: Hakibbutz Hameuchad, 1990.
———. *Mr. Mani*. Translated by Hillel Halkin. New York: Harvest, 1992.
Yiftachel, Oren. "'Anu meyahadim otakh moledet': Al nokhehuto shel ha-patriotizm ha-Yisra'eli ba-zemer u-ba-nof" [We Judaize you, our homeland: On the presence of Israeli patriotism in song and in the landscape]. In *Patriotizem: Ohavim otakh moledet*, edited by Avner Ben-Amos and Daniel Bar-Tal, 239–74. Tel Aviv: Dyonon, 2004.
Zertal, Idith. *Israel's Holocaust and the Politics of Nationhood*. Translated by Chaya Galai. Cambridge: Cambridge University Press, 2005.
Zerubavel, Yael. *Desert in the Promised Land*. Stanford: Stanford University Press, 2018.
Zierler, Wendy. "'In What World?' Devorah Baron's Fiction of Exile." *Prooftexts* 19, no. 2 (1999): 127–50.
———. *And Rachel Stole the Idols: The Emergence of Modern Hebrew Women's Writing*. Detroit: Wayne State University Press, 2004.
Zimmerman, Brett. "*Allegoria, Chronographia*, and Clock Architecture in 'The Masque of the Red Death.'" In *Edgar Allan Poe: Rhetoric and Style*, 51–62. Montreal: McGill-Queen's University Press, 2005.
Zlosnik, Sue. "The Gothic: Danger, Discontent, and Desire." In *The History of British Women's Writing: 1970 to the Present*, edited by Mary Eagleton and Emma Parker, 10:147–57. New York: Palgrave Macmillan, 2015.

INDEX

Abraham, Nicolas, 10, 230–31
Abramovitsh, S. Y., 107n21
Adaf, Shimon, 220n56
"Ha-adonit ve-ha-rokhel" ["The Lady and the Peddler"] (Agnon, 1943), 25, 38, 43, 66, 268–69; blood libel and, 60–63; gothicism in Agnon's vision of Jewish history, 40; gothic vision of the past in, 44; temporality and historicity in, 51–54; Wandering Jew figure in, 55–59, 63–64
Adorno, Theodor, 63, 115–16, 141n11
affective turn (mid-1990s), 11
affect theory, 11–13, 30n41, 99
African Americans, 223, 238, 255n4, 255n9
"Agadat ha-sofer" ["Tale of the Scribe"] (Agnon, 1919), 71n78
aggadah and *aggadic* literature, 82, 108n29
aginut, feminine genealogy of, 78, 80–84, 91–92
Agnon, S. Y., 2, 7, 8, 25, 37–73; critical receptions of Jewish gothic visions, 40–43, 69n17; historiography of, 43–48; Jerusalem and, 153
Agnon, S. Y., works of: "Agadat ha-sofer" ["Tale of the Scribe"] (1919), 71n78; "Agunot," 83; "Aliyat neshama" (Ascent of the soul), 37; "Ba-derekh" ["On the Road"] (1944), 45; "Be'era shel Miryam" [Miriam's well], 58n13; "Bein ha-bayit la-ḥatser" [Between the house and the fence], 45; "Bimtsulot" ["In the Depths"] (1917), 68n3; "Ha-ḥupa ha-sheḥora" [The black bridal canopy] (1913), 43; "ḥupat dodim" [The bridal canopy] (1931), 43; "Im knisat ha-yom" ["At the Outset of the Day"] (1943), 45; "Ir ha-metim" [City of the dead] (1907), 44, 68n3; *Ir u-melo'a* [*A City in Its Fullness*], 69n22; "Kisuy ha-dam" [Covering the blood] (1975), 71n78, 72n95, 72n100; "Kol ha-em" ["The Mother's Voice"] (1941), 43; "Le-veit aba" ["To Father's House"] (1941), 69n20; "Ha-lev ve-ha-einayim" ["Heart and Eyes"] (1943), 43; "Ma'agelei tsedek" ["Paths of Righteousness"], 70n41; "Ha-mikhtav" ["The Letter"] (1940), 69n20; "Ha-panas" [The lantern] (1906–7), 43, 44, 68n3; *Sefer ha-ma'asim* [The book of deeds], 68n11; "Ha-siman" ["The Sign"] (1943), 45; *Sipurey Polin* [*Stories of Poland*], 44–45, 48, 50; "Toitentans" [Dance of death] (1908), 44, 68n3; *Ve-haya he-akov le-mishor* [*And the Crooked Shall Be Made Straight*], 69n17; "Ha-yalda ha-meta" [The dead girl] (1932, 1935), 43, 63; "Yatom ve-almana" [An orphan and a widow] (1931), 43. *See also* "Ha-adonit ve-ha-rokhel" ["The Lady and the Peddler"]; "Meḥolat ha-mavet" ["The Dance of Death"]
"Agunah" (Baron), 109n50
agunah ("forsaken wife"), 81–84, 85–86, 108n38
"Agunot" (Agnon), 83
Aharonowitz, Yosef, 75
Ahavat Tsiyon [*Love of Zion*] (Mapu, 1853), 29n23
"Aḥot" ["Sister"] (Baron), 77
"Aḥrey esrim shana" [After twenty years] (Goldberg), 127
Aḥuzat Dajani [*The House of Rajani*] (Hilu, 2008), 1, 2
Aldana Reyes, Xavier, 12, 99
Alexander, Neta, 264
Aliya, First (1868–1947), 1
"Aliyat neshama" [Ascent of the soul] (Agnon), 37
allegory, 123, 182n29, 189, 192, 206
"Al oto ha-noseh atsmo" [On the very same subject] (Goldberg, 1939), 138
Alter, Robert, 181n8

297

298 | Index

alterity, 4, 16, 229, 272
Alterman, Nathan, 19, 21, 138, 142n63
Amichai, Yehuda, 153, 182n29
Amir, Eli, 234, 257n44
Amir, Gal, 28, 262
"Ana min al-Yahoud" (Behar, 2005), 28, 224, 226, 232–33; haunting and history of oppression in, 232; historical revision and, 237–38; limitations of language and, 246, 249–53; nonmemory in, 239–45; subjectivities of self and ghost intermingled, 233
"Annabel Lee" (Poe, 1849), 14, 141n13
Anolik, Ruth Bienstock, 84–85
Ansky, S., 76, 240
anti-Judaism, 31n54
antiquarianism, 189, 192, 193
antisemitism, 15, 32n61, 65, 67, 158, 216; in British gothic literature, 3; folktales used to subvert, 48; gender dynamics and, 60; in Germany and France, 45; Jewish history and, 22; Jew-vampire association and, 269; of Luther, 54; Nazi, 61; stereotypes of, 16, 53, 55, 61, 62, 63–64, 67; as undead phenomenon, 18; Wandering Jew figure and, 58. *See also* blood libel (ritual murder)
Anti-Semitism and British Gothic Literature (Davison), 32n60
Appelfeld, Aharon, 134
Arabic language, 243, 244, 249, 250; Arabic-accented Hebrew, 223, 225, 231–34, 239, 249–52, 254, 258n82; lost or silenced, 223, 252, 253
Arabic literature, 25, 253
Arbel, Michal, 46
archaeology, 165, 189, 201–2
Arendt, Hannah, 22
Arlozorov, ḥayim, 75
Armoni, Boaz, 263, 265
Arnold, Matthew, 71n63
art, 121, 125, 139; as antithesis of time and reality, 124; apolitical utopia of, 137; atemporality of, 26, 126; *ha-met ha-ḥai* ("living dead") and, 142n62; nation-sanctuary and, 136–39; past as sanctuary of, 127, 130; as politically engaged utility, 113; reality interdependent with, 114, 115, 116, 117, 118, 135
Ashkenazi Jews, 153, 159, 163, 230, 232, 237

assimilation, 55, 56, 58, 61
Auerbach, Erich, 116
Auschwitz, 23–24, 115, 138, 141n11, 201, 205, 216. *See also* Holocaust
Austen, Jane, 83, 134
authenticity, 1, 43, 194, 197; national identity and, 207; tension between counterfeit and, 2
authorship, 187, 213
"Auto-emancipation" (Pinkser, 1882), 17

"Ba'alat ha-armon" ["The Lady of the Castle"] (Goldberg, 1954), 26, 114–16; death (the past) as sanctuary, 129–32; dissent from Zionist vision, 133, 143n66; linguistic dynamics of, 141n24; nation-sanctuary in relation to culture, 136–39; revision of victimization and, 132–36; space and time in, 118, 119–22
"Ba-derekh" ["On the Road"] (Agnon, 1944), 45
Baines, Paul, 210, 213
Bakhtin, Mikhail, 75, 106n2, 120, 123, 142n37
Balfour Declaration, 150, 204
Ballas, Shimon, 234
Band, Arnold, 41, 69n17, 79–80, 194, 201, 220n70
Barnes, Deborah H., 236, 254
Baron, Dvora, 7, 26, 74–112; Hebrew and Yiddish versions of stories, 77; shtetls in works of, 107n21
Baron, Dvora, works of: "Agunah," 109n50; "Aḥot" ["Sister"], 77; "Bubbe Henya," 77; *Ha-golim* [The exiles], 82; "Kaddish" (1908, 1910), 76–77; "Shifra" (1927), 26, 76, 106-7n4
Baron, Salo Wittmayer, 22–23
Bartana, Ortsion, 21
Baruch, Tsiyon, 269
Bar-Yosef, Hamutal, 143n65
Ba-sa'ar [In the storm] anthology (1943), 37, 38
Basar totaḥim [*Cannon Fodder*] (film, dir. Gafni, 2013), 264, 267
"Bat ha-rav" [The rabbi's daughter] (Shteinberg, 1912, 1914), 77
bathhouse, as institution, 90

Bat-Shahar, hana, 134
Baudelaire, Charles, 31n53, 165, 167, 168
Be'er, hayim, 153
"Be'era shel Miryam" [Miriam's well] (Agnon), 58n13
Behar, Almog, 7, 8, 223–59; on "nonmemory," 227, 238–45. *See also* "Ana min al-Yahoud"
Beilis blood libel, 45
"Bein ha-bayit la-hatser" [Between the house and the fence] (Agnon), 45
Beloved (Morrison, 1987), 28, 224–26; haunting and history of oppression in, 232; limitations of language and, 246, 247–49; materialized ghost in, 225, 255n7, 255n9; rememory and disremembering in, 238–39, 241–42, 257n50; slave narratives and, 235–36, 257n36; subjectivities of self and ghost intermingled, 233–34; the uncanny and, 227–28
Be-mo yadav: Pirkey Elik [*With His Own Hands*] (Shamir), 139n2
Benjamin, Walter, 116, 151, 167–68, 170, 171, 173, 184n85
Bentham, Jeremy, 94
"Berenice" (Poe, 1835), 63
Berg, Nancy, 221n96
Bhabha, Homi, 228, 238
Biale, David, 59, 60–61, 71n74
Bialik, hayim Nahman, 75, 106n3
"Bimtsulot" ["In the Depths"] (Agnon, 1917), 68n3
Bitton, Erez, 257n44
Black Book, The, 235–36
"Black Cat, The" (Poe), 31n47
Blake, William, 181n27
Blesch, William, 267
blood libel (ritual murder), 16, 45, 60–62, 72n97, 72n100
Bondswoman's Narrative, The (Crafts), 232
Botting, Fred, 152, 160, 161
boundaries, 92, 124, 139, 171, 203; art as sanctuary and, 137, 138; crossing of multiple boundaries, 188; dissolution of, 160; elastic boundaries of the gothic, 5; emotions and, 12; of identity, 230; of Jerusalem, 149, 182n29; between Jewish and non-Jewish, 9; between persecuted and persecutors,

136; political, 155, 179; of the self, 233; temporal, 124, 238, 242; transgression of, 5–6, 163, 166, 168, 213, 238
Braddon, Mary Elizabeth, 99
breastfeeding, 93, 109n73
Brenner, Naomi, 107n15, 143n66
Brenner, Yosef Hayim, 182n28
Britain, 58, 217; national identity in, 55; supremacy as world power, 191–92. *See also* gothic literature, British
Brontë, Anne, 85
Brontë, Charlotte, 141n13
Brontë sisters, 83
"Bubbe Henya" (Baron), 77
Buber, Martin, 37
Buffy the Vampire Slayer (television series), 260, 267
Bund, Socialist, 32n61

Cain (biblical figure), 32–33n76
Campbell, Jill, 211
capitalism, 5, 229
Carmi, Oren, 263
Carmilla (Le Fanu, 1872), 59
"Cask of Amontillado, The" (Poe, 1846), 63
Castle of Otranto, The (Walpole, 1764), 1–2, 3, 9, 266; as archetype of gothic literary historiography, 189–91; as first gothic novel, 1, 133, 188; Hebrew translations of, 13, 262; historical context of, 191–92; incest in, 207, 209–10, 211, 214, 215; *Mar Mani* compared to, 27, 188, 191, 196–97, 207, 209–10, 214; nationalism and, 206–7; plot summary, 190–91; victims and villains in, 22
castles, 3, 22, 40, 134; chronotopes and, 120–21; of Dracula, 57
cemeteries, 40–41, 103, 109n60
Chekhov, Anton, 115
Chetrit, Sami Shalom, 257n41, 257n44
Christians, European, 15, 67; blood libel and, 60–61; crypts in early Christian Church, 161; Jewish converts to Christianity, 158; kashruth laws and, 62; time in Christian worldview, 131
chronotopes, 59, 75, 89, 105, 106n2; labyrinth and, 188; in Poe and Goldberg, 118–22, 131; of the shtetl in literature, 79–80

cinema/film, 5, 31n54, 260, 261; adaptations of gothic literature, 16; film noir, 263, 275n10; gothic affect in, 12; "Hebrew Horror" films, 28, 263–67; Nazi propaganda films, 55, 71n62; "New Violence" movement, 264
circumcision, 60
civilization, 46, 139, 159; British Mandate and, 150; clash of Hebrew and Hellenic civilizations, 71n63; performance of, 153, 155
Clery, E. J., 193
Cohen, Yisrael, 77
communism, 136
Communist Manifesto, The (Marx and Engels), 237, 257n42
Contested Castle, The (Ellis), 91
Copjec, Joan, 109n73
Crafts, Hannah, 232
cultural studies, 5
Culture and Anarchy (Arnold, 1869), 71n63
Cvetkovich, Ann, 99, 103, 111n107

Dacre, Charlotte, 58
Dajani, Salaḥ, 1
Dam kaḥol [Blue blood] (Tochterman, 2011), 28, 262
Daniel Deronda (Eliot, 1876), 99
danse macabre, 49–50, 70n41
Dargis, Manohla, 266
Davis, Colin, 10
Davis, Kimberly Chabot, 236
Davison, Carol Margaret, 6, 18; on antisemitism as vampire, 63; on Wandering Jew in British gothic literature, 16–17, 32n59, 54–55, 58, 70n58, 71n62, 71n75
Dayan, Yonatan, 263
death, 44, 65, 103, 106, 142n63; art and, 139; atemporality of art and, 126; culture of, 21; fictional distancing from threat of, 12; history and, 179; interment soon after, 63; love as transcendence of, 50; in *Mar Mani*, 212, 221n87; as refuge, 129–32; time as handmaiden of, 149; writing as act to ward off, 175
decadence, 19, 121
DeKoven Ezrahi, Sidra, 38, 46, 70n41, 72n100, 73n101, 182n29

de Lange, Nicholas, 180n1, 186n129
de Man, Paul, 123
Dent, Jonathan, 190, 196, 235
"departure metaphor," 78, 80–84
Derrida, Jacques, 10, 11, 228, 237, 247, 272–73
diaspora, 9, 18, 153, 158–59, 243; as antithesis of civilization, 159; "denigration" of, 115, 140n8; femininity associated with, 110n74; heritage of Hebrew language and, 252; nonmemory of diasporic histories, 253; vulnerability or powerlessness of, 21, 133
Dickens, Charles, 78, 161
difference, Jewish, 32n59, 53, 55, 57, 62, 67, 269
disremembering, 226, 238, 240, 243, 245, 247, 251, 254
Dolan, Elizabeth, 95
"domestic carceral," 33n95, 91, 93, 105
doppelgänger, 85, 93, 175, 208, 209
Dracula (Stoker, 1897), 13, 16, 129; Agnon's fiction compared with, 57; blood libel (ritual murder) and, 61; fear of Jewish takeover and, 70n58; Hebrew translations of, 262; Wandering Jew as vampire and, 59
DuBois, W.E.B., 224
dybbuks, 9, 76, 240–41

Edelmann, R., 54, 58
Egypt, 148
Eichmann, Adolf, trial of, 23, 24
electric power, 150, 181n12
Eliot, George, 99
Ellis, Kate Ferguson, 83, 84, 91
Ellis, Markman, 6
emotion: emotional excess, 41; feminism and role of affect, 99–100, 110–11n106, 111n107
Enlightenment, 7, 32n61, 143n66; gothic narratives as challenge to, 202; text-based historiography and, 192. *See also* Haskalah
Europe, Eastern, Jewish presence in, 25, 32n61, 66, 216; chronotopes and, 75; "domestic carceral" structures of women's experience, 26, 33n95; Jewish folklore, 241; Jewish past in, 4; lost world of, 39; place of women in, 79, 83; shtetl as shorthand for, 80; Yiddish folk culture in, 76
exorcism, writing as, 147, 162
expressionism, 77

fairy tales, 53
"Fall of the House of Usher, The" (Poe, 1839), 63
fascism, 19, 114
femininity, 26, 60, 77, 83, 169, 209; diaspora associated with, 110n74; Jewish and non-Jewish, 86; mother figure and, 84–89; "professional femininity," 84, 100
feminism, 5, 33n83, 97, 107n16, 220n71; critical theory and, 94; "gothic feminism," 26, 33n94, 84; on labyrinth and feminine psyche, 160; role of affect and, 99–100, 110–11n106, 111n107
Fiedler, Leslie, 168, 255n6
flâneur/flâneuse, 151, 166–74, 184n85, 184n88
forgetting, 153, 224, 225, 226, 232; cultivated, 28, 241; disremembering distinct from, 238; historical, 44, 45, 236; limitations of memory and, 238; nonmemory distinct from, 240; of one's own past, 233; rememory and, 239; time as agent of, 173, 176; willed, 231. *See also* memory; disremembering
Foucault, Michel, 91, 92
France, national identity in, 55
Frankenstein (Shelley, 1818), 13, 262, 263, 274n6
Freedman, William, 125–26
Freud, Sigmund, 154, 162; on the primal scene, 241; on the uncanny, 174–75, 227, 255–56n11

Gafni, Eitan, 264, 267
Gardenour, Brenda, 31n54
Garner, Margaret, 235
gender, 82, 86, 91, 104
genealogy: feminine, 78, 104, 105; illusion of, 207, 211; in *Mar Mani*, 187, 188, 189, 210, 213, 214; multigenerational, 89
genocide, 55, 247, 255n6
George III, King, 218n12, 218n22
German language, 37, 47
German literature, 25
Germany, 58, 204, 241; national identity in, 55; *Schauerroman* (terror-novel), 55, 71n62
Gertz, Nurith, 219n46
ghosts, 3, 5, 17, 27–28, 67; as conceptual metaphor, 10; exorcism of, 147; justice and, 228; language and, 246; as metaphor for historical trauma, 223; as representation of otherness, 18; revision of memory and, 227. *See also* haunting
Ghost Seer, The (Schiller), 71n75
Gilbert, Sandra, 107n6
"globalgothic," 5
Gluzman, Michael, 140n7
goblins, 76
Goddu, Teresa A., 29n9, 39, 71n77, 232, 255n7, 255n9
Goethe, Johann Wolfgang, 13, 70n44
Goldberg, Leah, 7, 26, 38, 113–44; criticized for cultural loyalty to Europe, 106, 183n46; "mobilized literature" rejected by, 138; on Poe and the writing process, 118; relationship with Zionism, 136–37; as translator of European literature, 141n13
Goldberg, Leah, works of: "Aḥrey esrim shana" [After twenty years], 127; "Al oto ha-noseh atsmo" [On the very same subject] (1939), 138; "Laila ve-yamim aḥronim" [Night and the last days], 127; *Mi-beyti ha-yashan* [From my old home] (1944), 140n7; "Ha-omets le-ḥulin" [The courage for the mundane] (1938), 115, 138, 143n65; "Oren" [Pine tree], 127; *Shir bakfarim* [Songs in the villages] (1942), 140n7; *Taba'ot ashan* [Smoke rings] (1935), 114, 127, 140n7, 140n9, 183n46; "Zman" [Time], 127. *See also* "Ba'alat ha-armon" ["The Lady of the Castle"]
Goldberg ve-Eisenberg [Goldberg and Eisenberg] (film, dir. Carmi, 2013), 263
golem, 9, 29n25, 72n97, 76
Ha-golim [The exiles] (Baron), 82
Gordon, Avery, 224, 228–29, 238, 247, 254
Gordon, Y. L., 109n50
Gothic America (Goddu, 1997), 29n9
gothic literature, American, 4, 224, 232; boundaries transgressed in, 5–6; comic effects in, 271–72; domestic setting in, 91; "female gothic," 84, 108n40; "first wave Gothics," 3, 272; in Hebrew translation, 13–15; imprisoned woman motif, 84; instability signified in, 6; labyrinth as convention of, 160–62; modes of subjectivity in, 85; paranoia as key motif, 154

gothic literature, British, 2, 11, 227; antisemitism in, 3; critical reception of, 20; identification with high culture, 58n14; villains/persecutors in, 134, 144n74; Wandering Jew figure in, 18, 32n59, 54–55, 71n75
gothic studies, 4–5, 12, 24, 29n9; "anxiety model" in, 275n15; ghost as key "generic marker" in, 11; surge since 1990s, 11
Gothic Studies (journal), 5, 256n21
Govrin, Nurit, 182n28
Greece, ancient, 59, 204, 217, 219n56
Green, Kenneth Hart, 47
Greenberg, Uri Zvi, 14, 19, 182n29
Gregg, Melissa, 12
Gubar, Susan, 107n6

Haberman, Abraham Meir, 45
Haggerty, George E., 12, 99
halacha (Judaic law), 81
Halkin, Hillel, 14
Hamilton, Cynthia S., 236
Hamlet (Shakespeare), 2, 228
Handelzats, Yisrael Eliyahu, 30n47
Haraway, Donna, 94–95, 163
Haskalah (Jewish Enlightenment), 30n26, 32n61, 63; image of conflict between light and darkness, 151; women and, 108n38
Hassidism, 37
ḥatsuya [Split] (film, dir. Kapon, 2009–12), 267, 268
haunting, 11, 27, 187, 233, 262; fragmentation of the self and, 152; hegemonic power relations and, 229; history and, 226, 228, 235, 237–38; in Jerusalem, 174, 217; language and, 239, 240, 241, 249; memory and forgetting in relation to, 224, 238, 254; Palestinian dispossession and, 223; prosopopoeia and, 176; return of the repressed and, 227; in the shtetl, 76; slavery and, 224, 225, 227, 234, 255n9; spectrality and, 10–11; temporality and, 150; transgenerational, 10, 28, 226, 230–31, 232, 245; Wandering Jew and, 55. See also ghosts
hauntology, 10, 11
Hawthorne, Nathaniel, 20, 141n13
"Hebrew Horror" films and TV series, 28, 260–76

Hebrew language, 1, 76, 136, 164–65; accented, 225, 227, 231–34, 239–40, 251, 253, 255n10, 258n82; association with Arabic, 249; biblical, 47; diasporic heritage of, 251; literary translations into, 9, 13–15, 29n23, 30–31n46, 68n5, 262–63; masculine sphere of, 77; poetry in, 18, 20, 75; as resurrected language, 9, 10, 30n26; transition from literary to spoken language, 47; Zionism and, 136
Hebrew literature, 8, 15, 37; adaptations of gothic elements, 8; contact with Yiddish literature, 77–78, 107n15; in global context, 25; gothic in development of, 2–3; women authors, 26
Hebrew Renaissance, 74, 81
Heidegger, Martin, 123
Henry, Katherine, 168
Herrmann, Leo, 37
Herzl, Theodor, 199, 204
heteroglossia, 123, 142n37
Hever, Hanan, 19, 137, 143n66
Hilu, Alon, 1, 2, 9, 15, 19
Hirsch, Marianne, 239
historiography, 3, 4, 24, 187, 214; of Agnon, 43–48, 67; American, 235; archive-based, 201–2; debates on Jewish historiography, 22; English history as Gothic history, 190, 191–92, 194; feminine, 103–6; injustice and, 28; limits of conventional practice, 223; perpetual return of 1948 war and, 180; reassessment of New Historians and, 194–96; revisions of, 7
history, 1, 7, 10, 187, 243–44; disengagement from, 205; gothic as mode of unofficial history, 6; as "grand scale" time, 124; Jerusalem and, 27; Jewish conception of, 3; Jewish presence in, 38; Jew's return to, 58; masculine temporality of, 105; nightmare of, 178–80; nightmares of, 39; "para-site" of, 4–9; representation of, 24; thematizations of history in *Mar Mani*, 202–6; transgenerational, 245
History of England (Hume), 190
Hitler, Adolf, 53, 203–4
Hochberg, Gil, 229
Hoeveler, Diane Long, 84, 100, 206

Hoffmann, E.T.A., 13, 41
Hogle, Jerrold E., 12, 13, 161, 165, 166; on dissolution of identity, 207; on labyrinth of narrative, 200
Holocaust, 4, 16, 18, 26, 270; Agnon's fiction and, 40, 45–46, 66, 73n101; in Israeli public sphere, 23–24, 33n87; child survivors of, 141n23; fragile sanctuary of art and, 139; gothic imagery in narratives of, 134; Israeli Jews' renunciation of Europe and, 115; Israeli state established in wake of, 23; Mizrahi Jews and, 33n92; persecution of Jews in Middle Ages connected to, 45; as subject of Israeli cinema, 264; traumatic memories of survivors, 239; Wandering Jew figure and, 58; Zionist perception of survivors, 133, 143n69. *See also* Auschwitz
Holtzman, Avner, 182n37
Homeland (Showtime series), 268
homosexuality, 206, 208, 209, 221n94
Horkheimer, Max, 63
Horner, Avril, 152, 172, 271, 272
horror, as genre distinct from gothic, 274–75n9, 276n37
Hume, David, 190
humor, 261, 265, 268, 272
"Ha-ḥupa ha-sheḥora" [The black bridal canopy] (Agnon, 1913), 43
"ḥupat dodim" [The bridal canopy] (Agnon, 1931), 43

identity, national, 4, 6, 8, 206–7; British, 32n59, 55, 137, 150; *ha-met ha-ḥai* ("living dead") and, 21; Jew as gothic figure and, 15; Wandering Jew as antithesis of, 54, 55
ideology, 30n41, 115, 116, 140n10
"Im knisat ha-yom" ["At the Outset of the Day"] (Agnon, 1943), 45
imperialism, British, 6
Industrial Revolution, 161
inheritance, 187, 188, 228
Inquisition, of Catholic Church, 59, 161
inside/outside spatial binary, 117, 119, 121, 122, 129
In Treatment (HBO series), 268
"Ir ha-metim" [City of the dead] (Agnon, 1907), 44, 68n3

irony, 39, 44, 46, 60, 257n50; Agnon and, 41, 67, 68n13; in Behar, 249; Dracula and, 59; in Goldberg, 118
Ir u-melo'a [*A City in Its Fullness*] (Agnon), 69n22
"Ir zara" ["An Alien City"] (Oz, 1968), 148, 178
Israel, 73n101, 132, 173; Archives Law, 195; establishment of (1948), 27, 180; gothic in popular culture, 260–76; haunted geography of, 223–24; isolation in international community, 265; secular, 217; as settler society, 230; war of independence (1948), 19; Zionist ideology and self-definition of, 23
Israeli Society for Science Fiction and Fantasy, 262
Israel-Palestine conflict, 2, 264, 267
Italian, The (Radcliffe, 1797), 133
"Ha-iveret" [The blind woman] (Shteinberg, 1923), 26, 76, 106n4; affect and expression of emotions in, 86, 101–3; gender-specific dynamics of, 110n74; as gothic horror story, 77; men absent from, 87–88; metaphor of staying in, 78; mother-daughter relationship in, 88–89, 109n54; plot summary, 86–87; significance of blindness in, 95–96, 97–98; uncanny feminine historiography in, 104, 105; women's experience of space in, 90–92

Jabotinsky, Ze'ev, 14, 30n46
Jaffee, Martin S., 23
Jane Eyre (Brontë, 1847), 141n13
Jay, Martin, 94
Jelen, Sheila, 77, 81, 108n26
"Jerusalem" (Blake, 1808), 181n27
Jerusalem, city of, 27, 147, 188, 204, 217; British Mandate period, 184n76; Central Zionist Archives, 1; emigre German-Jewish academics in, 159, 183n51; geopolitical fragmentation of, 149, 152; history of, 184n76; as labyrinth, 160–66, 177; as metonymy of Israel, 173, 176; as mythical space, 80; natural geography and, 149; nightmare of history and, 178–80; nighttime illumination and darkness in, 150–52; Old City, 155, 158, 163, 165, 184n76, 266; under Ottoman rule, 184n76; partition and paranoia in, 152–60; specter of

Jerusalem, city of (*continued*)
    1948 war and, 149; suppressed memory of violence in, 236; united under Israeli sovereignty (1967), 148, 178–79, 181n7; walking as flâneuse through, 166–74
JeruZalem (film, dir. D. and Y. Paz, 2015), 264, 266
"Jewish Question," 16, 17, 55
Jews. *See* Ashkenazi; Mizraḥi; Orthodox; Sephardi
Jordan, 148
Juda (television series), 268–71
Judaism, 59–60, 62, 153. *See also* Orthodox Jews and Judaism
"Judeophobia," 17, 18
justice, 10, 228

kabbalism, 63, 68n11
"Kaddish" (Baron, 1908, 1910), 76–77
Kalevet [*Rabies*] (film, dir. Keshales and Papushado, 2010), 263, 264
Kapon, Shai, 267
Kariv, Avraham, 106–7, 136
Kavka, Misha, 263, 274n9
Keshales, Aharon, 263
kibbutz, 173, 174, 182n37, 200, 212, 217
Kibbutz Hulda, 147
Kilgour, Maggie, 210
Kimhi, Dov, 182n28
Kinat David, 49–50
"Kisuy ha-dam" [Covering the blood] (Agnon, 1975), 71n78, 72n95, 72n100
Klein, Melanie, 154
Kokhavim baḥuts [Stars outside] (Alterman, 1938), 19
"Kol ha-em" ["The Mother's Voice"] (Agnon, 1941), 43
Komem, Aharon, 77
"Kotso shel ha-yod" [The point of the *yod*] (Gordon), 109n50
Kristeva, Julia, 105, 154, 206
Kurzweil, Baruch, 20, 21

labyrinths, 3, 91; in "Ba'alat ha-armon" ["The Lady of the Castle"], 134; chronotopes and, 188; feminine psyche and, 160; of Jerusalem, 149, 152, 160–66, 177; at Knossos (Crete),

203–4, 217; in *Mar Mani*, 200; in *The Monk*, 161; psychoanalytic theory and, 162–63
Lacan, Jacques, 94, 154, 175
Ladino language, 251
Lady Audley's Secret (Braddon, 1862), 99
Laila adom [Red night] (Amir, 2003), 28, 262
"Laila ve-yamim aḥronim" [Night and the last days] (Goldberg), 127
Lake, Crystal B., 192
language, 123, 227; abuse and power of, 246–53; reappropriation of, 28; spectral poetics and, 246
Laor, Dan, 46, 73n101
Lapid Press (Warsaw), 14
Lawrence, David, 236
Lebanon, 173
Lebanon War, 198
Le Fanu, Joseph Sheridan, 59, 276n37
"Le-nokhaḥ pesel Apolo" ["Before a Statue of Apollo"] (Tchernihovsky, 1899), 219n56
Lev, Dalit, 263
"Le-veit aba" ["To Father's House"] (Agnon, 1941), 69n20
"Ha-lev ve-ha-einayim" ["Heart and Eyes"] (Agnon, 1943), 43
Levy, Lital, 243, 251, 252
Lewis, Matthew, 3, 16, 22, 56
Leys, Ruth, 30n41
Lieblich, Amya, 138, 140n7
Liebrecht, Savyon, 134
Lingering Bilingualism (Brenner), 107n15
Literature of Terror, The (Punter), 271
Lithuania, 75
London, Jerusalem compared with, 153–55, 181n27; flâneur/flâneuse and, 170–71, 184n85; labyrinth and, 161
Lord, Audre, 110–11n106
Lubin, Orly, 82
Luckhurst, Roger, 11
luftmensch, 81
Luther, Martin, 54

"Ma'agelei tsedek" ["Paths of Righteousness"] (Agnon), 70n41
Mack, Ruth, 192
Madwoman in the Attic, The (Gilbert and Gubar), 107n6

Mahfouz, Naguib, 253
Mann, Thomas, 115
"Man of the Crowd, The" (Poe, 1840), 167
Mapu, Avraham, 29n23
Margaliyot-Kalvarisky, ḥayim, 1
Mar Mani [*Mr. Mani*] (Yehoshua, 1990), 27, 187–89; artifice of origin and sexual transgression in, 206–15, 221n96; *The Castle of Otranto* compared to, 27, 188, 194, 196–97; narrative disruptions in, 215–17; structures of history-telling in, 196–202, 219n46; thematizations of history in, 202–6
"Marshal, William" (Walpole pseudonym), 1, 193
martyrdom, 38
Marx, Karl, 10
Marxism, 228
masculinity, 60, 77, 110n74, 262
maskilim (Haskalah proponents), 32n61, 63
"Masque of the Red Death, The" (Poe, 1842), 26, 31n47, 117, 118–19, 123–26, 128–29
Massumi, Brian, 12, 30n41
Matalon, Ronit, 257n44
Maturin, Charles, 16, 56
"Meḥolat ha-mavet" ["The Dance of Death"] (Agnon, 1916), 25, 37, 66, 74; Agnon's revisions of, 68n3; blood as central symbol in, 64–66; gothicism in Agnon's vision of Jewish history, 40; gothic vision of the past in, 44; temporality and historicity in, 48–54
Meiton, Frederik, 150, 181n12
Melmoth the Wanderer (Maturin, 1820), 16, 56
memory, 10, 28, 153, 225; historical, 236; limitations of, 226, 238; of loss and catastrophe, 46; multidirectional, 244; nonmemory, 227, 238, 240–41, 243–45, 251–54; personal and historical, 172; politics of, 228; postmemory, 239; rememory, 226, 238–39, 241–45, 247, 254, 257–58n50; shared collective memory of trauma, 140n6; suppression of, 236, 245. *See also* forgetting; disremembering
Mesuvag ḥarig [*Freak Out*] (film, dir. Armoni, 2016), 263, 265
ha-met ha-ḥai ("living dead"), 16, 18–21, 32n76, 142n63

Mi-beyti ha-yashan [From my old home] (Goldberg, 1944), 140n7
Middle Ages, 45
Mighall, Robert, 161
Mikhael, Sami, 234, 257n44
Mikhael sheli [*My Michael*] (Oz, 1967), 27, 147–48, 180n1; Jerusalem as labyrinth, 160–66; Jerusalem at night, 150–52; partition and paranoia in Jerusalem, 153–60; time and the uncanny in, 174–78; walking as flâneuse through Jerusalem, 166–74, 184n88
"Ha-mikhtav" ["The Letter"] (Agnon, 1940), 69n20
Miles, Robert, 206, 207
Mi mefaḥed mi-ha ze'ev ha-ra [*Big Bad Wolves*] (film, dir. Keshales and Papushado, 2013), 264, 265–66
Mintz, Alan, 46
Miron, Dan, 20, 79–80, 107n21, 109n60; on "departure metaphor," 78, 80–81; on disruption of continuities, 222n97; on Jerusalem in modern Hebrew literature, 182n28; on widow and *agunah* figures, 82
Mistor [*Shelter*] (film, dir. Riklis, 2017), 263
Mizraḥi Jews, 33n92, 230, 232, 234, 255nn3–4; authors, 224, 226, 236, 257n44; cultural dispossession of, 235, 244; cultural kinship with Palestinian Arabs, 235, 237, 257n43; diaspora and, 243; Palestinian Nakba and, 254
Mizraḥim, 33n92
Mobley, Marilyn Sanders, 236, 257n36
modernism, 19, 40, 67
modernity, 8, 108n38, 141n13; ambivalent feelings about, 16; gothic shadows of, 40, 44; humor as mechanism for confronting, 261; inhospitability to the beautiful past, 129; spectralized, 11, 179
modernization, 16, 78, 81, 83; of Hebrew language, 47; vampires and fears linked to, 61
Molesworth, Jesse, 124
Molkho (Yehoshua), 194
Monk, The (Lewis, 1796), 16, 56, 134, 144n74; crypts and labyrinths in, 161; victims and villains in, 22
Ha-monolog shel Ikarus [Icarus's monologue] (Adaf, 1997), 220n56

Morris, Benny, 194, 195–96, 218n25
Morrison, Paul, 91, 95
Morrison, Toni, 28, 224, 230; on abuse and power of language, 246–47; on "rememory" and "disremembering," 226, 238, 240; "The Site of Memory," 235–36. See also *Beloved*
"Mot ha-zkena" [The death of the old woman] (Shteinberg, 1917), 77
mothers/motherhood, 26, 88–89, 109n54
Mulvey-Roberts, Marie, 31n54
Murnau, F. W., 16
Mystères de Paris, Les [*The Mysteries of Paris*] (Sue, 1842–43), 29n23
Mysteries of Udolpho, The (Radcliffe, 1794), 2, 22, 91, 133, 263
Mysterious Mother, The (Walpole), 210, 211, 213
mysticism, Jewish, 42, 47

Nakba (Palestinian catastrophe of 1948), 223, 236–37, 244, 245, 254, 254n1
Naqqash, Samir, 253
narrative, 189, 197, 202; cultural, 190; fetishization of, 196, 200; national, 39; personal and historical, 199
nationalism, 17, 26, 46, 137; electric power and, 150; Jewish, 19; as male narrative, 82; uprisings of 1848 and, 198–99. See also Zionism
Naveh, Hana, 92, 97, 98, 110n74
Nazism (National Socialism), 63, 71n62, 128, 136, 140n10, 270; blood libel and, 60–61; "discourses of blood" and, 71n74; Eternal Jew (*"Die Ewige Jude"*) figure, 55; national identity and, 55; sexual anxiety and, 60; Third Reich, 16, 54
Negative Dialectics (Adorno, 1966), 141n11
neoromanticism, 41
Neugroschel, Joachim, 241–42
New Historians, Israeli, 2, 27, 194–96, 202, 218n25
"New Jerusalem," 181n27
Northanger Abbey (Austen, 1817), 134
Nosferatu (Murnau film, 1922), 16
nostalgia, 39, 44, 140n6
Nostalgia and Nightmare (Band), 41

Omer-Sherman, Ranen, 224
"Ha-omets le-ḥulin" [The courage for the mundane] (Goldberg, 1938), 115, 138, 143n65
Ophir, Adi, 22, 23
"Oren" [Pine tree] (Goldberg), 127
orientalism, 156, 169, 177
Orthodox Jews and Judaism, 32n61, 155, 157, 172; in "Hebrew Horror" films, 263; in *Mar Mani*, 203
otherness/Other, 18, 58, 85, 229, 265
Ottoman Empire, 75, 181n12, 184n76
Oz, Amos, 7, 27, 147–86, 217; "Ir zara" ["An Alien City"] (1968), 148, 178; as soldier in Six-Day War, 178, 180. See also *Mikhael sheli* [*My Michael*]

Palestine, 2, 13, 37, 68n5, 74, 78; Agnon in, 42, 53; British Mandate period, 150, 152, 155, 198; creation of Hebrew culture in, 144n75; haunted geography of, 223–24; Hebrew literary scene in, 48; under Ottoman rule, 75, 181n12; partition of, 155, 176
Palestinian Arabs, 1, 156, 181n12; as characters in Israeli cinema, 264; in *Mikhael sheli* [*My Michael*], 155–56, 166, 169, 183n40; Mizraḥi Jews' kinship with, 235, 237, 249–50, 257n43; self-other binary with Israeli Jews, 229–30; as vanished ghosts, 231, 241; vocabulary of victimization and, 24. See also Nakba
"Ha-panas" [The lantern] (Agnon, 1906–7), 43, 44, 68n3
panopticon, 91, 94
Pappé, Ilan, 195
Papushado, Navot, 263
paranoia, 149, 151, 152–60, 165, 174, 263; in contemporary Israel, 265; disintegrating subjectivity and, 176; "feminine paranoia," 154; flânerie and, 173
Passover, blood libel and, 60
patriarchal society, 84, 85, 98, 109n54
Paz, Doron and Yoav, 264
Peeren, Esther, 11
Peretz, I. L., 75
Perry, Ruth, 211–12, 218n22
"Philosophy of Composition, The" (Poe, 1846), 118

picaro/picaresque, 20, 33n76
Pilar Blanco, María del, 11
Pinsker, Leo, 17, 18, 20, 32n61, 82, 105
"Pit and the Pendulum, The" (Poe), 31n47
Plato, 116
Poe, Edgar Allan, 14–15, 20, 30n47, 31n53, 68n5, 113–44, 262; live burial as theme in stories of, 63; as "the maniac of time," 116–17
Poe, Edgar Allan, works of: "Annabel Lee" (1849), 14, 141n13; "Berenice" (1835), 63; "The Black Cat," 31n47; "The Cask of Amontillado" (1846), 63; "The Fall of the House of Usher" (1839), 63; "The Man of the Crowd" (1840), 167; "The Masque of the Red Death" (1842), 26, 31n47, 117, 118–19, 123–26, 128–29; "The Philosophy of Composition" (1846), 118; "The Pit and the Pendulum," 31n47; "The Premature Burial" (1844), 63; "The Raven," 14, 118; "Silence," 31n47
Ha-po'el ha-tsa'ir (The Young Worker), 75
Ha-po'el ha-tsa'ir (Zionist weekly), 76
pogroms, 17
Poland, 39, 44, 48, 205, 217
Polish Jews, 50
postcolonialism/postcolonial studies, 5, 8, 94
powerlessness, 4, 9, 21, 86, 230; of diaspora, 23; of the flâneur/flâneuse, 168; Jewish conception of history and, 3; socioeconomic, 78; visibility and, 94
"Premature Burial, The" (Poe, 1844), 63
primal scene, 241
prosopopoeia, 176
prostitutes/prostitution, 165, 167, 168–69
Protestantism, 4
psychoanalytic theory, 22, 109n73, 154, 215, 220n71; labyrinth in, 162–63; on transgenerational trauma, 10
Punter, David, 6, 7, 12, 154, 271

queer studies, 5

race and racism, 60–61, 224, 265
Radcliffe, Ann. See *Mysteries of Udolpho, The*; *Romance of the Forest, The*
Ragussis, Michael, 16

"Rappaccini's Daughter" (Hawthorne, 1844), 141n13
"Raven, The" (Poe), 14, 118
"realgothik," 267, 275n30
repressed, return of the, 189, 252
Republic, The (Plato), 116
Requiem for the Night (film, dir. Blesch), 267
Reuveni, Aharon, 182n28
revolution, 10, 42, 115, 198, 214
Rice, Anne, 260
Ricoeur, Paul, 123
Ridenhour, Jamieson, 153, 154–55, 161, 170–71
Riklis, Eran, 263
Rilke, Rainer Maria, 115
Roberts, Nicholas E., 165
Robertson, Fiona, 196
Rody, Caroline, 236, 238
Romance of the Forest, The (Radcliffe, 1791), 91, 133, 263
Romanticism, 19, 41–42, 58n14, 274n6
Rosenzweig, Franz, 70n39, 252
Roshwald, Miriam, 40, 41, 68n11
Rothberg, Michael, 244
Rovner, Adam, 14–15
Rushdy, Ashraf, 241, 253–54
Russia, tsarist, pogroms in, 17
Russian literature, 25
Rutenberg, Pinhas, 150, 181n12

Sa'aroni, Y., 114, 121, 183n46
Sadan, Dov, 63
Sagal, Danny, 264
Sagiv, Yonatan, 264
Savoy, Eric, 176, 229, 230
Schauerroman (terror-novel), 55, 71n62
Schiller, Friedrich, 71n75
Schmitt, Cannon, 200
Schneour, Zalman, 45
Scholem, Gershom, 45, 47, 50, 67, 70n39, 252
Schulman, Kalman, 29n23
science fiction, 262, 263, 274n6
Sedgwick, Eve, 162, 178
Sefer ha-ma'asim [The book of deeds] (Agnon), 68n11
Seidman, Naomi, 77, 80, 107n16; on function of the *agunah*, 82, 83, 108n35; on women and the Haskalah, 108n38

Seigworth, Gregory J., 12
self, dissolution of, 22, 152
Sephardi Jews, 153, 159, 202–3, 212, 215, 220n70, 237
Setter, Shaul, 149
Seven Years' War (1756–63), 191–92
sexuality, 169, 206; blood libel and, 60, 61; incestuous, 207, 209–10, 211, 220n74. *See also* homosexuality
Shahar, David, 153
Shaked, Gershon, 41, 58n13, 127, 144n75, 201
Shaked, Malka, 70n41
Shakespeare, William, 115
Shamir, Moshe, 139n2
Shamir, Ziva, 77
Shapira, Anita, 33n87
Shavit, Zohar, 30n46
Shelley, Mary, 13, 262, 276n37
"Shifra" (Baron, 1927), 26, 76, 106–7n4; expression of emotions in, 86, 100–101; men absent from, 88; metaphor of staying in, 78; mother-daughter relationship in, 88, 89; plot summary, 87; surveillance in, 93; uncanny feminine historiography in, 104–6; vision/the visual in, 97, 98–99
"Shiratenu ha-tse'ira" [Our young poetry] (Bialik, 1907), 106n3
Shir bakfarim [Songs in the villages] (Goldberg, 1942), 140n7
"Shirey makot Mitsrayim" ["Poems of the Plagues of Egypt"] (Alterman, 1944), 21
Shlaim, Avi, 195
Shlonsky, Avraham, 138
"Shney ha-kvarim" [The two graves] (Tchernihovsky, 1942), 45
Shohat, Ella, 33n92, 237
Shouse, Eric, 30n41
Shteinberg, Ya'akov, 7, 26, 74–112; Hebrew and Yiddish versions of stories, 77–78
Shteinberg, Ya'akov, works of: "Bat ha-rav" [The rabbi's daughter] (1912, 1914), 77; "Ha-iveret" [The blind woman] (1923), 26, 76, 106n4; "Mot ha-zkena" [The death of the old woman] (1917), 77
shtetl, 41, 75, 106n1, 107n21; chronotope and history of, 79–80, 89, 105; "departure metaphor" and, 78, 80–84; metaphor of staying in, 80–84; social institutions of, 90
"Silence" (Poe), 31n47
Silver, Sean, 190
"Ha-siman" ["The Sign"] (Agnon, 1943), 45
Simḥat aniyim [*The Joy of the Poor*] (Alterman, 1941), 19–20
Singer, I. B., 75
Sipurey Polin [*Stories of Poland*] (Agnon), 44–45, 48, 50
Sipurim [Stories] (Poe in Hebrew translation), 14, 30n47
"Site of Memory, The" (Morrison), 235–36
Sivan, Avishai, 263
Six-Day War (1967), 24, 147–48, 157, 178, 212
slavery, 6, 224, 225, 228; American history haunted by, 253–54; dark interior landscape of, 235; escaped slaves, 235, 255n7; gothic texts about, 232; limitations of language and, 247; Middle Passage, 227, 234, 238, 242, 245; slave narratives, 235–36, 257n36
Smith, Andrew, 228
Smith, Charlotte, 83
socialist realism, 114
social justice, 75
social media, 260
Spain, Inquisition-era, 59
spatiality, 76, 120, 122, 131, 148, 161; chronotope and, 106n2; "domestic carceral," 91; of Jerusalem, 149, 160; of shtetl stories, 90; surface and depths, 162; of the Wandering Jew, 54. *See also* inside/outside spatial binary
Specters of Marx (Derrida, 1993), 10
spectrality, 10–11, 228, 237
"spectral turn," 10–11, 256n12
Spinoza, Baruch, 12
Spooner, Catherine, 38, 272–73, 274n3, 275n15
Stav, Shira, 210, 221n84
Stern, Rebecca, 95, 98, 151
Stoker, Bram, 13, 16, 22, 59, 71n62. See also *Dracula*
storytelling, 213, 225, 226, 246
subjectivity, 78, 85, 95, 99, 179; ambivalence about, 8; destabilized boundaries of, 242; embodied, 79, 86, 94, 99–103; flânerie and, 173; ghostly, 233; "gothic feminism" and,

26; labyrinth and, 160, 166; lack of, 89; maternal, 103; of narrator in *Mar Mani*, 197–98; origin in psychoanalytic theory, 154; "partial perspective" in female subjectivity, 95, 98, 99, 163; personal and historical narratives and, 199, 201; surveillance and, 91; transgressive, 166; the uncanny and, 175; urban subjectivity and the gothic, 152; victimization and, 229

Sue, Eugène, 29n23

Suez Crisis (1956), 152, 179, 180

Sugars, Cynthia, 230

supernatural events/figures, 2, 3, 9, 13, 116; in Agnon's fiction, 25, 40, 41, 43–44; in *The Castle of Otranto*, 209; in Yiddish folk culture, 77

surveillance, 91, 92, 94

symbolism, 19

synagogue, as institution, 90

Syria, 148

Taba'ot ashan [Smoke rings] (Goldberg, 1935), 114, 127, 140n7, 140n9, 183n46

Tarantino, Quentin, 266

Tchernihovsky, Shaul, 45, 153, 219n56

technology, 5

Tel Aviv, city of, 75, 182n28, 217; gothic fiction set in, 262; gothic-themed pop culture events (2017), 260

television, 28, 260, 261, 267–71

temporality/time, 4, 40, 47; in Agnon's fiction, 48–54; apocalyptic future, 166; clock as portal of the real in Poe and Goldberg, 123–29; confrontation between past and present, 8, 39, 47–48; cyclical, 26, 46, 53, 67, 104, 105, 202; death (the past) as sanctuary, 129–32; disjointed temporality of ghost, 228; fear of time, 148–49; geologic time, 162; linear, 106; masculine and feminine, 105; maternal, 105; of memory, 238; multitemporality (heterochrony), 123, 138, 142n37; in Poe, 116–17, 118–19; reassessment of present and future, 6; spatial component in representation of, 118–22; uncanny returns of, 174–78

Tenant of Wildfell Hall, The (A. Brontë, 1848), 85

terror, 3, 40, 89, 194, 263, 274–75n9, 274n6; comic Gothic and, 272; confrontation with darkness and, 7; emotion and, 99; fictional and real, 135; flânerie and, 167; Holocaust and, 139; horror films and, 263; in Israeli-Palestinian relations, 24, 249, 250; modern confrontation with the present, 43; patriarchal society and, 84; return of the repressed and, 189; slavery and, 232; temporality and, 126, 174; the uncanny and, 175, 271; victimization and, 6

textuality/intertextuality, 6, 44, 189, 207

Tikkun (film, dir. Sivan, 2016), 263

tlishut (departure), masculine genealogy of, 80–84

Tochterman, Vered, 28, 262

"Toitentans" [Dance of death] (Agnon, 1908), 44, 68n3

Tolstoy, Leo, 115

Torah, 59, 65, 86

Torok, Maria, 10, 231

"Totentanz, Der" (Goethe, 1815), 70n44

Treue [Fidelity] anthology (1916), 37, 38, 66, 74

True Blood (television series), 260, 268

Turcotte, Gerry, 230

Twilight films, 260, 267

Ukraine, 75, 241

uncanny, the, 104–6, 174–78, 227–28, 255–56n11, 263, 271

Union of Hebrew Authors (Agudat ha-sofrim ha-ivriyim), 37

United States, 237, 266, 273; as settler society, 230; slavery and racism in, 224

vampires, 3, 16, 20–21, 221n87; antisemitism as vampire, 63; breastfeeding babies as, 93, 109n73; erotica featuring, 28; intolerance for drinking Jewish blood, 52, 53, 58, 268–69, 270; Jew-vampire association, 16, 31n54, 59, 61, 269; language as vampire, 246; as representation of otherness, 18; in television shows, 267–71

Vampire TLV community, in Tel Aviv, 260

Ve-haya he-akov le-mishor [*And the Crooked Shall Be Made Straight*] (Agnon), 69n17

Verlaine, Paul, 31n53
victimization, 3, 6, 21–25, 28, 97, 135; *agunah* and, 85; haunting and revision of, 227–35; historiography and, 195, 215; as "professional femininity," 84; Six-Day War and shift in dynamics of, 24; time and revision of, 117, 132–36; "victim-community," 23; "victim fatigue," 24
violence, 3, 4, 21, 38, 52, 149, 194; in American history, 224; antisemitic, 45, 48; blood libel and, 60; in cinema and television, 267, 268; criminal, 262; in encounter of art and life, 124; hierarchies of power and, 216; of history, 190; intrusion of violent past into the present, 48; narrative of history and, 215; potential violence of the city, 170; religious and political, 27; suppressed, 151; suppressed narratives of, 228; urban civilization and, 153, 155
visibility, 95, 103

Walpole, Horace, 1–2, 3, 187–222, 276n37; antiquarianism of, 192, 193; as "Gothic historian," 190; *The Mysterious Mother*, 210, 211, 213; as Whig member of parliament, 192, 218n12. See also *Castle of Otranto, The*
Wandering Jew, 3, 16, 18, 44; Agnon's fiction and, 52, 63; Ahasureus, 33n76; blood libel and, 60; British gothic literature and, 54–55; British national identity and, 32n59; as counterpoint to British nationhood, 16; European national identities defined against, 54, 55; as vampire, 59
war of Israeli statehood (1948), 19, 27, 243; ambivalence about, 148; destroyed streetlamps in Jerusalem from, 152; historiographic reassessment of, 194–96, 218n25; nightmare of history and, 178–80; partition of Jerusalem and, 165; "speculative temporality" and, 149–50. See also Nakba
Warwick, Alexandra, 184n85
Wasson, Sara, 76, 150, 167, 168, 175
Wein, Toni, 190
Weisman, Anat, 115, 140n10
Weiss, Hillel, 46
Wilkes, John, 218n12
Wirth-Nesher, Hana, 161, 163

Wisse, Ruth, 261
Wolkstein, Oded, 31n53
women: *agunah* ("forsaken wife"), 81–84, 108n38; British women and the demonic Jew, 60; embodied subjectivity of, 78, 86, 94, 99–103; shtetl social institutions and, 90; women authors, 26, 74
World War I, 43, 61, 135, 198; Jewish soldiers in German army, 37, 38; Ottoman-ruled Palestine during, 75
World War II, 58, 73n101, 128; English national identity and, 150; German occupation of Crete, 198; Hebrew Brigade in British Army, 38

"Ha-yalda ha-meta" [The dead girl] (Agnon, 1932, 1935), 43, 63
"Yatom ve-almana" [An orphan and a widow] (Agnon, 1931), 43
Yehoshua, A. B., 7, 9, 187–222. See also *Mar Mani* [Mr. Mani]
"Yemei ha-beinayim mitkarvim" ["The Middle Ages Draw Near"] (Schneour, 1913), 45
"Yerushalayim shel zahav" [Jerusalem of gold] (Shemer song), 180–81n7
Yiddish language, 74, 240, 245; feminine sphere of, 77; folk tradition and, 9; Hebrew accented with, 251
Yiddish literature, 25, 37; contact with Hebrew literature, 77–78, 107n15; shtetl as key setting in, 75
Yishuv (pre-state Jewish settlement in Palestine), 30n46, 38, 74, 114
Yizhar, S., 2, 149–50
Youth Aliya, 119, 141n23

Zertal, Idith, 23
Zierler, Wendy, 107n16
Zionism, 4, 106, 121, 132, 171, 205, 215; ambivalence or skepticism about, 133, 143n66; birth of, 198, 199, 204, 216; Central Zionist Archives (Jerusalem), 1; diasporic weakness renounced by, 133; dispossession of Arab culture and, 225; haunted by specters of victims, 237; Hebrew as spoken language and, 30n26; Holocaust survivors

and, 133, 143n69; idealization of self-sacrifice, 21; Jewish intellectuals and, 32n61; language and, 251; masculinity associated with, 110n74; modernization of Hebrew and, 252; nonmemory and, 254; Palestinian tragedy as ghostly presence, 229; "pioneers" (*ḥalutsim*) of, 140n6; renunciation of victim identity and, 23; Revisionist, 14; socialist, 75; utopianism of, 173

Zlosnik, Sue, 84, 152, 172, 271, 272

"Zman" [Time] (Goldberg), 127

Zofloya, or the Moor: A Romance of the Fifteenth Century (Dacre, 1806), 58

zombie tales, 264, 266–67

KAREN GRUMBERG is Associate Professor in the Department of Middle Eastern Studies and the Program in Comparative Literature at the University of Texas at Austin. She is author of *Place and Ideology in Contemporary Hebrew Literature*.